The Secret She Carried

Also by Erich Eipert

Guy Going Under
Butterfly Powder

The Secret She Carried

A Perilous Odyssey Through the Time of Hitler

Erich Eipert

ErichEipert.com
ericheipert@gmail.com

Turnbuckle Press
Seattle, Washington

Copyright ©2015 by Erich Eipert

Publisher's Cataloging-in-Publication data

Eipert, Erich.
 The secret she carried: a perilous odyssey through the time of Hitler / Erich Eipert.
 p. cm.
 Includes bibliographical references.
 ISBN 978-0-9642349-4-9

1. Germans -- Czech Republic -- Sudetenland -- History -- 20th century. 2. Europe -- History -- 1918-1945. 3. World War, 1939-1945--Deportations from Czechoslovakia. 4. World War, 1939-1945 -- Personal narratives, German. I. Title.

DB2500.S94 E37 2015
943.086--dc23   2015911687

Cover Design: Susan Eipert

With the exception of brief quotations for book reviews, no portion of this book may be reproduced or used without the express written permission of the publisher. Although every effort has been made to ensure that the information in this book was correct at press time, the author and publisher disclaim all liability for any loss, damage, or disruption caused by errors or omissions, whether such errors or omissions result from negligence, accident, or any other cause.

Dedication

This book is dedicated to my mother, Maria, who rebuilt her life despite having experienced too much of the traumatic history that I describe.

Acknowledgments

For sharing their stories and information, and allowing me to make this material a part of my book, I express my gratitude to Oswald Lustig and Oskar Halusa. I wish I had met them earlier in life. This book might never have seen the light of day, or the glow of electronic reading devices, without the research assistance and editing of my wife, Susan. Acknowledgement is also due to my daughter, Annaliese, for her invaluable help. My thanks also extend to those who helped in various other ways, including friends Brian, Lenz, Esther, Sharry, Vernon, the Hajek family, Ingrid S., and many others. Any opinions expressed in this book are entirely my own, and should in no way reflect on them.

Contents

Introduction	9
1 First, a Bit of the Ending	12
2 A Lee County Farm	14
3 Of Three Soldiers in the Great War	20
4 An Empire Dying	30
5 The War to End All Wars	34
6 Hitler in the Trenches	40
7 Mitteleuropa	45
8 Out with the Old; In with the New	51
9 Johann at His Doorstep	55
10 The Goings-On at Versailles	59
11 Johann, the Second Blow	65
12 Misfortune	69
13 The Village Called Schömitz	80
14 A Community of Farmers	95
15 A German School	101
16 Hitler and Friends Step Up	112
17 Childhood's End	123
18 Hitler's Private Life	130
19 Of Czechs and Germans	134
20 The Expansion Begins	137
21 Helping Hands Across the Border	144
22 Life in the Reich	155
23 The Dark Side	163
24 War and Tears	171
25 Uniforms and Guns	182
26 Shortages on the Home Front	191
27 Front Lines	200
28 The Curtain Closes	216

Contents

29	Another Peace Found Wanting	222
30	Schömitz, Maria's Last Look	235
31	Schömitz Occupied	245
32	Oskar's Journey	255
33	Life Under the Knife	260
34	The Secret	271
35	The Czech Final Solution	277
36	Germany with Tears	284
37	Identity Entanglement	291
38	Wimmern, a New Beginning	299
39	Aftermath—An Accounting	315
	Maria's Cookbook and the Written Record	315
	Eduard Hajek	316
	The Hajek Family	317
	The Lustig Family	317
	The Halusa Family	318
	The Luksch Family	318
	Henriet	318
	Johann Caesar	319
	Mina	319
	The Stöffel Family	319
	The Geidl Family	319
	Lehrer Mauer	320
	The Neuspiel Family	320
	The Village of Wolframitz	320
	The Village of Schömitz	321
	The Village of Gubshitz	322
	Austria	322
	Adolf Hitler	323
	Joseph Stalin	324
	General Erhard Raus	324
	Edvard Beneš and Czechoslovakia	324

Contents

The Beneš Decrees	325
Central and Eastern Europe	326
Sarajevo	326
The Red Army	327
The Rape Epidemic	328
Germany	329
The Sudetenland	329
The Sudetenland Farms	331
Sudeten German History and Geography	331
The Numbers	332
Maria	334
Addenda	**337**
More About World War I: Ignition	337
More About World War I: Factors Leading to Conflict	339
More About World War I: Two Lesser Known Fronts of the Great War	340
More About World War I: Versailles—A Flawed Process	343
More About How the Minorities Fared in the New Czechoslovakian State: Reality Czech	346
More About Putzi: Hitler's "Friend"	348
More About Hitler: The Führer's Love Life	350
Author's Note	**353**
Image Attributions	**354**

Introduction

IN A SENSE, this book about the passage of a young ethnic German woman from childhood through World War II is a ghost story. The place she called home passed out of existence when the war ended, and the appalling violence that played out when her homeland's three million inhabitants were expelled haunts the displaced and their descendants still. Outside the collective memory of the dispossessed, the main record of the tragedy resides in a few yellowing volumes shelved in the D820.P72 section of research library stacks. This classification is the second place I turned to when I developed an interest in this subject decades ago. The first was my mother, Maria, for she was the young woman whose early life and experiences would become the focal point of this book. Like many others, she could never forget the war and the even more disastrous peace that followed. And neither could those close to her, the Sudeten German soldiers and civilians whose stories merge with hers. Of special note among her acquaintances in this anecdotal narrative are Oskar and Oswald, close friends of Maria's fallen brother—two boys who quickly had to become men to survive the intense fighting on the Eastern and Western Fronts.

Although Maria was never loquacious, she talked about her childhood when asked and even spoke of notable events such as Hitler passing through her rural village in an open touring car. But other things proved too distressing for her to address. The wartime deaths of many young men she knew was one. The violent Soviet Red Army and Czech partisan occupation that followed the war was another. At times she tried but found it too hard to proceed. With moist eyes, about all she could say then was, "you wouldn't believe the things they did to us." Not until later in life did I learn that she'd held back an important part of her story in order to guard a secret, and that this experience affected her far more than I could have imagined.

Her story begs for the context of history, for to relay such a chronicle in the absence of surrounding larger events would be to omit half the tale. However, because the account is steeped in war—something that produces winners and losers—that history has more than one perspective. Views through the lens of victory always differ from those seen through the lens of defeat. In the time of the Caesars, the situation was simpler; the victor dictated both the fate of the loser and the history. After World War II, the winners still decided the fate of the losers, but the record for posterity allowed a broader input—at least in the more democratic parts of the world. Still, governments, politicians, and generals did not altogether stop sculpting history when it served to enhance their own role or advance a national agenda. Viewpoints from the losing side are essential for rounding out the perspective.

In the territory controlled by the Soviet Union after World War II, objectivity countered the needs of the Kremlin, so a German purview wasn't allowed. And in the region administered by the western powers, the mad führer and his followers had so collectively tainted the nation that the plight of Germans didn't earn much sympathy or attention from the military government or the western press. Journalists here focused on Nazi atrocities, the punishment of war criminals, and the growing political dissension between the Western Allies and the Soviet Union. Because this emphasis crowded out the story of the suffering German populace, the western world learned little of their situation. The coverage became more inclusive over time, but the post-war story of ethnic Germans still remains largely unknown outside of Central Europe.

During Germany's reconstruction, when redemption in the eyes of the world required the new German government to repeatedly acknowledge the deeds of the Nazis, ordinary Germans gritted their teeth and accepted the ignominy because they wanted their reincarnated nation to leave that shameful era behind. But on a personal level, few individuals wished to revisit the Nazi past to confront their own interaction with it. Unfortunately, in entombing the past, Germans did themselves a disservice because they also interred the story of their own enormous suffering during and after the war and buried the crimes the victorious Allies committed against them.

Today, we have enough distance from the war to allow that lost conversation, even if it reflects unfavorably on some nations that have yet to do their own soul searching. The Nazi atrocities need no longer justify or excuse the victorious side's own war crimes and massive ethnic cleansing. Even though most individual perpetrators and victims are now dead, filling in the record is worthwhile as a reminder that one moral transgression, no matter how abominable, should never excuse the perpetration of another. Narratives that personalize the defeated, hated enemy do more than acknowledge injustice. They also counter the elements of extremism and revenge within the defeated. To describe how ordinary people on the enemy side became ensnared by events beyond their control is to show that this foe was not really so different from us. It is my hope that interlacing the experiences of Maria and others with the regional history of the period will accomplish some of the above.

Although this narrative is not intended to be a comprehensive academic work, I've referenced specific facts and quotes with academic and nonacademic books, papers, journals, and periodicals. However, I have chosen to cite more general topics in Wikipedia.org. Although subject to errors, Wikipedia articles are generally of a high standard and are a powerful resource in the digital age because they extend to the reader a ubiquitously available overview and a starting point for further research by supplying key words, search terms, and detailed sources.

1 First, a Bit of the Ending

THEY WEREN'T EXTRAORDINARY in any obvious way, the couple who in 1955 borrowed a pickup truck and moved their scanty possessions from a small-town rental house in Iowa to a farm in an adjacent county. However, sometimes people who appear quite ordinary turn out to be anything but. It was not intellectual achievement or an encounter with fame that set these two apart. Nor was it a background of privilege or hobnobbing with the well-connected, although they would once entertain as table guests on their Iowa farm a pair of Austrian counts, one of whom had a tie to the man who'd held the bleeding, dying heir to the Austrian Emperor's throne at the assassination that triggered World War I. Rather, what distinguished these two individuals from most of the people around them was their experiences—the extraordinary things they saw and endured in Europe during the apocalyptic period known as World War II.

Circumstances of geography relegated them and their families to the losing side in both of the devastating world wars. The First World War ended shortly before they were born and left them to grow up in the shadow of the ruinous Versailles Treaties forced upon the defeated nations. What prevailed throughout their childhood was called peace, but it was a tenuous, smoldering peace at best. The seething turmoil and impoverishment produced by the treaties all but guaranteed another war. That conflagration, which erupted just as these two reached adulthood, hurled them into an unprecedented vortex of brutality, violence, and deprivation.

Between them, they'd gazed upon the impassive face of Adolf Hitler, witnessed the cold-blooded execution of neighbors, beat back human wave attacks behind enemy lines, survived a bomb blast during a massive air raid, endured a filthy prison camp after a false arrest, and bore months of slave labor and the nightly fear of gang rape by a savage occupation force. As many less fortunate, and perhaps less stalwart, souls succumbed in the maelstrom, these two people independently grappled free, found each other, and rebuilt their lives.

However, to say they escaped is not to say they came away unscathed because for the rest of their lives neither could purge the disquieting memories accumulated in that barbarous time. Although they may have confided an incident or two to a close friend over the years, they sequestered most of their memories. They had their reasons, but guilt wasn't one. The most salient reason is not so difficult to understand for it is a defining characteristic of their generation. Deep in their marrow, they believed they needed to bury these distressful parts of the past in order to move on. And each had a particular part that wanted burying a bit deeper than the rest.

The individual secrets they kept, although not from one another, were the type many a person might opt to carry to their grave. Outside of its original context, the secret might be misconstrued, which risked having loved ones thinking less of them. To their credit, both decided someone ought to know, although one intended this *knowing* to be posthumous.

Had the couple remained in Germany—their place of exile after losing their homes, families, and possessions in Central and Eastern Europe—they would have been among others with like stories. In Germany, where histories such as theirs were more apt to be understood, they'd have been better able to desensitize those memories of cruelty, injustice, and violent death; however, in America they seldom rubbed elbows with others harboring similar experiences.

I know the more recent parts of this couple's story well because as a young boy I could have been considered one of the possessions they moved to the farm in the pickup truck that summer so long ago. Besides myself, my parents also brought to the farm my three younger siblings, a couple of crates of household items, a few sticks of furniture, a cow and two sows acquired while my father worked for a helpful and generous farmer, and a huge load of uncertainty.

2 A Lee County Farm

THE PARTS OF THE STORY predating my own memory came from asking my parents endless questions after I developed an interest in history as a young adult. The world wars and the period between them particularly intrigued me. However, before I relate that portion of the account, my interest in history compels me to mention the following.

The farm where my parents deposited me and their other possessions lay southeast of West Point, Iowa, a town situated near the middle of Lee County. Lee is the most irregularly shaped of the 99 counties that make up Iowa in part because it benefited from the addition of a piece of ground that in 1824 had become an historical oddity known as a Half-Breed Tract. Through a treaty with the Sac and Fox tribes, Congress declared what is now the southern part of Lee County a reservation and defined its borders as "lying between the Mississippi and Des Moines Rivers...bounded on the North by the prolongation of the northern line of Missouri." Congress designated this particular 119,000 acres and several other Half-Breed Tracts elsewhere as homes for Indian and European mixed-race people, who in those days did not fit in well with either the natives or the European settlers.

My parents never appreciated the appropriateness of their own settlement near the Half-Breed Tract, that triangular tip of land jutting down into northeast Missouri like a boat rudder steering the ship of Iowa westward. Although they arrived a century late, and the farm was a tad north of the Tract boundary, I like to think the placement was close enough to qualify as a partial fulfillment of the Tract's original purpose: a home for people caught between two cultures.

◆

In the 1950s the term ethnic cleansing had yet to enter the vernacular, but the crime had recently caused a great many people like my parents to lose their European homes, land, livelihood, community, and culture. The expulsion of ethnic Germans from Central and Eastern Europe was of such magnitude and consequence that it still stands as the largest forced migration and theft of property in history.[1] Yet, the plight of the 12 to 15 million violently uprooted victims is scarcely known outside of Germany and Austria despite the degree of responsibility the United States and Britain bear for approving the population transfer.

Eipert family portrait, complete with frowning author, circa 1951, Germany

My parents met as a result of the not-yet-recognized crime and then invested six years in rebuilding a postwar life from scratch in Germany. I believe the loss of their homeland imbued them with a subconscious need to establish a home in a place where something similar was unlikely to befall their children. At the time, Germany was the front line in the Cold War that began shortly after World War II ended. My parents knew that nuclear annihilation could occur anywhere on the globe, but at least America was unlikely to be invaded by its neighbors. Still, the decision to emigrate to a distant continent where they comprehended barely a word and would arrive penniless with two children in tow and a third well on the way could not have been an easy one to make. And they second-guessed the decision several times during the move when the trip did not go as planned.

Prior to settling in Lee County, we'd moved five times in three and a half years. In Germany my parents sold their household possessions when they received the call to report to Funk Caserne in Munich, a DP (displaced persons) exit camp. After some weeks in the camp we had to return to our former residence and rely on friends to get by because no more slots to America were available. My mother was well into the third trimester of her pregnancy when we were recalled to Munich. After another two weeks in a barrack where my parents nursed sick children, pretended strung-up blankets were real walls, and ate mess-hall meals far too abundant in cod, a slot finally opened.

Because of my mother's advanced pregnancy, our family's assigned mode of transportation shifted from sea to air. Any elation my parents felt over the quicker passage dissipated during the course of the seven flight legs it took to reach the eastern shore of the United States. At that time an airsickness bag was not just an unused item in a seat pocket. The noisy, unpressurized, propeller-driven passenger planes of that era flew through, not above, most air turbulence. Twice, the plane had to turn back and retrace its route. A harrowing failure of two of four engines over the iceberg-speckled North Atlantic accounted for one of the returns. Following this frightening and exhausting trip, our family barely got in a night's sleep before being hustled aboard a train for a five-day journey from New York City to Tulelake, California, where our sponsor lived and my father was to work.

A year later, when my mother had all she could take of the isolation and dust storms in this remote area and my father had fulfilled his one-year work commitment, the pair of them packed up again. This transplantation took us to the small town of Mediapolis, Iowa, where my father found work on a farm. Two years later, my parents rented the Lee County farm and began farming on their own. Compared to the earlier moves, the 40-mile haul between Mediapolis and West Point probably felt like child's play despite the addition of a fourth child. Easy or not, after so many relocations, my parents had a powerful aversion to ever moving again and were determined to make a go of the farm.

◆

Left: Location of Lee County (shaded) within Iowa.
Right: Location of Half-Breed Tract within Lee County (darkly shaded).

The new location suited my parents well. Their nearest farm neighbors were supportive and became lifelong friends. The town of West Point, where most residents came packaged with sturdy German surnames derived from ancestors who'd arrived several generations earlier, was also a complementary match. Like the villages my parents came from, the community was small enough for everyone to know everyone else, and most residents were Roman Catholics, like themselves. The timing of the move presented the biggest challenge. To start farming in the middle of summer with no crops to harvest for an entire year and no garden to draw upon in feeding six mouths proved a challenge. Money was in short supply for years. To get by, my mother sold dressed chickens, eggs, and cream while my father juggled jobs in town. In time, they swapped their rent payments for purchase installments and began to think of the farm as their own.

On that farm Maria and Fidel raised their four children and quietly lived out the next four and a half decades of their lives. In that span they made many friends—friends who no doubt believed they knew my parents well enough to conclude they'd left behind everything European but the German accent. However, Fidel and Maria could no more shake off the deeper traces of their old culture, lives, and toxic memories than they could shed their skins.

Victims of trauma often have compelling reasons for sequestering the memory of their experiences. For many, the painful recollections trigger uncontrollable emotions and evoke intrusive thoughts. This was certainly the case with my mother, and I believe it was true for my father too. Their anguish would have better stilled over time if not for the language barrier they couldn't cross. My mother grew up speaking German and

Czech, and my father, German and Romanian. In Germany after the war, both then also learned the local Bavarian dialect, which sounds like a foreign language to many other Germans.

Unfortunately, in America neither Maria nor Fidel ever grew facile enough in their fourth language to adequately convey their complex experiences and feelings. Like many adult immigrants with a limited education and no formal English instruction, they remained sentence people. Out on the farm they lacked the interaction and stimulation necessary to become the paragraph or chapter people the telling of their stories required.

Another reason my parents held back their experiences was the understandable expectation that Americans wouldn't be interested or sympathetic. As Germans they couldn't help but be aware that the popular culture in America during those postwar years was still charged with World War II patriotic fervor. Germans and Nazis—terms often used interchangeably in books, magazines, movies, and television shows—were synonymous with evil. So, my parents didn't expect compassion for the hardships Germans had faced.

Eipert Family on their Iowa farm, circa 1956

This patriotic America of the fifties and early sixties was also my childhood environment. Like all my friends, I grew up on a fare of World War II movies, magazine articles, and television shows. In those days Hollywood knew little subtlety when it came to the good guys. The heroes sounded like the characters played by John Wayne, Glenn Ford and Lee Marvin rather than Colonel Klink and Sergeant Schultz. When the Germans in field-gray uniforms were shot and blown up wholesale, at some level I was a little troubled for I knew my father had been in the war on that, the wrong, side and wore that very uniform. Yet, this awareness failed to pose a precipitous dilemma in my mind. I can only guess that even in those formative years I saw through some of the Hollywood shallowness and realized that not all the good people were on one side.

Years later, after I discovered that my parents came with stories every bit as compelling as those depicted in the popular media, a sense of responsibility set in and I felt compelled to extract the details before they were lost. Unfortunately, I moved too slowly and let some of the asking, and all of the telling, languish too long. I should have completed this saga years ago while my parents were still alive. In my defense I would plead that prolonged immersion in researching the indescribable acts of brutality and inhumanity that occurred in their part of Europe during and after World War II repelled me so much that I repeatedly shelved the project.

The Second World War is the most widely documented historical event of the modern era. Yet, the aftermath of the war to the east of Germany, the area my parents called home, has never received its proportionate share of attention. Because the Soviet Union made it difficult or impossible for objective western journalists to visit territory it captured unless propaganda value could be realized in the process, and because in Germany the high drama playing out as the top Nazis were collared and an ever ghastlier picture of Nazi atrocities came to light seized the public interest, the deadly and immense ethnic cleansing that occurred to the east scarcely received a mention. As a result it is not well known today. This narrative about my parents and some of the people and events around them is my small effort to tell a part of that story.

---

[1] R. M. Douglas, *Orderly and Humane: The Expulsion of the Germans After the Second World War* (Yale University Press, 2012), 1.

3 Of Three Soldiers in the Great War

ALTHOUGH MY PARENTS were not unduly complicated, their story is because it is inextricably tied to multiple historical events with both regional and global repercussions. The sequence began in a troublesome corner of Europe when an amateur terrorist upset the succession to the Austro-Hungarian Empire's throne and touched off something the world had never before seen. This deed, the assassination of Austrian Archduke Franz Ferdinand, plunged the world into a four-year conflagration of unprecedented scale. For two decades the war was known as the Great War, but today we know it as World War I because an even greater war followed. Tens of millions of soldiers and 28 nations participated in the First World War.

By the time the guns grew silent on November 11, 1918, a substantial part of a European male generation was no more. Ten million soldiers were dead and another 21 million had been wounded. Of those who came back, the lucky ones merely suffered physical damage. Many seemingly unscathed men were permanently affected by their experience and returned with deep emotional scars.

Among those millions of men who went off to fight in World War I, three play a prominent role in the early part of this narrative. All three of the veterans survived the war but none returned whole. Two of the men are intimately connected to my parents. Both were named Johann. I reference the third veteran for the impact he would have on the fate of the Johanns, their immediate families, their ancestral homes, and their descendants. All three men grew up under the flag of the Austrian Empire, fought for the Central Powers, and were ethnic Germans.

◆

Before proceeding, the meaning of the word *German* needs clarification because it bears so significantly on what follows. The term sounds simple enough, but its connotations are surprisingly complex. Although it is most commonly used to describe a German-speaking person from Germany, this is merely one type of German identity. In modern Europe, regions of both Switzerland and Italy speak German, as do the country of

Austria and the principality of Liechtenstein. So in a sense, residents of these areas might also be called German if we restrict the affiliation to language and possibly some aspects of culture.

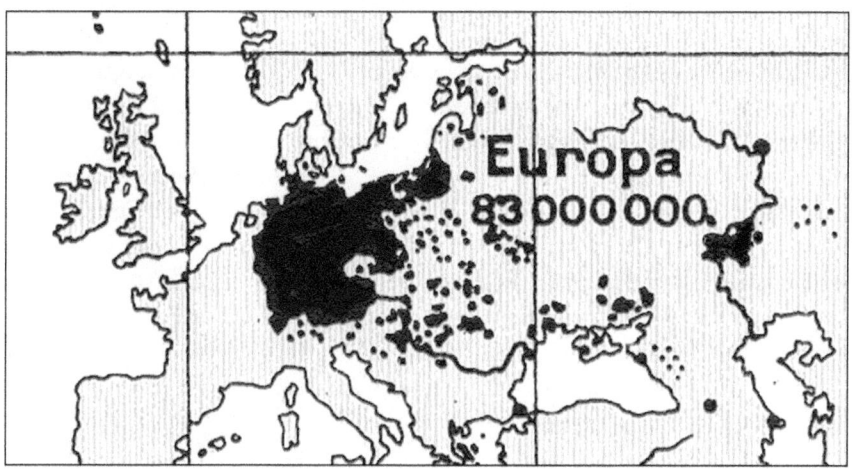

1930 distribution of the 83 million Germans in greater Europe

However, even using the term *German* in the sense of a language identity is not straightforward because the language itself is polycentric, meaning it is not one distinct language. Rather, German is a language with many dialects that differ in vocabulary and structure. With the exception of the standard German taught in schools and spoken on television and radio, the differences can be great enough that a German speaker from one region cannot understand a German dialect from a different region. Variety within the German language presents a stiff barrier to forming a cohesive "German" culture or a single identity.

With regard to nation, the situation is likewise complicated because the word *German* had different meanings at different times in European history. At first it denoted being "of a Germanic tribe". Later it came to mean "of the German feudal duchies" and then "of the German portion of the Holy Roman Empire." By the middle of the 19th century, *German* referred to someone "of the German Confederation". Only in modern times has the word come to designate someone "from the German nation" because only in this period was there anything that could be called a state.

The nationalism that caused so much woe in the 20th century did not exist for the vast majority of Germans in earlier eras. In the time of tribes, duchies, kingdoms, and provinces, Germans were ambivalent about national allegiance. Before the age of mass communication and education, and the regional homogenization this produced, allegiance was largely a matter of connectedness. Community, religion, and social class came first because those connections most directly affected people's lives. Not until the approach of the 20th century did Germans, along with other nations around the world, embrace the type of fervent nationalism so bound up with the notion of identity today.

The three returning soldiers, German in the sense of language and culture, came from German-speaking regions or pockets outside of Germany. German-speaking people had inhabited some of these regions for a very long time. In parts of Moravia, German had been spoken for the better part of two thousand years. In other regions of Central and Eastern Europe, Germans had arrived only two or three centuries earlier when several waves migrated east at the behest and request of monarchs and landowning nobles who sought to fill sparsely settled marshy and fever-ridden frontier lands with hard-working farmers. In the early 20th century, up to 15 million ethnic Germans lived east of present day Germany.

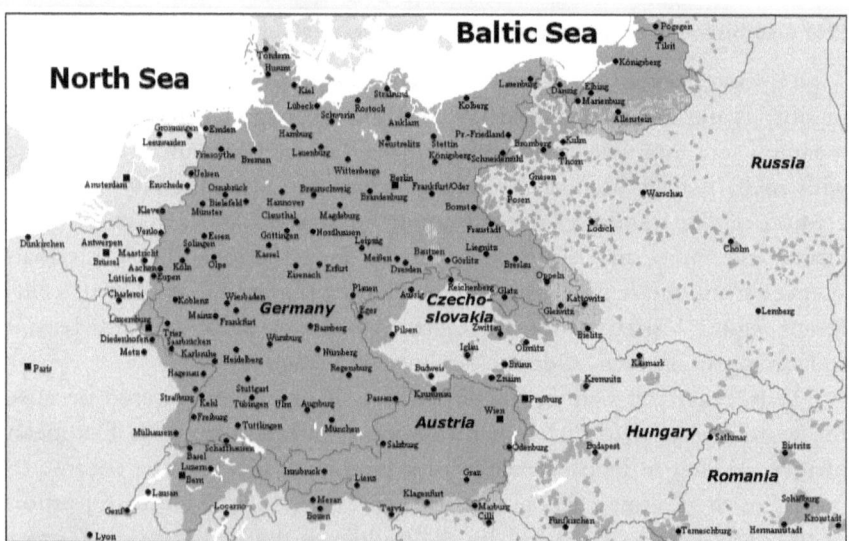

Linguistic map of Central Europe showing 1910 areas of German settlement imposed on 1937 national borders

◆

Although all three of the ethnic German soldiers returning from the war in 1918 had grown up within the Austro-Hungarian Empire, each returned to a separate region of Europe from different fronts of the war. The two Johanns headed back to Central and Eastern Europe, though not together. They didn't know one another, or even of one another, and would never meet because their homes were widely separated. One would have but a short time to live, and the other would withdraw into himself for the rest of his life. Neither of the Johanns would ever meet the third veteran either, and as far as is known, he has no descendants. The Johanns did have children, and two of their offspring would later meet, for these two veterans were my grandfathers.

Left: Johann Eipert. Right: Johann Hajek.

The Johann with but a short time to live, Johann Eipert, was my paternal grandfather. He returned from the Eastern Front to his home in the fertile plain known as the Banat—for centuries an integral component of Hungary, but about to be stripped away in large part and awarded to Romania by treaty. Johann was the descendant of Germans who nearly 250 years earlier had fled unhappy circumstances in what is now Germany and made great sacrifices in taming land retaken from the Ottoman Empire by the Habsburgs. Johann had much to live for, but fate dealt him a cruel hand when it let him pull through the war intact only to revoke his life a short time later. What little his survivors remember of him will be recounted in the subsequent book telling my father's story and his desperate measures to survive World War II.

The current chronicle involves Johann Hajek, my maternal grandfather. Despite the passivity and withdrawal the war left him with, he not only survived World War I, he also lived through World War II and half of the Cold War that followed. Because of what happened to him and his family, he couldn't forget the Second World War any more than he could forget the First. The home Johann Hajek returned to was in the southern portion of Moravia, an Austrian province just north of Vienna. In that borderland region, ethnic Germans had been the majority population for many centuries and considered themselves Austrians.

A sparsely populated Moravia first encountered Germanic and Celtic settlers in the fourth century. Other nomadic peoples joined them and Slavs migrated into the region some 250 years later. In the ninth century the descendants of these groups became part of a kingdom that rapidly grew to include neighboring Bohemia and part of Poland and Hungary. After a decline through several centuries, the Moravian kingdom eventually revived and expanded at the expense of Hungary and Austria, only to crumble once more in the 14th century as Hungary and Austria grew more powerful. The kingdom lost its independence in 1526 when it was incorporated into the Habsburg dynasty's Austrian Empire.

◆

The circumstances that brought my parents, the offspring of the two Johanns, together had everything to do with the third veteran because of the huge part he played in the calamity that became World War II and the dreadful "peace" that followed. This Austrian veteran's face is universally recognized; almost no one needs a photo to picture him. He would die by his own hand in the last days of World War II, a quarter century after World War I ended. Most would find it fitting that he shouldn't survive, for he was Adolf Hitler. The blame for the war and much of the unnecessary suffering it brought to even his own people falls squarely on him and his henchmen.

No one in my extended family ever actually met Hitler. My father came within a few miles of him when he traveled through the Berlin area during a reposting north of the city in the closing months of the war in 1945. However, Fidel had no chance to catch a glimpse of the Nazi leader because on January 16 Hitler retreated into the safety of his *Führerbunker* 30 feet beneath the Reich Chancellery Garden and seldom emerged after that. The adulation, public pageantry, and swooning crowds captivated by his oratory had long since vanished. The many assassination plots, incessant British and American bombing raids, widespread destruction, and extreme German war casualties ensured that Hitler no longer had the audience, or the stomach, for public appearances. By this time the führer's megalomania had led to the death of most of Fidel's schoolmates and heaped a mountain of misery on the rest of his family, not to mention the better part of a continent. So I'm pretty certain my father wouldn't have wasted any free time attending an appearance. If that wasn't reason enough, Fidel's passionate love of cards would have assured that he'd be engaged in a game in the barracks or a *Gasthaus* (inn).

Sudeten German areas (striped) of Bohemia and Moravia superimposed on the current Czech Republic, with location of Schömitz and Wolframitz marked.

My mother, on the other hand, did see Hitler when he toured a section of the Sudetenland in southern Moravia on his way to Vienna. The Sudetenland, which consisted of the German-inhabited border areas of Bohemia, Moravia, and Silesia, was incorporated into Czechoslovakia when that country was assembled at the end of World War I. The term *Sudeten Germans* or *Sudetendeutsche*, came into use in the early 20th century and was widely applied after 1918. Some believe the name comes from the Sudeten Mountains stretching along northern Moravia into Bohemia. Others insist the term was derived from the Roman expression *su de*, which means "so-called Germans," to distinguish the Germans living in the peripheral German sections of Bohemia, Moravia, and Silesia from those in the old territory of Germany.

Hitler's route on one brisk October afternoon in 1938 took him through my mother's village, right past her house. The residents had little advance notice of his coming because Hitler often made his travel plans whimsically and on short notice. He was very security conscious and enforced a strict rule that his security troops, the SS-Begleit-Kommando, were to keep his travel plans secret. To avoid attracting attention and to remain as inconspicuous as possible, Hitler didn't even allow the protection detail to disclose his route to the local police. He also often departed unexpectedly to foil assassination attempts.

Whether my mother had been working in the fields when word of Hitler's coming spread, she couldn't recall, but that afternoon she was one of several hundred residents who waited along the street to catch a glimpse of the world-famous leader. Her vantage point, just outside the door of her house, was only a couple of steps from the edge of the narrow street. The largest throng of excited onlookers assembled at the *Marktplatz* (marketplace) a little further ahead, around a sharp turn. This was the likeliest place for Hitler to address the crowd should he stop because it was next to the most prominent landmark in the village, the clock tower which fronted the *Rathaus* (town hall).

Wolframitz marketplace tower decorated for Hitler's visit

This large square-based tower was topped with a smaller hexagonal clock tower and reached a height of nearly 70 feet. The *Turm* (tower) could be seen from a considerable distance across the rolling landscape. My mother couldn't recall whether the local military garrison or an advance party for Hitler's entourage had hurriedly decorated the tower, but prominent Nazi symbols festooned it that day. Most conspicuous was a long vertical banner suspended from a horizontal flagpole jutting from a small window near the peak. The blood red banner sported a black Nazi *Hakenkreuz* (swastika) within a white circle. Below the banner on the whitewashed lower section of the tower's base, 12 feet above street level, hung two more dark swastikas. Mounted across the front of the tower, one above the other with six feet of space between, were three short inscriptions in black letters on a white background: **EIN VOLK, EIN REICH, EIN FÜHRER** (one people, one realm, one leader).

The assembled onlookers were disappointed when Hitler's party rolled right on through without stopping. Except for a few seconds when he stood and executed a partial salute, Hitler looked noticeably disinterested in the crowd. What the bystanders failed to appreciate was that after several years in power the novelty of being the center of attention in such a tiny setting had long since worn off for Hitler. Rousing speeches were wasted on small rural crowds when tens of thousands of ego-stoking admirers waited to be addressed in cities like Vienna and Prague. What's more, Hitler couldn't maintain a schedule if he stopped at every village and town along the route. Stops also made him more vulnerable to individuals wishing to change the course of history. He had no intention of exiting his seat of destiny via a bullet, the way Franz Ferdinand had. So the only satisfaction the townsfolk received from the man in the large, open-top, triple-axle, Mercedes-Benz touring car was a brusque salute.

My mother, Maria Hajek then, was captured in a photograph as Hitler passed by, but the copy she acquired didn't survive the war. During the war's frantic final days in 1945, with the Soviet Red Army poised in a neighboring village, Maria burned it because she feared it would put her in danger. This photo wouldn't have revealed details like the blue of her eyes or the green embroidery on her dirndl, since it was shot in black and white and taken at a distance. What it would have shown was a slender, attractive blonde 19-year-old amidst a scattering of spectators lining an unpaved street on a festive occasion—a typical teen, curious and excited about seeing one of the most famous people in the world.

The photo held no particular sentimental value for Maria for she'd never had any interest in politics or politicians. She was there that day because renowned and influential people did not happen by her remote rural village every day. And like most Sudeten Germans at the time, she regarded Hitler as the liberator of her people. Germany had taken over the Sudetenland only weeks before and the villagers were still jubilant over being freed from two decades of broken promises and oppression by the Czech government in Prague.

Teenage Maria in her dirndl

As time went on, Hitler proved to be anything but a savior. His policies and actions extracted a heavy toll of suffering and death from the people he'd "liberated." When the German military situation deteriorated midway through the war, Maria's photo became less a memento of happier days than one marking the end of normal life for her and her neighbors. By then nearly every ethnic German male between 18 and 45 had been stuck into a uniform and shuttled off to some distant front where he tried to keep from freezing or bleeding to death. The girl in the photo couldn't possibly have anticipated that the champion of the Sudeten German cause riding in the touring car would one day be the justification for the loss of everything dear to her. Nor could she have guessed that after this loss she would never see her homeland again, or even want to, because of the terrible things done there to her and those around her. But that is nearer the end of this story than the beginning.

4 An Empire Dying

WHEN THE FIRST WORLD WAR ERUPTED, Czechoslovakia did not yet exist and my mother's Sudmähren (southern Moravia) homeland was still part of the Austro-Hungarian Empire. And Maria's father, Johann Hajek, was still a robust young man of 26. As European wars go, this war was far from one of the longest. But four years of exposure to the new mechanized forms of destruction and killing were more than enough to ensure a man was spent and forever changed. This certainly applied to Johann.

With some allowance for vital occupations and the prevailing need, Austria required all fit 19-year-old men to serve three years in military service during peacetime. When conscripts resumed their civilian lives, they remained in an active reserve pool for 10 years and then in an inactive pool until age 45. In the latter, they were subject to active service recall into a replacement force called the Landsturm only in times of unusual need. World War I was such a time. To illustrate how dire the need became, the cutoff age for active service was raised to an unprecedented 55, and the military command sent 20 Landsturm brigades to the battlefield as regular combat units.

Johann's age in 1914 put him in the active reserve pool, so he'd have been called up early in the crisis. Men of his district reported to the garrison in Znaim (Cz. Znojmo), the home of the 99th Moravian Infantry Division (Mährisches Infanterie Regiment Nr. 99). The 99th was one of four regiments in the k.u.k. (kaiserlich und königlich) 4th Infantry Division, headquartered in Vienna. This Imperial and Royal Army combined men from all ethnic regions. The empire contained many ethnic groups speaking their own language, and even at the district level the military had several languages to contend with. To facilitate communication the empire concentrated men in units where most or all spoke the same language, when possible. Overall, the military was 26 percent German-speaking, 45 percent Slav (Czech, Polish, Ruthenian, and Serbo-Croat), 22 percent Hungarian, 6 percent Romanian, and 1 percent Italian. Johann's regiment was roughly two-thirds German and one-third Czech.[1]

The language of military orders and messages could be either German or Hungarian, depending on the location of the garrison in the empire's two kingdoms, but all soldiers needed to understand at least a few basic words of German. However, for any military unit to operate cohesively, communication has to extend beyond a few common words. Problems arose because in the Austro-Hungarian military, commanding officers frequently spoke a language not understood by the enlisted men, and a regiment could contain subunits of several ethnicities. Commanders were then challenged to find a common regimental language understood by everyone. The common language in one Slovak regiment was English, the language of the enemy. The officers had studied it in school and the enlisted men had learned some words because they hoped to emigrate to America.[2]

The mobilization of Austria's reserves, and Johann's call-up, came in response to the already mentioned assassination of the heir to the throne. The event occurred in Sarajevo, the capital of Bosnia—a troublesome Austrian province populated by Bosniaks, Croats, and Serbs. Serbian nationalists inside Serbia had tasked members of a terrorist organization with killing Archduke Franz Ferdinand. Both an emissary of the Serbian prime minister and Austria's own spies warned Ferdinand he was in danger, but the archduke refused to cancel his visit. He and his wife were shot and killed as they rode through the city in an open-top royal car belonging to a member of the archduke's retinue and bodyguard for the visit, Count Franz von Harrach. Von Harrach had positioned himself on the running board of the car as a shield for the Archduke. However, because he found himself on the wrong side of the car to prevent the shots being fired, he could only serve as a witness to what followed:

> As the car quickly reversed, a thin stream of blood spurted from His Highness's mouth onto my right cheek. As I was pulling out my handkerchief to wipe the blood away from his mouth, the Duchess cried out to him, "In Heaven's name, what has happened to you?" At that she slid off the seat and lay on the floor of the car, with her face between his knees. I had no idea that she too was hit and thought she had simply fainted with fright. Then I heard His Imperial Highness say, "Sopherl, Sopherl, don't die. Stay alive for the children!" At that, I seized the Archduke by the collar of his uniform, to stop his head dropping forward and asked him if he was in great pain. He answered me quite distinctly, "It's nothing!" His face began to twist somewhat but he went on repeating, six or seven times, ever more faintly as he gradually lost consciousness, "It's nothing!" Then, after a short pause, there was a violent choking sound caused by the bleeding.[3]

To read more about the event that triggered World War I, go to the addendum "More about World War I: Ignition".

◆

When I viewed Ferdinand's death car and the bloodstained uniform shirt he wore at the Heeresgeschichtliches Museum (military museum) in Vienna, I found it difficult to relate the artifacts with the enormity of the consequences this assassination triggered. Not long ago, after rereading several accounts of the killing and thinking about that car and its occupants again, I couldn't help but contemplate how different today's world might be had fate positioned von Harrach on the other side of the car, blocking Gavrilo Princip, the shooter, from his targets. Then the war might not have started in Austrian territory, or started at all, and my parents almost certainly wouldn't have met or found themselves in America.

The von Harrach name now also triggered a memory. I'd encountered it before during a long-ago visit to Rohrau, Austria—the village birthplace of Joseph Haydn, and the site of a palace adjoining a large estate owned by a branch of the von Harrach family. My parents, my wife, and I had received an insider's tour of the palace art gallery and farm because my father and the estate's farm manager were classmates and old friends. The count and countess were away at the time of our visit, so we didn't meet them.

However, my parents did meet the count the following year when he and another Austrian count stopped at their Iowa farm. Although Austria's nobility lost all special privileges in 1919 and retained only empty titles, European counts were a rarity in Iowa. And the Austrian variety of nobility had always been a cut above most of the rest of the continent's titled gentry. One author wrote of them, "No elite in Europe had a more venerable pedigree…they could impress even a star spangled bucko like Teddy Roosevelt. When asked what type of person had appealed to him the most in all his European travels he said unhesitatingly, 'The Austrian gentleman.' "[4]

From a snapshot of my father posing with the two men, I confirmed that one of the visitors was indeed from Rohrau. He was a count who'd married a von Harrach countess related to the archduke's personal protector in Sarajevo. What struck me was the improbability that someone tied to the family of the man who might have prevented World War I, and the long tragic chain of events that followed, should connect with my parents in their adopted land. In a way life had completed a full circle for the couple who were in America only because Franz von Harrach found himself standing on the wrong side of the archduke.

Years before I saw Ferdinand's car and uniform in Vienna, I stood at the spot in Sarajevo where Princip shot the royal couple. I tried to reconcile the events of June 28, 1914, with the insanity and scale of slaughter it brought about. I couldn't, despite the help of the unrepaired destruction still visible throughout the city from another recently concluded Balkan war initiated by Serbian nationalists. At the time, United Nations armored vehicles patrolled the streets, and sections of the city were still at odds with each other.

Sarajevo, which is very near where my grandfather faced his first bullets in World War I, lies in a beautiful valley surrounded by the Dinaric Alps. In the 1992–1995 Bosnian War those surrounding mountains left the city vulnerable to Serb artillery bombardment from their heights. The war ended three years before my visit, but much of the damage remained. One of the Serb targets was Bosnia's national library which housed irreplaceable, historic, ethnic Bosnian national and cultural records. The building has since been restored, but just one-tenth of the original 200,000 items in its special collections could be saved. Interestingly, in 1914 this grand edifice was the city hall, the place where Archduke Ferdinand delivered his speech minutes before his death. The assassination of this building is a legacy of the Bosnian War, much like the archduke's assassination is a legacy of World War I.

---

[1] Gunther E. Rothenberg, *The Army of Francis Joseph* (West Lafayette, Indiana: Purdue University Press, 1976), 128.

[2] Norman Stone, *The Eastern Front, 1914-1917* (New York: Scribner, 1975), 125.

[3] Luigi Albertini, *The Origins of the War of 1914*. (London; New York, Oxford University Press, 1952), 37.

[4] Frederic Morton, *Thunder at Twilight: Vienna 1913/1914* (New York: Scribner, 1989), 29.

5 The War to End All Wars

ALTHOUGH THE ASSASSINATION in Sarajevo armed the Johanns and millions of other men and ignited the Great War, the conflagration didn't erupt solely because of one act of terror. A large accumulation of fuel for the fire was already in place, and historians struggle to cram the causes into 500-page volumes. By 1914 none of the major European participants truly loathed the idea of going to war. They'd all recently built up their armed forces and felt confident they'd triumph in a conflict. This prevailing militarism exacerbated the distrust and hostile feelings that already existed. The leaders of the major nations, monarchs and politicians alike, anticipated great political dividends from a military campaign and consequently prepared the public for the eventuality of war.

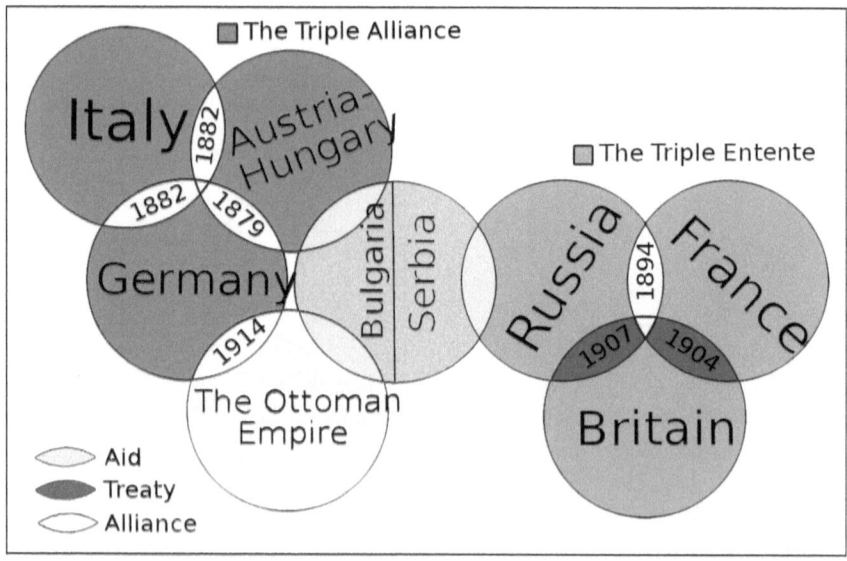

Diagrammatic illustration of European alliances at the start of the World War I, with the Balkans split between them. Overlap in circles represents treaties (indicated by date) and/or aid.

To read more about the causes of the Great War, go to the addendum "More about World War I: Factors Leading to Conflict".

In southern Moravia my maternal grandfather Johann Hajek would have donned his uniform in mid-July 1914, shortly before the heavy fighting began. The realization by Austro-Hungary's war planners that they needed to attack on two fronts, Serbia to the south and Russia to the east, required the rapid mobilization of active military reservists like Johann, but neither my mother nor her three younger sisters and brother in Germany could later recall anything about where he served. They all said he never talked about the war or his experiences and knew only that he'd spent some time in trenches. A name search at the War Archive (Kriegsarchiv) in Vienna, which contains various Austrian military documents dating from the 16th century through World War I, also failed to turn up any records. From other sources I learned that men in his military district served in the 99th Infantry Regiment (Infanterie Regiment Nr. 99 of 4. Infanterie Truppendivision, II Armeekorps), headquartered in Vienna.[1] Other references to this unit pointed me to where he'd have fought during the war.

A 1924 British book about the start of the war proved helpful in tracing the initial deployment of the 99th Regiment.[2] The following excerpt from a British diplomatic secret communique sent to London shortly before the onset of hostilities reports that Regiment 99 was initially rushed to the Balkans:

> Sir M. de Bunsen to Sir Edward Grey.
> Vienna, July 26, 1914. ...
>
> Following from Military Attaché, for the D.M.O.:
>
> Following is confidential: Only units of 2nd Vienna corps affected are 44th and 99th regiments, which left without waiting for reservists last night. It is believed that they are to replace two Austro-Serb regiments of 13th corps. Reservists for 44th and 99th regiments are now being equipped and will follow in batches. First day of mobilisation is 28th July. Mobilisation placards affecting 13th and 3rd corps (Trieste) are confirmed....

The 99th Regiment, as an element of 2nd Corps, dug in along the Serbian border and there probably did replace the less-than-totally-reliable Austro-Serb 13th Corps regiments mentioned in the British spy communique. If Johann hadn't caught up with the 99th's 3rd Battalion by the time it left its Znaim garrison, he likely joined it on the Serbian border and saw some fierce fighting in mid-August during the Battle of Drina. The Austrians had already begun shelling the Serbs across the border toward the end of July to cover their engineers as they built multiple pontoon bridges across the Sava and Drina Rivers for the upcoming invasion.

Shortly after 2nd Corps arrived at the Serbian border, Count Franz Conrad von Hötzendorf, the chief of staff for the Austrian Army, changed his mind about the deployment of this and other corps. The new intelligence he had received, indicating that Russia now almost certainly intended to join the war against Austria, required the Austrians to accelerate plans to open a second front far to the north and east.

Austria's rail system, which ran inefficiently even in peacetime, was already so overextended in moving its armies that when the 2nd Corps and other units were ordered to reposition in the north, the rail planners were unable to immediately comply. Redirecting or turning trains around would have caused gridlock across the entire rail system. Although this spared Conrad the public embarrassment of having to explain why troops he'd just sent south with great fanfare were suddenly coming back through Vienna in the other direction, it hindered the preparations of field commanders charged with confronting the frightening number of Russian divisions heading to Galicia in Poland.

◆

In World War I, soldiers commonly dealt with the complicated emotions they felt by composing songs and writing poetry, which often employed dark images and reflected death. From the words of such a song that originated with the 99th Regiment, I learned that the unit did indeed take part in the fighting along the Serbian border east of Sarajevo before it could be repositioned to face the Russians in the north. The poetic lyrics below came to me from a man named Oskar Halusa, who grew up in my mother's village and knew my mother and her family well. His name will come up many more times in the course of this narrative. Oskar found the song in a songbook assembled by his aunt, Agnes Ulreich, in 1918. The lyrics, which I translated into English, came from Agnes's brother, Corporal Hubert Ulreich of the 2nd Battalion, 99th Regiment. Ulreich had the misfortune to die on a battlefield a short time later.

Sarajevo on the Drina

By Sarajevo on the Drina in the bright moonlight
stands a brave 99er sentry, dutifully on guard.

A bullet comes flying, everyone feels the pain
one suffers on enemy soil, when struck through the heart.

At his side knelt his dependable comrade,
"Faithfully listen to what lies in my heart.

"Gather all the letters in my knapsack
and take them to my beloved back home.

"And if she should ask you, where I was left behind,
say I lie buried at Sarajevo on the Drina."

Sarajevo on the Drina in the bright moonlit night
The moon and stars shine on the soldier in the grave.

And sun, moon and stars with their silvery radiance,
light up the soldier's pallid face.

After the vacillating Austrian commander, Conrad, realized that disaster awaited if he didn't quickly rush the bulk of his forces to face the numerically superior Russian Army in the northeast, 2nd Corps's divisions boarded trains and headed back in the direction they'd come from as soon as rail cars and tracks became available. This repositioning nightmare meant troop transport trains seldom moved faster than bicycle speed. Over the course of days, the soldiers often could have advanced faster on foot. The trains were required to stop six hours each day so field kitchens could be set up. In typical army fashion, soldiers might go hungry all day and then be served two meals almost back-to-back late at night.

◆

The 2nd battalion of Austria's 99th Infantry Regiment in 1914 shortly before World War I. Hubert Ulreich, in the lower right corner, is marked with a cross.

In the first days of the war on the Russian Front around the end of August 1914, it looked as if the Austrian Army would perform well against the superior enemy numbers. The 1st Corps defeated the Russians in the Battle of Kraśnik and then four days later 2nd Corps did likewise at the Battle of Komorow. However, both sides suffered heavy losses.

Austrian troops positioned in a shallow trench

This fighting began almost immediately after the 99th Regiment's arrival in Southeast Poland. The unit fought one of its bloodiest battles near a village called Stary Zamość shortly after disembarking from the trains. Here, the first of the many soldiers from Johann's village who would die in the war met his end. That man was Oskar Halusa's uncle, Hubert Ulreich.

During the war, Austrian newspapers dutifully published long lists of soldiers killed in battle. Some of these listings are preserved today because they were subsequently republished in book form.[3] A search of this source revealed that the gruesome battle at Stary Zamość cost the 99th heavily. The death toll here was far larger than in any other battle the unit participated in during the early part of the war.

Again, the words of a song show the feelings of the soldiers. Like the song from the Drina River, this one too originated with the 99th Regiment, specifically the 2nd Battalion. Outwardly, the tone of bravado expresses the determination the soldiers needed to carry out their dangerous missions. But the lyrics also subtly reveal the underlying fear of what lies ahead. Later in the war the songs and poems of the soldiers were probably no longer quite as patriotic. Who the hero, Herzmannsky, was is probably lost forever. The term *yellows*, or possibly *yellowshirts*, appears to be a unit nickname. Below is my translation of a song that Oskar Halusa found in his aunt's songbook:

In Stary Zamość by the churchyard wall,
On all sides, by the enemy surrounded.
Oh, the horrors at the churchyard wall,
the bullet whistles and the shell explodes.
Who was there then, the world already knows,
it was the Second Znaim battalion.

High in the hills, the hills at Stary Zamość,
there the Russian line lies, firmly entrenched.
It must give way before the evening sun,
the yellows now have set bayonets.
To the assault sounds the horn's shrill call,
Stary Zamość will feel the onslaught of second battalion.

Always only forward, forward you gallant warriors,
fear not the bullet, nor the cool tomb.
It was the gallant hero Herzmannsky's voice,
that called us to fight, that called us to victory.
It endures steadfastly for Austria's imperial throne,
to the last man of the Znaim Battalion.

After Austria's successful military debut against the Russians, things never again went right for the Austrians. Johann's regiment remained on the Eastern Front in Poland until early 1917 when the equally hapless and ineffective Russian Army withdrew from the war. That allowed the 99th Regiment to redeploy to the Italian Alps north of Venice. There, Johann likely spent time in the trenches somewhere in the vicinity of the Isonzo Valley.

Austrian mountain troops scaling a rock face

---

[1] Oskar Halusa, Personal Communication.
[2] Great Britain, *British Documents on the Origins of the War, 1898-1914* (London: H.M.S.O, 1926), 118.
[3] Austria Kriegsarchiv, *Auf dem Felde der Ehre 1914-1915*, 1915.

6 Hitler in the Trenches

AS A YOUNG MAN, Hitler knew only failure in his chosen profession of artist. At times, he lived off breadlines and slept in homeless shelters. The little money he made came from odd jobs or painting picture postcards and advertising materials. He spent the bulk of his time during these formative years reading political material and arguing politics. The result was a young man with unusually strong political beliefs. In this time he came to admire a strengthening Germany and to despise Austria as an empire rotting away under the Habsburgs.

For five years, Hitler avoided registering for Austrian military duty. As soon as he passed the call-up age of 24 in 1913, he moved to Munich from Vienna in the belief that his identity papers now allowed him to exit the country without being detained for compulsory military duty. Before long, the Austrian police began to look for evaders like him when Austria's leaders began worrying more about its Slavic neighbors, Russia and Serbia, and extended the military service age. The police tracked Hitler down in 1913 and served him with a summons to report to Linz, Austria, where jail awaited him. With the aid of a lawyer, he avoided prison by agreeing to submit to a military physical in Salzburg, Austria. Hitler abhorred the thought of fighting for Austria but needn't have worried. He failed the February 1914 exam, and the Imperial and Royal Army rejected him. Years of poor nutrition had left him in wretched physical condition. The rejection stated, "Unfit for combatant and auxiliary duty. Too weak, unable to bear arms."[1,2]

The outcome pleased Hitler at the time but became a source of potential embarrassment years later. At the first opportunity after he assumed power in Germany and annexed Austria, Hitler sent agents to Vienna to find and destroy those records. He reportedly grew livid when word came back that the records had disappeared. A onetime friend stated that Hitler also had something else to hide when he wrote, "at the time of the Austrian *Anschluss*, the Gestapo made straight for the Vienna police headquarters and impounded certain dossiers. One of them, I am convinced, related to Hitler and dated back to his early youth in the city, although what the charges were, we shall probably never know."[3]

Hitler's rejection by the Austrian military left him free to return to Munich. When World War I began a short time later, the 25-year-old purposeless failure tried to join the German Army. Apparently, he wished to gain honor and respect for himself and at the same time perform whatever heroic fantasies swirled inside his head. He lacked German citizenship and was denied, but a petition to King Ludwig III of Bavaria earned him an authorization to join a Bavarian regiment.

In the 16th Bavarian Reserve Regiment, Hitler eventually rose to the rank of corporal and saw action in several battles in France and Belgium. He found himself in the midst of a dreadful slaughter almost immediately at the First Battle of Ypres, fought in October and November 1914. In this battle, outmoded infantry tactics allowed entire companies of men to be cut to shreds by new technologically advanced battlefield weapons. Almost half of the German force of 40,000 died over 20 days. By December Hitler's regiment of 3500 men was down to 600, and only 42 of his company of 250 were left standing.

As horrible as this fighting was, the carnage that followed later in the war was even worse, yet Hitler remained physically unscathed until the Battle of the Somme in 1916. There, the future führer was wounded in the lower abdomen and groin. This wound became topical years later at the outbreak of World War II when a ditty, which supposedly originated in a British propaganda ministry office, appeared amongst the ranks of British soldiers. The bawdy song, which proclaimed Hitler had just one testicle, was said to have infuriated the enemy leader.

Various versions of the ditty evolved. Perhaps the best known began "Hitler has only got one ball; the other is in the Albert Hall." The anatomical question remained alive even after Hitler's death, and from time to time further support for the song's validity emerged. One instance was a 1970s Soviet autopsy report on Hitler's incinerated remains. However, most experts dismissed the report as Soviet disinformation because Hitler's body was too badly burned to have allowed such a determination, and another part of the report was obviously wrong. Some experts argue Hitler was monorchid (the medical term for the one-testicle condition) from birth, probably due to a mild form of spina bifida.[4] However, the groin injury scenario gained some credibility when new evidence surfaced more recently. Notes of a conversation between a Polish priest who happened to be an amateur historian and the medic who treated Hitler's battlefield wound were discovered among the former's possessions when he died. This controversy may seem absurd but is relevant for those trying to understand Hitler's psychological development.[5] Whether or not the final word on the subject has been written is anyone's guess.

As the bloody fighting continued, the morale of soldiers on both sides plummeted, but Hitler held together and proved himself a good soldier. His job, *Meldeganger* (dispatch runner), was sometimes a dangerous one which exposed him to fire. Along with other decorations, he earned both a First Class and Second Class Iron Cross. Still, he was never able to connect with his fellow soldiers on a social level, and his quirks didn't help matters. Hitler never asked for leave, didn't take part in ordinary banter and lewd talk, and didn't like alcohol. One peculiarity was even more off-putting. A fellow surviving soldier from his company revealed that Hitler spent long periods sitting alone with his head in his hands, brooding. Then, right there in a trench, he'd suddenly jump up and spontaneously unleash a harangue about Jews, Marxists, and various political issues.

In light of what a Hitler friend wrote of Hitler's habits when both were in their late teens, this shouldn't be surprising: "I was often startled when he would make a speech to me, accompanied by vivid gestures, for my benefit alone. He...had to find an outlet for his tempestuous feelings. The tension he felt was relieved by his holding forth on these things. These speeches, usually delivered somewhere in the open, seemed to be like a volcano erupting. It was as though something quite apart from him was bursting out of him."[6] In the trenches Hitler was carrying on as before, but to a slightly larger audience.

Fellow soldiers respected Hitler for his soldiering but little else. In the superstitious world of the combat infantryman, he acquired an aura of mystique because he'd survived harrowing situations when others hadn't. Hitler had pulled through often enough that he came to believe he'd been spared by a higher presence for some important purpose. In his mind that purpose eventually became clear—he would save Germany. Later, Hitler asserted that in the trenches a voice once urged him to leave a crowded bunker minutes before an artillery shell killed everyone inside.

Hitler also claimed he was inexplicably saved on a second occasion after a battle in which he was battered, bloody, and caught in the smoking, shell-cratered wasteland known as no man's land. When his head cleared, he found himself lying in a trench and staring up at a British soldier with a rifle in the hands. The Tommy peering into the trench had an easy kill shot but inexplicably didn't pull the trigger. Although this story has many doubters, some version may have actually happened because Britain's most highly decorated World War I private, Henry Tandey of the 5th Duke of Wellington Regiment, reported such an incident near the French village of Marcoing. Tandey stated he couldn't bear to shoot a wounded man. Whether the man was truly Hitler, no one knows for sure, but both he and Hitler believed it. After the war, in honor of Tandey's exemplary record, his regiment commissioned a painting of him.

During his climb to the top, Hitler saw a newspaper story about Tandey and remarked that he recognized the face in the news photo as the soldier who'd spared him. In 1937 he asked Tandey's regiment for a large photo of the painting, which he hung prominently on a wall at Berghof, his Alpine retreat. In 1938 when British Prime Minister Neville Chamberlain met with Hitler to decide the fate of the Sudetenland, Hitler showed Chamberlain the reproduction and said, "That man came so near to killing me that I thought I should never see Germany again; providence saved me from such devilishly accurate fire as those English boys were aiming at us."[7,8]

Ironically, in 1940 during the German Blitz, Tandey barely escaped death at Hitler's hands in Coventry when German bombs destroyed the building he was in. At that time Tandey expressed regret that he hadn't known who that corporal was going to become, for had he known, his actions would have been different.[9]

◆

In October of 1918, just three weeks before the end of the war, Hitler's beaten-up and depleted regiment was again deployed near Ypres, the battleground where the unit had first been bloodied four years earlier. One night, a British mustard gas attack blinded Hitler. Hitler's condition worsened the next day and left him unable to stand, so he was evacuated to Germany to recover. When Germany surrendered, Hitler was in a hospital near the city of Stettin. There, he exhibited signs of what was then known as shell shock but is now called posttraumatic stress disorder (PTSD). He became apathetic, profoundly depressed, and probably developed hysterical blindness. During much of Hitler's confinement he ruminated in silence and stared at the wall. Sometimes he suffered bouts of crying and couldn't stop.

Horror, anguish, and suffering almost certainly left the two Johanns angry and disappointed as well, but they were somewhat better able to let go of their deepest anger once they reached their homes and families. Hitler, with no family or home to return to, had no such relief valve and his anger festered. He believed the army hadn't really lost on the field of battle; it had been stabbed in the back by the civilian leadership and the uncaring German populace. Although Hitler eventually recuperated from the mustard gas, he never recovered from his beliefs.

Upon release from the hospital in December 1918, he chose to stay in the army in Germany and briefly served as a POW camp guard in Traunstein, a town practically next door to the place where my parents found refuge after the Second World War, the war Hitler started. Within weeks Hitler returned to duty in Munich—a Munich very different than the one he'd known before the war. In the new Munich, the street scene flipped between mere discontent and all-out anarchy almost daily.

To read more about the eastern and southern fronts in World War I, go to the addendum "More about World War I: Two Lesser Known Fronts of the Great War".

---

[1] Diane E. Holloway, *Analyzing Leaders, Presidents and Terrorists* (iUniverse, 2002), 55.
[2] Morton, *Thunder at Twilight*, 59.
[3] Ernst Hanfstaengl, *Unheard Witness*, 1st ed. (Philadelphia: Lippincott, 1957), 109.
[4] Klaus P. Fischer, *Hitler and America* (University of Pennsylvania Press, 2011), 241.
[5] Wikipedia contributors, "Adolf Hitler's Possible Monorchism," *Wikipedia*, Wikipedia.org, 24 Mar. 2015, accessed 20 Apr. 2015.
[6] August Kubizek, *Young Hitler, the Story of Our Friendship*; Translated from the German by E.V. Anderson [pseud.] (London: A. Wingate, 1954), 10.
[7] Wikipedia contributors. "Henry Tandey." *Wikipedia*, Wikipedia.org, 9 Apr. 2015, accessed 20 Apr. 2015.
[8] "How a Right Can Make a Wrong," *Firstworldwar.com: a multimedia history of world war one*, Firstworldwar.com, accessed 20 Apr. 2015.
[9] "How a Right Can Make a Wrong."

7 Mitteleuropa

THE PLACE JOHANN HAJEK RETURNED TO was Schömitz, a tiny village in a region of tiny rural villages and towns with names that ended in *itz*. The village is some 25 km southwest of Brünn, once the capital of the large and powerful Moravian kingdom before Moravia became just another province of the Habsburg Empire. When Johann went off to war Brünn was no longer a seat of government; the center of power now lay 100 kilometers south of Schömitz in Vienna.

The farming village of Schömitz first turned up in written records around 1380. For most of its history, the hamlet belonged to monasteries and a family of nobles. Like all the surrounding settlements, it was extensively plundered and destroyed by armies that passed through or encamped in the area during several wars. The Thirty Years' War (1618–1648) was the most ruinous. Between 1623 and 1626, the pillaging armies reintroduced the Black Plague, which had already paid the village a devastating visit earlier in 1539. In the census of 1900, 520 years after the village was first noted in records, the community claimed only 256 male and 274 female residents. By religion, 522 of its 530 residents were Catholics and 8 were Jews. By language, 467 people considered themselves German, and 52, Slavs. The records fail to indicate the ethnicity of the remaining 11 individuals.

The village tax jurisdiction included 74 houses and 924 hectares (a hectare equals 2.47 acres or 10,000 square meters) of farmland. The Austrian census takers also precisely noted the usage of the surrounding land holdings. The breakdown in hectares reads: 845 plowed, 25 pasture, 4.5 garden, 9 vineyard, and 4 forest. The villagers owned 86 horses, 293 cattle, 322 swine, and 1 lonely sheep.

Schömitz was too small to merit its own policeman, but the residents seldom had a need of one. Usually its troubles were of a different nature. Throughout its history, Schömitz experienced brushes with survival. In 1872, during a celebration at an inn, a cooking fire roared out of control and set fire to the thatched roof. A storm blowing outside quickly dispersed the flames onto the roofs of the adjoining houses. With the limited firefighting equipment and water available, such a fire was unstoppable because the walls of most houses touched the walls of their neighbors' houses, and all had the same flammable thatched roofs. Half the town burned down that day. The villagers rebuilt their houses in the same adjoining fashion as before, but replaced the traditional thatched roofs with masonry roof tiles. The arrival of electricity to Schömitz and two nearby villages in 1921 further reduced the fire risk as lamps with flames became much less common.

Most of the houses in Schömitz bordered the north-south road that passed through the village. The remaining dwellings lined a second road that cut across the village near its north end. On a map, the village resembles a cross with arms slightly misaligned because the crossroads don't quite match up at the intersection. Three of the four streets lead to another -itz village. When house numbering became law across the empire under the reign of Empress Maria Theresa in the 1760s, sequential numbers were assigned. Thus later-built houses were out of sequence with respect to their neighbors. When I look at historical photos of the village, even such a small incongruity seems to violate the orderliness of the place because of the tidy and industrious nature of the residents.

Interestingly, the house numbering system (*Konskriptionsnummer*) was strongly resisted by nobles and took considerable time to implement. These elites saw it as a threat to their control and wealth for it allowed the state to more easily collect taxes on property lots.[1] Some villages and towns reconfigured their house numbers several times since Maria Theresa's day. But Schömitz, like much of the territory that became Czechoslovakia, stuck to the original numbers. This can make it difficult to find an address. It helps to know that the number sequence usually begins near the local church, in villages that have one.

In the way of comforts and possessions, the residents of Schömitz may not have been as well off as their city cousins in places like Vienna, but they were rich in culture, tradition, and friends. Schömitz had only two or three well-to-do families, so for all practical purposes everyone enjoyed the same social status. Cars were unaffordable for most, but few people needed one since neighboring villages were within walking distance, and when there was a need to go further, bicycles or horse-driven farm wagons sufficed. However, the subsistence farming of that day, with its small-scale machinery and the need to care for livestock, didn't leave farmers large blocks of free time to venture about.

Longer journeys for Schömitzers usually began several kilometers away in Bochtitz. Its railroad station was tiny in size but large in importance for the village because it was the portal to the outside world. Vienna was only two and a half hours away even though the train stopped at every other tiny station along the way. Local farmers didn't ride the train often even though many had relatives in Vienna. For them, it mainly provided a crucial link to farm markets.

Bochtitz was where Johann exited the local train he'd caught in the regional rail hub of Vienna on his way home from war in the late fall of 1918. The increasingly familiar landscape of the Austrian countryside rolling by would surely have caused him to ponder how he'd survived to see it again when so many men in his regiment perished. And he'd surely have begun trying to banish from his mind the misery and filth of the wet and cold trenches as he looked forward to reacquainting himself with his family and sleeping warm and dry under a roof once more.

◆

Whether or not Johann anticipated major changes within Austria, I don't know. But like everyone else in the empire, he certainly already knew the sun had set on the Habsburg dynasty, because on November 11, 1918, the day the war ended, Emperor Charles I renounced all participation in state matters. Johann also surely guessed the Czech nationalists had gained by the capitulation of Austria. Still, I doubt that he expected whatever new government came along would drastically upset the balance that had existed between Germans and Czechs for centuries.

Understanding the long relationship between the two groups is not simple and requires a look back at the history of Central Europe, which in the pre-World War I era loosely included most of the territory bounded by the Baltic Sea in the north, the Balkan states in the south, the Vistula River to the east, and the Rhine River to the west. North Americans did not know much about this area. Germans knew it as Mitteleuropa (Middle Europe), a name that denoted more than just a geographic region, for the word also had political and cultural facets. Before the breakup of the Austrian Empire, the name implied the existence of an economic sphere of German and Austrian domination and a protective buffer against Russian influence. For fundamental reasons, the evolution of those parts of Mitteleuropa lying outside the German states was very different than that of the great powers of Western Europe.

Centuries ago Western Europe, particularly the part that became Spain, France, and England, was not unlike Central Europe in its cultural diversity and multiplicity of languages. However, geography jammed these western cultures closer together and endowed them with accessible, but at the same time vulnerable, ports and coastlines. Military and political competition drove big change. The security of each of the alliances within the regions depended on the formation of ever-stronger central governments. Over time, the centers of learning and the glue of commerce gradually amalgamated the cultures and languages of each region until they coalesced around one main language and produced the national identities we recognize as countries today.

Central Europe too experienced clashes among the various expanding empires over the centuries, but the military rivalry was not intense enough to drive the same sort of change that occurred in the West. The outlying provinces were distant from the ruling centers, making communication slower and close oversight more difficult and expensive. Central Europe also lacked the same extent of vulnerable coastline. When the Austrian, Russian, and Ottoman empires clashed, sheer distance alone provided some degree of security. Distance also made it impractical or impossible for the emperors, tsars, and sultans to tightly govern their territories from an empire's capital, so to hold their domains together they ceded some power to regional and local authorities.

The regions of Europe

The Habsburg dynasty, which largely built its empire through dynastic marriages, was able to hold its dominions from 1276 until 1918 because it successfully converted nearly all its ethnic groups to Catholicism. The accepted doctrine of the day was *ubi unus dominus, ibi una sit religio* (one ruler, one religion). Religion couldn't become the nucleus of an ethnic rebellion when the vast majority of inhabitants shared a single faith. The Habsburgs tolerated a few exceptions such as the Balkan Muslims in lands formerly within the Ottoman Empire, protestant European settlers enticed to help tame the great river valleys, and Jews because of their economic importance to the empire.

To maintain their empire and wealth, the Habsburgs accepted political reform when faced with threats. One such threat arose when the ideas sparked by the French Revolution and the model of the nation-state seeped eastward in the last quarter of the 19th century. Although these concepts found their most fertile ground in the empire's Balkan provinces, the ideas took root elsewhere as well. The first crack in the empire appeared when the Habsburgs compromised with the Magyars in 1867 and allowed Hungary to become a nation-state within the empire. Not surprisingly, this encouraged a few Bohemian Czechs to agitate for a similar state. Although the occasional strike or riot did occur, most of the squabbling took the form of constitutional tussles in Vienna. Even as the empire struggled politically because of its outmoded form of government, it remained functional because it allowed Hungarians, Czechs, Poles, Croats, Jews, Muslims, and other minorities to fill critical military and civilian leadership posts.

In the more ethnically homogeneous countries of the West, politicians could promise ever more democracy or fan the flames of nationalism when necessary to gain support. For the Habsburgs to do the same, given their multiethnic populations, would have been political suicide. All they could do was rely on small internal reforms to hold back the tide of ethnic nationalism within their borders and give the minority populations ever-stronger constitutional guarantees of equality and opportunity. Along with more equitable treatment came universal education. Unfortunately for the rulers, mass literacy had the unintended consequence of giving the empire's subjects even more exposure to the ideas and ideals of the French Revolution. This helped the proponents of ethnic nationalism whip up resentment against the aristocracy and the old-fashioned idea of a monarchy.

A common perception today is that the various ethnicities within the Austrian Empire were at each other's throats for centuries. Such an impression is understandable given the violence, genocide, and ethnic cleansing that has occurred in the region during the last century. However, these extremes were an aberration. The Habsburgs had long realized that playing favorites raised discontent. To keep their empire stable, in

1781 they began legislating tolerance. Within limitations, their Patent of Toleration granted certain rights and recognized the existence of culture, language, and several non-Catholic religions. Enjoyment of civil rights gradually became independent of religious affiliation. Various ethnic and religious groups may have still held grudges, but by and large they rubbed shoulders on the street and kept disagreements in the alleyway.

◆

As for German-Czech relations, much has been made of a deep historical animosity. Although urban areas saw a degree of political activism and agitation by Czechs during the waning days of Austrian rule, until the end of World War II both groups lived together peacefully enough that intermarriage was common. My maternal grandparents' families are a case in point.

Johann's father, Jakob Hajek, came from a family whose ancestry chart largely bears Czech names. He'd married Rosalia Wewerka, a woman with primarily German names in hers. Since southern Moravia was overwhelmingly German, German was the language of business, government, and social life. Jakob and his parents almost certainly spoke at least some German, and he'd possibly attended a German school.

Johann married my grandmother, Maria Zawischka, in early 1913, the same year Adolf Hitler moved to Munich, just a year before World War I. Maria was the daughter of Rosina Wentzel and Johann Zawischka. The records reveal her mother descended from a family with German names in the preceding three generations. By contrast her father's ancestors had mainly Czech names, although he'd grown up among Germans and German was his first language.

In southern Moravia, the line between who was a German and who was a Czech was especially blurred because the two groups had lived in close proximity and intermarried for so many generations. It would be safe to say that most families had both German and Slavic ancestors. Names certainly weren't a reliable indicator of ethnic heritage here because a family's stated ethnicity could be considered a personal or family choice and often had as much to do with education, convenience, and economic opportunity as bloodline.

---

[1] Wikipedia contributors, "Konskriptionsnummer," *Wikipedia*, de.Wikipedia.org, 2015, accessed 20 Apr. 2015.

8 Out with the Old; In with the New

IN BOHEMIA, the highly industrialized and populous western Austrian province between Germany and Moravia, some degree of Czech nationalism had existed throughout most of the 1800s. But true hotspots didn't form and begin to smolder until the latter part of the century. This nationalism centered on regional administration and control of education and expressed itself as a political tussle between Czech and German representatives within the halls of government in Vienna.[1]

By contrast, in Moravia with highly German and Czech sub regions and a more agrarian economy, nationalistic expression was all but absent before the Great War because a satisfactory political arrangement between Czechs and Germans had been reached with the Equalization Agreement of 1905. The arrangement guaranteed "proportionate representation in the Diet [parliament] and separate Czech and German administrations for schools and cultural institutions."[2]

Bohemian Czech nationalism erupted into a blaze during the First World War. Yet even then, few Czechs favored an independent state until the final months of the war. Eventually, the advantages of exiting the war on the side of the winners rather than the losers turned the tide.[3] The concept of a Czecho-Slovakia (the name ultimately attached by the Treaty of Versailles) received a boost during the war when a Czech university professor from Vienna, Tomas Masaryk, saw opportunity in Austria's disastrous performance in the war.

◆

Masaryk grew up with the German language. While a penniless student studying in Germany, he became acquainted with a wealthy American student and married her. Through his wife he met many prominent American industrial, financial, and political leaders over the years, including people with connections to the American President, Woodrow Wilson. Masaryk's main partner in the founding of Czechoslovakia, Edvard Beneš, was another ambitious academic who fled Austria before the war. Although several competing nationalist groups formed during the war, they ultimately lost support to ultranationalists Masaryk and Beneš. Surprisingly, neither man had favored an Austrian breakup, and independence, several years earlier. Masaryk had written: "If Austria were defeated in a European conflagration and should break up, we would be integrated into Germany, alongside which we would have lived for a thousand years." As for Beneš, his 1908 doctoral thesis stated: "People have often spoken of a dismemberment of Austria. I do not believe in it at all."[4]

Both men did an about face and began a crusade to dissolve the Austro-Hungarian Empire when they sniffed opportunity in the internal divisions caused by the war. In 1916 they stated their intention to create a new homeland for northern Slavs living in the Czech and Slovak heartlands and began a campaign to win Allied support.

Edvard Beneš and Tomáš Masaryk

With his ready access to the elite of American society, Masaryk found no better place to promote his Czech Republic during the war than America. As good as he was at raising money in the United States, he was even better at winning support there. One way he kept Wilson's patronage was by flattering the president for his intellect and books.[5] Wilson had no desire to break up the Austrian Empire until Masaryk convinced him that the Czechs and Slovaks trapped within the Austrian Empire loved freedom just as much as Americans did and America's Czech and Slovak immigrants wholeheartedly supported a new Slav state in Europe.[6] Wilson knew little about the history or geography of Central Europe and confused the Austrian state of Slovenia with Slovakia. And he didn't learn until too late that Czechs and Slovaks were distinct ethnicities that didn't get along. A diplomat working for Wilson attested that as late as the president's Atlantic crossing to attend the Versailles Peace Conference the following conversation took place:

Wilson: "Bohemia will be a part of Czechoslovakia."
Bullitt: "But Mr. President, there are three million Germans in Bohemia."
Wilson (puzzled): "President Masaryk never told me that."⁷

To build their case for independence, Masaryk and Beneš accentuated injustices their people had suffered in the multiethnic empire. What they neglected to mention was that despite a mutual dislike among some groups, the multiethnic society had coexisted for centuries without war because guaranteed and enforced rights had maintained a balance. The Habsburgs took these protections seriously in order to hold their empire together.

In the United States Masaryk organized meetings between groups of Americanized Czechs and Slavs sympathetic to the idea of a joint Czech-Slovak state and promised the Slovaks a large degree of autonomy. He intimated to a sympathetic press that the Slovaks in Europe felt the same way as the Slovak-Americans at the meetings and ignored the inconvenient fact that the Slovaks profoundly distrusted the Czechs. A 1915 meeting produced a theatrical document called the Cleveland Document, which proclaimed the right to establish the Republic of Czechoslovakia. It promised the Slovaks their own administration, parliament, courts, as well as the use of their own language in public affairs and schools.

The true purpose of the exercise was to convince Wilson the Slovaks were not a distinct minority but simply Czechs who spoke another dialect of the same language so he wouldn't have cause to apply his much touted principle of self-determination. Masaryk later admitted that the American Slovaks had been fools to believe his rhetoric. He signed such agreements unhesitatingly, he wrote, in order "to appease a small Slovak faction which was dreaming of God knows what sort of independence for Slovakia."⁸

Eventually, in 1918, this document became the basis of a second document signed by Masaryk and US Slovak and Czech organizations, the Pittsburgh Agreement, which received Wilson's imprimatur and gave the Czech nationalists the endorsement they needed to get the other Allied leaders to sign on. Masaryk and Beneš now only needed to wait for the war in Europe to wind down before declaring Czechoslovakia's independence. In the interim, Masaryk was appointed president. Some cynics contend Beneš maneuvered the aging man into the largely ceremonial post so he himself could assume the post of foreign minister and wield the real power. When the Austrian Empire's military fortunes precipitously declined in October 1918, Masaryk declared Czechoslovak independence.

When they'd begun their campaign, Masaryk and Beneš had cast their eyes only on Slovak-dominated territory. It wasn't until later in the war that they envisioned including the adjoining Sudetenland for its valuable industries and other assets beneficial to the Czech-populated area. By the end of the war in November of 1918, Masaryk and Beneš were in a strong enough position to react when Sudeten Germans declared their own independence. In December the new leaders ordered their soldiers to overthrow the self-declared Sudeten German government and seize the Sudetenland and Slovakia and suppress any self-determination ideas. And before anyone else could do so, the Czech military also occupied a chunk of Hungary's fertile Danube plain to improve its border there as well.

---

[1] Kurt Glaser, *Czecho-Slovakia: A Critical History* (Caldwell, Idaho: Caxton Printers, 1961), 13.
[2] Glaser, *Czecho-Slovakia*, 16.
[3] Glaser, *Czecho-Slovakia*, 19.
[4] Glaser, *Czecho-Slovakia*, 16.
[5] Robert Ingrim, *After Hitler Stalin?* (Kessinger Publishing, 2006), 79.
[6] Ingrim, *After Hitler Stalin?*, 78.
[7] David Fromkin, *In the Time of the Americans: FDR, Truman, Eisenhower, Marshall, MacArthur—the Generation That Changed America's Role in the World* (New York: A.A. Knopf, 1995), 272.
[8] T. G. Masaryk, *The Making of a State; Memories and Observations, 1914-1918* (New York: Frederick A. Stokes Company, 1927), 220.

9 Johann at His Doorstep

MY MOTHER HEARD as a child that Johann resembled a scraggly beggar more than a soldier when he came home at the war's end. Fleas and lice infested his filthy, ragged uniform, and he was terribly hungry. The rheumatism in his back from the muck, dampness, and cold of the trenches made walking painful and left him with a stoop. He was scarcely recognizable as the same man who'd departed four years earlier.

Having returned from a war myself, I can't help but conjure up a picture of my haggard grandfather as he stepped from the train and hobbled home those last few kilometers. I picture him as a man bearing a haunting sadness and uncertainty—lineaments that even the joy of coming home couldn't totally mask. His weathered, lined face would have looked years older than a 30-year-old man's should. He could still respond to Schani, his old nickname, but inside he knew the name's playfulness no longer comfortably fit his demeanor. Around those he came back to, he'd have struggled to hide how remote and distant he felt. These people could never understand the world he and his comrades had occupied, and he'd never be able to tell them. He certainly couldn't yet comprehend how profoundly his experiences had altered him. He'd survived, but was not whole. No one who'd absorbed such violence, and parceled it out too, remained untouched. Particularly someone on the losing side.

Johann's mental and physical state couldn't have been helped by the way the war ended. When his government and army collapsed abruptly, the absence of any authority produced chaos on all Austria's fronts. Particularly affected was the southwestern front, where Johann found himself. The dissolution left soldiers with but one purpose—to make it home. Discipline disappeared as hundreds of thousands of soldiers threw down their weapons, ammunition, and gear, abandoned their stations, and stampeded to the rear areas. Bases, ammo dumps, supply depots, artillery, and armor were all left behind. Trains were jam-packed with men desperate to get home. Those who couldn't push their way inside cars climbed up onto the roofs. In the Alpine tunnels, many men were brushed off and killed. Only a few military units held together and made their way back in an orderly way. Some needed their weapons to exit enemy territory.[1] Because Johann never talked about the war, or its end, the story of his return is lost forever.

Chaotic state of rail yard in Trento, Italy, as one of the last trains returning Austrian soldiers home departed in 1918

Probably few of the people who welcomed him home would have thought him lucky, but the war's statistics argue otherwise. Of the men who put on the various uniforms of the Austro-Hungarian Empire in the war, 90 percent ended up a casualty: wounded, missing, captured, or killed. Approximately 1.2 million of the 7.8 million men mobilized were corpses by Armistice Day, the eleventh hour of the eleventh day of the eleventh month of 1918.[2]

Johann was among the 10 percent who had somehow managed to dodge the bullets and shrapnel, avoid capture, and evade even the silent assassin—contagious disease. On the Eastern and Southern Fronts, where battle lines were generally less static than on the Western Front, microbes were the deadliest killers. The most lethal of all was typhus, which is not to be confused with typhoid fever. The disease, which kills up to 40 percent of its victims, is caused by a microbe hosted in the body lice infecting rodents. Rodents, particularly rats, find an ideal breeding ground in the unsanitary conditions of field armies. For much of recorded history, this disease was the curse of campaigns and often routed armies that the opposition couldn't defeat.

General Typhus, as the disease was sometimes known, devastated Napoleon's army during the invasion of Russia. In Johann's period of service, it particularly plagued the Russian and Serbian encampments. The most deadly typhus outbreak of the 20th century began in Serbia shortly after Austria's initial attack. Typhus spread throughout the country of three million people and killed over 200,000. Among the dead were 70,000 Serbian troops and half of Serbia's 60,000 Austrian prisoners of war (POW). After the outbreak began, Austria refrained from attacking Serbia for the next six months to keep the epidemic from spreading to its own army.

◆

Johann grew up in another *-itz* village, Klein Seelowitz, several kilometers from Schömitz. He'd met his wife, Maria Zawischka, at the large farm known as the *Meierhof* (manor farm) in Schömitz where both worked. Unfortunately, my mother was unable to tell me anything about the circumstances of her parents' meeting or how long they courted. I did learn both had a similar background. Neither was a stranger to poverty or misfortune, and both were raised by widowed mothers. Maria lost her father when she was 10, and Johann lost his when he was a baby. At the time Johann and Maria met, both still lived with their mothers—Maria in Schömitz and Johann in Klein Seelowitz. Johann didn't get on well with his mother, Rosalia, so there was never a question of taking up residence in her house when he and Maria married and couldn't afford a place of their own. The newlyweds set up housekeeping in the home of Maria's mother, Rosina.

Within a year of the wedding, a daughter was born to them and baptized Rosa. The young family was content and optimistic about the future right up until the Sunday of Franz Ferdinand's assassination. There is a good chance that like many other Germans in their locale, they were attending a large gymnastic festival in the village called Wostitz that day. Many local gymnastic clubs participated in this popular sport and the annual event provided an outing with entertainment, music, and dancing. Out of respect for the assassinated royal couple, the merriment stopped immediately when the news arrived. Before the day ended, the entire empire knew the lovely 50-year era of peace was probably over.[3]

Johann had only months to savor fatherhood. On August 1, 1914, right in the middle of the harvest season, Austria mobilized its military. Farmers had to drop everything and report almost immediately. About a hundred Schömitz men, most of the workforce, donned uniforms and left the women, children, and old men to fill in.

Maria and her mother shouldered the extra load in their household and carried on as women in Europe had throughout the ages when their men left to fight in the all-too-frequent national conflicts. Like much of the public throughout Europe, Johann and Maria probably believed the war would present little more than a short term inconvenience and be over by Christmas. The leaders in power who knew better didn't dare share their view too openly as they beat the war drums and readied their populace for perseverance and sacrifice.

In all likelihood, Johann had long forgotten that naïve hope when he reached his family's doorstep again in 1918, for he surely anticipated embracing Maria, hugging his daughter, and reclaiming his old job and a sense of purpose. However, fortune was not smiling on him when the door to house number 48 opened. He got to hold his wife, but cruel disappointment awaited his other expectations. Fate had three major blows in store for the ex-soldier. Two would find him in due course, but the first struck straightaway when Maria, deep in grief, broke the news that he'd returned too late. Johann would never again hold his little girl close for Rosa had died of diphtheria a short time before. She was five years old. Johann never had a chance to make her laugh, see her walk, or hear her tiny voice say "Papa."

---

[1] Rothenberg, *The Army of Francis Joseph*, 219.
[2] Wikipedia contributors. "World War I casualties." *Wikipedia*, Wikipedia.org, 20 Apr. 2015, accessed 20 Apr. 2015.
[3] Rudolf Mauer, *Schömitz* (1950, unpublished manuscript edited by Oskar Halusa), 33.

10 The Goings-On at Versailles

THE FORMAL PEACE TREATY NEGOTIATIONS attended by representatives of all 10 victor nations began in January 1919 at the Versailles Palace in France. However, the real negotiating and decision making occurred outside of open sessions and involved the Big Three leaders: French Prime Minister Georges Clemenceau, British Prime Minister David Lloyd George, and American President Woodrow Wilson. Because the representatives of the losers were not consulted, the proceedings were denounced as a travesty by many, even during the session. Since then, it has often been said that World War II began the day the Versailles Treaty was signed.

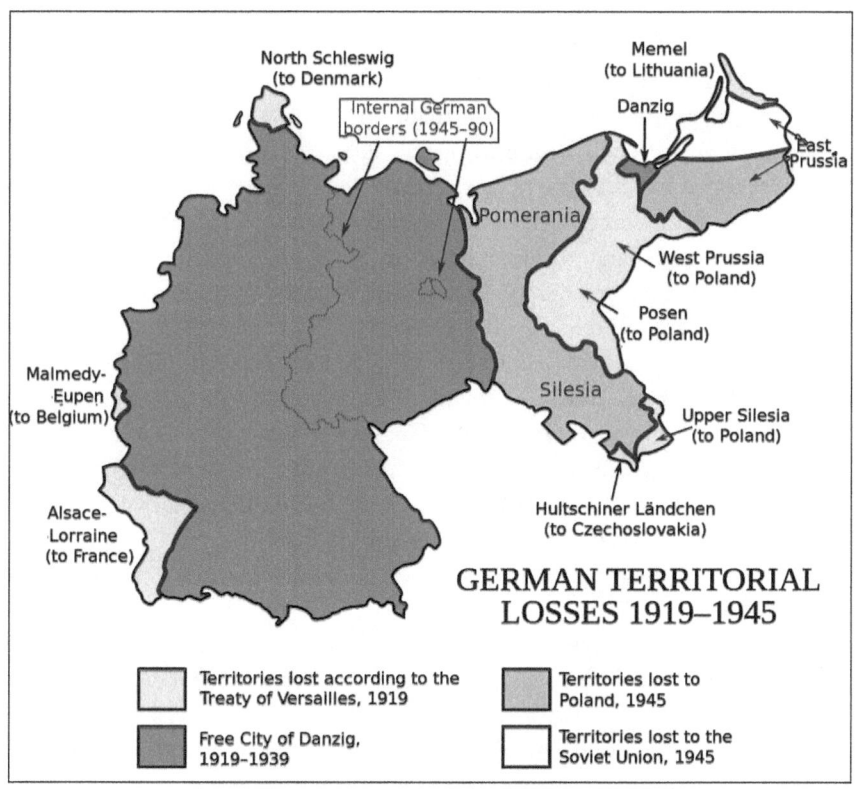

German territorial losses from two world wars (1919-1945)

To placate their constituents, French and British diplomats needed to be seen punishing Germany severely. Hence, Germany was assigned most of the blame for starting the war even though the other major European powers had all contributed. Germany's hostile neighbors emerged from the conference with a large amount of German strategic territory, assets, and population. Germany also lost its colonies and overseas possessions, its naval and commercial shipping fleet, many business enterprises, and many valuable commercial patents.

Beyond this, Germany was severely restricted in future military strength and saddled with an astronomical reparations debt, at French insistence. The reparations totaled nearly 40 percent of the country's national wealth, or the equivalent of $400 billion in 2010 dollars. Germany's refusal to sign the agreement would have resulted in occupation by the Allied Powers. Germany didn't finish paying off these reparations until a decade into the 21st century. The debt burden quickly bankrupted the country and before long nearly a third of Germany's workers lost their jobs.

◆

Of more immediate pertinence to the Johanns was the fate of Austro-Hungary. The empire was dismantled in separate accords called the Treaties of Trianon and Saint-Germain-en-Laye. It was bad news for all Germans when French Prime Minister Clemenceau became president of the conference because his political career was largely based on one issue summed up in the words of a conference observer: "He hated Germany and he hated Germans; to him they were incarnate bad, all of a piece, the eternal enemy. To him there was only one future, that of a France secure forever against a repetition of the assault."[1] Clemenceau delegated the Austrian territory settlement duties to a deputy named André Tardieu, who hated Germans nearly as much as Clemenceau. Because gutting the Austrian Empire and cleaving the German-inhabited Sudeten territory from Austria to make it part of Czechoslovakia fit the designs of the French government, Tardieu and Beneš worked hand in glove. Masaryk and Beneš had already so effectively lobbied the western powers that when the peace negotiations began they encountered little opposition to their demands.

The reason Masaryk and Beneš had strived so hard to convince the Allies that Slovaks were little more than Czechs in different clothes rather than a separate Slavic nationality like Russians or Poles was because the Slovaks provided the key to acquiring what the pair really wanted—the valuable additional territory populated by Germans, Hungarians, Ruthenians, and Jews. Without the Slovak population, they couldn't swallow the Sudetenland and the other minority lands and still make a case for a Slav homeland because the proposed new nation would lack a Slav majority.

To gain the popular support of Slovaks before the peace conference, the Czech nationalists had repeatedly pledged that their new republic would be a real federation and not just a smaller Czech-led Austrian Empire. But the Czechs didn't rely entirely on quiet acquiescence. At the very time that Beneš was assuring the Allies his new country would model itself on Switzerland and its ethnic Cantons in democratic structure and tolerance, behind the scenes he was ruthlessly suppressing the Slovak voice in his "republic." After he ordered the Czech military to occupy Slovakia, most Slovaks turned against the union because of his heavy-handedness.

When Masaryk and Beneš pitched their borders to western leaders, they refused to let facts and figures stand in their way. No one at the conference used deceptive documents better than Beneš. Some of his documents were outright forgeries, notably the maps minimizing Sudeten German and Hungarian territory and population.[2] The war's losers never had an opportunity to rebut and present maps based on actual census data because they weren't allowed to attend the sessions. The treaty principals had many experts, researchers, and fact checkers on hand but these specialists were seldom consulted, lest inconvenient facts interfere with political arrangements. The non-Slav areas Beneš demanded contained an astounding 70 to 80 percent of all industry in the Austrian Empire—enough to instantly make Czechoslovakia one of the world's top 10 industrialized countries.

Wilson's chief negotiator at Versailles later wrote of the deceptions: "Each one of the Central European nationalities had its own bagful of statistical and cartographical tricks. When statistics failed, use was made of maps in color. It would take a huge monograph to contain an analysis of all the types of map forgeries that the war and the peace conference called forth. A new instrument was discovered—the map language. A map was as good as a brilliant poster and just being a map made it respectable, authentic. A perverted map was a life-belt to many a foundering argument."[3]

The deliberations that started full of hope and promise for international diplomacy and justice devolved into a sad spectacle when President Wilson and the idealistic words he'd spouted back in the United States butted up against the reality of entrenched politics. He'd promised the Congress on February 11, 1918: "There shall be no annexations, no contributions, no punitive damage. Peoples are not to be handed about from one sovereignty to another by an international conference or an understanding between rivals and antagonists."

However, in Paris Wilson learned that his former leverage had dwindled once the critical need for American money and troops passed. As the French and British politicians ran roughshod over him and his idealism, Wilson's voice and health faded away. And so did the principles he'd championed. Domestically, he was able to jettison the Sudeten German self-determination issue because after America entered the war against Germany and Austria in 1917 the vicious nature of the new warfare turned American public sentiment strongly against anything German. Back in the United States the Senate was so disgusted with the outcome at Versailles that it refused to sign the Treaties or join the newly established League of Nations. Unfortunately, by then it was too late to change the outcome.

◆

It appears that nearly everyone of note at the peace conference subsequently published a book about it. Some accounts were more forthright and observant than others. One British delegate, in a book consisting largely of his diary notes, captured the lively essence of how business at Trianon was conducted. Some entries flow almost poetically:

> During the afternoon...final revision of the frontiers of Austria...in that heavy tapestried room...with the windows open upon the garden and the sound of water sprinkling from a fountain...the fate of the Austro-Hungarian Empire is finally settled. Hungary is partitioned by these five distinguished gentlemen—indolently, irresponsibly partitioned—while the water sprinkles on the lilac outside...Balfour, in the intervals of dialectics on secondary points, relapses into somnolence—while Lansing draws hobgoblins upon his writing pad—while Pichon crouching in his large chair blinks owlishly as decision after decision is actually recorded. After some insults flung like tennis balls between Tardieu and Lansing, Hungary loses her South. Then Czecho-North and East...then tea and macaroons.[4]

The chief of the American delegation's field mission described the contradictions and misrepresentations in the outcome: The Czech nationalists "base their claims to the two halves of their territory on opposite principles. In Bohemia, they demand their 'historic boundaries' without regard to the protests of the large number of Germans who do not wish to be taken over in this way. In Slovakia, on the other hand, they insist on nationality rights and ignore the old and well-marked 'historical boundaries' of Hungary."[5]

Masaryk and Beneš got nearly everything they wanted in binding up a disparate population of 13.5 million and creating a smaller version of the Austro-Hungarian Empire. Both men were immediately hailed as national heroes by their fellow Czechs. The French leaders also got what they wanted—revenge against the Germans and Austrians and a deeply indebted ally installed between the two.

Hungary, the other kingdom within the Austrian Empire, was also dismantled after its neighbors demanded most of its territory. The American delegation supported a plebiscite to let the residents decide their own fate, but the British and French delegations wanted a weak and small Hungary. Allowing a vote would set a dangerous precedent. Tardieu, the committee chairman, consequently stated he had a choice of organizing plebiscites or creating Czechoslovakia. He insisted no pity be shown to Hungary, so over 70 percent of the Hungarian Kingdom's land was awarded to hostile neighbors Czechoslovakia, Romania, and Serbia. Even the least deserving ally, Romania, who'd performed miserably in the war and supported the Allies only halfheartedly, was given a huge portion of the very valuable Banat plain.

The new national boundaries after the dissolution of Austria-Hungary by the Versailles Treaties. The dotted line indicates the border of the old empire; the solid lines demark the territory left to the rump states of Austria and Hungary after the treaty.

This award changed the nationality of the other Johann, my paternal grandfather. Shortly after his homecoming he found himself a Romanian farmer instead of a Hungarian farmer. And a poorer one at that, for when the Austro-Hungarian Empire was whole, the agricultural bread basket and the industrial heartland complemented each other and allowed the whole region to prosper. With Austria stripped of her industry, banks, and skilled work force, and Hungary's farmers and huge grain mills stranded from their traditional markets, Central Europe was knocked into a devastating depression.

To read more about what went on at Versailles, go to the addendum "More about World War I: Versailles—A Flawed Process".

---

[1] Roger Burlingame, *Victory without Peace* (New York: Harcourt, Brace and Company, 1944), 188.
[2] Glaser, *Czecho-Slovakia*, 24.
[3] Edward Mandell House, *What Really Happened at Paris; the Story of the Peace Conference, 1918-1919* (New York: C. Scribner's sons, 1921), 142.
[4] Harold Nicolson, *Peacemaking*, 1919, (New York: Grosset & Dunlap, 1965), 328.
[5] Glaser, *Czecho-Slovakia*, 22.

11 Johann, the Second Blow

THE SOUTHERN MORAVIA JOHANN RETURNED TO in November 1918 was no longer the quiet, stable place he'd left at the start of the war. The frightening rhetoric of the Czech Nationalists induced anxiety in the German population and led to much anger. Rumors abounded. The political situation couldn't have helped my grandfather's transition back to civilian life—not when he was already deep in grief and struggling with his wartime demons.

Much of the hope Johann and his fellow residents of the *-itz* villages retained for an independent Sudetenland or a state associated with Austria faded a month before the peace conference began when armed Czech soldiers, wearing the same Austro-Hungarian uniform Johann had recently discarded, invaded the villages in December. For a man who'd just borne four years of hardship and buried many friends, the extinction of the nation he'd fought for surely came as another great blow.

Under the heavy shadow of the Czech flag, self-determination dreams all but died. The only prayer the Sudeten Germans had of escaping Prague's yoke was the Versailles Peace Conference, set to convene early in 1919. They had a chance if President Wilson held steadfast to his principles of self-determination during the Treaty of Saint-Germain-en-Laye proceedings. The Sudeten Germans would have shuddered had they known the main concern of the conference's chairman and many of the delegates was distributing the territorial prizes and reassembling the Austrian Empire's ethnic jigsaw pieces into new, smaller puzzles. The diplomats ensconced in fine hotels and dining in fancy Paris restaurants were obliged to please the home constituents who paid the bills and cast the votes, not the distant minorities in the *-itz* villages.

Although the aggressive Czech takeover and its subsequent endorsement at Versailles angered Sudeten Germans, they didn't anticipate the change in government would much alter their relationship with Czechs in everyday life. Not when Masaryk and Beneš had repeatedly assured the Allies that the Prague central government would respect the rights of all the minority ethnic populations. So, Johann surely wouldn't have expected the Meierhof farm where he worked, and all other large estates and private enterprises owned by ethnic minorities or the Catholic

Church, to be appropriated by the Czech government. Nor would he have expected the minority protection policy of the new government to be used one-sidedly to benefit only Czechs—in regions where they were a minority. Under the guise of this policy the new Meierhof manager in Schömitz fired all his German workers, which cost both Johann and Maria the jobs they'd held for years.

I was unable to learn exactly when the job replacement at the Meierhof occurred, but indications are that it happened soon after nationalization of the enterprise. Some of the workers replacing the Germans lived in nearby villages, but most were transplanted into the community from elsewhere.

The Meierhof estate had belonged to aristocrats for centuries and in 1908 passed to the House of Kinsky, a prominent Central European family associated with the Habsburgs. The 350-hectare farm, substantial in size for an area where typical farms consisted of only a handful of hectares, was by far the largest employer in the village. Maria, along with a number of other village women, helped milk the farm's 100 cows while Johann worked as a horse handler. Now, not only were they childless in their new nation, they were also unemployed.

Similar scenarios played out throughout the Sudetenland. Germans were frightened because it portended that the new government aimed to convert ethnic villages like theirs into Czech communities. German fears increased with subsequent dictums from Prague. These actions included throttling the German language by constraining German schools, eliminating Germans from public administration and civil service jobs, dismantling German self-administration, and appropriating Sudeten German capital and industry.

German unemployment soared when only Czechs could fill government, police, and public service positions or were eligible to work at state-owned businesses and enterprises regulated or assisted by the state. Some of the German workers were simply fired outright; others lost their job when they failed Czech language tests deliberately made difficult. Even the Slovaks, the people Beneš called Czechs in different clothes, weren't spared from the discrimination. During the country's first parliamentary session, when Slovak representatives demanded the autonomy pledged by the Czechs in the Pittsburgh Agreement—their own Slovak administration, parliament, and courts—they were told the document was invalid because it had been signed by American Czechs and Slovaks. Ultimately, Slovaks filled only 200 of the 8,000 civil service jobs in their homeland and just half of the teaching posts.[1]

The Czech government pushed hard to transfer control of business and industry from German to Czech hands. German businesses were required to borrow from Czech banks and given credit only if the company employed a sufficient quota of Czechs. Sometimes banks required the replacement of all German workers. Meanwhile, Czech firms were nurtured with government contracts as German companies lost their markets. The government also transferred German industries out of the Sudeten borderlands to facilitate Czech control. Public works contracts were let almost exclusively to Czech firms with Czech workers, even in German areas. German industrial plants were strangled with restrictive production quotas, and German export products were hobbled with tariffs while Czech products were subsidized.[2]

◆

As Johann and Maria quickly learned, the demands of daily living don't pause for grief and suffering. With no source of income, dwelling on their privations was a luxury they couldn't afford, so to squeak by they maximized what food they could grow on Rosina's small parcel of land when the planting season began in March and competed with all the other Germans thrown out of work. They survived through enterprise and whatever odd jobs they could find.

My mother didn't know what work her mother found in this place where most jobs for women, like for men, consisted of farm labor of some type. Johann knew horses and now worked seasonally as a horse handler when farmers needed extra help. Because many men had died in the war, and others were incapacitated or hadn't yet returned from captivity in Russia, Italy, and other places, there was some need for part-time laborers. Johann also assisted the village blacksmith from time to time.

After the dust settled in 1919, Czechoslovakia managed to stay out of the international spotlight until in 1938 it was forced to relinquish the Sudetenland to Hitler's Third Reich. (The preceding "Reichs" or empires had been the German Empire (1871–1918) and the Weimar Republic (1919–1933).) When Germany also took over the core Czech state a few months later, Czechoslovakia disappeared from the map. Although that first iteration of the state vanished, it was never forgotten. History texts still portray the First Czechoslovakian Republic as an island of democracy surrounded by a sea of intolerance and totalitarianism. It may have been perceived as a democracy by Czechs and the outside world, but to Johann and his neighbors this "democracy" was more legendary than real. Its Sudeten Germans, Hungarians, and other minorities existed as second class citizens. Mistakes made at Versailles eventually provided an irresistible invitation for intervention and exploitation to Johann's fellow Great War veteran, Adolf Hitler.

To read more about how the Sudeten Germans and other minorities fared in the new Czechoslovakian state, go to the addendum "More About How the Minorities Fared in the New Czechoslovakian State: Reality Czech".

---

[1] Glaser, *Czecho-Slovakia*, 30.
[2] Bertram De Colonna, *Czecho-Slovakia Within*, (London: T. Butterworth, 1938), 58.

12 Misfortune

THE PEACE CONFERENCE DELEGATES, with their pens and political motives in hand, arrived in Paris at the lavish setting of the Versailles Palace in January 1919, weeks after Czechoslovakia had already asserted military control of the territory it coveted. Czech troops made sure the mosaic of ethnic homelands Masaryk and Beneš demanded at the conference couldn't build independence movements as they themselves had. When the dust settled, Sudeten Germans and five other groups that had once been the ethnic majority in their ancestral homelands found themselves a captive population.

This was a difficult time for Johann and Maria. They grieved for their daughter and struggled to put food on the table, but some good news finally came their way in the spring when Maria learned she was going to be a mother again. It probably didn't occur to her that her baby and her new country were conceived at about the same time. Had she and Johann been students of history, they might have been aware that the development of nations and babies is not so different. In both, character manifests itself early and is often a good indicator of what lies in store. If they'd known this, the behavior of the infant republic would surely have alarmed them even more.

Maria gave birth to a baby girl before the year was out. As was the tradition, the child received her mother's forename, Maria. This child, my mother, always wished that she had asked more about the circumstances of her birth and infancy when she was young. All she knew was that she was born at home in her parents' bedroom. She might have learned considerably more had I examined her birth certificate years earlier, rather than when she was ninety. At that time I noticed that her godmother, a woman named Marie Halusa, was listed on the form. By coincidence I'd been in Vienna interviewing Oskar Halusa, the man who provided me the songs of the 99th Regiment, only days before. Oskar was one of the last surviving Schömitzers to have grown up in the village and he had also been a close school friend of my mother's half brother, Eduard Hajek. Marie Halusa turned out to be his aunt. Had I known decades earlier, I could have located this woman and helped my mother learn more about her earliest years.

In this period predating antibiotics, childbirth was hazardous. The joy my mother's birth brought was soon tempered by a complication. Her mother never recovered her strength after the birth and lay sick in bed with a lingering infection and recurring fever. The baby's grandmother, Rosina, cared for both mother and baby. In April 1921, a year and a half later, the third major blow struck Johann when his wife, age 29, succumbed to gangrene. Baby Maria wasn't yet old enough to retain a memory of her mother. Decades later just three small photos she'd managed to hang on to through the post-World-War-II turmoil were all that she had to remember her mother by. Two are portraits showing her mother holding Maria's deceased sister, Rosa. Maria had no pictures of herself with her mother, probably because the family had been too poor to afford one.

Two portraits of Maria Hajek Sr. holding daughter Rosa

Rosina had to put aside her grief and become the child's surrogate mother because Johann couldn't properly take care of the toddler. He lacked homemaker skills and was too busy scratching out a living. Rosina already knew how hard it was for a single parent to raise children because she'd been through it herself. But when her husband had died, she was young and had much more energy. Now she was 64. Fortunately, help was nearby when needed. One benefit of farmers living together in villages was the proximity of neighbors, relatives, and friends. Rosina had all three in the adjoining house.

The floor plan of Rosina's small, single-story house was simple, and similar to that of nearly every other small house in the community. The largest and most-used room was the kitchen, where everyone spent their indoor waking hours. The kitchen was certainly the coziest room in the colder months because its masonry wood- and coal-burning cook stove doubled as the heat source. In this room residents ate their meals, entertained visitors, read, played games, and sewed or mended clothes. For Rosina, this room also served as a bedroom. With the exception of the bathroom, the house had only one other room. While Johann was away at war, that room served as a storage space and guest room for visitors. After his return, it became a bedroom once again.

Rosina's house was constructed of stucco-coated brick topped with a red tile roof, like the majority of the approximately 90 dwellings in the village. Its walls touched the adjoining houses on each side. And like most farmhouses in southern Moravia, the longer side, rather than the gabled end, faced the street with a large two-section window and the *Hof* (farmstead) gate. This entrance was the size of a modern single garage opening and could be closed off with two hinged doors. The front door of the house was located off the street, just inside the gated entrance.

The Hof extended back behind the house on a deep lot which accommodated the farm's equipment, livestock, and feed. Nearly all village houses had such a setup, since they either belonged to a farmer or had once belonged to a farmer. The stable in a typical Hof stretched back off the rear of the house and sheltered a cow or two, several pigs or goats, and poultry. Larger farmers might also have horse stables. Behind the stalls stood a small detached shed or barn with a workshop and storage for feed and farm implements. A tall masonry wall surrounded the entire Hof.

Many farmsteads also had an old tree or two for shade. Mulberry trees were a longstanding tradition. Children played under them or climbed their branches. In season, the abundant and tasty berries that fell to the ground were a delicacy for the ducks, geese, and chickens that scavenged the Hof. During World War II, with its shortages, villagers throughout southern Moravia supplemented their income by using these trees to breed silkworms so they could harvest the cocoons for silk.

When Rosina's husband was alive, the family kept a cow. Cows provided milk, and on small landholdings did double duty as draft animals pulling plows and other farm implements. Rosina had to give up the cow because an impoverished widow couldn't afford the expense. Cows involved considerable work. They needed to be taken out to graze daily during the growing season and required hay and straw be put up for the winter. Cows also needed to be milked twice a day and have their manure hauled out periodically. Goats were far more practical and provided enough milk for cheese. Rosina also kept chickens, geese, and a hog or two to fatten.

Rosina's land was less than a kilometer northwest of Schömitz on a south-facing slope once part of one of the municipality's historical vineyards. The hill, called Semmelbeiser, was renowned for the excellent wine grapes it grew because its sun-facing orientation resulted in early warming of the soil each spring. Cherry and apricot trees grew exceptionally well there too.

Pocket-sized even for a place where most farms were compact, Rosina's plot wasn't more than a hectare in size and really too small to be called a farm. However, because the land was fertile, drained well, and was and easy to cultivate, she could raise nearly everything she needed on it. She grew a wide variety of vegetables, fruits, nuts, and berries, and enough wheat and barley to keep her in flour for the year. She also grew potatoes and corn as well as any of four or five varieties of hay. Occasionally she also planted a few sugar beets as a cash crop. Rosina's next door neighbors, using their milk cow, plowed the field for her and helped with the heavy work.

◆

By custom, in Schömitz all children shared in the inheritance and received a portion of the land when it was passed on. Although the custom was equitable and progressive, the result was ever-smaller farms for the succeeding generation—farms less able to provide their owners with a living. In Schömitz and the surrounding area, fields consisted of long thin strips delineated along their length by stone markers set in the ground at intervals. Some families owned strips only a few meters wide. They accessed these ribbons of earth from a common lane that ran across one end. Because farms were so small, even before my mother's time, many children beyond school age left for the city or took up non-farming professions. Since these emigrants no longer had a need for their land, the strips sometimes ended up in the hands of outsiders.

The principle agricultural product of the village was once wine. However, in the late 19th century phylloxera, an almost microscopic aphidlike insect that feeds on the roots and leaves of grapevines, destroyed the wine industry here as in much of the world. Only after 1918, with the use of phylloxera-resistant rootstock, did vineyards make a comeback. Cereal grains, hay, and sugar beets, which also thrived in the fertile clay and humus soil, replaced the ruined vineyards. Farmers also grew several varieties of wheat, rye, oats, clover, potatoes, corn, and alfalfa. Although some farmers raised various varieties of barley for large breweries, the king of local cash crops was the sugar beet, thanks to the demand from two large processing plants nearby in the village of Pohrlitz.

Narrow strip fields typical of the region around Schömitz and Gubschitz

In the 20th century the profits in growing fresh vegetables for the tables and restaurants of Vienna began to entice some of the more enterprising local farmers. Raising such produce was feasible because these industrious farmers knew their land and had an agronomy education that allowed them to surmount the problems presented by unfamiliar crops. As a result, many a Viennese consumer enjoyed fresh tomatoes, cucumbers, melons, berries, spinach, salad greens, early potatoes, varieties of cabbage, and a potpourri of fruits from Schömitz and surrounding communities. Schömitzers boasted that not one square meter of usable land was wasted. Even the roadside ditches were used productively. Fruit and nut trees lined both sides of all four roads leading out of Schömitz, and the villagers took much pride in cultivating them. As far back as anyone could remember, the village had shipped its fine plums to Vienna. This once meant a 100-kilometer journey of several days by horse and wagon, but those days ended in the mid-19th century with the completion of a rail line between Brünn and Vienna.[1]

◆

By the 20th century, arranged marriages in Schömitz were as dead as the horse-and-wagon trip to Vienna. However, when Johann showed no inclination to find a new wife on his own, Rosina and her next-door neighbor and niece, Emma Luksch, took matters into their own hands. In their view, baby Maria needed a young mother. Both the child and Rosina would benefit, so they determined which local women were eligible, made inquiries, and winnowed the list down to three names. After much discussion, they decided on a woman named Karolina Haas, Emma's first cousin. Perhaps it was mere coincidence that Karolina's brother conveniently owned a house and small farm the couple could rent. But they did think Karolina would cherish little Maria all the more because, at the age of 25, she was rather old to still be unmarried and hence was less likely to bear as many children as a younger woman.

How well any of the candidates knew Johann is open to question, since Johann had never been a man of many words and the war certainly hadn't made him any more loquacious. Also, he'd grown up in a different village, socialized little, and was absent for four years during the war. After Karolina accepted the proposal, the two women needed only to persuade Johann. Whether Johann's assent came from loneliness, the desire to give his child a mother and ease the burden on Rosina, or his inability to say no, my mother didn't know. The wedding took place in early 1923, but as so often happens in human affairs, things didn't quite work out as planned.

The problem wasn't the living arrangement since Johann and his bride were indeed able to move into the house belonging to Karolina's brother, Fritz Haas. Nor did it have to do with the couple feeding themselves, since Johann and Karolina were also able to rent the small farm owned by Fritz. Karolina's brother was given both properties while his mother was still alive because he'd been her favorite among seven children. He could afford to let out the properties because he liked working for one of the large farmers in the community, and his job came with a dwelling.

What the matchmakers hadn't anticipated was Karolina's refusal to accept Maria, now three years old, into her house. Either the bride hadn't been forthcoming about her intentions or the matchmakers were too lax in questioning the candidate about mothering a stepchild. Of course, Johann was not blameless either. He could have saved everyone a lot of trouble by being a little more communicative, or insistent, with his intended in settling such a crucial matter before the wedding. Perhaps the war had something to do with Johann's passivity, or maybe it was just his nature, but Karolina took control of the marriage from the start. Years later Emma apologized to Maria, saying she and Rosina had made a big mistake in arranging this marriage. Although Emma was years older than Maria, the two of them became good friends. Emma, born with a club foot, herself never had a suitor or the opportunity to marry.

Not only did Karolina stun Emma and Rosina by rejecting Maria and dominating Johann, she also dumbfounded them with her fertility as she went on to bear six children. The underemployed and landless Johann surely hadn't anticipated this. When the plan to help Maria backfired, Rosina went from being the little girl's surrogate mother to becoming her fulltime parent and sole means of support. Johann might as well have lived in another village for all his involvement.

Other relatives could have offered to take Maria in, yet didn't. Maria's father had three sisters. The oldest lived in a nearby village and had a daughter. Another also lived in the vicinity, and the other resided in Switzerland. Johann also had an older brother who lived in Austria, but Maria never met him because he'd died as a young man—presumably in the war.

Another close relative who could have taken young Maria in was her mother's brother, Hans, who after finishing elementary school in Schömitz, went to Vienna as a tailor's apprentice. There he married and fathered two children. Professionally, Hans became successful and rose to the position of head tailor in a large department store. He was in charge of the store's many other tailors, a job Maria thought suited his authoritarian disposition well. Hans did invite Maria to join his family in Vienna when Maria reached school age, but by then his stern and aloof nature frightened Maria. Moving there would also have meant abandoning her grandmother and the home she knew for life in a large city among strangers. At the time, she wanted Schömitz to be her home forever.

Rosina's next door neighbors did offer to take Maria in. This was the Luksch family—Rosina's sister Theresa, husband Franz, and daughters Marie and Emma. Franz was Karolina's uncle, and Emma had been Rosina's co-conspirator in arranging the matrimonial match. Like nearly all small local farmers, the family was getting by but not prospering under Czech rule. When Rosina left the choice of where to live up to her, Maria chose to stay with the person she knew and loved best, her grandmother. Perhaps her grandmother wasn't entirely disappointed with the decision because Maria was a precious connection to the daughter she'd lost, and she'd mothered the girl for so long already that little Maria had become a daughter to her.

◆

With the death of her mother and the rejection by her new stepmother, Maria's childhood didn't begin idyllically. And life didn't get much easier for her. Rosina was a loving parent, but strict. Her limited means meant Maria began working quite early in life, so the little girl didn't have as much play time as most of the children around her. Housework, farmyard chores, gardening, and minding the grazing geese her grandmother raised to sell often took precedence after school. Maria adapted by playing while

Franz and Theresa Luksch inside their Hof gate

Middle-aged Emma and Marie Luksch in postwar Germany

she worked. At least a couple of other young unfortunates in the same situation were often also to be found in the village communal grazing area where she watched the geese. There Maria played house, hopscotch, marbles, or made toys of whatever was at hand. Luckily, the geese didn't require Maria's full attention as the mother geese did most of the work in keeping the goslings close.

As many other young girls, Maria liked dolls. Her Vienna relatives gave her several nice ones during her childhood. And with three doting female relatives next door, relatives skilled at sewing, these dolls never lacked for custom outfits. The dolls were well made, but for some reason they never outlived their clothes. Every one suffered accidents and broke beyond repair.

Broadcasting was a new technology when Maria was small, and radios fascinated her. After a neighbor brought home the first radio in the neighborhood, she became so entranced by the magic box that she gravitated to the open kitchen window of the owner's house to listen. She was still too short to peek through the window and view the device spewing out the voices, music, and the marvelous crackles and pops, so she'd sit and dreamily listen.

As Maria grew a little older, the baby boom in her father's new household became a torment. This wasn't a matter of pique or jealousy. Rather, it was the work that accompanied caring for so many babies that bedeviled her. Most days her grandmother sent Maria over to her stepmother's house before school to help get the children dressed, fed, and off to school. Then, after school Maria returned to babysit the smallest ones and take them out in the baby carriage. The worst chore was helping to wash the children's clothes and diapers. And none of it was for pay! Few people in Schömitz could afford washing machines, so laundry was done by hand. These responsibilities, and later events, curbed Maria's childhood much too early.

Although Maria wasn't always pleased with her situation, she had two close friends and came away with many fond memories. She particularly remembered the day her grandmother bought her a bicycle. The bike came with a lot of sacrifice on Rosina's part, and possibly the help of her relatives too, but it widened Maria's world considerably and allowed her to accompany her two friends who already had bikes. Sadly, an unhappy fate my mother refused to ever disclose would befall both of those friends. But this was several years in the future.

Sledding in the winter was one of Maria's favorite pastimes as a small girl. She never forgot the time when she stayed out until well after dark with her friends. Rosina expected her home at six, when the evening bell tolled, but the little girl couldn't tear herself away from the fun. When she finally returned, her grandmother punished her by making her kneel and pray for a good long while. Although this doesn't sound very harsh, for an active child like Maria it was extremely boring and tiring. And because she had to kneel on a chunk of firewood, it also became painful. Mostly, she prayed her grandmother wouldn't also spank her. At least this wish was granted. But the next day the sledding was still excellent, and she stayed out late with the other children once again. She decided the fun was worth whatever price she'd have to pay in punishment. However when she returned home, her grandmother, apparently feeling remorse over her earlier harshness, didn't say a word.

Postcard of early 1900s Schömitz. The bell tower at the street's far end is opposite Maria's home. Oskar Halusa's father appears at the far right in front of his house.

◆

The young Maria was no stranger to kneeling because the former subjects of the Austrian Empire were overwhelmingly Roman Catholic. And Catholics had much practice kneeling. Since nearly everyone shared this faith, the Church played an important role in the life of the community. Schömitz was too small to support its own priest or church, but it did have a bell tower situated opposite Maria's front door on the far side of the street. A villager faithfully rang the bell three times a day—at 6 a.m., 12 noon, and again at 6 p.m.—and at other times on special occasions. The saddest of these was always the knell that accompanied the recently departed on their final journey to the church cemetery in neighboring Lodenitz.

Maria sometimes attended Mass in a chapel in the nearby village of Gubschitz, but usually walked to Lodenitz, a larger and more well-to-do German village four kilometers north. This church also ministered to Czech congregants from two nearby villages. The parish priest, a Czech fluent in German, said both an early and a late Mass each Sunday morning. Although the Masses were Latin, the sermons and hymns were either Czech or German. The priest alternated the language of the early and late services each week.

Most priests in the district, whether German or Czech, were bilingual. However, according to Oswald Lustig, another close friend of Maria's brother, when Czech civil servants, managers, and policemen replaced Germans in their jobs, many Czech priests also supplanted German priests. In the local area, four of these Czech priests subsequently needed to be removed due to scandals. Although the replacement of the original German priests by Czechs might have been due to political pressure, Oswald speculated the Brünn Diocese found it expedient to send their problem Czech priests to remote German areas at this time. One of these dysfunctional clerics was an alcoholic who smoked 60 to 80 cigarettes per day. This priest, after accusing Oswald and Eduard of laughing in church when they hadn't, grabbed their forearms and banged their elbows hard on a table. The other three priests fathered children with German women. Two each sired two children and the other, one. When such priests became too much of an embarrassment, the diocese shuffled them off elsewhere.

Unlike most ethnic Germans in the community, Maria spoke Czech fluently and could sing the hymns and recite the prayers at either of the Masses in Lodenitz. She learned Czech through a pal she made when her grandmother befriended a Czech woman who'd moved into a nearby rented house. The woman and her husband were brought to Schömitz to fill two of the German jobs at the Meierhof. As most women employed at the farm, Rosina's friend milked cows as young Maria's mother had. Although the woman spoke German, her husband only knew Czech, so Czech was the language used in their home. As a result their daughter, who attended the new Czech school established in the village, spoke very little German. The two small girls spent much of their free time together and they soon picked up each other's language. Unfortunately, when Maria was in the third grade her friend moved away.

---
[1] Mauer, *Schömitz*.

13 The Village Called Schömitz

TINY SCHÖMITZ, with just 91 houses and 530 residents at the start of the 20th century, supported a school, several cultural organizations, and a number of businesses, including a barbershop, a blacksmith shop, a brickyard, and two groceries. One of the latter also housed a bakery. Two inns served food and drink as well as provided local men a place to play cards. One inn also maintained a popular outdoor bowling court. The list of village craftsmen included a wagon maker, several masons and carpenters, a butcher, and two shoemakers. Schömitz also supported three dressmakers and a midwife. However, farming dominated the local economy.

Despite its sleepy appearance, the village had a turbulent history and was not always a peaceful place to live. During the 1419 to 1434 Hussite Wars, Schömitz experienced much suffering and destruction. From 1618 to 1648 the village endured even worse as Catholic and Protestant armies clashed throughout Europe in the conflict called the Thirty Years' War. During the war, entire regions were ravaged by transiting armies that supported themselves by looting, extortion, and foraging. During this, one of the longest uninterrupted wars in modern history, many villages in southern Moravia were completely obliterated.

Two villages near Schömitz were never rebuilt after being devastated and in Maria's day were remembered in folklore as the desolated villages. Besides gaining salvaged building material, Schömitz added to its landholdings in the demise. Even more than two centuries later, farmers still occasionally plowed up the remains of houses and military artifacts. One farmer found a portion of a spear and a helmet whose crest identified it as belonging to a Swedish cavalry officer. Following a decisive 1620 battle in the Thirty Years' War, the Meierhof passed to the House of Liechtenstein.

The local peasants were hit hard again during the Napoleonic wars. The worst suffering occurred in late 1805 when French soldiers occupied the village and consumed most of the grain, wine, cattle, hay, and straw. The villagers had little left to see them through the winter. The soldiers also raped many women in the village. Much the same recurred in 1809 when the Austrian Army passed through in retreat. A period of devastating inflation followed. Later, fire destroyed much of the village at least twice.

In feudal days all the ground surrounding Schömitz was held by three landholders and the farming was done by serfs. Two of these manors were monasteries, located at Kanitz and Znaim. The third large estate, the Meierhof, changed hands among various noble families over the years. The situation changed in 1781 when Emperor Joseph II attempted to rid the Habsburg Empire of serfdom by power of decree. Austrian subjects already enjoyed freedom of marriage, learning, occupation, movement, land ownership, and some degree of protection from punishment by nobles. However, it took another 70 years to implement total reform. When the last burden—the requirement for peasant farmers to perform unpaid work in order to remain on the land of nobles—was removed in 1848, Schömitz thrived. However, the prosperity didn't last long. In 1866 the Prussian Army pursued a vanquished Austrian Army through the region and Schömitz was again overrun by ransacking soldiers. Along with them came cholera, which doubled the misery and claimed many lives.

Then Schömitz experienced a golden era. Farmers and local businesses flourished, and cultural organizations came into their own. This era of peace ended abruptly 50 years later with the 1914 terrorist attack in Sarajevo. As described earlier, many area residents were that day enjoying themselves at the large gymnastics festival that rotated annually among regional towns. When the news of Archduke Franz Ferdinand's assassination reached them, the villagers instinctively knew this deed, in combination with the existing European tensions, probably meant the end of their lovely peace. Their worst fears were realized when the first mobilization call came four days later and caught farmers midway through their harvest. They had to drop everything and report to their regiment. Before the killing ended, Johann and about a hundred other Schömitzers had donned a uniform. Many didn't return whole, and nearly a quarter never returned at all.

In an unpublished memoir Schömitzer Oskar Halusa described how the village mourned its dead during that war. He wasn't yet around to experience it himself, but learned of it many years later from his aunt, Agnes "Otti" Ulreich. Otti, the youngest of nine children, was 12 when the war began and had particular cause to remember it because her brother, Hubert, was the first Schömitzer to die in the war. Otti recited a poem called "Für Uns" ("For Us") at her brother's memorial service held in the school on a Sunday afternoon. The poem made such a powerful impression on the mourners that there was not a dry eye in the room after her recitation. Oskar jotted down the words as she recited it from memory when an old woman. My translation reads:

> Far—far to the east, there looms a grave,
> into which thousands of dead were lowered—for us!
>
> In the west, many a cross rises simple and small,
> where they lie silently in long rows—for us!
>
> And where the wind echoes the roar of the sea,
> they gladly gave up their lives—for us!
>
> To sacrifice the future and the happiness of youth,
> they never returned home—for us!
>
> They gave their all, their life, their blood,
> with holy courage they sacrificed—for us!
>
> And we? We can only weep and pray
> for those who lie there, pale—bloody and broken—for us!
>
> For there is no word that can thank the fallen,
> and there is no thanks for those who fell—fell for us!

Otti could still recite the poem from memory 77 years later because her recitation became a fixture in the memorial service of each fallen soldier after that day. Every family in the community lived in dread of the day she might have to recite it for them. That day came for many families, and for some it came more than once. The young girl recited it two dozen times in the course of the war.

◆

Changes to the village name occurred over the centuries as regularly as the wars. The recorded variants are Schempnicz in 1442, Semnytz in 1676, and then Semnitz, Schemnitz and finally Schömitz. In 1945, following the world's greatest war, the most drastic change of all took place after the village was ethnically cleansed of Germans. The new Czech residents made it Šumice.

One relic that survived the earlier changes was the village crest of 1676, an ornamental metal shield painted with a seal. At its center was an implement with a broad base and a sharp point at the top, representing a vineyard knife or perhaps a plowshare. Beneath the tool is the inscription **WAPPEN DES DORFES SEMNYTZ 1676** (Crest of the village Semnytz 1676). The German ex-residents do not know if the crest survived the destructive rampage by Czechs and Russians in 1945, but fear the worst because the crest bears witness to the German history and ancestry of the village. Fortunately, Rudi Mauer, a son of the last head teacher at the school, was able to later draw the shield from memory because he'd seen it every day for years on end as it hung on a wall in the school.

Left: reproduction of 1676 Semnytz (Schömitz) village seal. Right, drawing of the Schömitz village crest that hung in the German school.

◆

Before Schömitz became Šumice, and the village still possessed its old crest and German residents, it sustained many old rituals and traditions. Most were connected to the villagers' Catholic religion. Although the community did not have its own church, it celebrated religious occasions and civic holidays by ardently ringing the bells of the village *Glockenturm* (bell tower). The bells also served as an audible clock and were particularly helpful to workers toiling in the fields, for they sounded at the beginning, middle, and end of each workday.

The Schömitz Glockenturm was dedicated to St. Florian, the patron saint of Austria. In the days of the Roman Empire, Florian joined the Roman Army at a young age, advanced rapidly to become an officer, and reached an elevated rank. Toward the end of his career, he held an important administrative post in a territory that centuries later became a part of Austria. During the reign of Diocletian, Florian converted to Christianity—not a sound career move at a time when the authorities hunted down and persecuted Christians. Florian hid for a time, but eventually gave himself up to the soldiers of Governor Aquilinus. The legend goes that following a confession, he was twice scourged, flayed alive, and set on fire. He survived these severe tortures because of his unyielding faith, but his faith could not save him when flung into the river Enns with a millstone tied around his neck. After a pious woman retrieved his body from the river, an eagle watched over the corpse until it was buried.

◆

In Schömitz the first great bell-sounding celebration of the year occurred on Easter Sunday, following the solemn weeks of Lent. The ringing was preceded by complete silence from the bells on Thursday through Saturday of Easter week. At the times the bells would normally ring during the day, and at three in the morning, all Catholic school-age boys gathered in front of house number 47. From there they marched through the streets and stopped to pray at three stations along the way. Each boy wore a traditional hat and carried a *Ratsch*, a mechanical ratcheting noise maker constructed by village craftsmen. When rotated by a circular swinging motion, the instrument emitted a marrow-piercing sound. The cacophony of many ratchets reverberated loudly through the whole village. The village girls accompanied the procession and held the boys' hats whenever they stopped at the stations to rattle. In Maria's youth the procession always ended at the southern end of the village in front of a World War I monument atop the hill known as Kellerberg (Cellar Hill) where the villagers had their wine cellars and grape-press houses. The rattling took so much energy that the younger boys were exhausted when they reached the Kellerberg.

Boys beyond elementary school age participated only at 3 a.m. and formed their own separate procession. The participants gleefully looked forward to this event because at night the noise they created was truly deafening, particularly when their path crossed the path of the younger boys' procession. When they stopped at the three stations and mothers emerged from their houses to beg the boys not to wake their small children, the boys rattled all the more fiercely for tradition forbade them to comply with the request.

On Easter Monday the boys canvassed the village and knocked on each door with a bundle of eight willow branches to collect a reward for the rattling. They greeted the woman of the house with a traditional expression in the regional archaic German, saying, "Madam, give me a red egg; if no red egg, then a blue one; if no blue one, then a white one, laid by a hen." The woman then presented the boys with Easter eggs, baked delicacies, oranges, and sometimes even money. The recipients took in far more eggs than they could possibly eat, so the excess ended up mixed with feed for goslings, ducklings, and chicks.

May Day was the second annual festival celebrated in Schömitz. Unlike in Vienna and other large cities of Europe where on this day the working class marched through the streets in huge numbers and struck fear into the hearts of the establishment, here the occasion was joyous and festive. Residents first decorated a *Maibaum* (maypole) in the outdoor dance area with ornaments and then began the festivities with a morning parade. Women and girls wore seasonal Sunday outfits. Some women simply wore their best dress or skirt, but most wore a dirndl and a large flower. The dirndl is a traditional dress in parts of Germany and Austria and consists of a long- or short-sleeved blouse, an apron gathered into the waistband of the cylindrical skirt, a bodice that varies in style, and an underskirt. Men and boys dressed in shorts and white shirts. Trailing the village musicians were the *Burgermeister* (mayor) and other local officials. In a tiny community, a parade can only last for so long, even when it pauses for drinks at each Gasthaus. Following a break for the noon meal, the music began in earnest and dancing commenced.

For Maria, and most other residents, the highlight of the year was Kiritag. For this festival, the bells got a workout. In Schömitz Kiritag was celebrated on the first Sunday after September 8, the Feast of the Birth of the Blessed Virgin Mary. Except for the beet crop, the harvest was usually finished by then and farmers were ready to celebrate. To prepare for the holiday, women and girls cleaned house fastidiously, applied fresh paint where needed, and took no nonsense from the men of the household while doing so. The latter were delegated to tidy up outside. This festival played no small part in the neat and well-maintained appearance of the local German communities of the region.

Many relatives and people with some past connection to Schömitz, including a few Czechs, returned each year to attend the festival. The visitors stayed through the weekend or longer, so many families put up guests. Maria's Uncle Hans, along with his wife and two children, usually came for a whole week from Vienna and made it their annual vacation. When their train arrived, Rosina would send a hired horse cart to retrieve them and their luggage from the station in Bochtitz. Although her home wasn't large, everyone made do. Rosina and Maria slept in the all-purpose kitchen as usual, while Hans and his wife used the spare room. Maria's two young cousins stayed next door with the Luksch family.

On Sunday morning of the festival weekend, the entire family strolled to Lodenitz in their best summer clothes to attend Mass. After some post service socializing, they sauntered back to Schömitz for the midday meal. In Maria's house, and throughout the village, the women spared no effort for this special Kiritag feast. Soups were commonly served first at the main meal of the day—soups such as *Rindsuppe* (beef soup) or *Knochensuppe* (bone soup), perhaps with *Griesnockerln* (semolina dumplings) or *Leberknödel* (liver dumplings). Popular meat dishes like *Gulasch* (goulash), *Wiener Backhendl* (Viennese fried chicken), *Paprikahendl* (chicken paprikash), *Gespickter Hasenbraten* (spiked roast hare), and *Gebratene Gans* (roast goose) followed. For Kiritag, Rosina bought the best beef or pork she could afford and served it with dumplings, potatoes, and fresh vegetables from her garden.

A village specialty prepared for this day was *Kirtagsflecken*, sweet yeast rolls filled with soft cheese, plum jam, or a cooked poppy seed or walnut filling. However, the village women took such tremendous pride in their baking that they seldom made just one sweet to cap off such a meal. They might also prepare such treats as *Schneeballen* (snowball pastries), *Faschingskrapfen* (Fasching doughnuts), *Vanillekipferln* (vanilla crescent-shaped cookies), *Wiener Apfelstrudel* (Viennese apple strudel), or *Topfenpalatschinken* (crepes with soft cheese filling).[1]

The formal festivities, which continued through Monday, began early Sunday afternoon when the village musicians—mainly farmers—honored the mayor, the head teacher, and the city council by playing before them. Then they led the luminaries around the village in a parade. The scenario was repeated the following day to honor other local notables. The event afforded the honorees a chance to be seen and to exhibit their latest attire. When the parading ended, the band assembled by the dance area in front of the Gasthaus across the street and two doors down from Rosina's house.

On Sunday only young unmarried people danced. The dancing began with another ritual. After the older village boys gathered at a meeting spot, the most senior carried a special banner and led the group to the house of the oldest girl, where the girls had all assembled. From there, the boys escorted the girls to the dance area. As they arrived, the musicians, from atop a large farm wagon specially decorated for the occasion, began to play. Most married men sat at the Gasthaus tables and drank beer while the wives, who'd brought their own chairs and refreshments, gathered at other spots. From their seats, everyone could view the dancers, who began with a traditional dance. As soon as it ended, the dancers walked to an adjoining area to the accompaniment of music and escorted the assembled young people from other villages to the dance area. Then the real dancing began. On Monday, married people danced.

The band instruments typically consisted of a drum, an accordion or two, a flute or clarinet, and a couple of horns. The musicians paced themselves with breaks throughout the long afternoon and evening so they too could socialize and help reduce the supply of beer and wine. Their repertoire consisted largely of waltzes and *Ländler*s. A Ländler is a folk dance that originated in what had been known as Upper Austria (the province bordering the German state of Bavaria), and the name, which means "of the peasant or farmer," reveals its ancestry. The dance is long, smooth, and done in slow waltz time. Because different regions, and sometimes individual villages, developed their own traditional Ländler, most dancers only knew their local version.

The Germans here didn't dance Polkas much, but the local Czechs did. Maria and her friends enjoyed polkas as teens, so they attended dances at the two Czech villages near Lodenitz and at tiny Bochtitz, where the train stopped and most of the local vineyards were concentrated. Since Bochtitz was closer to Maria's later home in Wolframitz, she and her friends went there most often.

Fall was a busy time for social events. One informal, but enjoyable, tradition was the work party. Oskar Halusa's favorite took place after the corn was harvested and the ears had dried sufficiently in a bin at the Hof that the shelled kernels would store well without becoming moldy. Family and friends gathered in the storage building and shelled the corn by hand under lantern light. Songs were sung, stories told, local gossip exchanged, and practical jokes played during the evening. And as always, the women provided plenty of food and drink. These gatherings, delightful for children and adults alike, continued well into the night. The following night it would happen all over again at someone else's Hof.

For the men, a cherished harvest festival tradition with primal ties was the annual hunt. Small game was plentiful in the region, so the village took pride in inviting men from nearby villages to participate. Not everyone carried a gun; many men and boys participated as beaters instead of shooters. This was also an exciting time for dogs. Rudolf Mauer, one of Maria's teachers, wrote about the event years later. Sometimes 30 rabbits would break from cover at once when rousted by the beaters—far too many for the shooters to bring down at once. The day's total might number as many as 500 or 600 rabbits in addition to a scattering of pheasants and other game birds.[2]

As the hunt progressed, the hunters loaded the game on carts. At the end of the day the carts were secured in barns until the next morning when area residents and meat buyers purchased the bounty. The proceeds went into the community coffers. The rest of the day was filled with song, dance, and eating. Again, the women plied the hungry hunters with baked delicacies and other treats. In time it became a tradition for the hunters to attend a post hunt feast at Johann Caesar's inn, where the fare was crispy browned goose with liver dumpling soup.

As best as I could determine from Johann's offspring, my grandfather occasionally took part in the hunt. However, he participated as a beater, not a shooter, for he was a poor man and couldn't afford ammunition. Johann was not known to have joined any of the community's clubs or taken an active part in its social life, aside from a visit to the nearby inn each Sunday afternoon to play cards and sip beer. Even then, he never drank much because he had little money.

The year's final dance took place in November, just before Advent began. The very last of the year's traditions commenced at twilight on Heiligen Abend (Christmas Eve) when the town's watchman made his way down the street with a special noisemaking whip and a sack in which to collect small presents from each home he passed. The gifts consisted of baked sweets and the occasional bottle of wine. Now and then a celebratory volley of gunfire into the sky punctuated the night and startled other revelers. The next morning nearly the entire village trekked off to Lodenitz to attend Christmas Mass.

◆

Schömitz established a small library in the late 1800s. After the Great War, when the city council agreed to expand the library and assessed each household a small sum for new book purchases, the collection grew substantially. For many, reading became a popular winter pastime. Johann was one of them and spent many hours reading library books in his kitchen.

The community also offered other recreational activities. Outside the Gasthaus, boys played *Fußball* (soccer) and *Schlagballspiel*, also known as *Kaiserall*, a game similar to softball. In the warm months, young people enthusiastically participated in *Turnverein* gymnastics, a sport organized and propagated by Deutsche Turnverein (a Sudeten German cultural organization) and founded specifically to help small communities set up local gymnastics clubs. By the 1930s the organization had brought gymnastics to nearly every German village in the country.

Schömitz lacked the resources to build a gymnasium or buy equipment, but the sport flourished because the local young people had transformed an overgrown patch of boggy ground that previously sported only mud holes and a manure pile into a beautifully landscaped outdoor facility. There, in the wooded setting near the community wine cellars, coaches and participants spent countless hours practicing. Maria enjoyed the social aspects of Turnverein both here and later in neighboring Wolframitz. The entire town turned out for the public performances held several times each year. The undisputed Turnverein season highlight was the district regional summer gymnastics festival—the event in Wostitz cut short by the assassination of Franz Ferdinand in 1914.

Because the *Volksschule* (a combined primary and lower secondary school) didn't offer girls any extracurricular athletic activities, when Turnverein came to Schömitz, Maria and many other girls jumped at the opportunity to participate. Their uniform was a blue skirt and a white blouse with a loose neckerchief tie. The participants, both girls and boys, made good use of the of the gymnastics field to practice and hold performances. Sometimes they performed in other villages as well.

Music played a large role in the cultural life of Schömitz. The instrumental musicians who entertained at dances and festivals were certainly an important part of the music scene. However, the local musical interest was not confined to this band. The German Cultural Association was another national organization founded to keep Sudeten German culture alive when it came under siege by the Czech government. The organization became so popular that again virtually every village embraced it. In Schömitz almost every household had a member or two that sang or performed at cultural events staged by the various singing groups.

The most talented and popular singing group in the village was an older one, founded in 1897 through the inspiration of a local teacher. The Männergesangsverein Schömitz (Men's Vocal Group of Schömitz) dissolved in 1914 when most of its members went off to war. But it sprang back to life in 1920. I suspect Johann never participated, even before the war. Members often sang with bands and talented performers from neighboring communities. Eventually the group expanded and evolved into a mixed chorus that received invitations to perform in many other venues and communities. Schömitz had no space large enough to accommodate all the people who wished to attend their concerts, so performances had to be held in larger and wealthier villages.

◆

Maria never forgot one other annual event of a different nature. This was the coming of the Roma, people she knew as the *Zigeuner*. Every language and country in Europe had a variation of that name. In English these people are often known as Gypsies. The Roma had always provoked social tension because they put a greater emphasis on the family than on work outside the family. The low worth they placed on regular employment and literacy, and their high birth rate, burdened them with perpetual poverty and a high crime rate. This, along with their roaming lifestyle, language, and dissimilar appearance fostered a low regard for them in the general population. Nomadic Gypsies roamed throughout much of Central and Eastern Europe during Maria's childhood. Most of Czechoslovakia's 200,000 to 300,000 Roma called eastern Slovakia home, but to the consternation of the government, many of them wouldn't stay in one place. In the mid-19th century, the horse-drawn wagon became the center of their nomadic lifestyle. Young couples typically began their married life by buying the wagon that became their home.

A band of these unannounced visitors passed through Schömitz twice yearly during the warmer months. They first headed west away from their home territory in Hungary and then later trekked back. Their caravan consisted of about 10 wagons, each drawn by a pair of skinny, decrepit horses. Every wagon, or *vardo*, was a little house on wheels. Although the wagons of relatively prosperous Roma groups were quite fancy, or even ornate, the band migrating through Schömitz was poor.

Their wagons were run down and quite plain, with a window on each side and an arched, hard roof shaped like the tops of the covered wagons pioneers used to migrate across the American West. The uppermost part of the roof extended out in the front and back to provide extra cover from the sun, rain, or snow. However, because the families tended to be large, and the wagons were not, the migrants pitched dome-shaped tents at their campsite for sleeping.

Whenever the villagers spotted the caravan, they sent their children scurrying home to secure doors normally kept unlocked. Maria recalled being out in the field more than once when her grandmother passed her the house key and sent her racing home as fast as her legs could carry her. "And don't lose the key," Rosina always shouted after her.

The Roma visitors understood little German or Czech and didn't trade with the residents. Nor did they practice any cash-earning trade such as pot mending. In southern Moravia Czech tradesmen known as *Hausierers* had a monopoly on this concession and went door to door mending cookware and other household items. On the road, these Roma supported themselves by begging. They spread out, trudged from house to house, and efficiently canvassed the whole village. If no one was home and a door or window happened to be unlocked, they felt free to donate food and other items to themselves on behalf of the owner. Rosina always gave them something to eat.

No one could argue that these people didn't educate the local children during their brief stays. Schömitz's horse pond, the swimming hole for village children in the summer, was where the Roma also swam when they passed through. However, they frolicked in the water sans bathing suits. So many of them congregated at the pond that the local children became frightened and left. Still, the nudity was an eyeful and made for quite a spectacle. For Maria, the coming of the Roma was like the arrival of a carnival. To the relief of the adults, the law limited their camping near villages to 24 hours, so the visitors were constantly on the go. From the viewpoint of the farmers, a day was still too long because of the band's many horses. The animals had to graze somewhere, which sometimes was in fields along the road. Most local farmers owned plots so small that they had no forage to spare.

◆

Unlike the Roma, most Schömitz farmers were stay-at-homes. The adults Maria knew never took real vacations, and few ventured far beyond the next village. All they knew how to do was "work, work, work," she said, with the hint of a grin across her face. Maria did venture out though. Even before she got the bicycle, she walked to other villages to visit relatives. One of her favorite relatives was her Pauli *Tante* (aunt) in Leipertitz. During summer vacation she sometimes stayed with Pauli for several days. Pauli, unlike her younger sister Karolina (Maria's stepmother), was fond of Maria. Maria also walked to Klein Seelowitz to visit her fraternal grandmother, Rosalia Hajek. Rosalia hadn't approved of her son's second marriage and disliked Karolina. When Maria was still small, Rosalia would walk to Schömitz to see her granddaughter and Rosina. But later Rosalia's health deteriorated and she was often sick in bed.

Rosina never went anywhere, so the only traveling Maria experienced as a child was the occasional solo trip to Vienna to visit her relatives. She made the trip three or four times as a school girl, during summer vacations. The train ride was always exciting for her. Maria believed Rosina didn't accompany her because she couldn't afford to spend any money on herself.

In Vienna Maria stayed with two different relatives—a cousin on her mother's side and her uncle Hans. The two didn't live near each other, but streetcars made it easy for Maria to hop back and forth between them. Maria's relatives ferried her all over the city to see magnificent sights such as the grand Hofburg and Schönbrunn Palaces. These lavish Habsburg winter and summer residences were the centers of power for centuries. Her uncle's apartment in the 13th *Bezirk* (district) was conveniently near Schönbrunn, so this excursion wasn't a long one. But it was one Maria always highly anticipated because a visit to the palace grounds was never complete without a visit to the marvelous nearby Schönbrunn Tiergarten, the world's first public zoo. Years later my father, Maria's future spouse, would also see Schönbrunn, but in a more intimate way because for a time during the Second World War he lived in a building in that large complex.

The outings also brought Maria to cemeteries where the wealthy and powerful had built huge ornate monuments for themselves or their family. Once or twice she even went to the opera. These experiences were exciting and otherworldly compared to those she knew in sleepy little Schömitz, so upon returning home, the pace of rural Sudmähren life would seem exceedingly slow. But the feeling only lasted a few days. Back among familiar surroundings and her friends, she quickly regained her equilibrium and found she didn't really miss Vienna all that much. In streetcar-less Schömitz, walking became a good-enough mode of transportation again. It suited the pace of life there. Although walking was not always such a joy for older people with ailments, Maria found strolls pleasurable. With both sides of every road lined by fruit and nut trees, and seldom a motorized vehicle to disturb the silence, the serenity and beauty was idyllic. Never was this truer than in the spring when all the roadside trees were in blossom.

During Maria's childhood mature apple trees lined the road to Lodenitz. When peach, apricot, and cherry trees later replaced them, the road to Gubschitz became the main source of apples. After World War I, the Czech government took the ownership of these trees away from Schömitz and other communities. From then on, Czech caretakers in shacks along each road guarded the trees when the fruit ripened and sold it to the public. Buyers picked or gathered the fruit themselves. Often a family bought the fruit of one entire tree to can or preserve. However, all this good fruit proved a terrible temptation to young children. Maria recalled one caretaker in particular who took his job very seriously. If anyone stole so much as one apple or peach, he ran after them like a man possessed and flailed away madly with the stout stick he always carried.

◆

The serene environment notwithstanding, the combination of the raging Great Depression and a government that treated its ethnic minorities as second-class citizens kept life in Schömitz difficult for families. Fortunately, Rosina could count on her relatives next door for assistance. The Luksch family always willingly helped out, despite having little themselves. Marie, the seamstress and the older of the two daughters, made many of young Maria's clothes. When Maria grew a bit older, she repaid the favor by delivering Marie's finished garments to her customers.

Front from left: Maria, Rosina, Theresa Luksch and two relatives. Rear from left, Emma, Franz, and Marie Luksch

Rosina's goat provided enough milk to make cheese, but cow's milk for drinking and cooking came from the Luksch family. Franz's two cows served as draught animals for farming as well as for milking. The milk the families didn't consume was delivered to the cooperative collection station in the lower part of the village each day. Maria laughed fondly when she recalled a story about one of the Luksch cows. She was accompanying Franz *Onkel* (uncle) on foot, helping him drive the two cows he'd sold to a buyer in Pohrlitz. On the outskirts of the town, shortly after Maria began to hear a radio playing music loudly through an open window, Franz Onkel burst out laughing and pointed ahead. The hindquarters of one of the cows was swaying and keeping perfect time with the music.

Franz was one of those rare and delightful people who couldn't help but laugh and make others laugh, too. He even enjoyed laughing about things that hadn't been the least bit funny when they happened, like the incident that drove his family out of their house after his redheaded nephew, Johann, became a carpenter. This young man was Karolina's youngest brother. Maria found him likeable and pleasant even though some of his other siblings, particularly Karolina, didn't. No relative in the village stepped up to help him out when he wanted to set up a workshop, so Rosina allowed him to convert her storage shed near the back of her lot into his shop. For heat, Johann installed a wood stove and cut a hole in the wall for the stovepipe. But when he fired it up for the first time, the smoke from the pipe funneled right into the Luksch house through the rear door and windows and chased the gasping and coughing occupants outside. Franz Onkel laughed about that for years.

As a child, Maria wished Rosina could have become infected with some of the same lightheartedness, but grew to understand why this would never be. Her grandmother's hard life had molded a disposition that did not easily lapse into laughter. Fortunately, children are flexible and can overlook many shortcomings in the adults around them. Even though Maria found her situation wanting in some ways, she appreciated and dearly loved those who gave her so much when they had so little themselves.

Maria didn't mind helping her grandmother or delivering finished garments for Marie next door, but she increasingly came to resent having to help her stepmother. Lending Karolina a hand was a never-ending job, and the thought of that woman still agitated her 70 years later. Maria saw her as a selfish person who took and took but never gave back. Particularly galling was how Karolina used Rosina. Maria's grandmother was old and worked hard to support herself and Maria, yet Karolina selfishly added to the old woman's workload and never showed any appreciation.

Karolina regularly sent dirty clothes to Rosina for laundering. This annoyed Maria to no end, and she was obliged to pitch in. Maria knew Rosina put up with it because Karolina wielded an unspoken threat. If Karolina didn't get her way, she'd cut off contact between Maria and her father. Although Johann was largely absent from Maria's life anyway, he was still her father. More vexing to Maria than the laundry was the other demand. The woman had refused to take Maria in under her roof, yet had no qualms about insisting Maria help care for her own large brood. Maria started helping when she was still quite young herself and hadn't liked the job then. Her resentment mounted as her duties grew, but her loathing extended only to Karolina. Maria liked all the children and got on well with them.

It frustrated Maria that despite all the time she spent working at her stepmother's house, she wasn't able to talk to her father there because of Karolina's domineering character and Johann's passivity. She and her father chatted only when well out of Karolina's sight. Maria was far too intimidated to rebel for she'd witnessed more than one of Karolina's dish-smashing temper fits.

Karolina wasn't alone in her behavior. Right across the street from her house lived another domineering wife who treated her stepchild, a girl about Maria's age, the same way. Her husband too was passive like Johann and had little say in family matters. These two women seemed to learn from, and feed off, each other. Fortunately for the girl, sympathetic relatives eventually took her into their home and created a happier environment for her.

---

[1] Oskar Halusa, Personal Communication.
[2] Mauer, *Schömitz*.

14 A Community of Farmers

THE BREAKUP OF THE AUSTRIAN EMPIRE impacted Sudeten Germans financially because the new borders isolated traditional industrial and agricultural markets and fragmented the transportation network. The plight of this population worsened when Prague's nationalization and redistribution reforms took away German enterprises, capital, and jobs. The Great Depression, which began in 1929, finished the impoverishment. Because Germans were largely ignored when it came to support and assistance from the Czechoslovak government, it was not surprising that the unemployment rate for Germans soared and became several times that of Czechs.[1]

Schömitz survived as a functioning German community because of its agricultural heritage. Growing food ran in the blood. There, nearly everyone was a farmer regardless of whether farming was the family mainstay or not. Acquiring the skill and knowledge to make things grow was certainly driven by pride, but more importantly, eating well demanded it. In growing food, Schömitzers understood the benefits of mutual cooperation. Most farmers shared ideas, equipment, and labor. This cooperative spirit had allowed recovery from the many calamities in the past, and the practice allowed neighbors and friends to scrape by in the current difficult times.

Schömitzers realized that only their own initiative and guile could keep their community alive and vibrant, so they joined or established cooperative ventures. Adequate drinking water was one longstanding problem they tackled in this period. Although most houses had rock-lined wells, an unpleasant mineral taste made the local groundwater undrinkable. In the early 1800s, the village had laid a small wooden pipeline to bring in drinking water, but the system could only deliver it to one outlet in the lowest part of the village. In the first community water project of its type in Moravia, Schömitz in 1888 replaced the wooden pipe with a more modern cast-iron pipe that fed three outlets, but the system still lacked enough pressure to pipe water to individual houses.

In the 1920s residents tired of lugging water home in vats slung on their backs and mounted a community-wide effort to further modernize. The community raised taxes and in 1927 constructed a modern pipeline and pumping station able to serve the entire village. Schömitz had previously been a pioneer in introducing electric lighting through a joint cooperative with Lodenitz and two other villages in 1921. It also participated in co-ops with other villages for milk marketing, veterinary services, banking, and sugar beet storage.

1927 Dedication of new water works. Head teacher Rudolf Mauer is fifth from left in front row; Johann Hajek is in last row just to right of SCHÖMITZ.

Although much of the village infrastructure was built and maintained cooperatively, like nearly every other southern Moravian community, Schömitz employed a city worker to perform certain duties. This *Gemeindediener* (community servant) had many responsibilities and often held the job for decades, so the man chosen for the job was selected for his dedication and efficiency. His most visible duty, to deliver public announcements from the mayor, was carried out by beating a small drum and shouting out the message as he trudged through the streets. The Gemeindediener was a respected and important man in the community and attended official meetings as well as announced them. He was seldom off duty because as the night watchman he also patrolled the village streets.

The Gemeindediener also had responsibilities regarding the community's livestock. A small stream flowed through town via a roadside ditch and emptied into the masonry-enclosed horse watering pond at the lower edge of the village—the pond that did double duty as the swimming hole for local children and the roving Roma. In the days of serfdom, this little stream fed a string of large fish-rearing ponds that the village women attended to for the lord. In Maria's era the pond overflow ran into a second pond in the communal fowl-grazing area. Each morning the Gemeindediener blew a horn signaling residents to open their farmyard gate and turn their ducks and geese loose. In the street these birds joined a long orderly procession heading to the pond. In the evening the flow reversed as the birds all waddled back in the opposite direction. Seldom was there a lost bird. After the harvest each year, the Gemeindediener directed the fowl to the fields to forage the grain left on the ground.

When the community fell under Prague's control, the antagonistic nationalistic policies damaged the smooth functioning system that had provided a living for everyone in Schömitz for so long. The Gemeindediener's salary came from the community, so that job remained in German hands, but when the Meierhof was nationalized the Germans thrown out of work faced fierce competition in finding other jobs. Men like Johann had to get by with part-time work because only large farms employed full-time workers, and in the period between the wars Schömitz had only three such farms.

◆

A pair of brothers named Judex owned one of the three large farms. They employed two or three full-time hired men and a few seasonal workers. A second farm with several parcels of land near the town of Pohrlitz was somewhat larger and employed more laborers. It belonged to Simon Dukes, a small man with a larger-than-average house near the German school. Dukes, a Czech with a Czech nationalistic outlook, wanted nothing to do with his German neighbors socially. Because he was neither likeable nor friendly, his neighbors reciprocated and had little to do with him. Yet oddly enough, Dukes liked Fritz Haas, Karolina's brother. Fritz tended Dukes's livestock and handled long-horned oxen in fieldwork. Dukes was the man who provided Fritz lodging in a nearby house, enabling Fritz to rent Karolina and Johann the house and farmland given him by his mother.

Besides being a large landowner and a Czech, Dukes stood out in another way too. He was a Jew. Many of the villages and towns throughout the district had at least a sprinkling of Jewish residents, but few Jews were farmers. Most practiced professions, ran shops, or owned businesses. Pohrlitz, where Jews owned most of the businesses, had a thriving Jewish community.

Dukes's wife was also Jewish, but German rather than Czech. The couple's son and daughter attended school in Pohrlitz and mingled little with the other children in Schömitz. But the family did do some business in Schömitz. Maria's grandmother often sold geese to the family for their table, and Maria's seamstress cousin, Marie, made most of their clothes.

A second Jewish family in the village offset Dukes's disagreeability. The Neuspiels were German Jews and operated a small grocery store. They were friendly, outgoing people who were well liked and respected. Their children, Ilse, Robert, and Erhard attended the German school and the family actively participated in festivals, celebrations, and other aspects of village life. Maria and Ilse were friends, and on Jewish holidays Maria sometimes went to her house and ate matzo. On Saturdays the Neuspiels left for their synagogue in Pohrlitz.

Later on during World War II, one of the local innkeepers, Johann Caesar, inherited considerable land and also became a large farmer. He too was a small man with a sometimes grumpy disposition. At least that was Maria's impression when young. Maria recalled that he was one of the few farmers who used POW laborers from Russia, Croatia, and Serbia during the war years. Ernst Hajek, Maria's youngest brother, came to know these POWs as well as anyone because as a boy he spent considerable time with them during the harvest season. Several of the Croats and Serbs spoke good German, and he was on friendly terms with them. However, he learned to stay out of their way when they were drinking because they often got into fights with each other. Like the Czechs and Slovaks, the two nationalities disliked one another.

◆

The Meierhof was the largest local farm. Before nationalization, it had been but one parcel of 1500 square kilometers owned by the Liechtenstein family in Moravia, Bohemia, and Silesia. A decade prior to Czechoslovakia's founding in 1918, Graf Rudolf Kinsky, a nephew of the reigning prince, inherited the Meierhof and several other properties. When the new Czech government nationalized the farm, it also took the sugar-beet-processing factories in Pohrlitz. Seizing these valuable assets allowed Prague to control the local economy and pack more Czechs into the German villages.

The Meierhof compound contained the largest buildings in Schömitz. The hub of the enterprise was located at the south end of the village down a 75-meter lane that led through a large gate. The spacious Hof resembled a fort in that its long farm buildings surrounded a square open space. In this Hof the cows were milked, the hay and grain were stored, and the livestock and machinery were housed. Much of the land east of the road to Lodenitz belonged to the farm, as did more land nearer to Pohrlitz. With the large modern machinery of today, an operation of that size could be farmed with minimal workers, but in Maria's day it required many laborers.

The Hof became a beehive of activity each morning and evening, and for the entire day at certain times of the year. During the summer grain harvest, the threshing machines sent out a cacophony of sound for weeks on end. In the fall the intensive effort moved to the beet fields. Sometimes the sugar beet harvest lasted into December or January. Oxen plowed up the beets. Workers picked them out of the overturned soil by hand, cleaned off the dirt, and shoveled them into wagons. At the peak of the harvest, columns of horse or ox-drawn wagons loaded with beets clogged the roads to the processing plants in Pohrlitz and Mährisch Kromau. In wet years this traffic turned the unpaved portions of these roads into nearly impassible mud pits.

The small triangular Kellerberg plot directly across the road from the Meierhof held special significance for Schömitz residents because for centuries it had been the site of the village wine cellars and press houses. The Meierhof's new Czech managers defiled the place when they built new wagon roads adjacent to the cellar area and dug large silage pits into which they dumped the waste pulp brought back from the sugar factories by the beet wagons. Not only did the silage fermentation process smell, but the encroaching access roads and stinky discharge from the pits destroyed many beautiful chestnut trees.

In the days when mainly Germans worked at the Meierhof, the farm only needed to house the seasonal Slovak laborers who tended the beet crop. However, after 1918 the influx of new permanent Czech workers created a need for further housing. Some found accommodations in the village, but most boarded in a large residential structure built on the eastern edge of Schömitz. Like the Meierhof, this residence also enclosed a central courtyard. Because the Czech and Slovak residents didn't get along, they occupied separate wings of the building. The Czechs received better accommodations. Their small apartments made up three wings of the building while the Slovaks occupied cramped dormitory quarters in the remaining wing. The Slovak migrants arrived each spring to plant and thin sugar beets, and then departed right after the beet harvest ended. The married couples among them left their children at home with relatives because working in the fields all day didn't allow enough time for child care.

On Sunday the Slovaks dressed up in the colorful, traditional peasant attire of their region. Since they were devout Catholics, Maria saw them each Sunday on the road to the church in Lodenitz. The women wore billowy, white skirts adorned with colorful patterns, lace, and embroidered designs. Many tied aprons over the skirts. Some wore vests with embroidered designs over blouses that frequently came with puffy sleeves. When the Slovak women washed their clothes on the wall of the horse pond, Maria always wondered how they got their Sunday finery so white with that dirty water.

On the farm the pecking order was also obvious in the clear division of labor. Czech men drove the long-horned oxen used for soil preparation, sowing, and other field work, while Czech women milked the cows. The Slovaks, men and women alike, tended to the backbreaking thinning, cultivating, and harvesting of sugar beets. As the wagons loaded with beets from the large storage piles of the harvested crop made their way to the processing plants, the Slovaks prepared to leave. Maria remembered their departure ritual well. Once their belongings were packed, they toted their straw mattresses out into the courtyard and dumped the contents onto a pile. Then someone lit the straw with a match. When the smoky, fiery spectacle was over and the bedding was reduced to a pile of ash, the workers hurried away to rejoin their families and resume their lives until spring called them back to the drudgery.

The Liechtenstein monarchy has been trying to get the Meierhof and its other large land holdings back ever since the new Czech state seized them. Although it reestablished diplomatic relations with the Czech Republic in 2009, at this writing its claims are still active. Since the breakup of the Holy Roman Empire in 1806, Liechtenstein has existed as a small independent state sandwiched between Switzerland and Austria. Its ruling princes were at one time high-ranking members of Austria's imperial court and resided on their lands in the Czech areas and in Vienna. However, in 1938 just before the start of hostilities, they wisely relocated to Liechtenstein.

No description of agriculture and farming in this area is complete without mentioning the remarkable farm community of Lodenitz, whose fields bordered Schömitz to the north. Here, farmers passed their land on to the oldest son instead of dividing it among all their offspring. This kept farms large enough (typically 20 to 50 hectares) to be prosperous if managed well. And well managed they were, as evidenced by the lovely paintings and artwork many of these farmers owned. There were 40 to 50 such farmers, the majority of whom had earned advanced academic degrees. This concentration of expertise made it possible for the village to maintain a prestigious school of agronomy. The farmers were affluent enough to offer their children higher education, and the children made use of the opportunity. Oswald Lustig showed me a list he'd compiled of their impressive education achievements. The farmers included professors of math and science, veterinarians, and holders of doctorates in various other disciplines.

---

[1] Wikipedia contributors. "Sudeten Germans." *Wikipedia*, Wikipedia.org, 5 Apr. 2015, accessed 20 Apr. 2015.

15 A German School

MARIA'S DAILY WALK TO SCHOOL was a short one. As might be expected of a small village that had been German for nearly a millennium, the *Volkschule* (elementary school) too was German. Prior to 1790 when it was first set up in a local house, any children fortunate enough to attend school walked to Lodenitz. Important improvements came about in 1869 when the Austrian Empire reorganized its education system, allocated more resources to communities and teachers, and made education compulsory.

In 1883 the community demolished a large farmhouse and erected a new school building in its place. The ground floor provided an office for village administrators and a residence for the head teacher. The second floor contained two spacious classrooms and an apartment for a second teacher. Behind the school was a playground, a garden for the teachers, a stable, and a shed for coal and firewood. In 1918 the school began to provide free books and supplies to all children because many families could no longer afford to buy such things. The community also began to host an annual Christmas party at which low-income families were given a quantity of baked goods and a new pair of leather shoes for each child.

When Prague's actions packed Czechs into German communities like Schömitz, local harmony suffered. Because the large number of newcomers brought with them their own customs and priorities, they did not fully integrate into the local culture and diluted the community's ability to support its existing institutions. More significantly, as early as 1919 the influx provided the government the justification to start a government-supported Czech school when there were only seven Czech children in the village. The children would have been better served had they been transported several kilometers to a larger existing school, and it would surely have been more cost effective. However, as the village was to learn, the government had other reasons for establishing an alternative to the existing community-supported German school.

By law, communities were due compensation when properties were nationalized and removed from the tax rolls, but Schömitz's claim for recompense for the loss of the Meierhof was ignored by Prague. Despite many attempts to collect the money, it was never paid. This greatly impacted the community's tax base and indirectly further hurt the privately supported Volkschule by impoverishing the German taxpayers who needed to make up the shortfall.

◆

The German school, and many others like it, survived largely because of the efforts of a Sudeten German by the name of Dr. Rudolf Funke. He recognized the danger posed by the new Czechoslovak government's policies and founded a nonpolitical private organization to aid German schools. The Deutsche Kulturverband's stated mission was to respect the rights of others and at the same time vigorously defend the rights of Germans by supporting their traditional schools, language and culture. For the next two decades the organization helped poor villages pay their teachers, cover expenses, and provide scholarships for children in need. By the start of World War II, the group had nearly 3400 local branches. In communities that hadn't fought to save their schools, German children had no option but to attend a Czech school.

The Czech government quickly built many new school buildings throughout the minority areas. In larger villages like Lodenitz and Wolframitz, it constructed a campus. To boost Czech enrollment, Prague transported in many children from distant Czech communities each day by car. In countless German communities, Czech schools were established for as few as a handful of children in order to supplant local ethnic schools. Administrators devised new rules and screened family ancestries to raise enrollment. The parents of children with Czech grandmothers were shocked to receive official orders to enroll their children in the Czech school. Germans wondered whatever happened to the Masaryk and Beneš promise of a tolerant and benevolent democracy emulating Switzerland and its ethnic cantons.

Schömitzers became embittered in 1919 when Czech authorities evicted the Schömitz school board from its quarters so their new Czech school could take over the space. Similar dictates and actions upset Sudeten Germans throughout the country. The Schömitz head teacher between the wars, Rudolf Mauer, anecdotally described how infuriating the government policies were. A local man named Anton Kopischte enrolled his small son, also named Anton, in the Schömitz Volkschule, the same school the father had attended. When questioned, Kopischte told the Czech authorities that he spoke, felt, and thought only in German. Yet, because his wife came from a neighboring Czech community, the administrators ordered Kopischte to withdraw his son from the German school and send him to the Czech school. He refused. Fines of 10 crowns, then 20, and finally 50 didn't cause him to change his mind. Since the fines had no effect they jailed Kopischte for a week. When he still refused to comply, they barred little Anton from attending the German school, so the child attended no school at all.[1]

After a legislator intervened two years later, the authorities relented and allowed the boy back into the German school. Because his parents were farm workers and not well educated, the boy had received no home schooling during this time. Fortunately, young Anton was gifted and quickly surpassed his classmates. He went on to a secondary school in Pohrlitz and then to a teacher-training institute in Brünn. However, World War II pulled him in, as it did all young German men, and Anton received a commission as an officer. He didn't survive the war.

Prague's policies continued to deliver a steady stream of new Czech workers, so the Czech school enrollment grew through that means as well. Then the local authorities required kindergarten-age children, as well as the older children, to be screened for Czech ancestry. When the enrollment hit 35 to 40 students, there were enough students for the government to justify allocating money for a fine new facility able to entice even more students from mixed-marriage families. To stem the erosion and keep its Volkschule competitive, the Germans undertook a major renovation of their school, funded through donations. Despite the community's poverty, the frightened German residents threw their full support behind the project and paid off the debt in just two years.

At the opening ceremony for the new Czech school, the German villagers were shocked to hear loud chants of "Long live Czech Schömitz."[2] This came as a rude awakening to the Germans who hadn't yet understood the nature of the threat to their community. Encouraged by the regional government, a small but confrontational Czech faction was now firmly established in the community. Actions such as this made Germans throughout the Sudetenland fear for their future. They reacted by supporting the new Sudeten nationalistic political parties.

The German Volkschule in Schömitz, with its limited resources, did the best it could to compete with the government-supported Czech school, but never regained its former lofty enrollment. Although the absence of so many men during the World War I years resulted in lower numbers of school-age children several years later, the establishment of the competing school and the loss of German jobs also took a toll. The numbers tell the story. From 1880 until 1919, the school averaged over 100 students. The 1919 enrollment of 104 fell to 74 in 1920, and dropped to 55 in 1923, just before Maria started school. The numbers finally stabilized and remained in the upper forties until 1938 when the Sudetenland became part of the German Reich.

Czech and German children usually got along despite the political differences of their parents. Yet, occasionally a Czech child would taunt German children with name-calling. And the German children retaliated. Of course, the taunting also sometimes came from the other side.

◆

Until the teacher shortage of the German Reich era, the Volkschule provided one teacher for the lower four grades and another for the upper four. Both lived in apartments within the school building. In Maria's time, neither originated from Schömitz. She knew the two teachers didn't much like one another because they sometimes bickered in the hallway like an old married couple.

Rudolf Mauer, the *Oberlehrer* (head teacher) was a father of six. His children, along with Johann's, made up a sizeable portion of the student body. Five of the Mauer children were boys. Their names were Franz, Helmut, Otto, Rudi, and Erhard. Maria was considerably older than the daughter, Erica, but liked the young girl and sometimes spent time with her in the family apartment. Maria seldom saw Herr Lehrer Mauer there because he always sequestered himself from the hubbub and domestic activity in his study. The Mauers lived comfortably and employed a housekeeper to help with the cleaning, laundry, and cooking. Maria's cousin made most of the family's clothing.

The Mauer children derived certain benefits from residing in the school building. They never had to brave inclement weather on the way to or from school, or walk far to retrieve forgotten homework. And they had a playground right outside their back door. However, spending two periods in this yard each school day probably lessened their enjoyment of it, particularly since one of those periods consisted of conditioning exercises. The younger children, exempted from this structured activity, were always allowed to use the play equipment. Maria sometimes lingered on the playground with her friends, or Erica, after school when she didn't have work to do at home or at her stepmother's house. Sadly Erica died of tuberculosis in 1945 at age 16.

In the classroom the children were clustered by age. The teachers circulated among the groups and spent a few minutes with each when not lecturing. The normal school day ran from eight to four, six days a week, with a break for lunch. Since the students all lived in, or close to, the village, they walked home for lunch. Religion was taught because this was a private school and nearly all students were Catholics. For a time a *Katechet* (seminarian studying to be a priest) came from Lodenitz to provide the religious instruction. Maria remembered him well because he showed no hesitation in applying a ruler to misbehaving boys.

A German School

Although the school's budget limited outings and field trips, in good weather the teachers sometimes took their classes outdoors or on walks. In March 1929 when Maria was nine, the entire student body assembled outdoors to watch the hydrogen airship Graf Zeppelin soar overhead. The dirigible passed low enough for Maria to see the outline of passengers gazing through the windows on the return leg of a flight which had taken them to Palestine and Egypt.[3]

A few months later in August, the rigid airship made its famous around-the-world flight. The Graf Zeppelin's circumnavigation of the globe covered 20,651 miles in 12 days. Coincidentally, my wife's mother watched the zeppelin pass overhead during that flight. Her view was from northern Illinois near the end of the voyage. The trip was commercially backed by flamboyant American newspaper publisher William Randolph Hearst who, to glean maximum publicity from the flight, stipulated that the journey begin and end in the United States at the Lakehurst Naval Air Station in New Jersey. Lakehurst was the hangar base for the Graf Zeppelin's sister ship, which the Zeppelin Company had been required to build for the US Navy as a war reparation.

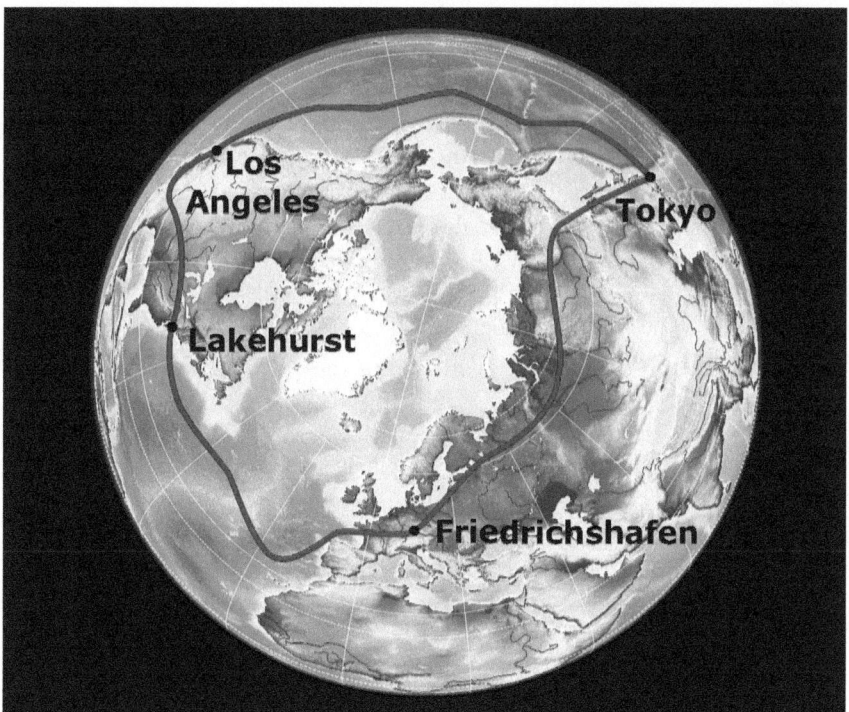

The route of the Graf Zeppelin 1929 global circumnavigation

Constructing such airships was a complicated process and Germany had the best technology. Not only were the rigid frames hard to construct, producing the bags to hold the hydrogen was difficult also. No material could adequately contain hydrogen gas until the Germans discovered how to bond together pieces of cattle intestine. The process of making the many huge gas bags required for a zeppelin was extremely labor intensive. Each dirigible needed upwards of 250,000 intestines. During World War I, when Germany built many dirigibles for military use and bombed London with them, the country suffered a severe sausage shortage because the intestines that normally served as sausage casings went to dirigibles.

The only school field trip Maria recalled was to a natural wonder near the city of Brünn. Tropstein Höhle, one of several caves in the Moravian Karst formation, was a locally famous cave featuring impressive stalagmites. On the outing, the cave was less memorable for Maria than the Macocha Abyss, a large sinkhole within the same formation. Macocha is a Slavic word for "stepmother." The name came from a 17th century legend in which a woman threw her stepchild over the edge of the abyss.

The legend held that in the village of Vilemovice, when a widower with a small son remarried, all was well until his wife gave birth to her own child. From then on, she sought to get rid of the stepson. One day she ordered the boy to accompany her in gathering the fruits of the forest. She deliberately led him to the abyss and there flung him over the edge. He was spared from death only because he became entangled in tree branches at the bottom of the abyss. Several woodcutters working nearby heard his cries and came to his rescue. After the boy told his story, and the men repeated it to the other villagers, an angry mob seized the stepmother and threw her into the abyss. The trip left Maria with vivid thoughts about her own stepmother.

◆

Maria's school-day routine varied little throughout the week, with the exception of Wednesday afternoon when the boys were dismissed or received some type of practical instruction outside the classroom. At that time, girls from grades three through eight participated in *Handiweit*. A woman named Frau Braun came from Lodenitz each week to instruct this class. Cooking wasn't a part of this instruction, and not just because the building lacked a facility for food preparation. Such a class wasn't necessary because no girl could avoid picking up that skill at home. The handcraft Frau Braun taught was needlework—sewing, crocheting, and knitting.

Girls spent the entire school year completing a chosen project. As a girl's skills improved each year, Frau Braun expected her to take on ever more difficult challenges. The projects, which remained in the classroom until year-end, were then graded and displayed. The year Maria learned to use a sewing machine was the most satisfying for her. However, she admitted it was not the most memorable one. That honor went to her knitting project. Although she managed to save a couple of her projects in the aftermath of World War II, she chose to leave that one behind. She'd brought her knit stockings home at the end of the year and immediately took them to the Luksch house to show Marie, an accomplished knitter. When Maria unfolded them in the kitchen, Marie couldn't contain herself and burst out laughing. Although Maria was taken aback at first, when Marie remarked that if the stockings were any longer they'd fit over stilts, Maria had to laugh herself.

Maria enjoyed Handiweit tremendously. This was not the case for the sole Czech girl in her class, whose family lived just outside of town to the east. Maria felt sorry for her because she was all thumbs and couldn't seem to make anything. The law allowed her and her brother to attend the Volkschule because their mother was German. The family was so poor that the boy came to school barefoot much of the year. The children's father worked as a laborer at the brickyard that fired clay roof tiles and bricks in ovens. Because the children spoke poor German, they did badly in school. The boy also had serious learning problems that left him distracted and mischievous, resulting in frequent disciplining by the teachers. The girl got much more out of school because she was well behaved and gradually grew more competent in German.

The family's poverty provided the children one thing in abundance—head lice. Although the lower grade teacher routinely examined heads for lice in the morning, her screening wasn't foolproof and other children kept getting infested. Maria had to have her head treated several times as a result. The treatment called for the application of a potent, foul-smelling insecticide that left her hair smelly enough the following day to keep her home from school.

The lower level teacher, Elsie Kniefel, was a redheaded spinster from Brünn. Maria described her as a grumpy old thing who came down hard on students caught copying work, not paying attention, or unable to recite their lessons. Although Maria was usually a good student, on occasion Elsie gave her grief too. Maria never forgot the time Elsie kept her after school for not completing her homework. At some point during the detention, Elsie left for her apartment down the hall and forgot about Maria sitting quietly in her seat. After an hour alone in the classroom, the little girl sneaked out and ran home. Her grandmother didn't show much sympathy when Maria explained her tardiness. The next morning Maria dreaded returning to school, knowing she'd slipped out without permission. But Elsie said not a word about it, probably because she felt guilt for forgetting a child in the classroom.

The German measles epidemic was another memorable event during Maria's younger years. The outbreak hit during the school year and nearly every child caught the illness. Before immunization for the disease was available, such epidemics struck regularly every few years. Although the disease is generally mild and not life threatening, pregnant women who contract the virus risk passing on congenital rubella syndrome to the developing fetus. The potential consequences are serious and include mental retardation, heart and eye malformations, growth retardation, deafness, and a whole host of liver, spleen, and bone marrow problems. Consequently, the health authorities closed the school and quarantined the village children in their homes for six weeks. Those children with pregnant mothers or preschool siblings who hadn't previously had rubella were quarantined at a relative's house.

That epidemic was bad enough, but another highly infectious epidemic common in the early 20th century—scarlet fever—closely followed it. This childhood disease can cause serious complications such as rheumatic fever or kidney inflammation. By the time the second quarantine ended, three months of the school year were lost. Maria was alone in the house most of the day during this time as her grandmother worked in the fields. Neither Maria nor her friends had telephones, so to keep from going crazy, she and Marie next door gouged a hole in the common wall between their houses to allow the two of them to chat while Marie worked at her sewing.

Maria also talked to her dog, Max. Max wasn't allowed in the house, but she could speak to him through the window and back door, or out behind the house. Cats lurked about too, but because no one in the village kept them as pets, they weren't tame enough to be good listeners. Maria was much relieved when the quarantine finally ended and she could again leave the house and see her friends.

◆

In the entire school year, the two most dreaded days were those set aside for testing. The government mandated twice-yearly exams covering all subjects, which were administered orally by an outside examiner. The examiners always looked friendly enough on arrival, but their demeanor didn't fool the students. These people were to be taken seriously. They intimidated the students. The examiner quizzed the children individually in front of the entire class during this all-day process, and no one dared act up during the testing.

What students feared most about a poor showing was their teacher's reaction. Such a result reflected poorly on the teacher, and when students underperformed, the teacher exacted revenge the next day. The exams always raised a terrible anxiety in Maria. Even though she didn't do particularly well in math and found history and geography boring, she generally earned good marks on her quarterly report cards, did well on the comprehensive exams, and liked school.

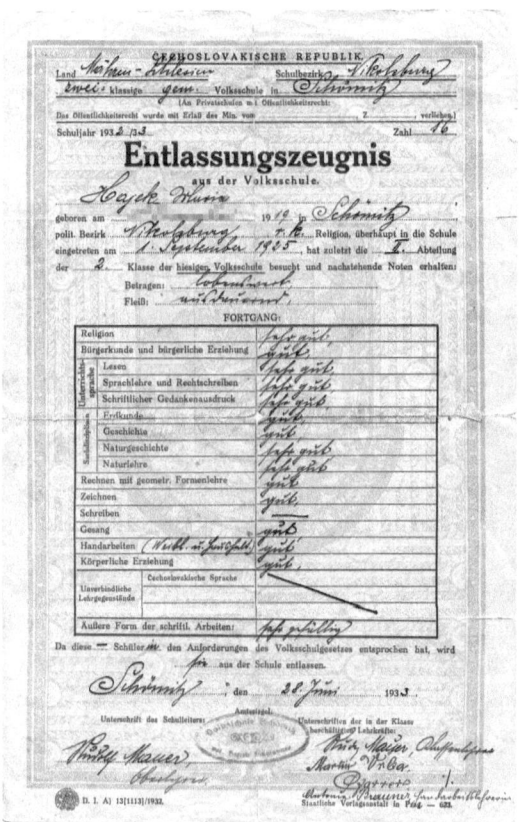

Maria's eighth grade graduation certificate

Students feared Herr Mauer, whether it was exam day or not. He brooked no nonsense and rigidly enforced discipline with a small riding whip. Troublemakers, and those who hadn't prepared their lessons, soon felt the sting of his riding crop across their hands. The victims were usually boys. Occasionally, perhaps for variety's sake, he rapped knuckles with a ruler. Mauer wielded both instruments with gusto and to great effect, but the little whip was his favorite. Once, when a group of boys were reported to Herr Mauer for stealing apples from trees along the road, the culprits paid dearly for their misdeed when he laid the whip to their hands. That was the last incident of apple larceny Maria heard of.

Although most children attended school for only eight years, much was packed into those years, thanks to a six-day school week, short holiday and summer breaks, and a no-nonsense instructor. Whether a student liked him or not, by the end of eighth grade nearly every graduate agreed they'd really learned something from Herr Mauer.

Maria's formal education ended at age 14 because her grandmother didn't have the money to send her on to Pohrlitz for further schooling. It was the same for most children in Schömitz and nearby villages. While poverty was usually the reason children didn't continue their education, some parents just didn't want their children to leave home at such a young age. Others were concerned that if their children did leave for a larger town or city they might not choose to return.

The parents of an academically gifted child had to make choices even earlier. If they could afford to pay for schooling and did decide to send the child on to a more academic preparatory school, they also had to determine at what age the child should go. With the Czech government's policy of trying to squeeze out minority schools, parents were mindful that sending their child elsewhere lowered the enrollment in the Volkschule and weakened the position of the community in keeping its school. On the other hand, not sending their child away lessened the child's chances of admission to an institution of higher learning.

When Oswald Lustig's parents in Gubschitz confronted this issue, they decided to enroll Oswald in the *Bürgerschule*, a preparatory school in Pohrlitz. Oswald started there as soon as he was old enough to walk a considerable distance. Because his grandparents in Wolframitz lived closer to the school, he stayed with them during the school week. Even so, 12 kilometers each day on foot or by bicycle was a substantial distance for a youngster.

In October 1938, after 20 years of Czech rule, Prague's efforts to close German schools and turn Germans into Czechs ended when Germany, France, and England negotiated the Munich Agreement without Czech consent and allowed Hitler to annex the Sudetenland. The agreement, viewed by most historians as an act of appeasement, split the Sudetenland from the core Czech region. The Reich's new local administrators wasted no time in addressing the school situation. Within days they directed the Schömitz Volkschule to relocate to the Czech school building.

Before the Czechs hastily abandoned their building, they came in trucks and stripped it of all its furniture, desks, and supplies. The Schömitzers didn't fret because the new school desks they'd bought after remodeling the old German school fit right in with the stylish parquet floor in the new building. To the Germans, who'd struggled to maintain their old school, the landscaped new building, bound by rose gardens, orchards, and the sugar beet fields beyond, seemed like a palace.

More changes quickly followed. German children who desired to learn a trade or skill suddenly gained access to a wide variety of training programs, and all academically gifted German children wishing to attend the Bürgerschule in Pohrlitz were subsidized by the Reich government. For higher education, the district offered more than 10 secondary schools choices. These included academic high schools for winemaking, teacher training, and agricultural sciences. More schools were soon added to the mix. Before long, a bus shuttled 30 students between Schömitz and the railroad station each day. Unfortunately, these changes came too late to help Maria further her education, for she was already 19 at the time the Sudetenland came under German administration.

---

[1] Mauer, *Schömitz*.
[2] Mauer, *Schömitz*.
[3] "Contrary Winds: Zeppelins Over the Middle East," *Saudi Aramco World*, 45 No. 4 (1994).

16 Hitler and Friends Step Up

Throughout Maria's childhood in the 1920s and early 1930s, great changes were occurring in Germany. As Johann's voice in household matters faded away in tiny Schömitz, in Germany the voice of his manipulative fellow veteran, Adolf Hitler, became stronger and more strident. Although the voice of Johann's wife, Karolina, also became ever more strident and manipulative, her influence didn't extend beyond her family. Hitler, far more astute, ambitious, and devious, came to play on a much bigger stage—one so large that it expanded to encompass both Schömitz and the family of my other Johann grandfather farther to the east in Romania.

Johann and Karolina wouldn't have heard of Hitler yet when their first children came along. But a few years later, after Hitler linked the Sudetenland's fate with that of Germany's, he'd made himself the most famous and feared man in Europe. Understanding how such a thing could come about and how that subsequently affected Maria, Johann, and millions of other ethnic Germans east of Germany requires a closer look at the man and the circumstances that allowed him to come to power.

Unlike the Johanns, rootless Adolf Hitler had no incentive to return to the region of his birth in Austria after the Great War. His childhood there had been unhappy and troubled. He'd hated his authoritarian and abusive father and was relieved when he died. He felt the opposite for his mother, but she'd died of cancer when Hitler was 19. His war experience did nothing to help him regain any sense of belonging to the now fragmented Austrian Empire, so he returned to Munich.

◆

Many historians believe World War II would not have happened without the crippling terms imposed on Germany and Austria at Versailles. The punitive measures in the treaty did more than merely humiliate Germany. They also guaranteed its impoverishment because the treaty cost Germany 6 million citizens, 13 percent of its territory, 10 percent of its industry, all its foreign colonies, and a large share of its coal, iron ore, and other natural resources. The treaty also severely crippled Germany's armed forces and allowed for just the barest excuse for a navy and a tiny army of 100,000 men. Submarines, armor, aircraft, and military conscription were all forbidden. Coupled with the extreme reparation payments, the treaty measures drove Germany to such a state of anarchy and chaos that extremists and revolutionaries attracted a great following.

Britain exacerbated Germany's postwar troubles when it imposed a seven month tight naval blockade on German ports in 1919 to force acceptance of the treaty. Not only did the blockade destroy a maritime shipping competitor, it also created a scarcity of food and goods that helped fuel a staggering hyperinflation within Germany. About 500,000 people starved to death and hundreds of thousands of women suffered miscarriages.

Few took the loss of the war harder than Hitler, who never relinquished the idea that it wasn't the German Army who'd lost the fight. In his mind the German politicians were responsible, for they'd betrayed the military. The injustices of the treaty only intensified his outrage. As for his extreme views on political conspiracies, Jews, and communists, those were formed before or during the first war and hardened as he accumulated influence. Eventually he became even more unhinged than he'd been in the trenches.

Had Hitler merely been rootless and not also ruthless, things might have turned out differently. But unlike the Johanns, with no family to return to and no obligations to fulfill, he saw no better alternative than to remain in the army where, for the first time in his life, he tasted pride for being successful at something. Still, this pride alone would not have done much to advance the career of a fanatical nonentity if the Versailles Treaty hadn't broken Germany to such an extent that civil war raged in its cities. The combination of the chaotic milieu and Hitler's lack of morals made it possible for such an extremist to rise from lowly army corporal to totalitarian dictator in little more than a decade.

Politically, the nightmarish economic conditions led to many communist and left-wing revolts around the country and secession attempts by states. The chaos drew in the involvement of the Russian Communists in Moscow. Hitler's back yard, Bavaria, turned particularly chaotic. At war's end the Independent Social Democratic Party of Germany (USPD) declared an end to the 700-year-old Bavarian monarchy. After the USPD failed to win the parliamentary election and its leader was assassinated, the group compounded the anarchy when it attempted to consolidate control by declaring Bavaria a Soviet Republic in the spring of 1919.

The bedlam produced a string of would-be leaders and reformers. At one point Bavaria's Foreign Affairs Deputy, a man in and out of psychiatric wards for years, tried to declare war on Switzerland because the country wouldn't lend his Soviet Republic a large number of locomotives. That government collapsed after only a few days.

The successor government, the Communist Party, wanted to do away with paper money entirely and redistribute housing and factories to workers. The group's undoing was the enlistment of unemployed workers into a Red Army paramilitary force that arrested and executed counter-revolutionaries. Germany's conservative military leaders feared this threat might get out of hand. With the aid of an anticommunist, army-officer-led, paramilitary force called the Freikorps, which liberated several cities and ports in Germany from leftist groups, the military confronted the Red Army in Munich and killed a number of leftists. During the anarchy the army arrested Hitler and many other soldiers espousing ideas of revolution. Hitler saved himself from execution by persuading the arresting officers he was on their side. To prove his loyalty, he snitched on fellow soldiers who supported the socialists and soon became a political operative, lecturing and converting other soldiers to the army's political philosophy. The assignment in effect paid him to deliver the very sort of political harangue his comrades in the trenches had shrugged off as lunacy.

No one could have dreamed up a better environment for political fanatics, idealists, crazies, reformers, revolutionaries, and opportunists. In 1919 Hitler was directed to infiltrate and spy on the Deutsche Arbeiterpartei (DAP; German Workers Party) because certain of his commanders were convinced the DAP members were left-wing revolutionaries. The tiny talk group met in local beer halls. The would-be spy found his opportunity when he got into a raucous argument during a meeting in a Munich beer hall. Anton Drexler, a DAP founder, spotted Hitler's raw oratory talent and offered him a membership.

Drexler might also have been drawn in by what a friend of Hitler during their teen years saw: "The eyes were so outstanding that one didn't notice anything else. Never in my life have I seen any other person whose appearance…was so completely dominated by the eyes….it was uncanny how these eyes could change their expression."[1]

Hitler accepted the offer when he saw how closely Drexler's views on Aryan superiority and nationalistic, anticommunist, antimonarchist, and anti-Semitic ideas meshed with his own. Working more for himself than for his military superiors now, Hitler wangled his way onto the DAP executive committee and before long recruited other soldiers. One was Captain Ernst Röhm, who had access to manpower, guns, and army political funds.

◆

In 1920 Hitler persuaded the DAP to change its name to the Nationalsozialistische Deutsche Arbeiterpartei (NSDAP; National Socialist German Workers' Party), despite disliking the general idea of socialism. Socialism was a popular political concept in Germany, and Hitler felt the label was necessary in order to draw in more skilled and educated Germans. *Nazi* is the German pronunciation for the first two syllables of the word *National*.

Although Hitler never intended implementation, his party's platform became the redistribution of major industry income and war profits, free education, more generous pensions, and the nationalization of major trusts. Hitler never felt any genuine empathy for the working class and secretly promised wealthy industrialist contributors that measures harmful to them would never be employed. Hitler's brand of socialism, unlike the Russian Bolsheviks', didn't play one class against the other. His National Socialism consisted of a single Aryan society that excluded Jews.

Hitler soon manipulated his way into sole leadership of the NSDAP and chose the title *Führer*. His ruthlessness emerged as he transformed a gaggle of beer-hall roughnecks and ex-soldiers into a paramilitary group called the Sturmabteilung (SA), or brownshirts. Under the command of Ernst Röhm these storm troopers acted as bodyguards for the NSDAP leaders as well as intimidated and beat up the opposition. The organization eventually enlisted three million members and played an important role in Hitler's ascension to power.

In the early days, Hitler's party thrived because Germany brimmed with desperate unemployed workers. The appeal stemmed from Hitler's oratory skill, the population's disaffection with the more liberal parties, and free beer. In time, the beer became unnecessary. When small businessmen defected from other parties, the extra money and influence they brought allowed the NSDAP to offer brownshirt recruits a paycheck and authority. The rapid rise of the National Fascist Party in Italy, a similar fascist movement led by Benito Mussolini, helped shape the public face of the party. Mussolini seized power through a coup and gained popular support by promising territorial expansion. Hitler borrowed both of these ideas as well as the straight-armed salute Mussolini introduced. However, Hitler required his salute to be accompanied by a spoken "Heil Hitler."

Hitler's attempt to make his militarized salutation the universal German greeting didn't quite work because the public tired of this annoying formality. Since "heil" can also mean "heal" as well as "hail," some Germans would make fun of the greeting by treating it as a command. They could then reply, "Why, is he sick?" or "Heal him yourself, I'm no doctor."[2]

Germany's extreme hyperinflation also provided Hitler a tremendous boost. The German mark was valued at four to the dollar until the sum of the astronomical war reparation debt became public. That news quickly dropped the mark to 75 per dollar. By 1922 the exchange rate was one percent of the initial rate. When France refused to grant a payment postponement, the German government defaulted and the French sent its army to occupy Germany's industrial Ruhr Valley. Within months the mark fell to 160,000 per dollar. Before the year ended, the mark collapsed to a stupendous four billion per dollar. Bank accounts lost all value and the population grew desperate because their money was no good. The employed received a worthless paycheck that couldn't buy food, even had it been available. Food riots erupted and mayhem spread.

◆

In the fall of 1923 party members turned restless when they saw little action accompanying Hitler's oratory. Under pressure, Hitler decided to grab power in much the same way Mussolini had. That November the Nazis invaded a big political gathering in the Bürgerbräukeller, one of the largest beer halls in Munich. Vast beer halls, some of which could accommodate thousands, were a natural forum for political gatherings. On cue, hundreds of brownshirts, backed up by a machine gun, moved in and blocked the exits. Hitler, protected by about 20 of his followers, rushed in and leaped up onto a chair. He fired a pistol into the ceiling and stunned the crowd into silence.

The crowded Bürgerbräukeller beer hall on the night of Hitler's attempted putsch

Surrounded by a phalanx of bodyguards, Hitler pushed his way up to the stage and shouted, "The National Revolution has begun. No one may leave the hall. Unless there is immediate quiet, I shall have a machine gun posted in the gallery. The Bavarian and Reich governments have been removed and a provisional national government formed. The barracks of the Reichswehr and police are occupied. The army and the police are marching on the city under the swastika banner!" Of course, his statements were a bit optimistic and premature.

Hitler then rushed into a room where his followers had sequestered the Bavarian politicians attending the meeting. At gunpoint he tried to coerce Bavaria's leaders into pledging allegiance to him. When they balked, Hitler hurried back to the stage to deliver a short but dramatic speech that was stirring enough to provoke wild cheers and to cause the crowd to erupt into song with "Deutschland über Alles."

The performance attested to the oratorical dexterity Hitler had acquired by then. A well-connected, Harvard-educated German named Ernst "Putzi" Hanfstaengl said about that skill: "What Hitler was able to do to a crowd in two and a half hours will never be repeated in 10,000 years. Because of his miraculous throat construction, he was able to create a rhapsody of hysteria. In time, he became the living unknown soldier of Germany."[3]

Putzi Hanfstaengl, Hitler, and Herman Göring

On one occasion, as Putzi banged out Harvard fight songs on a hallway piano for his friend, Hitler grew excited and exclaimed that this sort of rally song was exactly what his movement needed. So Putzi converted some of the material into cheers and marches for Hitler. Harvard's "Rah! Rah! Rah!" became the Nazi mass-meeting chant "Sieg Heil! Sieg Heil! Sieg Heil!"

To read more about Putzi, go to the addendum "More About Putzi: Hitler's 'Friend' ".

Hitler had been able to hijack the fledgling DAP so quickly in 1920 because of the effective speaking technique Hanfstaengl described. People joined the party to see and hear him. The founders knew without Hitler's draw, their party was just another group of radicals. As Hitler became more confident and experienced in speaking, he boosted his appeal with a few podium tricks. He showed up late to build audience tension and then waited for complete silence before launching his dialog. After connecting with the audience, he swayed from side to side and used his hands and arms to gesture emphatically and dramatically.

As his facial muscles grimaced with expression and his eyes bulged with each further pronouncement, beads of sweat trickled off his face. His voice, already dripping with passion as the shouted words poured forth, would break as he laid out the injustices done, the cruelties perpetrated, and the conspiracies inflicted on the German people. At the close, with his audience in a frenzy, he'd quietly slip off the stage without fanfare to add to his persona of mystery.

♦

However, on the night of the so-called Beer Hall Putsch in 1923, the drama and speaking technique alone weren't enough to take over Germany. The attempted coup collapsed the next day when Hitler and 3,000 supporters marched down the street. Only a hundred armed policemen stopped them by firing their weapons into the pavement. A few rounds ricocheted and wounded or killed several marchers. Hitler dislocated his shoulder when the bodyguard he'd locked arms with dragged him down after being hit. According to Hanfstaengl, the only thanks the bodyguard got for taking a bullet for the führer was dismissal from his job.

A shaken Hitler left his comrades to fend for themselves and fled to the home of his confidante Hanfstaengl in a Munich suburb. Hanfstaengl, still close to Hitler then, had already learned of the failed coup and gone to Austria. But his wife, Helene, was home. Hitler arrived in a terrible state, convinced the police had targeted him to be shot. After he hid for 24 hours in an attic room, the police arrived to arrest him. Hanfstaengl described what happened next:

My wife hurried up to the attic and found Hitler in a state of frenzy. He had pulled out his revolver with his good hand and shouted, "This is the end. I will never let these swine take me. I will shoot myself first." It so happened that I had taught my wife one of the few jujitsu tricks I know, for wrenching a pistol out of someone's grasp. Hitler's movements were awkward with his dislocated shoulder and she managed to get the thing away from him and fling it into a two-hundredweight barrel of flour we kept in the attic to combat the recurrent shortages. Hitler calmed down somewhat and in the few moments left sat down and scribbled out a political testament on a piece of paper.[4]

Oddly enough, the failed Beer Hall Putsch worked in Hitler's favor. Although Hitler faced the death penalty at his trial, his supporters in the government made sure this would not be the outcome. The trial resulted in a propaganda victory when Hitler turned it into a stage and spoke interminably. His words and ideas were reported daily in the press throughout the country. Hitler so impressed the judges that he received only a light sentence for treason, to be served in a comfortable cell with a liberal visitation policy. There, Hitler realized order-loving Germans didn't favor military takeovers, so he decided to seize power politically. And there, Hitler wrote his famous manifesto, *Mein Kampf*. Hanfstaengl claims some credit in this endeavor. A relative said, "He had a hand in editing the memoir Hitler wrote in prison, *Mein Kampf*, 'crossing out his worst adjectives and the excessive use of superlatives' but leaving the deranged core largely intact."[5] The book eventually earned Hitler a comfortable income. Hitler never paid the income tax bill on the profits—a bill he was conveniently able to forgive himself when he assumed national power. He also garnered many sales by having the state present a copy to all newlyweds and military recruits.

Upon release from prison, Hitler reorganized the party and expanded its reach throughout Germany. Rousing speeches, pageantry-filled Nazi rallies, violent underhanded tactics, and voter dissatisfaction with other nationalistic parties all contributed to an increase in Nazi Party membership. Yet, the best thing Hitler and his party had going for them was the start of a new economic disaster—the worldwide Great Depression.

◆

Hitler understood propaganda. He kept his message simple enough for the least educated member of the audience to understand, and hammered it home relentlessly. He also effectively used the latest tools, the radio and airplane. In the early stage of the Great Depression in 1930, when the government had no answers for the high unemployment and ever rising number of business failures, the Nazi Party won 18 percent of the vote. In the next two years the economic situation deteriorated further, and the majority party couldn't form an effective majority coalition. Hitler ran for president. He came in second to the war hero incumbent, Paul von Hindenburg, by then 84 and in poor health.

New parliamentary elections were soon called because Germany's middle class, frightened by the grim economic situation and the violence in the streets, demanded solutions. Hitler promised to rebuild the economy and restore law and order. The latter was a cheeky promise because his brownshirts constantly battled the paramilitaries of the Social Democratic Party or the Communist Party and were the main instigators of the street violence. The Nazis pulled in 37 percent of the vote, which was still far short of a parliamentary majority. The communists came in second, but their masters in Moscow banned them from entering into an alliance, so again no effective coalition government could be formed. In new elections the Nazis dropped to 33 percent as voters became increasingly wary of the strong-arm tactics.

The party's falling appeal frightened Hitler. He realized he needed to assume power quickly, so he directed his surrogates to get the aged and doddering Hindenburg to appoint him Reich Chancellor. They assured Hindenburg Hitler couldn't subvert the government with only a minority of the cabinet positions in his party's hands. Meanwhile, the Nazis spread rumors the communist party planned a coup, which so frightened the nation's top industrialists that they too appealed to Hindenburg to appoint Hitler. In 1933 Hindenburg gave in.

After Hitler maneuvered deftly to prevent an opposition majority coalition from forming, he persuaded Hindenburg to call again for new elections. This time the Nazis eliminated the rival Communist Party from contention by blaming them for an arson fire in the Reichstag, the parliament building in Berlin. Although this convenient "communist conspiracy" churned up anticommunist hysteria, it didn't buy the Nazis a majority in the election, so Hitler turned to legislation. His government asked the Reichstag to approve the Enabling Act, a measure giving the cabinet complete powers of legislation for four years. Under chaotic conditions Hitler's brownshirt thugs seized control of the Reichstag and blocked certain members from entering during the vote to give the Nazis the required two-thirds majority they needed.

With both legislative and executive powers in his pocket, Hitler eliminated all political competition by declaring the Nazi Party the only legal party. He next annihilated all labor union opposition by forcibly integrating the unions into the party. Then he incorporated all of Germany's state governments into the party, leaving only two potential rivals—the army and Hitler's own SA brownshirt paramilitary. The SA worried Hitler most because of its large and well-armed membership, and the socialist demands its leaders were making. The SA's head was still Ernst Röhm, the man Hitler brought into the party. Hitler felt no gratitude toward Röhm and the SA for doing his dirty work for years, so with his usual ruthlessness Hitler devised a plan to destroy the SA and at the same time eliminate the army as a power rival.

Hitler accomplished both aims by decapitating the SA with a raid on its headquarters. History books call the purge the Night of the Long Knives, or Operation Hummingbird, but Germans know it as the Röhm-Putsch. As justification, Hitler devised a bogus conspiracy threat, like he'd done with the Reichstag fire, and told the public the SA was attempting a coup. Two of Hitler's shadowy Nazi political entities, the Schutzstaffel (SS) and the Geheime Staatspolizei (Gestapo) killed several hundred SA members and arrested many more in the raid. The German regular military, which had feared subjugation by the SA, was so grateful for removal of the threat that its top officers agreed to take an oath of personal allegiance to Hitler. With the demise of the SA, the SS expanded and assumed many of the SA's enforcement functions.

◆

Because Hitler appreciated the importance of information, or rather disinformation, one of his first acts after consolidating power was the establishment of the powerful Reich Ministry for Public Enlightenment and Propaganda. The ministry controlled not only the German press, but all cultural activities. Its loyal, fawning, and womanizing head, Dr. Joseph Goebbels, worked closely with Hitler until the end of the Nazi era.

When von Hindenburg died in August 1934, Hitler stacked the cabinet with Nazis and drafted a law that combined the office of president and chancellor into one position with the title *Zamość und Reichskanzler*. Hitler violated the constitution by assuming the president's office, but by then no one could do anything about it. With head-of-state powers, he now commanded the armed forces, but to gain an even deeper hold on the military Hitler required all service members who'd only sworn allegiance to the state to transfer their allegiance to him.

To legitimize the new arrangement and ensure nothing short of a coup or assassination could remove him from office, Hitler scheduled a voter plebiscite. When von Hindenburg's last will and testament inconveniently appeared and revealed a desire to see the return of a constitutional monarchy, the document quickly disappeared and a political testament of von Hindenburg's accomplishments, sprinkled with favorable references to Hitler, turned up. It was almost certainly forged to win favor in the upcoming plebiscite. And it worked. Voters overwhelmingly approved the structural leadership change.

Hitler continued to concentrate power and by the time World War II began, Germany was the Nazi Party. Like all canny dictators, Hitler kept his deputies from collecting too much personal authority by forcing each deputy to build, and then hold onto, his turf. This resulted in a large bureaucracy rife with corruption that soon disaffected many Germans. Unfortunately, Hitler's larger-than-life, propaganda-enhanced persona, the revived economy, a restored national pride, and a new German world standing kept Hitler personally popular until the war began to go badly.

Germany experienced a huge industry and infrastructure growth under the Nazis. Hitler's vast expansion of the armaments industry and the military was the driving force. Both figured into his plans to reacquire the territory Germany lost at Versailles, and then some. However, debt and currency manipulation financed so much of the growth that industrial workers paid for the gains with a standard of living lower than their peers in other western industrial countries.

---

[1] Kubizek, *Young Hitler, the Story of Our Friendship*; Translated from the German by E.V. Anderson [pseud.] With an Introd. by H.R. Trevor-Roper., 13.

[2] Wikipedia contributors. "Nazi salute. " *Wikipedia,* Wikipedia.org, 15 Apr. 2015, accessed 22 Apr. 2015.

[3] "Ernst Hanfstaengl." *Wikiquote,* Wikiquote.org, 4 Feb. 2015, accessed 20 Apr. 2015.

[4] Hanfstaengl, *Unheard Witness,* 108.

[5] "The Harvard Nazi," *Boston Magazine,* Bostonmagazine.com, Mar. 2005.

Schömitz was convenient for Karolina because the girl would be less able to cause trouble over her grandmother's house and the income from the land. Late in 1934 Maria left for Wolframitz with the expectation she'd do housework and help a farmer's wife take care of two young children.

◆

Wolframitz wasn't anything like Vienna, but Maria found the place more cosmopolitan than Schömitz. The village adjoined three additional villages that had fused into one larger village and straddled a minor highway that linked several larger villages and towns. Years before, the government had constructed a Czech school there as in Schömitz, even though the community was overwhelmingly German. This school's capacity was much too large for just the children of the new Czech workers, so to fill it the officials bused in children from Czech communities and made attendance mandatory for German children with a Czech grandmother.

Wolframitz had seen several famous and important visitors over the years. Austrian Emperor Franz Joseph came to the village in 1848. And according to Oswald Lustig, Vladimir Lenin and his wife enjoyed a pleasant stay there when four local communists attending a conference in Vienna invited him to return there with them. Oswald gave me a photograph showing their names in Cyrillic scratched into the hard-sand cellar wall of the house where they stayed. I was unable to affirm Lenin's informal visit from other sources, but Lenin did live in the Austrian Empire for a time. When in Vienna he frequented Café Central, a coffeehouse gathering place for intellectuals. It was said that in January 1913, he, Adolf Hitler, Leon Trotsky, Josip Broz Tito, and Sigmund Freud all visited the café at various times. Joseph Stalin, who was also staying in Vienna at the time, avoided such intellectual gathering places.[1]

Conceivably, Hitler could have encountered Trotsky, Tito, or his future archrival Stalin in Vienna. A few people contend Hitler played chess with Lenin. A controversial etching depicting this scene, signed by Hitler's Jewish art teacher, Emma Löwenstamm, was auctioned in 2009. Pencil markings on the back of the drawing are supposedly the signatures of Hitler and Lenin.[2]

In the 1920s the beauty of the Wolframitz area enchanted a successful Berlin artist by the name of Karl Säwert enough that he returned in 1928 and spent the summer painting local scenes. Coincidentally, one of his subjects was the little house bearing the Lenin inscription in its cellar. To some, the artist is best remembered for a painting he didn't do. According to Oswald, when Säwert was asked to paint Hitler's portrait in 1938, the artist refused.

Wolframitz also produced a successful and highly effective World War II general. Erhard Raus, the son of a long-serving mayor of Wolframitz, was assimilated into the German Army from the Austrian Army when Hitler integrated Austria into the Third Reich. Raus rose to the rank of Generaloberst, the second-highest German rank, and assumed several senior command positions on the Eastern Front. He played an important role in preventing the capture of the 23rd Corps at the outskirts of Moscow early in the war during the extreme winter of 1941–1942 when his 6th Panzer Division was assigned the difficult task of holding the territory to the corps's rear and keeping the supply lines open. One military historian wrote, "His performance during the Soviet winter counteroffensive earned him the sobriquet *Der Nochdenker* (the farsighted one)."[3] According to another military historian and biographer, his soldiers admired him because "he was especially skilled in extricating troops from desperate situations" and gave him the moniker *Raus zieht heraus*, by which the men meant "Raus pulls you through."[4,5]

Raus became a defensive tactician because through most of his wartime commands his side was in a continuous retreat. By war's end he'd built a reputation as one of Germany's best and most innovative armored-warfare commanders. He was not the best known of Germany's Eastern Front generals, but some tacticians consider him among the ablest to command on that front. Although the general himself hadn't lived in Wolframitz since joining the army years before, most of his family resided there. The homes of Raus's parents, siblings, and grandmother were just a few doors away from Maria's new home. She came to know the family, but I didn't discover this until dementia had obscured the details in her memory. I learned of Raus's origins through Oswald Lustig who, for the six years he attended school in Pohrlitz, lived with his grandparents in Wolframitz one house away from Raus's grandparents and other family members.

Oswald thought so highly of Raus that he humbly implored me not to even mention his own modest connection to the general, but I will do so anyway. Oswald met Raus only once, in 1942 shortly after turning 19. The general was visiting his grandparents in Wolframitz. When Raus heard young Oswald, also visiting his grandparents, was about to be inducted into the German Army, the general invited Oswald to drop by at his leisure. Oswald was so nervous that his hands shook as he walked over. What struck him most was Raus's humility—he put on no airs and acted like an ordinary villager instead of a powerful general. Raus told Oswald to let him know if he could be of any service, but Oswald never contacted him.

Oswald Lustig at age 86

◆

Like Schömitz, the four-village cluster that included Wolframitz consisted largely of farmers. But because the town was several times the size of Schömitz and more prosperous too, it had more going on. The municipality even employed two or three policemen. Wolframitz also had a Gemeindediener who served as the mayor's messenger as well as night watchman. He walked the dark streets and kept a wary eye out for thieves, but mainly he watched for house fires and pranksters.

The house and farmstead that became Maria's new home belonged to a farmer named Rudolf Geidl—a middle-aged man with two small children and a wife several years younger than himself. Although Maria found Geidl rather old to have such small children, she wasn't surprised for in Wolframitz farmers often delayed marriage until they came into their inheritance. What did catch her off guard though was Geidl's temperament and immaturity. By his stage of life, most farmers had acquired some degree of levelheadedness. But not this man. The deficiency was compounded by his exceptional stinginess and insensitivity toward other people. Having just one such boss would have been bad enough, but Maria soon learned her job came with two. Geidl's mother, obviously his role model, was constantly underfoot. Fortunately, the woman returned to her own house at night.

Maria arrived expecting a relatively short stay and then a return to a more agreeable living situation in Schömitz, away from her stepmother. But nothing about the new job was as described. Karolina, or perhaps Hoffman, had misrepresented the situation. Geidl almost certainly perceived that Karolina didn't care about the teen's welfare or want her back, so he took advantage of the situation. At first the outdoor portion of the "housework and childcare" only consisted of milking the cows. Geidl soon tacked on other farm chores and by spring had her toiling long hours in the fields. Maria said he paid her next to nothing when she started and refused to increase the meager pay after adding all the heavy labor.

Geidl's medium-sized farm required the use of large draft horses instead of cows or oxen. Unfortunately, Geidl had made his horses as mean and bad tempered as he was, which posed another difficulty for Maria. Working near the beasts was dangerous. Maria couldn't enter their stalls because they kicked. To feed them, she had to climb the stall partitions to toss in their hay. She wasn't the only person afraid of those horses. Geidl's wife also refused to go anywhere near them.

In Wolframitz Maria felt cheated out of her inheritance and exiled into bondage among strangers. She remained homesick and lonely for months because she missed the Luksch family and her old friends. Since she only had one day a week off, she no longer saw much of them. The thought of how many more years she'd be subject to her stepmother's guardianship added to her misery.

On hearing all this, I expected my mother to admit that one of her greatest disappointments was her meek father's failure to protect her. Yet she refused to criticize him. I can only guess she saw him sympathetically as a man broken by the war. And one intractably dominated by the woman he'd married.

Maria would have despaired even more had she known she'd be stuck working for Geidl for four years. She told me she'd have left, given an opportunity, but jobs were hard to come by. Over time, whenever she'd saved any money from the pittance paid her, she had Franz Onkel deposit it for her in the Raiffeisen Kasse, a branch of a cooperative bank in Lodenitz. Not long before she died, I found her old bank account book listing these deposits. The booklet was among the few documents she was able to save after World War II.

Childhood's End 129

To get through her ordeal, Maria liked to think of the things she had to be grateful for in Wolframitz. One was Geidl's wife. Emilie was such a nice person that Maria felt sorry for her and the children because of their difficult life with the man they were stuck with. Another consolation was having a degree of privacy. The Geidl house was newer than many in the village and larger, so Maria had her own bedroom. But the greatest positive was not being around her stepmother.

◆

In time Maria adapted to her situation and learned to detach herself from her job at the end of the workday. Strolling with new friends became one of her greatest pleasures. On warm Sunday afternoons, she liked to walk to Miskogel, a large, wooded, parklike hill several kilometers west of Wolframitz along the road to the town of Mährisch Kromau. Vineyards and hay fields flanked the hill. From the village the contrast of the verdant forested slope against the intervening undulating cropland held a powerful allure, one highly anticipated throughout the long work week. The Miskogel's paths, hiking trails, and valley views provided a wonderful respite. During the summer, when the sun was curing nearby cut clover, the teen believed Miskogel was the sweetest smelling place on earth.

Wolframitz had its own church barely a couple hundred paces from Maria's doorstep, so she no longer attended Mass in Lodenitz. The village marketplace and the handsome Rathaus (town hall) weren't much farther away than the church. In my two visits to Wolframitz, I saw for myself how compact and convenient everything was. Because of what happened to the village after World War II, these sites lost both their luster and their importance to the community. At least they still exist, which is more than can be said for many of the houses. In the years since 1945, many houses were demolished because they'd become decrepit after abandonment by the Czechs who took them from their German owners. The empty space between the Rathaus and house to its right was once filled by five houses. The still standing house was formerly the home of Oswald Lustig's grandparents. It survived because its walls of fired brick held up better against neglect and moisture than did the dried clay brick walls of the other houses.

---

[1] Frederic Morton, *Thunder at Twilight: Vienna 1913/1914* (New York: Scribner, 1989), 6.

[2] Dylan Loeb Mcclain, "Based on Life or Fantasy, a Picture Goes to Auction," *The New York Times*, September 30, 2009, sec. Arts / Art & Design.

[3] Erhard Raus and Steven H Newton, *Panzer Operations: The Eastern Front Memoir of General Raus, 1941-1945* (Cambridge, MA: Da Capo Press, 2005), 90.

[4] Erhard Raus and Peter Tsouras, *Panzers on the Eastern Front General Erhard Raus and His Panzer Divisions in Russia, 1941-1945* (London; Mechanicsburg, Pa.: Greenhill; Stackpole Books, 2002).

[5] Dennis Showalter, *Hitler's Panzers: The Lightning Attacks That Revolutionized Warfare* (Penguin, 2009).

18 Hitler's Private Life

AS A 15-YEAR-OLD shoved out into the adult world to fend for herself, Maria was far too preoccupied with the drastic changes in her life to take note of what was happening in distant Germany. But by 1937, three years later, the German political scene and economic rebound could no longer go unnoticed by Maria or anyone else in the Sudetenland.

This transformation cannot be understood without a look at the psyche of the Johanns' fellow veteran—the man behind the changes. By then the nation Adolf Hitler took over mirrored his own dark soul. When Hitler first entered politics, he was a conscienceless, clownish little man full of ambition, delusion, hate, and self-doubt. As he acquired a beguiling oratorical skill and cultish following, his public persona masked these faults. But even at the height of his power, Hitler remained insecure and anything but the confident heroic figure seen by the public. One major weakness was an inability to connect with people on a personal level. Despite his humble origins, he couldn't empathize or engage with ordinary individuals. When conversing one-on-one he spoke as if looking over the other person's shoulder and addressing an audience.

Perhaps to compensate, Hitler insisted on being addressed formally, like royalty. Even his oldest cronies and top lieutenants, men like Goebbels and Göring who'd known him as a rising nobody, had to comply. At gatherings and dinners he regularly monopolized the conversation and loosed lengthy monologues. He tried to be witty but lacked a real sense of humor. Often, he picked up what others said and later repeated the thought as if it were his own. Those closest to him heard him retell the same anecdotes and stories about himself countless times. When he did stop conversing at dinner, he was not offended when his neighbors chatted among themselves as if he were not there. At such times Hitler pretended to be mulling over weighty matters, but missed nothing.

For Hitler money was never a problem after he established himself as the head of the Nazi Party. This set him apart from the common people, the class he believed he was destined to lead out of the economic morass and into greatness. Money flowed in from both industrialists and the military because the donors expected to exert influence should the party ever gain power. Hitler was personally unsavory to many of these contributors, yet they coveted the social standing they stood to gain as he ascended to power.

Although he sought their cash and support, Hitler was uneasy around the well-educated or accomplished and avoided contact with diplomats, journalists, and academics as much as possible. They made him uncomfortable and unsure of himself. Hitler was much more at home with the misfits, scoundrels, and hypocrites that comprised his inner circle. Despite the rhetoric about Aryan purity and principles, he tolerated criminality, deviancy, and corruption in his associates, stating that their private lives were their own business. All he demanded was loyalty—something he never felt bound by himself. He wouldn't hesitate to eliminate anyone if it proved useful to him.

Except for his military service, Hitler kept his past, especially his youth and early adulthood, hidden in the shadows. Details of that period are still murky, and little from that time presented him in a favorable light. He'd failed in school, in attempts at a career, and in relationships with females. His vow to never drink again after he got drunk once at 15 was one of his few positive accomplishments.

◆

Nothing in Hitler's life lacked peculiarity. His sex life was no exception. Several of the early Nazis leaders who ascended along with Hitler were homosexuals, which caused some to believe Hitler too was homosexual. But his sex life, if he had one, remains an enigma. He liked pornography and eagerly consumed the dirty stories and cartoons in *Der Stürmer*, a Nazi propaganda paper that printed the closest thing to pornography allowed in the Third Reich. In his private studio, Hitler enjoyed lewd movies. At times he also liked to associate with pretty actresses. Whether any sex was involved remains unknown.

Hitler's sex life is likely to remain a fertile field for discussion because facts are in such short supply. As a powerful leader, he could have had countless women, but his disturbed makeup prevented him from becoming a celebrity ladies' man. Although he had numerous superficial dalliances, just two women (Geli Raubal and Eva Braun) were known to have had any sort of deeper relationship with him until some 15 years after his death when details of a romance with a girl named Maria Reiter emerged. According to Hitler's sister, she was the only woman Hitler ever truly loved.

They met in 1926, walking their dogs in a park. He was 37 and she was 16. The girl immediately attracted Hitler, so he invited her to hear him speak. Her name was Maria, but her friends called her Mimi. Hitler told her to call him Wolf. He explained he'd like to marry her and have blond children, but his need to save Germany took precedence. They continued to meet off and on but Hitler ended the relationship in 1928 because he feared the romance was affecting his mission.

Hitler's next known entanglement began in 1928 at age of 40 when he rented a summerhouse in Obersalzberg and persuaded Angela Raubal, his half sister in Vienna, to join him as his housekeeper. Hitler soon became infatuated with one of the two daughters she brought with her. At first Geli, a vivacious 20-year-old with a Viennese allure, reveled in the attention brought to her by being in the company of such a famous man with an endless string of subordinates to do his bidding. Putzi Hanfstaengl considered Geli lazy and something of a slut. Hitler took her to cafes, the theater, concerts, and even political events and publicly passed it off as a doting uncle indulging a favorite niece.

In time the relationship turned stormy and developed a dark side. Some evidence suggests Hitler had a proclivity for perverted or sadomasochistic sex, and Geli grew disgusted with him. The relationship wasn't helped by Hitler's possessive and controlling nature, which kept the girl from seeing her friends or having an outside life. Geli so missed the company of her friends that she began to argue with Hitler. Hitler, unable to keep a constant close watch on the girl himself, assigned two trusted underlings to accompany her everywhere. Eventually Geli needed Hitler's permission just to leave the apartment. Somehow, despite the resentment, Geli could still feel jealousy. It flared up when Hitler took a 17-year-old girl for a ride in his car. She was an admirer named Eva Braun, whom he'd met in 1929.

Just before Hitler departed on a trip in 1931, a tremendous argument ensued when he ordered Geli to stay in the apartment instead of visiting Vienna. The next day Hitler learned Geli had killed herself with a gun. Not everyone believed the "self-inflicted" official ruling. Vicious rumors circulated.

Hitler, deeply depressed after the death, paced the floor for days and wouldn't eat or sleep. Again, he threatened suicide. Some of his acquaintances believed he never recovered from this tragedy. One visible change was his sudden conversion to a vegetarian diet. Eating meat, he said once, reminded him too much of eating a corpse. However, he occasionally did make an exception and eat meat..

The same year Geli died, Hitler invited Eva Braun, now 19, to his Berchtesgaden retreat. This started a 14-year relationship. Exactly what kind of a relationship Braun and Hitler shared, few knew. Hitler, uncomfortable with displays of intimacy, didn't allow their relationship to become public or visible. Eva was in love with Hitler to the end, but whether the reverse was true is hard to say.

Eva spent most of her time waiting for Hitler. Her lonely and sad existence resulted in bouts of depression. She had to be kept a secret because during the early years of his rise, Hitler was strangely captivating to women and needed to be chaste to draw their votes. For much of their time together, Hitler stashed her at his Berghof estate in Berchtesgaden where she acted as his hostess whenever he was there. The rest of the time, she stayed in Munich. In both places Hitler allowed her presence only around old party acquaintances.

Those who knew Braun said she seemed intimidated by Hitler. Albert Speer, a man close to Hitler and often referred to as the architect of the Third Reich, said it was painful to see how Hitler humiliated her. Speer told one of his biographers that at dinner one evening Hitler asserted an intelligent man should always choose a primitive and stupid woman so she would not be a bother when the man was trying to relax. Braun was seated next to Hitler at the time and couldn't have failed to hear.

Hitler sometimes found himself attracted to well-known film actresses, and after his power and fame accumulated, he could put himself in their company. One such figure was Renate Müller, who to her misfortune was one of the top German film actresses when Hitler came to power. Müller's story ended tragically. This behavior likely also affected Braun. In 1932 she attempted suicide by shooting herself in her chest. In May 1935 she swallowed 25 sleeping pills and nearly died before her sister discovered her unconscious. Whether Hitler felt a twinge of remorse or simply wanted to avoid further problems is unknown, but he then bought her a nice apartment in Munich near his own and put a car with a Nazi chauffeur at her disposal.

Braun, who filled her time between Hitler's visits with sports, watching film romances, reading romance fiction, and keeping fit, never talked about politics or the war, even when Hitler's plans went drastically wrong and his health deteriorated. When the Red Army closed in on Berlin in April 1945 and Hitler had to confine himself to his bunker, Eva came from Berchtesgaden to join him. He advised her to escape in those last days, but she refused. They were married April 29, one day before committing suicide together. On Hitler's prior orders, guards carried their bodies outside to a pit, doused them with gasoline, and threw in a match. Even in death, Hitler couldn't bear the humiliation of falling into the hands of the Russians.

To read more about the private life of Hitler, go to the addendum "More About Hitler: The Führer's Love Life".

19 Of Czechs and Germans

EVEN WHILE BASKING in the Sunday-afternoon blue skies at Miskogel during the mid-1930s, Maria and her new friends couldn't completely banish from their consciousness the political storm clouds gathering. The increasing alienation of Sudeten Germans from the Czechoslovak government, political confrontations in Bohemia, and Adolf Hitler's powerful influence in a rising Germany were hard to ignore. Competition for influence between Germans and Czechs was nothing new. Although under Habsburg rule equilibrium had existed, the Czech population never showed any real enthusiasm for a German-speaking monarchy. After the Allied Powers fragmented the empire to punish the Austrians, the situation reversed and left the formerly Austrian Sudeten Germans chafing under Czech rule. The war's victors had been warned that the creation of a nation with a central Slavic core enclosed by a ring of ethnic German territory was a prescription for trouble. Yet, largely at the insistence of the French, they proceeded anyway and precipitated a disastrous chain of consequences.

The Habsburgs converted their multiethnic empire to Catholicism to prevent religion from becoming a focal point for revolt, but never dared attempt anything as incendiary as pressuring their ethnic populations to become German-speaking Austrians. However, the Czechoslovak leaders didn't show a similar reluctance to Czechify Germans. Despite the Masaryk and Beneš's pledges to emulate Switzerland's canton system of government with its ethnic administrative districts, they continued to pressure German schools, limit German influence in important ministerial government positions, and prohibit local government business to be conducted in the local language. In Maria's part of Moravia, Germans were infuriated when thoroughly German districts were gerrymandered in order to give them enough Czechs to place German communities out of compliance for public service jobs. Wolframitz had to turn over all three police positions to Czechs. The story was the same in factories and facilities that received any sort of government loan, contract, or regulation. Even private movie theaters subsidized by Sudeten German cultural organizations had to be turned over to the Czech minority one night each week.

The government's policies led to an influx of Czechs, as intended. In Wolframitz and Schömitz some of the newly open jobs were filled by residents of three nearby small Czech communities; however, many Czech workers were resettled from more distant Czech areas. Some of these newcomers were able to buy a house, but most were poor, ill educated, and didn't speak German. In the vicinity of Wolframitz, these workers filled railroad, factory, and agricultural jobs such as those at the Meierhof. The Germans couldn't blame the economic immigrants for the government's actions, but they did distinguish these people from the Czechs who'd long been part of the community and had come by their job or livelihood fairly. Maria mentioned several such families—enterprising Czech families who made brooms and other household items and sold them door to door. One family produced dill pickles and marketed them around the villages from a barrel on the back of a horse-drawn wagon.

The loss of jobs, lack of social benefits, and the siphoning of German children to the many new Czech schools rankled Germans, but these government actions earned wildly popular support from the Czech majority. As a result, Czechs idolized the founders. Especially Masaryk, their president. On national holidays they paraded through the streets in celebration of their independence. Maria recalled that once when President Masaryk passed through Schömitz, Germans were required to display Czechoslovak flags for the occasion. Few residents owned one, so flags were handed out, along with instructions to wave them as the president drove through. The flag waving would have been more enthusiastic had the German residents not felt the government existed mainly to benefit their Czech neighbors.

◆

The economic problems introduced by Czech nation building brought troubles enough to the minorities, but the worldwide Great Depression which began in 1929 greatly exacerbated the ills. Massive unemployment in the highly industrialized Bohemian part of the Sudetenland resulted. Nearly a third of the Bohemian German worker force became unemployed. When Sudeten Germans failed to receive adequate help from the government, they lost confidence that they'd ever be treated equally and concluded they'd be better off seeking a degree of autonomy or associating with more prosperous Germany. Sudeten German voters increasingly flocked to Sudeten nationalistic parties and abandoned the Czech political parties as well as the two main Sudeten German political parties.

The Sudetendeutsche Heimatfront (Sudeten German Homeland Front), founded in 1933 by Konrad Henlein, benefited from the discontent and gained many members when Prague banned a long-existing party, the German National Socialist Workers Party. Although the name was similar to Hitler's NSDAP, the two were unrelated. Henlein stated he wanted equality for Germans through the Czechoslovak Parliament, espoused loyalty to the government of Czechoslovakia, and kept his distance from the Nazis during the early 1930s. When Henlein's efforts bore little fruit in Prague, Hitler sniffed opportunity and exploited the situation by backing elements of the organization sympathetic to the Nazi Party. In 1937, when struggling Sudeten German workers in Bohemia began to respond strongly to the anti-Czech message of the pro-Nazi faction within the party (now called the Sudetendeutsche Partei), Henlein realized the Nazis would destroy him if he too didn't support Hitler.[1]

---

[1] Wikipedia contributors. "Konrad Henlein." *Wikipedia*, Wikipedia.org, 21 Oct. 2014, accessed 20 Apr. 2015.

20 The Expansion Begins

HITLER'S ACCEPTANCE BY SUDETEN GERMANS was probably served by his Austrian origins. He came from the Waldviertel (Wooded Quarter) in lower Austria where his family had ties to four small farming villages: Döllersheim, Strones, Spital, and Wirnharts—villages not so different from the villages Maria knew. The farmers might have been a little more uneasy about the führer had they known Hitler ordered Döllersheim, the birthplace of his father and the burial place of his grandmother, to be obliterated and turned into an army training area as soon as Austria was annexed in 1938.

Hitler hated his father and was paranoid about his past, so it is likely he got rid of the village to try to erase a less than glorious part of his history. He succeeded, insofar as today the führer's origins and lineage remain obscure. The village of Strones, another piece of his childhood, met a similar fate. Hitler arranged for this community to disappear from the map when the Nazis enlarged the military training base. The village was on the outermost perimeter of the facility and minimal effort could have saved it. Instead, Hitler ordered it blasted to pieces by artillery fire, leaving behind only desolation and craters. Its residents received a photo album of what had once been their village and were resettled elsewhere.

New training bases like these presaged Hitler's vision of a great *Lebensraum* (living space) enlargement of Germany. In his view, Germany had to expand or confront a crisis of overpopulation because of the territorial losses from the Treaty of Versailles. The Aryan master race's new territory would come from the *Untermenschen*, the "inferior" masses to the East.[1]

Toward this end he began to build up Germany's infrastructure and military for the time when he'd have the political muscle and weaponry to advance his megalomaniacal vision. As he rearmed, he told the outside world he wanted peace, but those listening carefully could detect ominous nuances buried within his domestic speeches. His address to the National Labor Front in Nuremberg on September 12, 1936, offers a prime example. In this speech he complained about how hard Germany had to work to gain a little land from the ocean while others had a glut of land they didn't know how to make productive. "If the Urals with their vast wealth of raw materials, Siberia with its rich forests, and the Ukraine with its vast fields of grain were in Germany, it would be swimming in surplus under National Socialist leadership."[2]

Hitler projected his power outward long before Germany had any real military muscle. Over a weekend in March 1936, Hitler ordered nineteen German battalions to march into a section of the demilitarized zone east of the Rhine River on the French border and take back this section of Germany lost after World War I. The commanders of Hitler's still impotent German Army begged him to back off because their men stood no chance against the French Army, but Hitler didn't listen. For the actual showdown, a mere three battalions crossed the river into the western border area of the Rhineland. These troops were a token force—soldiers on bicycles, armed only with rifles and orders to pull back quickly if French forces moved in.

Hitler's anxiety over the French response caused him several days of stomach cramps and sleeplessness as events unfolded.[3] Unfortunately, France's lack of will handed Hitler an easy success, fed his ego, and encouraged further adventures. More than one high German official of the day believed French intervention could have finished Hitler politically and prevented World War II. Hitler could probably have recovered the Rhineland by quiet negotiation, but diplomacy alone didn't provide enough drama to divert the public's attention from the latest economic crisis and the Nazis' growing reputation for domestic heavy-handedness.

In November 1937 Hitler convened a secret conference that only he, his top military commanders, his foreign minister, and an aide attended. After swearing everyone to secrecy, he shocked the generals by laying out the arguments for why Germany was entitled to Lebensraum at the expense of its neighbors. His vision left no doubt where he saw the most space for the least cost. The timetable laid out several scenarios based on prevailing conditions. Crucial to his plans were the acquisition of Austria and Czechoslovakia. Without them, Germany's flanks were vulnerable. He believed Germany would have to act between 1943 and 1945 before Nazi hold on power waned, Germany's new weapons became obsolete, and the postwar baby boom pool of military recruits declined. Hitler had already concluded that rather than risk war, Britain and France would renege on the mutual defense agreement with Czechoslovakia and abandon the country.

Left unstated by Hitler was an important personal factor. He was convinced he'd die early like both his parents and had already shown signs of Parkinson's disease. So his war for territory had to happen while he was still healthy. He often said privately, "I would rather have the war when I'm 50 than when I'm 55 or 60."[4]

Hitler wasted little time in putting neighboring Austria into play. In early March of 1938, during Maria's fourth year working for Geidl, Hitler and his propaganda machine placed severe pressure on Austrian Chancellor Kurt Schuschnigg. In an attempt to foil Hitler, Schuschnigg announced a referendum to decide whether or not Austria should remain independent. Schuschnigg fully expected the mandate outcome would favor independence.

Hitler became furious when he found out. With his usual behind-the-scenes, divide-and-conquer tactic, he outmaneuvered the chancellor and forced him to resign before the vote could take place. The Austrian National Socialists, already an appendage of Hitler's Nazi Party, seized power and formed a new government. German troops crossed the Austrian border only three days after the announcement of the referendum. A day later, Hitler traveled to Linz, Austria, and announced legislation to formalize the Anschluss (annexation) of Austria. An enthusiastic crowd, excited at the prospect of an economically revitalized Austria that could regain some of the prominence it lost at Versailles, greeted him. Hitler told the audience: "If providence once called me forth from this town to be the führer of the German Reich, in so doing it must have charged me with a mission, and that mission could be only to restore my dear homeland to the German Reich."[5]

◆

In Czechoslovakia, Beneš succeeded Masaryk as president in 1935. He still refused to make any substantial concessions to Sudeten Germans despite the ominous rise of the German nationalistic parties. As a result, these parties attracted ever more support. With direction and funds from Germany, the Nazis gradually subverted the various Sudeten German parties and factions. The activism was centered in the industrialized urban parts of Bohemia where most Sudeten Germans lived. Yet even in southern Moravia, where there was no history of political activism, voters aligned with the nationalistic parties and listened to what was being said in Germany. After nearly two decades of Czech rule and stagnant prospects, they too sought change.

As the divide between Sudeten Germans and Prague widened, the Czechoslovak government grew alarmed enough to bulk up its military and build border defenses. In 1936 it began construction of a heavy line of fortifications opposite the German border and a lesser line along the Austrian border to the south. When Germany took over Austria in 1938, Beneš initiated emergency construction of a second bunker line parallel to the one facing Austria. The earliest bunkers were already finished when French consultation resulted in a design change modeling the surface fortifications of France's Maginot Line. The huge undertaking called for 10,000 small concrete and steel bunkers and over 250 large fortresslike bunkers. Most were in an advanced stage of construction when the Czechs ran out of time.

In mid-March 1938, shortly after Maria and her neighbors learned German troops had entered Austria, they could see Prague was very worried about its exposure to the Austrian border. Two months later, during what was called the May Crisis, the government ordered a partial military mobilization and called up many young reservists, including Sudeten Germans. Simultaneously, the government commenced the emergency bunker-construction program and conscripted other young ethnic Germans, men and women alike, for the hard bunker tunnel and trench shovel work. Maria's impression was that the Czechoslovak government still believed it could stop Germany by political means, thanks to its alliance with France and Britain. If Germany did attack, Prague thought the army could fend off any German push until France and Britain rushed to help.

Maria recalled that in Wolframitz and the surrounding communities, the Czechoslovak Army commandeered local farmers to work on the bunkers strung across their fields. The army employed two basic Maginot Line bunker designs. The larger, a small fortress, could hold hundreds of defenders and featured deep exit and entry tunnels up to several kilometers long. In Maria's locale, only the smaller type was built. It consisted of a partially buried rounded mass of concrete with two machine-gun ports and a heavy steel door. The structure barely held two or three soldiers.

So many bunkers survive to this day that the Czech Republic has been trying to sell them to Czech citizens. The government donated some of the fortress type to local municipalities and organizations. Although old bunkers in other places are often used for such purposes as vegetable storage and mushroom growing, the small bunkers are so cramped inside that they have little practical value. I can attest to the size of the latter for I located and inspected a number of them on my second visit to Wolframitz.

Late in the summer of 1938 when the political situation deteriorated, the Czechoslovak Army mobilized fully and sent large numbers of troops to finish the bunker construction and man the border fortifications. Oskar Halusa recalled that an entire army regiment was posted in Schömitz. Every house had to billet soldiers. He estimated 10 to 15 percent of them were Sudeten Germans. Oskar's farmstead alone quartered

30 soldiers in the barn. However, the Czechoslovak Army did not station Germans inside the bunkers.

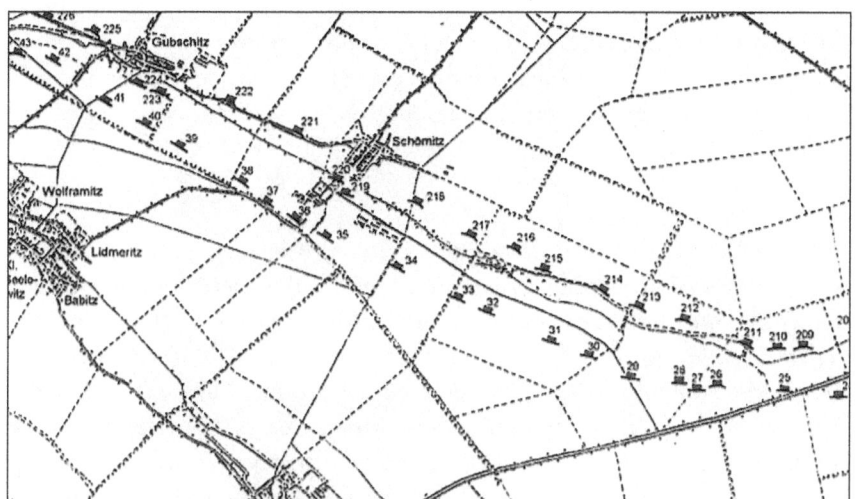

Map of Czech bunker lines near Wolframitz

◆

At the time of the construction, the police confiscated all radios and guns from southern Moravia's Germans. Taking the guns in particular angered Schömitzers for it meant the end of the community's popular and traditional annual hunt. Innkeeper Johann Caesar, an avid hunter and a former policeman, knew it was hopeless to attempt getting the weapons returned anytime soon, but he did try to get the town's radios back. From his inn, which had the only telephone in town, he rang up the police station in Lodenitz. After stating he'd learned some radios had already been returned in nearby Wolframitz, he asked if Schömitz might expect its radios back soon as well.

A few minutes later Czech policemen pulled up in a car, stormed into the inn, and arrested Caesar. Later his family learned the police had whisked him off to Brünn and imprisoned him in Spielberg Castle, an infamous prison closed by the Austrian monarchy in 1855. Prior to then, it had held some of the old empire's most dangerous criminals and political prisoners, many of whom never left alive. The Austrians used the castle again during World War I, but its barbarous reputation as a prison wasn't revived until after World War II when Czechs condemned the Nazis for committing atrocities there during the war. The Wikipedia entry, in reference to the first year of the Nazi occupation of Czechoslovakia reads "Several thousand Czech patriots suffered in Špilberk at that time, some of whom were put to death."[6]

What the entry neglects to mention is that the Czechoslovak government had already put it back in service as a prison before the war began. Caesar found himself in one of its cells for simply making a phone call. Inside, he crossed paths with an acquaintance from Lodenitz who'd been arrested too. If Caesar hadn't been confined to a cell, he'd probably have recognized more German prisoners because those who'd resisted induction into the Czechoslovak Army were imprisoned there.

◆

In September 1938 the Sudeten crisis came to a head. The Czechoslovak military labored feverishly to complete the bunker defense line because the command staff still expected their fortifications to fend off the German Army until help arrived from their allies. Unfortunately for Beneš, on September 30 his allies stepped around him and ceded the Sudetenland to Hitler by signing the Münchner Abkommen (Munich Agreement) in Germany. Neither Britain nor France was willing to go to war over Czechoslovakia. Beneš's government protested, arguing the country's economy would be ruined since along with the Sudetenland would go the majority of the country's industry. Beneš knew the argument well for he had conveniently covered up this point in 1919 at Versailles when it was Austria's loss. When Beneš's protestations were ignored, he dropped his complaint until large Czech public demonstrations forced him to show some backbone. At this point he declared he would defy the agreement and resist. As a result, the bunker construction continued night and day.

Gubschitz resident Oswald Lustig described what occurred in his village and recounted how the Czechs crumbled a week later. On October 7, when Czechoslovak soldiers working on the bunkers still filled Gubschitz, a military vehicle stopped at Oswald's house. Two officers emerged. One carried a heavy suitcase-like pack and ordered Oswald, 14 at the time, to lead him into the house. Once there, the officer walked across the room, stopped at the door of the food pantry, and commanded Oswald to open it. The officer entered, placed the case on the flour-storage bin, and sat down in front of it. As the officer opened the pack, the boy saw it contained a military communications radio. When the radio was set up, the soldier picked up the hand mike, turned some dials, and spoke into it. Twenty minutes later he jumped to his feet and exchanged a few quick words with the other officer. The two men then packed up the radio and departed abruptly. Within half an hour every Czechoslovak soldier was gone. The abrupt departure mirrored what happened in neighboring Schömitz and all along the bunker line—the army hastily retreated to the interior of the republic. That was the extent of Beneš's military resistance. The Czechoslovak generals were willing to fight but Beneš showed no courage and gave the order to fall back. Consequently, the Czechoslovak Army didn't fire a single shot when the smaller German force marched into Bohemia and Moravia October 6 through October 10, 1938.

With the exception of German communists, social democrats, and other antifascists, Sudeten Germans displayed tremendous enthusiasm and joy upon liberation from their 20-year nightmare. No one was happier than Johann Caesar. The day after the Czechoslovak retreat, a car returned him to his village. He'd been away just a few days but was nearly unrecognizable when he emerged from the vehicle. Bruises covered his entire body, and his swollen face was a mosaic of black and purple from the beatings delivered by his jailers in Spielberg Castle—the prison the Czechoslovak government complained about after the war for Nazi abuse of prisoners.

---

[1] Wikipedia contributors, "Untermensch." *Wikipedia*, Wikipedia.org, 12 Apr. 2015, accessed 20 Apr. 2015.

[2] Adolf Hitler, Max Domarus, and Patrick Romane, *The Essential Hitler Speeches and Commentary* (Wauconda, Ill.: Bolchazy-Carducci Pub., 2007), 835.

[3] Alan Bullock, *Hitler, a Study in Tyranny*, Completely rev. ed., Harper Torchbooks (New York: Harper & Row, 1964), 135.

[4] "The History Place - Triumph of Hitler: Conquest at Munich," *The History Place; The Past into the Future*, Historyplace.com, accessed 20 Apr. 2015.

[5] "The History Place - Triumph of Hitler: Conquest at Munich."

[6] Wikipedia contributors. "Špilberk Castle." *Wikipedia*, Wikipedia.org, 11 Jan. 2015, accessed 20 Apr. 2015.

21 Helping Hands Across the Border

At the time Hitler became their chief advocate on the world stage, the Sudeten Germans he championed didn't realize his motives extended far beyond their cause. The short time between the Anschluss of Austria in March of 1938 and the acquisition of the Sudetenland in September seemed to say that their plight had been an urgent concern for him. They didn't guess they were little more than pawns in his game to neutralize Czechoslovakia and cover Germany's exposed southern flank for the upcoming land grab in Eastern Europe.

Months before he took over the Sudetenland, Hitler had secretly ordered his military commanders to draw up a plan to attack Czechoslovakia. The leak of this Case Green plan was what had triggered the May Crisis and caused Prague to mobilize its military and confiscate Sudeten German radios and guns. Hitler, angered by both the leak and the mobilization, told his military chiefs his decision to crush Czechoslovakia was unalterable.

Had Beneš been more a more flexible politician and tried to win some Sudeten German support, Hitler could have found it much more difficult to take the Sudetenland. Back in April, Konrad Henlein and his Sudetendeutsche Partei had presented Beneš an eight-point demand for limited Sudetenland autonomy within Czechoslovakia. But Beneš rigidly refused to make any substantial concessions despite the ominous precedents Hitler had set when through his machinations he regained control of the Rhineland and took over Austria.

In the game of wits, Beneš was constantly on the defensive. By the time he realized military escalation was unavoidable if he didn't bend, the demands had increased. Limited autonomy within the Czech state would likely still have satisfied most Sudeten Germans, but after Nazi subversion of Henlein's party, Hitler was asking for far more. Autonomy had never been in his plans. The Sudetendeutsche Partei's slogan now became the slogan of the Nazi Party: "Ein Volk, ein Reich, ein Führer!" And Hitler's familiar tactic, creating turmoil by demanding more than can be expected and then ratcheting up the demands at the first sign of weakness, was now Henlein's tactic too.

Hitler's deft maneuvering left Beneš in a difficult bind because if Czechoslovakia lost the Sudetenland, it would also lose its ring of defensive fortifications. Hitler upped the pressure by arousing public sentiment at home and abroad with passionate speeches. He and his propagandists cited both real and manufactured reasons why Czechoslovakia needed to cede the Sudeten areas to Germany. To further rattle Beneš's government, Hitler allowed the secret provision of old Austrian rifles to a Henlein-led Free Corps paramilitary group. By this time Henlein had visions of liberating the Sudetenland through a coup. However, Prague easily snuffed out his little insurrection.

◆

Hitler's ministers and military commanders had been horrified when Hitler first revealed his intent to seize Czechoslovakia because they knew an attack on Czechoslovakia could lead to yet another disastrous war with the western powers and the Soviet Union. The relative military strength of the two countries particularly frightened them. Germany had only 31 fully armed divisions and 7 in reserve while the Czechs possessed a heavily fortified border and fielded 45 well stockpiled divisions. And France, which was obligated to help Czechoslovakia, possessed three times as many divisions as the Germans. However, Hitler didn't tolerate questioning. When his war minister and military chief of staff protested the plan early in 1938, engineered scandals cost both men their jobs. The führer's military audacity also resulted in the resignation of his foreign minister after he too voiced his fear that Germany wasn't yet militarily ready to take such a step.

Some months later the German chief of the general staff took his fears to the commander in chief of the army, who convened a secret conference of top generals. The generals unanimously agreed they should take action. The chief of staff suggested a mass resignation, but only he resigned and Hitler quickly hushed up the incident. However, the replacement chief of staff shared the same view and with a number of co-conspirators devised a plan to arrest Hitler and his top Nazi henchmen when the order came to invade Czechoslovakia. The group planned to blockade Berlin to keep the SS from aiding the top Nazis while the conspirators seized the most important government buildings and rounded up the Nazi leaders. Success depended on the western powers keeping pressure on Hitler in the interim by threatening a military mauling.

The plotters sent several special agents to Britain to apprise Prime Minister Chamberlain of their plan and to urge him to take a strong stance against Hitler. Unfortunately, two factors worked against the conspirators. The German Army had given Hitler such strong backing that the German agents didn't appear credible. And Chamberlain, already convinced that diplomacy and negotiation were the best course, met with Hitler in Germany in late September. When he returned from that famous meeting, he said about Hitler, "in spite of the hardness and ruthlessness I saw in his face, I got the impression that here was a man who could be relied upon when he had given his word."[1] As many others had already learned, Hitler's word was worthless, and today Prime Minister Chamberlain's name is synonymous with appeasement and naiveté.

As Hitler's game of nerves sent England and France scrambling to avoid another costly war and find a face-saving way to satisfy Hitler's demands, optimism about the future mounted in small farming communities like Schömitz and Wolframitz. The army's mad scramble to finish the defensive bunkers with the help of conscripted German laborers didn't abate, but Maria and her neighbors sensed Prague no longer felt as confident in its army's ability to hold off a German attack.

On September 30, 1938, the Czechoslovak government had been appalled to learn Britain and France had signed a negotiated agreement giving Hitler what he wanted. The Munich Agreement ceded the Sudeten territory to Germany, and officially recognized the territory as Sudetenland. Becoming part of Germany was not quite the self-determination Sudeten Germans had sought and thought they deserved at Versailles, yet the majority gladly accepted it in exchange for relief from Czech oppression. However, 20,000 German Social Democrats and communist antifascists did not. To escape the claws of the Nazis, they fled to Czech areas where they expected sympathy, but during the next several years Czechs turned most of them over to the Nazis.

Czechs felt humiliated when Beneš had shown no stomach for a fight and capitulated without firing a shot despite his military advantage and huge armaments industry. Two hours after Hitler signed the Munich Agreement, the first German troops crossed the border to occupy the Sudetenland.

Since Hitler's rise, the western powers had discounted him at each clash and lost. Britain's German ambassador had fallen into the same trap during the crisis when he advised Chamberlain to give the Sudetenland to Hitler in exchange for peace. Ambassador Neville Henderson finally came to understand the danger Hitler represented the following year when he wrote: "From beginning to end the world has made the fatal mistake of underestimating Hitler. At first he was either a mountebank or a kind of Charlie Chaplin, an Austrian house-painter or inferior sort of Corporal and now he is a madman or a paranoiac. While in fact he is one of those extraordinary individuals whom the world throws up from time to time, sometimes for its ultimate good but generally for its immediate misfortune."[2]

Sudeten Germans celebrated on becoming part of what they believed was a rising Germany. The promise of prosperity was welcome after two decades of broken promises, injustice, and economic starvation. But they too would learn they'd misjudged Hitler by failing to grasp the extent of his deviousness and ambition. For Hitler, the Czech oppression had been little more than a convenient issue that helped him eliminate the Czechoslovak military threat.[3]

Following the Munich Agreement, Beneš and most of his government ministers abandoned their countrymen and fled to London with millions in American currency, leaving others to face the Nazi threat. Several Sudeten German communist leaders and politicians who opposed the Nazi takeover also fled with Beneš. In London, Beneš appointed himself head of the government-in-exile despite bearing much responsibility for bringing his country to its knees through his inflexibility in dealing with Hitler and his orders for the military to lay down its arms. At least one journalist critic asserted he was able to assume leadership because he had sole control of Czechoslovakia's gold reserves and for years had used his official position to compile files on the dirty secrets of rival politicians.[4]

For political reasons, Beneš couldn't exclude the antifascist ethnic Germans who'd fled with him, so his exile government began with a semblance of democracy. However, he'd already decided to get rid of all Germans after the war, so didn't tolerate this "democracy" any longer than necessary. The British, who in large part bankrolled his exile government, insisted he resign and hold elections as soon as the war was won. It is unclear if Beneš actually resigned after the war, but once all personal danger had passed and he did return, he simply reclaimed the presidency, formed a new unelected "democratic" government, and in collusion with Czech communist leaders eliminated opponents by branding them as collaborators.[5]

Throughout the war Beneš had lobbied for Allied approval to nullify the Munich Agreement, employing secrecy and intrigue in the process. The total expulsion of Sudeten Germans became integral to his postwar plans. He worked relentlessly to sell the Allies on the collective guilt of the Sudeten Germans in "collaborating" with Hitler and destroying the Czechoslovak state. The guilt had to be collective because to differentiate between Nazi supporters and ordinary citizens risked allowing many Germans to stay, which would pose another political problem in the future.

On September 30, 1938, after Hitler and Chamberlain signed the Munich Agreement, life changed drastically for Sudeten Germans. In Bohemia, German soldiers had simply crossed the border from Bavaria to take control of the new territory. In more remote areas such as where Maria lived, the German troops arrived several days later. Oswald Lustig watched the advance party enter Gubschitz on the night of October 9. In Wolframitz Maria found German soldiers in place when she arose on the 10th. They'd come across the border from Austria.

The son of Schömitz Volkschule head teacher Rudolf Mauer wrote in a short memoir that when the Czechoslovak soldiers fled, a number of Czech civilians left as well. However, when the new German administrators didn't expel the remaining Czechs or fire them from their jobs, some of those people returned. He also reported the German troops at this time strictly observed ethnic borders. After recognizing they'd mistakenly occupied a neighboring Czech village, they quickly withdrew.

According to Maria, the locals were wary and distrusted the German soldiers at first. One reason was their foreignness. The unit came from Prussia, and the Prussian-German dialect was so different from the Austrian dialect that the villagers could barely understand them. The people were particularly wary of the high ranking officers for no one knew who might be a Nazi to be feared.

At first the situation was very fluid. Soldiers came and went, and no one knew what they were up to. Some of the unit's soldiers were based in the nearby towns of Mährisch Kromau and Pohrlitz, but the main body was split between Znaim and Nikolsburg, the two nearest district seats. Although Wolframitz was not large enough to warrant a sizeable garrison, the army did set up some administrative offices in the fancy new Czech school. Maria never learned exactly what function the offices there had; it was best not to be curious about such things. Within days of the takeover, a few soldiers were billeted in the village. The Gasthaus in Klein Seelowitz, one of the villages in the Wolframitz cluster, was the most popular spot.

In Schömitz, as in Wolframitz, most of the distrust evaporated once the residents grew accustomed to the presence of the soldiers and their Prussian speech. A number of the soldiers grew so fond of the area that they said they'd like to settle there when their military service was over. Some of the senior officers didn't wait and brought their families soon after arrival.

Hitler toured southern Moravia in triumph after the 1938 takeover. The region's Sudeten Germans were still jubilant over their deliverance and had yet to get a taste of the sacrifices they would have to make. Oswald Lustig was in the eighth grade and followed the news closely. The boy had such a keen interest in history and politics that seeing Hitler promised to be the experience of a lifetime. His idealism and high expectations would later make his disappointment in Hitler all the more bitter. When he told me about Hitler's visit years later, he said he could still picture the event as if it had happened yesterday.

My mother also saw the führer that day. She needed only to step outside her front door as his limousine passed by a few feet away on the street. The excitement in the air was palpable, but after five years of laboring to support herself the 19-year-old was considerably less idealistic than Oswald. Consequently, her recollection of the visit was less keen. When I asked her whether Johann had turned out to see his fellow war veteran, she was unable to recall.

In Gubschitz on October 27, 1938, the news quickly spread up and down the street. Neighbors and friends emerged from their houses and gathered to discuss the impending event. Oswald grew very excited upon hearing Hitler's motorcade would arrive in Wolframitz late that afternoon. Although a record covering many of Hitler's day-to-day activities stated that Hitler "briefly visited Pohrlitz and Wolframitz" before delivering a midday speech in the district seat of Nikolsburg,[6] Oswald clearly recalled the visit occurred in the late afternoon after Hitler's motorcade left Nikolsburg by way of the Kaiserstrasse, a highway connecting Vienna and Brünn.

Oswald's mother wasn't interested in seeing the führer, but the boy and his father couldn't wait. They hurried to Wolframitz to stake out a prime vantage point on the main street through town. When they arrived, a scattering of people already lined the street. The largest knot had assembled in front of the Rathaus and on the opposite side of the street in the Marktplatz. Oswald and his father decided if Hitler stopped to speak, it would surely be there, so the boy positioned himself at the street's edge to be as close as he could get. He was in total awe of this hero who'd addressed the entire world's youth by radio at the grand 1936 Olympic Games in Berlin and then spectacularly topped this by liberating Sudeten Germans from Czech oppression. In the boy's view, Hitler took on Western Europe's most powerful leaders—men who had ignored the Sudetenland's oppression and even denied a problem existed—and made them come to Germany in order to correct the situation.

Eventually several large, open-top Mercedes limousines arrived bearing high ranking SS officers sitting with an arm draped across the sides of the cars. The insignias on their uniforms read **LEIBSTANDARTE ADOLF HITLER**. Oswald impatiently scanned each car as it neared, but none held Hitler. Then at last, two more cars pulled into view, and he made out the form of Hitler through the windshield of the first. As the vehicle drew close, most bystanders raised their arms in the stiff-arm Nazi salute.

Hitler's arrival in Wolframitz. Oswald's arm is somewhere among other outstretched arms in front of Rathaus on left.

Hitler's reaction perplexed Oswald. The crowd of about 300 was paying homage to its liberator, yet unexplainably the liberator was looking on without expression or feeling.

Nevertheless, Oswald was thrilled to be able to see his hero pass close enough that he could almost reach out and touch the car. It looked as if Hitler would ride by without any acknowledgement of the crowd, but just before reaching Oswald, the führer stood, raised his right arm, and returned a lazy German military salute, just like Oswald had seen in newspaper photographs.

The crowd was not raucous, so everyone in the vicinity was astonished when they saw the parish priest, positioned next to Oswald and in front of Oswald's father, raise his arm and hysterically scream, "Heil, Heil, Heil!" The shout caught Hitler's attention for a moment, and the führer, still standing, half turned and glared down at the priest. Hitler then sat back down and seconds later disappeared from view when his car rounded a curve. After two more identical cars full of Wehrmacht (armed forces) officers passed by, the event was over. The spectacle of Hitler's passage was so brief that some of the bystanders hadn't even seen the man.

Hitler curtly acknowledges crowd in front of Wolframitz Rathaus

Oswald arrived home only minutes behind his father. As he stepped inside the house, he could hear his father complaining to Oswald's mother about the despicable behavior of the Wolframitz parish pastor. The priest's behavior was odd because although he'd been the pastor of the German community for years, he'd always maintained he was a loyal Czech. What upset Oswald's father most though was that the priest's antics had blocked his view of Hitler.

◆

Not much later, Oswald learned that the motorcade had stopped outside of Wolframitz near a bunker along the hastily built Czechoslovak Army defensive line. There, the military set up a roadblock so Hitler and his staff could inspect a bunker. As Hitler looked on, an army officer explained how such bunkers could be defeated. He demonstrated the maneuver by breaching the bunker's protective wall with an explosive charge, and then flinging a hand grenade into the steel-reinforced machine gun port to knock out any defenders inside. Several local community members had been present. Oswald was disappointed he hadn't been among them.

The Czech bunkers turned out to be useful for the German military. The army used them to devise methods to defeat such structures and to train soldiers in neutralizing them. German attackers applied that knowledge in 1940 when they invaded the neighboring Low Countries and encountered similar fortifications in Belgium as well as along France's Maginot Line. German familiarity with the large fortress-type bunkers proved pivotal at the Battle of Fort Eben-Emael in Belgium. A few handfuls of German airborne soldiers in gliders landed on the roof of the supposedly impregnable fortification and captured it, which allowed German invasion forces to skirt other Belgian defensive positions in the drive to secure the countries along the coast.

Overgrown Czech bunkers in fields near Wolframitz, 2010

When I explored the bunkers near Wolframitz, I searched for the one where Hitler's demonstration took place. Neither Oswald nor Oskar could identify it on the map they had carefully plotted and marked with each bunker's position and identification number. I examined a number of the structures in the hope of finding a damaged one, without success. Most lay in large farm fields. Several were along roads. The majority had become dense little islands of trees and brush over the years, making access and entry difficult. These dots of greenery are even visible on web-based satellite images of the area. The most logical location was along Hitler's route west of Wolframitz near where the road began to climb the slope to Miskogel. None of bunkers there were damaged. However, I did find a spot that looked as if it might once have been the site of a bunker. If so, it had long since been razed and the debris removed.

After the bunker-busting demonstration, Hitler and his entourage continued along the road to Mährisch Kromau and the palace of Graf Rudolf Kinsky, who owned the Meierhof manor in Schömitz and participated annually in the autumn hunt there. The palace was located at the edge of town near the former location of a castle built by the Knights Templar in the days of the Holy Wars. The Renaissance palace was built in 1512 by the Liechtenstein family. Napoleon was but one of the famous personages who'd stayed there. The Kinsky family had owned this handsome building, and until the formation of Czechoslovakia, a considerable amount of farm land throughout the region. The German takeover allowed the family to get it back.

Interior courtyard of Schloss Kromau in town of Mährisch Kromau during Nazi rally of Nov. 24, 1938. Here, a month earlier, Oswald came to catch a second glimpse of Hitler on the evening of the Wolframitz visit.

Many local residents gathered in the garden of the palace courtyard in the early evening following Hitler's arrival. Hitler appeared with the host family on the grand extended second-floor balcony, and there Graf Kinsky formally honored Hitler with a short welcome speech. Oswald was among the throng of onlookers. He'd made his way to Mährisch Kromau when he learned the führer would be staying there overnight, for he still hoped to hear Hitler speak. Oswald waited expectantly, only to be disappointed once again when Hitler did nothing more than thank the assembled for coming. When it became clear there'd be no speech, the crowd broke into nostalgic song and sang several favorite German melodies, but didn't shriek hysterically as the crowds in Vienna and the other large cities had when Hitler visited.

The excitement didn't end for Maria either after Hitler's entourage departed Wolframitz, for she learned the revelry would continue that evening. For Moravian Germans, that meant a dance. No celebration was complete without one. The village cluster had no indoor gathering place large enough to hold this event because of all the additional soldiers and civilians who'd arrived to see their leader, so it was to take place outside a large Gasthaus. The military band added excitement for it had some excellent musicians and a repertoire new to the Wolframitzers. Maria looked forward to the dance while she finished the workday. Unfortunately, things didn't work out as planned. She recalled standing in the doorway of her residence with a friend, highly disappointed because an approaching thunderstorm caused the event to be cancelled.

---

[1] Graham Macklin, *Chamberlain* (Haus Publishing, 2006), 68.
[2] Nevile Henderson, *Failure of a Mission; Berlin 1937-1939* (New York: G. P. Putnam's sons, 1940), 39.
[3] Valdis O Lumans, *Himmler's Auxiliaries: The Volksdeutsche Mittelstelle and the German National Minorities of Europe, 1933-1945* (Chapel Hill: University of North Carolina Press, 1993), 85.
[4] Sidonia Dědinová, *Edvard Beneš the Liquidator: Fiend of the German Purge in Czechoslovakia* (Mountain View, Calif.: Ready for Print Publications, 2001), 220.
[5] Dědinová, *Edvard Beneš the Liquidator*, 222.
[6] Hitler, Domarus, and Romane, *The Essential Hitler Speeches and Commentary*, 1231.

22 Life in the Reich

SHORTLY AFTER THE GERMAN ANNEXATION of the Sudetenland, Maria left her job at the Geidl farm when Geidl informed her he didn't need her help any longer because the children were four years older now and able to tend to their own needs. His reason was absurd because housework and childcare had never been a big part of Maria's job. The truth was she and Geidl had grown sick of each other. Maria had just turned 19 and was at long last legally free of her stepmother's control. She considered moving back to Schömitz to live with the Luksch family but ultimately decided to stay in Wolframitz. The thought of living near Karolina again was too much, so she agreed to work for a farmer just down the street. This job didn't pay well either, but did allow Maria to remain where she had many friends and now felt at home.

Her new boss, Alois Stöffel, was nothing like Geidl. Not only was he closer to her own age, he was pleasant to be around and fair. This time she knew from the outset that housework was but a small part of the job. Yet, once again the job came with an unpleasant surprise—the farmer's wife, Aurelia, was extremely lazy and soon began to think of Maria as a personal servant. Having someone to boss elevated Aurelia's self-image and let her think of herself as more of a lady than a farmer's wife. The source of these notions was no mystery to Maria; they came from Aurelia's interfering mother. Whenever Maria was not in the field helping Alois, Aurelia assigned Maria every bit of labor she herself no longer wished to do.

The Geidl farm hadn't been small, but Stöffel worked even more land. By custom, each community in the region provided the parish church a farm whose rent supported the parish priest, and Alois farmed this ground in addition to his own. For Maria this meant there was always too much work to be done.

Although Maria disliked the endless hard field work, the inadequate pay, and Aurelia's laziness, she had come to embrace Wolframitz. Socializing with her friends in the evening allowed her to release most of the tensions and irritations accumulated during the day. Maria still liked to stroll, but by this time had saved enough money to buy herself an adult bicycle. The new mobility allowed her to venture out to dances, festivals, and social gatherings of all types with her friends. The group went everywhere together and sometimes even rode their bicycles all the way to Mährisch Kromau for a movie.

Maria with her bicycle

◆

Mobility was not the only change in Maria's social life after the integration into the Third Reich. All of a sudden the number of sports activities available for young people exploded under the mantle of the Hitler Jugend (Hitler Youth Organization) and the Bund Deutscher Mädel or BDM (League of German Girls), the girls' equivalent of Hitler Youth. In Germany membership in the latter became mandatory for girls after 1936, but it was not compulsory in Maria's rural area of the Sudetenland. Maria had been out of school for several years already, but she and her friends joined for the camaraderie and activities. They found participation in sports novel and fun. On weekends, which for a farm worker meant Sunday after Mass, she often joined a group going to Miskogel, the recreation area on the hill several kilometers out of town. There, the girls trained and participated in track and field events.

Maria around the time she left the Geidl household

In Wolframitz participation in BDM recreational activities came without any formal political indoctrination, which suited Maria and her friends fine. But for one Schömitz girl, the younger sister of one of Maria's former classmates, the BDM constituted much more than simple recreation. This girl had had serious learning problems as a student, and the teachers were unable to teach her to read no matter how hard they tried. They rapped her knuckles and thumped her head with a ruler countless times to no avail. Yet surprisingly she thrived in the BDM and became one of its top local leaders.

For boys, Hitler Youth was not the same sort of benign experience. Boys were required to join the organization, for its primary aim was to toughen and prepare them for the military. Maria's stepbrother Eduard was introduced to it when he left Schömitz to attend school in Znaim. Eduard enjoyed the new sports activities that came with it, but not the persistent regimentation and physical training. As far as Maria knew, her younger brother Erich never had to join because Schömitz was too tiny to form its own chapter.

German administration of the Sudetenland was very positive when it came to education, at least for the German communities. Suddenly they no longer had to fear the loss of their schools. Capable students, even those from poor families, gained immediate access to advanced schooling. Although this came along too late to benefit Maria, Eduard was the right age. His parents, even with their extra income from renting out Rosina's house and land, couldn't have afforded further education. With the support the government now provided for students such as Eduard, people jested that scholars need bring only their pants and a pen—everything else was provided.

In Johann's second family, Eduard was closest in age to Maria and the sibling she grew closest to. With misty eyes Maria remembered him as "the nicest person you would ever want to know." Their friendship deepened after he left home to attend a secondary school. The amount of land Johann farmed had never been large enough to require much help from Eduard, so his parents had sent him away to stay with a relative and work during summer vacations. This experience expanded the boy's horizon beyond the little village of Schömitz; he developed academic ambitions. After the Sudetenland's educational opportunities widened, Eduard was able to attend the Bürgerschule secondary school in Lodenitz, joining his good friends Oskar Halusa and Oswald Lustig. All three boys were good students and scored well enough on their oral exams to be accepted by the *Lehrerbildungsanstalt* (teacher training institute) in the old town of Znaim. The older residents of the region's communities knew Znaim well as it was the home garrison of the old Austrian Army's 99th Regiment in which Johann and many other local men had served during the First World War

Eduard, or Eddo as his friends knew him, thrived in his new school despite the militaristic regimentation the Nazis imposed as the price for free education. Here Eduard and Oswald developed an interest in a pair of sisters named Mitzi and Franziska, who were also students at the school. Maria visited Eduard in Znaim a time or two by bus, but couldn't recall meeting the girls.

Oskar and Eduard, in the back row from the left, at the teacher training school in Znaim

◆

At that time Znaim was a charming old German town on the left bank of the River Thaya. Now the town is called Znojmo, the River Thaya has become the Dyje, and the original prosperous German inhabitants are no longer even a memory because they were driven out or killed and the record of their former presence erased. In the absence of this history, about the only reminders left are the old buildings and a few historic landmarks.

The most notable of the latter lies beneath the city's streets—a 30-kilometer network of tunnels and catacombs built through the centuries for purposes both venerable and deplorable.

Znaim is also associated with a famous scientist. Gregor Johann Mendel began his academic career here as a substitute teacher. He arrived as a young priest who'd just learned he was not psychologically equipped to minister to the sick and dying. Mendel proved a capable teacher but to the benefit of science failed a teaching certification exam because he was self-taught and lacked a formal grounding in the sciences. To remedy the situation, his religious order dispatched him to the University of Vienna to study math, physics, plant physiology, and anatomy. As a result he acquired the empirical and scientific methodology he so successfully used when he applied statistics to a biological problem and discovered the two principles of genetics now known as the laws of segregation and independent assortment.

The most notable historic event in Eduard's new locale was a battle without a victor. In 1809 the Austrian Army fought Napoleon's forces to a standstill here and then negotiated a settlement known as the Armistice of Znaim. No monument still exists to commemorate the battle; however, Znaim does have an obscure and modest monument of a different sort—the Rabenstein Menhir. A menhir is an upright, prehistoric stone megalith. Folktales associated with this particular stone have endured since before local history was recorded. The Rabenstein Menhir's original significance is unknown but earns a mention here because it led to the occult awakening of perhaps the strangest denizen in the Nazi stable of weird supporting cast characters.

Like my grandfather, Karl Maria Wiligut served in Austria's 99th Infantry Regiment and was garrisoned in Znaim. Wiligut, like his father and grandfather before him, was a career officer in the Austrian Army. In 1900, at age 34, he became intrigued with the Rabenstein Menhir. He'd already dabbled in the occult, but the folklore attached to this find sent him down that path in a determined way. Soon Wiligut claimed to be a direct descendent of a long line of Germanic mystics with special occult powers. His gift enabled him to recall precepts, beliefs, and traditions from his race's Nordic past by way of genetic memories passed on through his ancestors. Rather remarkably, and conveniently, this memory reached many thousands of years into the past. His ancestors, he declared, practiced something called Irminism and worshiped a Germanic god named Krist, which Christians later turned into their Christ. Of course, this also implied the original language of the Bible was German.

Wiligut's insights didn't stop there. He maintained that his lineage passed through the lost continent of Atlantis and other eminent civilizations. His powers enabled him to see back hundreds of thousands of years to a time when the earth still had three suns and was the dwelling place of mythical inhabitants. During a three year confinement in an asylum for schizophrenia, Wiligut convinced himself that the Catholic Church, Jews, and the Freemasons were persecuting him and that these entities were also behind Austria and Germany's loss in World War I. Given the similarity of his beliefs and those of a certain former German corporal experiencing a meteoric rise to power in Germany, it should not be surprising to learn Wiligut developed an affinity with this politician. Alignment was almost inevitable after destiny delivered Wiligut to Munich following his release from the asylum.

In Munich he changed his name to Weisthor and set up shop anew. During those tumultuous days after the Great War, many Germans had lost faith in the government, the church, and traditional institutions. Because people desperately wanted to believe in something, wild and irrational beliefs flourished, and occultism became a growth industry. Weisthor/Wiligut found he could meet that need by writing for occult magazines. Before long he was inventing prehistory as fast as his audience could swallow it. With the help of other occultists, Weisthor became a Germanic prophet to many, including Heinrich Himmler, Hitler's *Reichsführer* and head of the SS.

Himmler never wearied listening to his new friend expound on the history of Atlantis, the Holy Grail, and mythical ancestors. Himmler was an ambitious man who, like Hitler, lacked moral constraints. He saw in Weisthor the basis for a new state religion to replace Christianity in Hitler's Thousand Year Reich. Weisthor saw in Himmler a golden chance to legitimize Irminism as well as an opportunity to boost his own career and immortalize his place in the new religion.

Weisthor eagerly joined the SS and as a Himmler favorite rapidly advanced in rank. Weisthor's plan to establish Irminism as the state religion included the restoration of ancient pagan sites and monuments as well as the destruction of Christianity. Additionally, Weisthor designed the runic symbols used on the black SS uniforms and flags, and devised the sinister Totenkopfring (Death's Head Ring) which Himmler bestowed on favored SS officers. The runes and mystical symbols covering the ring were important for establishing an aura of mystique and building a mantle of obscurity around Himmler's near-medieval brotherhood of SS knights. Himmler bestowed the ring on officers with the stipulation it would be forfeited if the SS discipline code were violated.

A year before the war began, Himmler decided that the rings of SS men who died should be returned to permit a mystical union of the dead. Orders were issued that comrades of the fallen should make every effort to retrieve the rings to keep them out of the hands of the enemy. Just how fastidiously the order was followed in light of the extreme Waffen SS (combat field force of the SS) losses late in the war is unknown, but by January 1945 nearly two-thirds of the 14,500 issued rings had come back. In the final days of the war Himmler purportedly ordered the rings hidden in a cave and blasted shut. Today surviving rings are a highly prized collector's item.[1] In 1939, when Himmler learned of his mystic's asylum stay, word quietly went down that it was time for Weisthor to return his Totenkopfring. The official explanation for the sudden retirement was ill health.[2]

◆

Eduard likely never heard of the inspirational connection between the obscure Znaim monument and the mystical awakening of the man who has been called Hitler's Warlock and Himmler's Rasputin. He would have been far too busy with his studies and new athletic activities. One of these new activities was ski touring. When the ground was covered with snow, Eduard enjoyed skiing all the way home from Znaim with Oswald, Oskar, and several other local boys. He'd stop first in Wolframitz to visit Maria, and then continue on to Schömitz and his family. At other times of the year, he biked or took the bus.

This love of academic studies was not shared by Eduard's younger brother Erich, who chose a different path. On graduation from the eighth grade in Schömitz, Erich decided he'd had enough of classrooms and apprenticed himself to a carpenter in Lodenitz—his Uncle Johann. This was the same Johann who years earlier had built the carpentry shop in Rosina's storage shed and smoked the Luksch family out of their house with his stove. Erich remained with Johann for two years until the latter was called into the military. The boy was then fortunate enough to locate another carpenter in Lodenitz who agreed to take him on until he finished his final year of the apprenticeship.

---

[1] Wikipedia contributors, "SS-Ehrenring," *Wikipedia*, Wikipedia.org, 8 Feb. 2015, accessed 21 Apr. 2015.
[2] Wikipedia contributors, "Karl Maria Wiligut," *Wikipedia*, Wikipedia.org, 14 Apr. 2015, accessed 21 Apr. 2015.

23 The Dark Side

IN THE HEADY DAYS AFTER ASSIMILATION into the German Reich, Sudeten Germans believed they were better off with their new allegiance. Many could still recall their stable, prosperous lives in the Austrian Empire before the Great War. When positive changes came about quickly and their schools, culture, and jobs were no longer under assault, they believed Hitler had restored this life.

One of the most welcome changes involved transportation. For the first time ever, many rural villages and towns became connected as public buses began operating between towns. The transportation especially benefited children because it gave them access to more schools and advanced academic and technical education tracks. Buses also allowed older people to visit friends and relatives elsewhere as well as reach markets and shops in larger towns. In Wolframitz the improved mobility rapidly stimulated commerce. A thriving weekly farmer's produce market sprang up in the Marktplatz where only a monthly public market had existed before. Not only did this give housewives a wider variety of fruits and vegetables to choose from, it allowed enterprising farmers to earn some extra income.

Local merchants in Wolframitz, particularly the proprietors of the beer-drinking establishments, benefited almost immediately from the payroll of the recently arrived Prussian military. The district army posts also contributed something everyone in the community appreciated—a military band. As in Schömitz, bands comprised of local residents had always provided the music at festivals and dances. The arrival of the military band with more musicians, a new repertoire, and a greater variety of instruments excited local residents. Wolframitz now held more dances because the soldiers stationed in the vicinity needed leisure activities. Most of these dances took place outdoors near the large inn in Klein Seelowitz, but the Wolframitz Marktplatz or old Gasthaus hosted dances for some of the festivals such as Rosenmontag (the German equivalent of Mardi Gras), which featured activities and partying for weeks prior to the main celebration. Even many Schömitz residents came to Wolframitz for these dances. On the day of a dance, soldiers began arriving in the afternoon from outlying posts. Sometimes officers used the opportunity to make speeches, but the men came for the dances.

♦

Despite these improvements, the honeymoon with Hitler didn't last. Before long some residents began to quietly question the benefits of joining the Reich. Military service, compulsory for Germans but not for Czechs, was an early irritant. Under the former Czechoslovak rule, both Germans and Czechs had to serve. The induction of young single men began almost immediately. By the time World War II started on September 1, 1939, the military also tapped young married men who operated farms or businesses and had children. These men had responsibilities and thought they'd already fulfilled their military obligation. This imposed hardship on everyone, particularly the wives, who were left to do a man's work on the farms even as they maintained a home and took care of their children.

Girls and young women began to have a difficult time finding local dance partners. At first a few could still be found because they occasionally returned home on leave during training, but when the war began in earnest, it was a rare soldier who made his way back on furlough. Maria had had a couple of boyfriends in the prewar period and was seeing a young man steadily at the time of the takeover. He returned a couple of times during training, and the two of them talked about marriage. Then Hitler invaded Poland and mobilized the military. The new uncertainty caused many young couples to put their marriage plans on hold. Maria, because she'd just recently gained her independence, wasn't prepared to rush into marriage, so she and her soldier agreed to wait and see what happened. She didn't tell me of this until her final years, and even then revealed it only reluctantly and in the most general terms. The memory was obviously still painful.

A further burden imposed now on Sudeten Germans, as members of the Reich, involved identity documentation. The Nazis required most adults to complete an official ancestry document called an *Ahnenpass*. The form, a passport-sized booklet, required verification of family lineage through several generations. The person or office in charge of a community's records recorded the entries. For Maria and those around her, this person was typically the parish priest and his assistants. Combing the parish birth, death, and marriage records for this information entailed an incredible amount of effort.

In Germany this testament of a Jewish-free ancestry became an ever more onerous requirement. Racial status was everything in the Nazi world, and the Ahnenpass document served as quick proof of Aryan racial acceptability. The document was necessary for party membership, business ownership or transfer, marriage, higher education matriculation, the mandatory Labor Service, numerous professions, Hitler Youth, name changes, government aid, child support, and membership in many organizations. The document was required of men called up for military service. Married military inductees even needed proof of their spouse's racial purity. And children put up for adoption needed an Ahnenpass.

Eventually the list of statutes and regulations relating to the Ahnenpass numbered some 2,000. One modern scholar wrote, "It is probably not an overstatement to say that by 1945, aside from the very old and the very young, virtually every Reich citizen, or would-be citizen, had made an ancestral proof at one time or another."[1] Maria's form listed information reaching back six generations. Since Schömitz had so few Jews, and Jews seldom intermarried, few in the community had reason to worry about an unacceptable ancestry.

Even after the war began most Sudeten Germans were still relieved enough by the removal of the threat to their schools, culture, and institutions to hold their noses and accept the more sinister aspects of Nazi control. Neither Maria nor anyone around her talked openly about these darker facets. She confessed anxiety about the Gestapo, especially after area Jews began disappearing. Although she didn't know of any Gestapo agents in Wolframitz, like everyone else she avoided talking about the subject, except in private. Historically, Jews had resided in the region almost as long as Slavs and were tolerated. In Wolframitz Maria knew of only one Jew, a cattle buyer who supplied local butchers with cattle he bought from farmers. One morning he was gone. Whether he fled or the Nazis whisked him away, no one seemed to know.

The nearby prosperous village of Pohrlitz had the greatest concentration of Jews. There, they owned nearly every store and business. Maria didn't know any Jews there personally, but heard that not long after they'd all disappeared some of the local Nazi officials and senior military officers obtained new housing. At some point Maria learned both of the Jewish families in Schömitz had also vanished. Her Luksch relatives told her that one morning the little grocery store didn't open, and the owners were gone. No one seemed to know what happened to them, or weren't talking. The news about the Neuspiel family and her old school friend disturbed Maria. The Neuspiels were good people and well liked. She hoped they'd fled quietly in the night as a whispered rumor suggested, but she feared the Nazis had snatched them up and sent them to a work camp.

To Maria the thought of imprisoning these people was disturbing enough. The idea that in the future the Nazis would kill many of them was unthinkable. Despite the Nazi anti-Semitic propaganda campaign to exclude Jews from civil society, the actions troubled many residents and left some wondering who might disappear next. Again, few people felt safe talking about such things for the village had several known fascists who could be informers. Maria had particular reason to be cautious. One suspected snitch lived right across the street. His wealthy son down the street was known to belong to the Nazi party, so everyone surmised the father belonged as well.

Although the fighting during the war barely touched Czech territory, Czechs throughout the Sudetenland and the Czech core did have to endure a harsh Nazi administration. The Berlin Nazi government intended to Germanize a large portion of the Czech population and settle Germans among them, much like Beneš and Masaryk had done to Czechify German areas. However, the German plan wasn't to begin in earnest until after the war, so fewer than 10,000 Germans were ever resettled. When the war effort brought about shortages of consumer goods and food, rationing was imposed on Czechs, but they received the same ration allowances as Germans. Still, the Czech state suffered in other ways. In November 1939, two days after large Czech student protests, Berlin ordered the closure of Czech universities. The Nazis executed several students and sent about 1200 others to concentration camps. Many Czech workers were forced to fill jobs in mines and war-critical industries. Without doubt, Czechoslovak Jews and Gypsies suffered the most for they were largely eradicated.

◆

The rapid, decisive military successes Germany enjoyed early in the war encouraged Hitler to speed up the launch of his grand territorial acquisition plan. The troop strength required for this venture quickly depleted the supply of young men in southern Moravia. The call-up age for military conscripts climbed in order to meet the demand, which put a terrible strain on the agricultural sector. In the absence of the farmers who knew the land and farming, wives, daughters, and elders not only had to take on the heavy work, but also had to make crop and management decisions that they were ill equipped for.

The German Wehrmacht (armed forces) inducted men through a military district system in which the Reich was divided up into Wehrkreis districts. Germany established seven districts after the Treaty of Versailles restricted the German Army to 100,000 men. During the period of Nazi power consolidation, the Nazis vetted the allotted men so when the time came, this small but professional core could form the leadership of a competent and rapidly expandable military force. From 1934 to 1938, the number of military districts increased to thirteen as the Reich took additional territory. After the annexation of Austria and the conquest of

Poland, the number climbed to eighteen. Although the Wehrkreis inducted only *Volksdeutsche* (ethnic Germans) from the new territories, the millions of ethnic Germans living in these areas swelled the number of fighting men.

Each district supplied the manpower to form two military corps through an assigned recruitment allotment. A corps is a unit made up of at least two divisions, so each district supported multiple Wehrmacht divisions. Each German division, including field units, depot components, and replacement regiments, drew its recruits and replacements from its associated Wehrkreis. Before the all-out war mobilization of June 1939, each Wehrkreis headquarters provided two administrative sections—a tactical component serving as the corps headquarters when the corps deployed to the field and a garrison administration to handle training and replacement. Less fit or older men filled slots in the rear areas, which allowed a medium-sized country like Germany to mobilize a disproportionately large field force.

Unlike the Czech nationalists who took over the Sudetenland in 1918, the Nazis allowed most Czech civil servants and other workers to keep their jobs in the Sudetenland. The German planners were not being altruistic; they anticipated a labor shortage when Germany went to war. Because Czech males didn't face military service, they were available to take jobs vacated by the Germans called up into the military.

◆

In Wolframitz Maria saw the Czech policemen work openly with, and even appear to be sympathetic to, their new German superiors. She wasn't in a position to know whether this was because they wanted to avoid trouble or whether they found little difference in their masters. In Pohrlitz Czechs kept their jobs at the sugar beet factories, and in Schömitz, Czechs and Slovaks continued to work at the Meierhof as they had for the previous two decades. When the Nazis eventually took over the core Czech area and called it the Czech Protectorate, Czech workers there kept their jobs as well and cooperated with the German administrators. The Nazis didn't even have to bother vetting them for their political views or loyalty. Even in the armaments factories, labor problems and sabotage were practically unheard of throughout the war.

On farms, Czech workers from Czech areas filled some of the German labor needs. However, after Hitler and the Soviet Union signed the pact that divided Poland's territory between them, Germany's new acquisition provided a much larger labor pool. Many Polish girls and young women eagerly came to the Sudetenland to work. Maria recalled that eventually nearly every household acquired a Polish maid because they willingly worked for low wages. The extra help was a godsend for many women. With the men away, they struggled to mind the children, take care of the house, and labor in the fields also. The Stöffel family hired a Polish girl, but not until four years into the war.

Berlin also provided another labor source to farmers as the war expanded. Early in the fighting on both the Eastern and Western Fronts, the German military took many more prisoners of war (POWs) than they could handle. On the Eastern Front, many of them died. To ease the need to house, feed, and guard these men, the military parceled many out as laborers. Prisoners were not widely used in Maria's locale, because most farms were small. Where they were used, POWs commonly remained at the same farm for years and bonded with the families they worked for. Some of these men even stayed on for a time at the end of the war in an attempt to protect the family from reprisals.

Another minor source of farm labor was ethnic Germans from points further east. In 1940 the Nazis, by prior agreement with the Soviet Union, removed ethnic Germans from the Soviet zone of Poland and other recently acquired territory and resettled them elsewhere in the Reich. In this exchange, Maria's part of southern Moravia ended up with a number of ethnic Germans from Dobrudscha near the Black Sea. A camp in Mährisch Kromau housed them until they received a permanent placement. Several of these families were given farmland the Nazis appropriated from the vicinity of two Czech villages near Wolframitz. This land confiscation was on a smaller scale than the Czechoslovak land redistribution scheme that had placed Czech farmers on German land in the previous two decades, but it raised the same sort of resentment among Czechs as it had earlier with Germans. German farmers also hired Dobrudscha Germans as workers. The Stöffel family employed a married couple for a year. They lived in their own room in the Stöffel house until the wife became pregnant. When they left, Aurelia hired the Polish maid, who lived in the house from 1943 to 1945.

Maria didn't mind her job when Alois was in charge. He was a hard worker and a fair employer, and he was able to keep Aurelia's demands on Maria in check. So it was a dark day for her when Alois received his notice to report for military duty. After he left, life was much less pleasant. Maria's workdays began early and often ran well into the evening. Aurelia expected her to milk the four or five cows twice a day, work in the fields, and help with the children too. Sometimes Maria also had to cook the meals. Because of all the cheap foreign labor available, Maria had no other job prospects.

In the fields, the crop Maria despised most was hay. Larger farms like the one she worked on relied on heavy horses to handle the field work.

Feeding these animals entailed raising three or more special varieties of clover. Haying was hard, labor intensive, and dirty. The main crop on the two Stöffel farms, grain, also translated into heavy labor at threshing time. Like Maria's previous employer, Alois owned his own thresher. Operating it required many laborers, so he relied on small-farm neighbors to get the job done. In exchange for their labor, Alois then threshed their grain, which also required Maria's help.

Soon after Alois's departure, Maria learned that demanding, lazy Aurelia wasn't her only problem. Alois's father, who took charge of the farming, was just as hard to tolerate. Anton Stöffel was a disagreeable man who'd burned through two Czech wives. Not only was the man overbearing and obnoxious, he was greedy and a workaholic too. The day never had enough work hours to suit him. Maria argued with Anton often because she and the other workers could never get enough done to please him. However, there was nothing to be done; the characteristics ran in the family. Anton's brother was much the same, only rich. The only saving grace was that Anton returned to his own house on the other side of the street in the evening.

Anton was often at odds with Aurelia too. In spite of his best efforts, he couldn't get her to do any work. Maria disdained both bosses equally at first, but as time went on her contempt for Aurelia moved to the fore. The woman occasionally condescended to help with breakfast, but not often. And when she did, she worked little for the rest of the day. Not until 1943, when the young Polish maid arrived to help with the housework, did the domestic load ease for Maria. However, the maid's presence would later have a negative consequence.

After the long days of hard work during the growing and harvesting seasons, Maria was often too weary to meet her friends in the evening. At times she even had to work Sundays. Nothing could be done, so she tried to make the best of it. Fortunately, in between the intense field seasons she had more time to socialize. On Sundays and holidays with free time, Maria occasionally biked to Schömitz to stay with Emma and the Luksch family.

The loss of Rosina's house to avaricious Karolina still rankled Maria. Were it hers, she wouldn't be slaving away so hard in Wolframitz. Maria always intended to talk to her father about getting back what should have been hers, but she seldom saw him. And when she did, the two of them couldn't talk freely because Karolina was around. However, deep down Maria knew it was pointless. Karolina would deny him any say in the matter. Even the house furnishings were still beyond Maria's reach, as was the rent money from Maria's plot of land. Franz Onkel had offered to buy the land from Maria to keep it in the family and to build up

Maria's savings, but Karolina opposed the sale. Franz didn't want to cause more trouble for Maria's relationship with her father, so he dropped the idea.

---

[1] Eric Ehrenreich, *The Nazi Ancestral Proof: Genealogy, Racial Science, and the Final Solution* (Indiana University Press, 2007), 61.

24 War and Tears

SHORTLY AFTER SECURING the Sudeten sections of Bohemia and Moravia, and incorporating them into the German Reich, Hitler insisted he was still interested only in peace and used the following allegory in a speech. "Regrettably, there are people who hate the hedgehog merely because it has quills. Well, all they have to do is not bother the animal. No hedgehog has ever attacked someone lest he was threatened himself. Let this be our code of conduct, too."[1]

Even as he said this, the peaceful hedgehog was already pointing its quills east toward Poland and the territory that the Treaty of Versailles stripped from Germany at the end of World War I. When ongoing negotiations with the Poles broke down in January 1939, Hitler decided to seize Poland militarily. However, doing so presented a problem—Czechoslovakia still possessed a sizeable army. To eliminate this vulnerability before invading Poland, he needed control of the remainder of Czechoslovakia. He hoped to solve the problem through political means, but ordered his military to draw up a contingency plan to seize the Czech part of Bohemia and Moravia in case the first option failed. The Ides of March, March 15, was to be the launch date.

To soften up his target Hitler dusted off the political divide-and-conquer strategy he'd used so successfully in the past. With some behind-the-scenes maneuvering he coerced Hungary, to the southwest, and the Slovaks in Czechoslovakia to break up the rump Czech state. These neighbors cooperated because they'd suffered at the hands of the Czechs and also feared Hitler. By prearrangement, on March 14 the Slovak Diet voted unanimously to declare Slovakian independence from Czechoslovakia. Simultaneously, Hungarian troops moved in to occupy the predominantly Hungarian portion of eastern Slovakia and the Carpatho-Ukraine region stripped from Hungary at Versailles. In the west along the Czech Bohemian border, the Germans massed their own invasion force. With all parts of the plan in place, Hitler sprung his trap.

He summoned Emil Hácha, the aged caretaker president of Czechoslovakia, to Berlin that night, and badgered and threatened him until he signed the document handing over governance to Germany. At three in the morning, Hitler was so jubilant upon returning to his office that he invited his secretaries to kiss his cheeks as he gloated: "Girls, Hácha has signed! This is the greatest day of my life. I shall be known as the greatest German in history."[2]

Only hours later, German troops rushed into what the Nazis called the Czech Protectorate, or the Protectorate of Bohemia and Moravia. Again, not a shot was fired against them. The führer himself arrived in Prague the same evening and spent the night of March 15 in what had once been the royal residence of the Bohemian Kings, Hradčany Castle. The next morning, to the wild cheers of Prague Germans, Hitler proclaimed Bohemia and Moravia a possession of the Reich. The ethnic Germans of Prague wouldn't have greeted the führer so enthusiastically if he'd appeared later when the call-up of German men was unrelenting and the list of military casualties was long.

In Hitler's address to the Reichstag the following month, he revealed just how valuable his latest acquisition was. The yield was two huge armaments manufacturing complexes, military bases, aircraft, and enough war materiel to equip 40 divisions. The Czechs, after seizing the bulk of their industrial manufacturing capacity from Austrian and German ownership in 1919, had put the armament plants to use manufacturing huge quantities of arms. Although most of the Czech military hardware wasn't as advanced as the latest German equipment and weaponry, the German military was able to use it.

Hitler regarded this triumph as something less than a spectacular achievement six years later. Near the end of the war when his earlier glories had dissipated along with Germany itself, he recognized that the takeover of the Czech core was the first major step leading to Germany's defeat, for that was the first time the country put itself wrong in the eyes of the world. By taking this territory he'd broken his agreement with Chamberlain and stepped beyond his oft-stated goal of uniting all Germans only through the acquisition of territory containing substantial numbers of Germans.[3]

◆

World War II formally began on September 1, 1939, when Hitler for a second time broke his pledge to Chamberlain to take no more territory after the Sudetenland. German forces mounted a surprise attack on Poland. As in Czechoslovakia, Poland had treated ethnic Germans harshly in areas formerly belonging to Germany. But there too, Hitler was less interested in the welfare of Germans than in territorial gain. To justify an invasion domestically, he needed a pretext his propaganda machine could disseminate. The final act in the series of phony outrages against Germans was a staged attack on a German radio station carried out by several SS men disguised in Polish uniforms. The charade didn't fool any governments, but Hitler didn't care. The story was meant to stir patriotic fervor and was good enough for domestic consumption.

The invasion of Poland gave the German military a chance to test its new *Blitzkrieg* (lightning war) tactics. The mobile warfare proved so successful that the Germans overran Poland in a matter of days. As the operation unfolded, the world was shocked to learn the Soviet Union was in on the deal. In the summer of 1939, Hitler and Stalin had secretly negotiated the Molotov-Ribbentrop Pact. The agreement divided up Poland and gave half to each invader. The Polish Army, although large, was ill equipped and found itself completely overwhelmed. Britain and France promptly declared war on Germany, but failed to act for months despite a pledge to defend Poland.

In April 1940, six months later, the Germans seized Denmark and Norway to preclude a sea attack from the north once the shooting war began. Hitler's blitzkrieg machine thereafter rapidly took Luxembourg, Belgium, and the Netherlands. France found itself in Hitler's gun sights next because the large French Army posed an obvious threat to German forces. Between the wars France had spent a huge sum to build a strip of heavily fortified defensive positions 12 to 16 miles deep along the German border—the defensive line Czechoslovakia tried to emulate. However, faith in this "impregnable" Maginot Line proved unwarranted. When the Germans attacked on June 5, they simply detoured around the barrier and threw the French forces into disarray. German divisions raced through France and on June 14 entered Paris without resistance. Three days later, French military resistance ceased entirely.

Hitler insisted the signing of the armistice with France be done at the same location where the Allies had forced Germany to sign the armistice ending World War I. He even ordered the rail coach used then be brought from a museum. After reading the opening section of the document, Hitler in a calculated gesture of disdain exited the car and left the proceedings to a subordinate. The following day he triumphantly entered Paris to view a few sights he'd selected. One was Napoleon's tomb because he longed to be compared to this emperor. "That was the greatest and finest moment of my life," he told his entourage upon leaving.[4] Apparently this greatest day superseded all the previous greatest days in his life.

Hitler's final challenge in Western Europe was England. The island nation posed a threat that necessitated elimination. To soften up the target, in July 1940 he ordered the Luftwaffe to begin a campaign to destroy the Royal Air Force. A month later, as air battles raged, Hitler launched a sea blockade and ordered his Navy to sink ships ferrying American aid across the North Atlantic to Britain. In September Hitler initiated the Blitz, a massive bombing campaign directed at London. The British held out, and the attack ended in May of the following year.

At the beginning of 1941, Hitler sent German troops to Africa under the command of an able and formidable German hero, General Erwin Rommel. Hitler's Italian ally, Mussolini, had tried to secure North Africa but ran into trouble when Britain sent troops to keep Egypt from falling into fascist hands. Egypt was crucial to the British because the Suez Canal was a vital link for raw materials, oil, and supplies between Britain and its most important colonies. The German help was too little, too late, and by May 1943 the British, with the help of the Americans who had now entered the war, defeated the Axis forces in Africa.

To Hitler's dismay a second Mussolini adventure, directed against the Serbs in the Balkans, also ran into trouble. To protect his own flank, in March 1941 Hitler had to send another German force to drag the hapless Italians out of the second hole they'd dug for themselves. This proved a major military blunder. Although the Germans captured Yugoslavia and Greece in short order, the operation held up the launch of a much larger and more important undertaking. The delay in launching Operation Barbarossa, the invasion of the Soviet Union, would have devastating consequences for Hitler and Germany.

◆

Operation Barbarossa began June 22, 1941, when the Germans smashed through the Soviet border at three in the morning. Over three million men, 2,000 aircraft, 3,500 tanks, 7,200 artillery pieces, and 750,000 horses took part. The German force had three components: Army Groups North, Center, and South. Stalin's troops, because they were largely concentrated in static positions along the border and not deployed in smaller tactical units throughout the Soviet half of Poland, were unable to present an effective defense. Some historians believe Stalin concentrated his army so he could spring a surprise attack on Germany after Allied forces in the west had weakened the Germans.

Regardless of whether or not Hitler unleashed his offensive to forestall an eventual Russian attack and remove a major threat to Germany's domination of Europe, there is no question that he'd long intended to invade the giant neighbor to the east. Capturing the European portion of the Soviet Union would more than satisfy his call for German Lebensraum. At the same time, the conquest would destroy the threat the Communist political base posed. Hitler expected the Soviet Union to collapse in a matter of weeks as its military forces disintegrated. He felt confident this would happen if Army Group North captured the important industrial port of Leningrad, Army Group Center took the capital Moscow with its concentration of armaments factories, and Army Group South seized the Caucasus oil fields and Russia's Black Sea coast. The Soviet Union's industry and natural resources were vital in sustaining his war machine and empire.

The Luftwaffe caught most Soviet planes on the ground and largely bombed Russia's air power out of existence. With total German air superiority assured, all three army groups pushed ahead so rapidly that they easily outmaneuvered and encircled the opposition. The static deployment wasn't the only reason the Red Army performed so poorly; it also suffered from a leadership vacuum because Stalin had initiated a vicious purge in the thirties. In his paranoia Stalin murdered many of the military's top leaders. Others, he sent to Siberia. The combination of the poor positioning of Soviet forces and the deadly speed of the German blitzkrieg left the Red Army reeling and unable to react quickly enough. As a result, the Soviets suffered hundreds of thousands of casualties and lost enormous amounts of equipment.

The German operation proceeded so well at first that it had the Red Army on the verge of collapse as Hitler hoped. By the end of 1941, the Red Army had lost three million men—nearly the equivalent of their entire western army at the start of hostilities. The military evacuated its headquarters in Moscow, and Stalin suffered a nervous breakdown. But the German forces were not without problems. If anything, they suffered from too much success. Stalin's willingness to sacrifice 10 Soviets for every German killed spooked the average German field soldier. Luckily, these men didn't have to annihilate all the Russian soldiers. During the early stage of the offensive they took hundreds of thousands of Russian prisoners. However, even as POWs the Russians posed a massive problem because of the chokehold they placed on the already strained German supply capability. The shortages led to mistreatment and starvation of many of these prisoners.

Supply and communication lines all but collapsed because the German Army advanced so swiftly and the attack front broadened so rapidly both north and south. Supplies often couldn't catch up to the attackers. The army didn't have enough transport to support such a distant front, and the long supply routes left the trucks and trains easy targets for sabotage and attack by the many fierce partisan guerrilla units that sprang up behind the German lines in both Poland and the Soviet Union. In the northern Soviet Union, another difficulty was the lack of roads and other infrastructure. The Russians had deliberately left this area undeveloped as a defensive shield to protect their capital against an invasion.[5]

Hitler's Eastern Front, where most of the called-up men Maria knew were sent, brought sorrow to many Sudeten households. Heinrich Himmler, as commander of the SS, played no small part in this because of the fanaticism of his SS—the feared political and paramilitary organization that grew out of a small force of armed guards who protected the führer and other Nazi Party members in the early days. Himmler had resolved to build his all-volunteer political army into an organization to rival or surpass the regular military. Initially, officers and recruits were either Nazi stalwarts or individuals who believed strongly in some aspect of its philosophy, so these early joiners tended to be aggressive and fanatical in their actions. For the most part, the SS field units performed exceptionally well as soldiers on the battlefield, but at the price of heavy losses.

SS units fought alongside the Wehrmacht in the invasion of Poland as well as the Soviet Union. In the latter, various SS units, both combat and noncombat, perpetrated many well-known war crimes related to the execution of partisans, Jews, Gypsies, and Soviet POWs. These actions earned the SS a notoriety, fear, and hatred their enemies exploited through propaganda. This hatred greatly instigated brutality by Soviet soldiers and in turn led to many atrocities against German soldiers and civilians. The political units the German leadership called Einsatzgruppen (deployment groups) committed a disproportionate share of the SS crimes.

On the Russian front, the Einsatzgruppen consisted of noncombat battalions that were little more than mobile killing units. These groups operated behind the battlefront and were outside the control of the Waffen SS (SS field combat forces) and Wehrmacht generals. The Einsatzgruppen personnel, consisting of police units, SS men drawn from other units, and camp guards, killed whoever the Nazis leadership deemed a racial or political enemy. In addition to Jews and Gypsies, on the Eastern Front they also targeted intellectuals and officials of the Soviet Communist Party or the Soviet State. Einsatzgruppen killing ranged from small executions of a few individuals to large operations requiring a day or two to complete. By 1943 these killers had coldly murdered over a million men, women, and children and disrupted the lives of many more.

At the Nuremberg Trials both the Waffen SS and the political SS units were labeled criminal organizations. However, the court also recognized that beginning in 1943 many men, men like my father, were forced to join the Waffen SS and served only as ordinary combat soldiers. Such conscripts were excluded from the criminal group.

The Nazis' targeted killing is indeed damning, but when it came to mass slaughter, Allied hands were also dirty. The American and British bombing of German civilians, particularly the firebombing of entire cities, killed tens of thousands of noncombatants at a time by fire or asphyxiation. In firebombing raids, bombers drop both high explosives and incendiary devices. The explosives destroy roofs so incendiary phosphorus bombs can better penetrate buildings and ignite fires. Dresden, Hamburg, and Tokyo were the sites of the most successful and infamous firebombing of the war. These cities were selected by the bombing campaign planners because they offered ideal conditions for massive firestorms.

And in the Soviet Union, Stalin's massive political, class, and ethnic killing took a toll numbering in the millions. The Soviet military was complicit in mass murder and behaved no better than German forces. Throughout the war, Soviet Commanders meted out harsh punishment to civilians, POWs, and their own soldiers.

Erhard Raus of Wolframitz was a colonel in the 6th Panzer Division when Hitler attacked Russia. In recounting the offensive, Raus described a disturbing incident as the fighting began. When his unit suffered a temporary setback at an Army Group North bridgehead, Russian tanks intentionally rolled over seriously wounded German soldiers. After the Germans retook the bridgehead they "discovered that all of the wounded and captured soldiers left behind…were murdered and mutilated."[6]

He also reported that as the Soviets retreated through the Baltics toward Leningrad, they destroyed everything in their wake, leaving only "ashes and ruins." They executed thousands of "undesirables" and abducted thousands of other residents in the retreat. Raus saw incidents of German POWs killed and mutilated throughout the war and commented that the Russians "sought to impress the German troops and lower their morale by committing numerous atrocities upon them. The great number of such crimes, committed on all sectors of the fronts tends to support that presumption."[7]

Many of the Soviet war crimes were committed by the NKVD (People's Commissariat for Internal Affairs). While the organization is best known for its secret police activities, the massive bureau's divisions also included intelligence, military counterintelligence, traffic and railroad police, firefighters, state security, prisons, public order, vital records, state archives, and border security.

While Himmler's Waffen SS boasted 38 divisions at its peak strength, the NKVD fielded over 50 armed military divisions. These Soviet units functioned mainly as a barrier force during the war to keep the Red Army in line and fighting. NKVD units were assigned to every major Soviet combat group to brutally put down mutinies and keep soldiers from retreating. The soldiers feared the NKVD troops to their rear as much as the enemy. The NKVD killed thousands of their own soldiers and citizens along with undesirables and Axis prisoners of war. Destruction battalions, troops specially trained to inflict large-scale devastation, performed some of the heavier killing. Mass graves of their victims are still being uncovered today.

One notable NKVD atrocity first made the news in 1943 when Germany's propaganda ministry announced German forces had uncovered enormous mass graves in the Katyn Forest, located in the portion of Poland seized by the Soviet Union after the secret Molotov-Ribbentrop Pact in 1939.

The remains were those of Polish military officers, police, and intellectuals who had disappeared into the hands of the Russians. The Soviet Union used its propaganda machine to blame the Germans. These executions occurred at several secret locations, not just Katyn. The chief executioner, Vasili Blokhin, went on to become a major general in the NKVD. The murders the NKVD admitted to during just Stalin's reign stand at nearly a million. During Blokhin's 26-year career he personally killed at least 50,000 people, for an average of over five executions per day.

The killings at Katyn occurred in a specially designed soundproof execution building. After Blokhin's assistants led the handcuffed prisoner into a red-painted room to be identified, they had him face a log wall in the next room. There, Blokhin put a bullet into the base of the man's skull. The man's blood was hosed down the sloped concrete floor into a drain while the body was dragged out the back door and thrown on a truck. The whole process took less than three minutes per victim and allowed Blokhin to kill 6,000 men in 28 days.

Each night Blokhin put on shoulder-length gloves and a butcher's apron before he began to practice his trade with the briefcase full of German Walther pistols he'd brought to work. The Russian service pistol wasn't reliable enough, and the German pistols were also forensically convenient for blaming the murders on the Germans if the bodies were ever discovered.[8]

◆

In September Erhard Raus was promoted to *Generalmajor*. His battle group, as part of Army Group North, fought its way through the difficult Baltic forests and swamps, captured vital bridges and railheads, and finally pressed through the dangerous six-mile-deep defenses of Leningrad. To capture the city, Hitler had halted Army Group Center's push to take Moscow and sent its armor forces to support Army Groups North and

South in their objectives. But just when Leningrad and control of the Baltic Sea lay within grasp, Hitler ordered the city to be starved to death by siege and sent Raus's division and other panzer (tank) units south to resume the capture of a less strategic but more symbolic target—Moscow. Now Leningrad had enough breathing space to reorganize its defenses, but not until the winter of 1943, after 900 days of siege, would a Russian troop buildup finally drive the Germans back. This breakout plays an integral part in my father's story.

At the close of summer in 1941, when Hitler's invasion front stretched over 1,000 miles north to south, the Germans learned how vulnerable they were. The supply line wasn't their only problem. Hitler found the Red Army possessed vastly superior tank numbers. Later he admitted he'd never have invaded the Soviet Union had he known. When Hitler had initially intervened in his generals' war plans and sent Army Group Center's panzer units to support Groups North and South instead of proceeding with the capture of Moscow, the redirection and delay in reaching Moscow didn't seem important. Then the Germans encountered an enemy they had no chance against—the weather. Now, the earlier three-month delay in invading the Soviet Union that came from sending troops to save Mussolini from defeat in the Balkans cost dearly.

In the north the first snow fell in mid-September. When heavy rains set in across the entire front in October, the roads and fields turned to muck and the attack all but halted. Russians called this season *rasputitsa* (the time of no roads), and it saved the Red Army. This taste of winter made Hitler realize that Moscow now had to be captured quickly before the really deep winter—the icy phenomenon called General January—stopped all advancement.

Group Center finally got its panzers back in October, two months after they'd left, and resumed the push toward Moscow. But because the unusually cold and fierce winter weather set in early, tanks and trucks became locked into frozen mud and the troops were caught without proper winter clothing. Temperatures dropped so low that machinery wouldn't operate. The German psyche and its penchant for dark humor soon had soldiers calling the 1941 Winterschlacht im Osten (Winter Battle in the East) medal and the Ostmedaille (East medal) the Frozen Meat Order and Frost medals.

On December 6, Raus and his 6th Panzer Division sat just nine miles from Moscow and 15 miles from the Kremlin itself. However, the unit was down to only a handful of tanks and a few men. A Russian counterattack and a sudden drop in temperature to −30 degrees F ended the Group Center offensive and the Germans began their first retreat. Raus rounded up what soldiers he could find and captured sufficient territory on either side of the withdrawal route to hold off the Russians through January, during which nighttime temperatures averaged −30 to −40 degrees F. In the process Raus lost all of his tanks and heavy weapons, 80 percent of his infantrymen, and most motorized vehicles. When his frostbite cases approached 800 per day, he ordered his engineers to blast holes in the frozen earth for shelter so the men could partially cover the holes with lumber and build fires to warm themselves up.

The weather also slowed Group South's offensive. In the summer of 1942 that force received orders to race for Stalingrad, a key industrial transportation hub. Hitler wanted the city as the staging point for the capture of the Caucasus oil fields Germany desperately needed. The winter allowed the Red Army to replenish its manpower and armaments so now they were better able to engage the Germans. They understood that Germany's tactical advantage—mobility—was useless inside the city, so they rushed to fortify Stalingrad.

The heavy combat in Stalingrad began on September 1, 1942. Twice during the next six weeks Hitler called for a final offensive as ever more Soviet troops converged on the city. In November the Russians broke through the outer ring of Axis defenses held by Italian, Hungarian, and Romanian troops. The 350-mile gap this opened allowed the Red Army to encircle and trap the entire German 6th Army inside Stalingrad.

General Raus and his 6th Panzer Division, who had been sent to France to rebuild after the Moscow withdrawal, was ordered to Stalingrad to help relieve the trapped 6th Army. That just the transport of this one panzer division required an incredible 87 trains of about 50 cars each illustrates how costly and complicated redeployment was.[9]

Raus's division spearheaded the drive to help the trapped 6th Army break out of Stalingrad. After a series of heavy engagements the general established a bridgehead just 20 miles from the city. He saw little Soviet opposition left before him, but the order for the final thrust never came. Raus believed if he'd gotten the go-ahead, the trapped army, despite its short supplies, could have fought its way out and linked up with his panzers. But when Hitler ordered the trapped German Army to hold the city, Raus's division was redirected to another hotspot: Karsk. Stalingrad was the bloodiest battle in history and produced about two million total casualties. Of the nearly 100,000 prisoners taken when Germany surrendered after months of fierce engagement, only five to six thousand survived their captivity.

---

[1] Hitler, Domarus, and Romane, *The Essential Hitler Speeches and Commentary*, 1232.
[2] Joachim C. Fest, *Hitler* (Houghton Mifflin Harcourt, 2013), 571.
[3] Martin A. Allen, *Himmler's Secret War: The Covert Peace Negotiations of Heinrich Himmler* (Da Capo Press, 2005), 47.

[4] Martin Gilbert, *The Second World War: A Complete History* (New York: H. Holt, 1989), 102.
[5] Showalter, *Hitler's Panzers*, 175.
[6] Raus and Newton, *Panzer Operations*, 22.
[7] Raus and Newton, *Panzer Operations*, 38.
[8] Wikipedia contributors, "Vasily Blokhin," *Wikipedia*, Wikipedia.org, 15 Apr. 2015, accessed 21 Apr. 2015.
[9] Raus and Newton, *Panzer Operations*, 137.

25 Uniforms and Guns

OSWALD LUSTIG, OSKAR HALUSA, AND EDUARD HAJEK, the three close Schömitz and Gubschitz friends attending the teacher training institute in Znaim, were split up in 1942 when Oswald and Oskar turned 18 and received their Wehrmacht conscription notices. Oswald was the first to leave. Following three months of training late in the year, the army assigned him to the 44th (44. by German convention) Infantry Division (Infanteriedivision), also known as the Hoch und Deutschmeister Division. While in transit to the Soviet Front, his assignment changed because the 44th was destroyed at Stalingrad and no longer existed.

The 44th had successfully fought its way into the Caucasus, but then received orders to turn around and attach itself to the 6th Army for taking Stalingrad. During the fierce urban fighting for the city, the 44th, along with the entire 6th Army, became trapped in the Stalingrad pocket. In February 1943 after the 105,000 surviving men of the 6th Army surrendered, the 44th Division officially ceased to exist.

Oswald's new orders directed him to the 45th Infantry Division, a part of the German 2nd Army. A year and a half earlier this division had nearly reached Moscow, but when Oswald joined it in early 1943, the greatly outnumbered German forces were in retreat across the whole front. As Oswald described what he saw, he couldn't help but use the word *unglaublich* (unbelievable). A nearly continuous line of destroyed tanks and vehicles—German, Russian, and even American (supplied to the Soviets)—littered the sides of the roads. After the Red Army demolished the German force in Stalingrad, the offensive had shifted north and smashed into the Germans here. The 45th Division became encircled, but fought its way out and then limped a considerable distance westward. By this time Oswald was just as exhausted and sleep deprived as the men he joined.

In July the crippled division became a reserve component of the 9th Army and participated in Operation Zitadelle near Kursk. The German command hoped to halt the Red advance by trapping the large Soviet force occupying a pocket intruding well into the German lines. Success would shorten the German front line and free up some German troops badly needed on the Western Front. Because the Germans had to repeatedly delay the engagement, the Soviets had four months to abduct German soldiers and extract the plans from them. The Kursk engagement became the largest armor battle ever fought. The vastly outnumbered Germans inflicted five times as many casualties on the Red Army as they themselves suffered, yet the loss of irreplaceable equipment and men was another disaster for them. As a result, in late 1943 the division teetered on the brink of collapse.

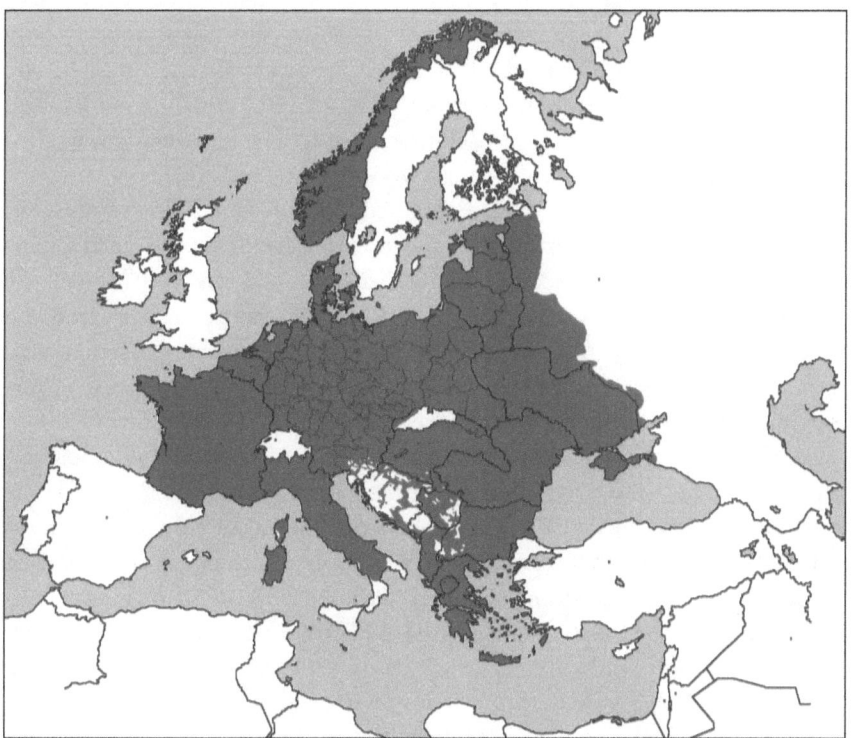

Area of Europe still under German control in September, 1943 after the Eastern Front had begun to collapse

The 45th suffered extreme casualties in this battle. Yet the German front was stretched so thin that the division couldn't be relieved. In the summer of 1944 the German command gave the depleted skeleton force of a unit a few replacements and changed its name to 45. Grenadierdivision. A short time later it changed again to 45. Volksgrenadierdivision. Chaos reigned as the Russians relentlessly pushed the division rearward. During Oswald's endless struggle to stay alive, one harrowing night he fell asleep on the side of a large straw pile. When he awoke he heard soldiers nearby in the darkness, but they weren't speaking German. He somehow sneaked past the Russian troops and for the next two days, alone and frightened, struggled to catch up to his own retreating lines. At one point he had to discard his gear to cross a stream, but eventually reached the retreating Germans and found his company.

The front continued to crumble, and by autumn 1944 the German line had collapsed all the way back to Poland. There, in the southeast sector of the front the men of the broken 45th engaged in heavy defensive combat along the Vistula River and again suffered heavy casualties.

Oswald was wounded three times on the front. The first time, an injury to his jaw resulted in the loss of several teeth. The second time, shrapnel peppered one entire side of his body. The third injury nearly proved fatal as shrapnel pierced his chest and arm. Oswald told me he thought himself a dead man when he regained consciousness and found himself lying in the snow, bleeding profusely. The temperature was so low that the blood flowing from his wound froze and formed a thick icy crust on his chest. The heavy fighting around him kept help from reaching him as he lay there drifting in and out of consciousness. In his conscious moments he expected he'd bleed out and die, but eventually someone loaded him onto a small sled. In the frantic rush to pull the wounded out of the fighting zone and to an aid station, Oswald's sled upended on a large snow bank. He tumbled down and came to rest buried in soft snow. Again, he believed himself finished. However, two Ukrainian women braved the fighting and dug him out. After reloading him aboard the sled, they dragged him to the field dressing station. He was forever grateful that these women from the other side saved him at considerable risk to themselves. Others were not so lucky and many men from both sides died there. Several days later Oswald regained consciousness and found himself aboard a westbound evacuation train already well into Poland.

Oswald told me that on the front in Russia all the men around him confessed their sins to a priest before a major action. He was the only one who didn't, yet he alone survived.

◆

In October 1942, not long after Oswald left for military training, Oskar Halusa received his own induction notice. Oskar kept a journal during the war and in his eighties assembled an account of his wartime service from his journal entries. His story is a compelling one and conveys the dreadful position Hitler's megalomania placed Germany's soldiers in from 1942 until the war's end in 1945.

Oskar's orders sent him to the Western Front after training. The conditions and climate of southern France were much to his liking; however, the easy duty didn't last long. Upon his return to France after a home leave to Schömitz, he learned his unit had departed on a troop train and was heading to the Eastern Front. As he set off in pursuit, one of his most vivid recollections was of children in Poland running alongside the train, begging for food. Like packs of hungry wolves, they pounced on the bread and other rations the soldiers threw out. He caught his company just before its dispatch to the vicinity of Kharkov in the Soviet Union where it was to confront the Red Army on the far side of the Donets River. In subsequent operations there, artillery exchanges frequently sent Oskar and his fellow soldiers scrambling to dig foxholes. Oskar was thankful that the digging was easy in the rich black soil "with barely a stone in it."

The incoming artillery was particularly unsettling when it consisted of Katyusha rockets, a weapon that saturated the impact area. It was fired from racks of parallel launchers mounted on vehicles, even tractors and trains. The ferocity of this weapon belied its innocent name, which is the Russian equivalent of Kate or Katy. The name Katyusha came from a song popular in Red Army at the time and is about a girl pining for her Russian soldier. German troops called the weapon *Stalinorgel* (Stalin organ) because of the sound the rockets made and the vague resemblance of the clustered launchers to church organ pipes.

One night Oskar also experienced a memorable exchange of a different type, notable because it didn't involve bullets or explosive ordinance, at least at first. A German loudspeaker directed east at the Russians blared out a beautiful German song, "In der Blauen Mondnacht" ("In the Blue Moonlit Night"), and then several other melodic songs. Following the music, a Russian-speaking German invited the Soviet soldiers to defect to the German side. The spell collapsed when Russians answered through the muzzle of a machine gun.

In the following weeks as the front moved westward, the two sides engaged often with artillery, snipers, grenades, mortars, and small arms. In their relentless retreat, the outnumbered and outgunned Germans also endured occasional strafing from Russian fighter planes. Oskar left many friends behind in the ground during this time. September and October served up some of the young soldier's blackest days. He endured days without sleep, the deaths of his closest friends, and nightly pullbacks with Russian soldiers in hot pursuit. Men dragged one another through mud or linked arms to keep each other from falling asleep as they slogged rearward.

The wide Dnepr River with limited bridges became a chokepoint for the Germans as over a dozen divisions and their supplies jammed up at Kremenchug, a Ukrainian town with only a wooden bridge and a single-track rail bridge. A crossing guard of a thousand men of various specialties, under the control of General Raus as the local corps commander, untangled the chaos to fully utilize the bridge capacity. His men had to prevent the approaching columns of soldiers from crossing paths and at the same time allow ambulances and emergency vehicles periodic access in the reverse direction. To buy time, rearguard troops staved off large concentrations of Russians for 10 days until the tens of thousands of soldiers in the bottleneck crossed the river. Six panzer divisions, five infantry divisions, and their 70,000 vehicles ultimately passed over the highway bridge. The railway bridge, in addition to trains, allowed another three infantry divisions and their transport to cross when planks were laid down.[1]

Raus's engineers also constructed a crude floating bridge alongside the railroad bridge for 30,000 civilian vehicles to cross. Many horses and cattle were herded west to deny them to the Red Army. Most were diverted further downstream to swim across at a point where army engineers built a crude bridge of motorboats, logs, wagons, and miscellaneous other material. Ultimately, 64,000 horses and 80,000 cattle swam the river.[2]

However, the Red Army was also on the move. Many units crossed the river in places the Germans hadn't yet reached to defend and established bridgeheads. German artillery fired at the Russian forces but had a limited supply of ammunition. Raus reported that the Russians drove large groups of civilians ahead of their soldiers so the German infantry would expend its limited ammunition on them.[3]

Because so few men were left in Oskar's company by the time they crossed the Dnepr River, the survivors were reassigned to fill out other companies. Before long, the Russians attacked Oskar's new unit and hit it relentlessly for days with both artillery and infantry. One day when Oskar scrambled to switch positions as tank shells whizzed by, something tugged at his leg and he felt warm blood filling his boot. Instinctively, he lunged for the cover of a straw stack to shield himself from the heavy enemy rifle and machine gun fire while he examined his injury.

Although Oskar was relieved to find his femur hadn't been hit, he knew he needed to get out of there quickly before the German side pulled back and he lost the strength to move. To stay meant death. The Red Army's medical stations refused to treat Germans, and Russian soldiers shot or clubbed wounded Germans to death before they ever reached such stations anyway. The fierce tank battle raging around him kept any German aid from arriving, and his wound wouldn't allow him to get far on foot.

Oskar realized his only real hope lay in clambering atop a panzer. Desperation and an adrenaline surge enabled him to hobble his way to a firing German tank, where he caught the eye of the tank commander. From deep within, he summoned enough strength to hoist himself up onto the tank's deck. With a higher view of the battlefield, he saw how terribly vulnerable he was. If the tank's armor took a hit, the impact would fling him off. As the tank fired its cannon and darted about, Oskar bounced around and hung on for dear life. Out to the front he saw smoking Russian tanks. At one point, the tank commander shouted "Volltreffen!" (hit) when he took out an enemy tank. In short order, he disabled two more Russian tanks.

The two most telling adjectives Oskar used in relaying this experience were "indescribable" and "lucky." Many other wounded and bleeding men lay scattered about the battlefield and cried out for help, but the fighting was too intense for anyone to reach them. Eventually Oskar's panzer ducked behind an embankment where the commander shouted for Oskar to dismount because he had to refuel and rearm. There, where he was out of the line of fire and back on the ground, infantry soldiers put him aboard another vehicle and took him to a farmhouse already sheltering several other wounded men. Not long after his arrival, a Ukrainian woman brought the men a pitcher of milk. To staunch the flow of blood, Oskar reached into a pants pocket for his handkerchief. His wallet was in the same pocket, and both items were soaked with blood. He discovered shrapnel had passed through both the leather and the wad of folded money inside. Oskar believed his femur would have shattered if the wallet hadn't absorbed much of the force, and then he'd have been too seriously hurt to save himself. At length, a horse cart transported him and the other wounded men to a dressing station in a small village called P'yatykhatky.

◆

This P'yatykhatky is not to be confused with another Ukrainian P'yatykhatky, near Kharkov, which is the site of a large mass grave associated with the Katyn Forest Massacre in 1940. After Russian NKVD killers executed Polish military, police, and intelligentsia captives at Kharkov, they needed to hide the bodies. Sparsely populated P'yatykhatky became the disposal site. When the population of the P'yatykhatky area grew after the war, local children, who "would find on the surface and in shallow graves bones, skulls, pieces of uniform…and bring them home and to school," discovered the gravesite. Local residents already knew the spot was the grave of many Poles as well as Ukrainian intellectuals Stalin's killers had shot before the war. During the Cold War the Soviet KGB (Committee for State Security) had the audacity to build an employee recreation facility at the site. Today, the place bears a monument to the thousands of Ukrainians buried there by the NKVD.[4]

At the P'yatykhatky Oskar arrived at, he saw two makeshift casualty evacuation trains waiting on the tracks. Although they consisted only of cattle cars, he was surprised to find rail transport so close to the chaotic fighting. He considered himself especially lucky when the medical orderlies loaded him onto the front train, since the second had no locomotive. Only after he was aboard did he finally think he might actually live to see another day. However, when the train still hadn't moved by nightfall and artillery shells began impacting around it, he and the others grew fearful. As they waited, the orderlies squeezed ever more wounded men aboard—some gravely injured. Only when the shelling grew more intense and houses in the vicinity caught fire did the train start to roll. The doors of the cars were wide open, and in the light of the burning houses Oskar spotted Russian tanks closing in and firing on the train. The train hadn't gone more than 300 meters when it crashed to a halt. The abrupt stop drew fierce cries of pain and fear from the wounded.

Oskar said his heart nearly stopped when he looked out through the door and in the firelight spotted a formation of mechanized Russian infantry troops closing rapidly. Following a loud nearby explosion, a soldier shouted, "Everyone on the floor!" Someone else screamed, "Out of the car!"

Oskar's proximity to the door allowed him to roll out. He hit the ground painfully and tumbled down a steep embankment. Others were right behind him. From the fierce cries and panic above, he knew many of the men unable to move or exit in time had been shot by Russian soldiers. When the train rocked with another terrific explosion, Oskar and the others below the embankment knew they were dead men if they hung around. No one had any idea in which direction safety lay. Some men fled alone into the night, but Oskar and a small group stuck together and headed toward a light they saw in the far distance. He described this light as a beacon drawing him on, something like the Star of Bethlehem. His wounded leg made walking a tricky balancing act. Because his leg muscles couldn't raise his left leg, he improvised by looping a rope around the sole of his boot so he could lift it with his arm, marionette style. In his right hand he gripped a sunflower stalk as a cane.

Eventually the group reached a branching railroad track. Since it appeared to head west, they hobbled along on it. Sometime later they heard a locomotive approaching. They had no idea if it was German or Russian. Someone shouted, "Take cover!", so everyone scrambled to the side of the tracks and dropped. When no one fired at them as the lone engine swept by, everyone breathed a sigh of relief. But the extra exertion exacted a toll. Several of the men were so weak they couldn't rise, and those already upright didn't have the strength to pull them up. Only the pleas of those on their feet gave these men the wherewithal to rise and trudge on.

At length the group spotted a different light, a dim one, ahead and recognized it as a railroad signal station, so they stumbled on. When they banged on the door, a Russian woman inside asked if they were Russians. Whether she was more wary of Germans or Russians, Oskar didn't speculate. However, like the other woman, she gave the men milk when she saw their sorry state. After they'd rested, some of the wounded again didn't think they could go on. But the others convinced them the Russians would shoot them if they stayed, so everyone resumed the trek toward the Star-of-Bethlehem light, still visible in the distance. Movement was painful and difficult. They wondered how long one night could last, but the eastern sky eventually began to lighten. Soon, they heard horses and vehicles ahead. Whether the source of the sounds was Russians or German, they couldn't tell at first. All they knew was they had to keep going and trust to luck. The commotion turned out to be retreating Germans, which gave them the stamina to plod on. Oskar had no idea where they ended up because he passed out the moment he reached safety and didn't regain consciousness until his stretcher was unloaded from a vehicle at a dressing station.

After Oskar and the others were bandaged and fed, they were taken to another train. Unlike the makeshift one at P'yatykhatky, this one was a dedicated evacuation train made up of real passenger cars painted with large red crosses and already crowded with wounded soldiers. On the journey to safe German soil, guerillas attacked the train in a forest as it passed through territory that had been part of Poland before the war. The attendants on the train had already warned the wounded soldiers the red crosses had no meaning for the enemy here, so the train carried a manned weapons car. Those men able to drop to the floor did so as the engineer opened the throttle and the train's gunners returned fire with automatic weapons.

To Oskar, the trip seemed endless. In what is now Lvov in Ukraine, medics deloused and bathed the wounded while other attendants baked their uniforms in a hot room to kill the lice they harbored, for no German soldier was to return home with lice. Oskar reported each wounded soldier also received what was supposed to be a one-time *Führerpaket* and an entry in his pay book (*Soldbuch*) noting he'd received the gift parcel of food items. The packages contained items such as flour, honey, jam, butter, cereal, and sardines. Oskar called it a Führerpaket, but today some confusion exists between it and a similar package called the

Führergeschenk. The Nazis had originated the führer gift programs as a means of recognizing the sacrifices of soldiers and citizens in the war effort, but in time it took on another purpose. When the men presented the führer gifts to their families, it was supposed to show how well things were going at the front.[5]

Oskar ended up at a field hospital in Bad Altheide (Polanica-Zdrój) in western Poland. The place had formerly been a hotel called Zwei Tannen. While undergoing treatment there, he welcomed a surprise visit from his father, who then went on to visit Oskar's wounded older brother, Alfred, in another hospital in Poland. A few weeks later, in December 1943, Oskar received a two-week convalescent leave that enabled him to spend Christmas in Schömitz with his family.

While he was at home, an official mail packet arrived from his unit headquarters. He was reluctant to open it, fearing it bore orders to return to the front immediately. To his relief it held an Iron Cross Second Class and a *Verwundetenabzeichen* (Wound Badge). However, what he valued most was the additional two-week extra-leave notification that came with the medals.

While visiting relatives in Vienna, he was on his way to the movies one evening when a military patrol stopped him and grilled him about his papers. He'd drawn their attention because of the civilian neck shawl he wore over his uniform. Although Oskar explained that he'd been unable to get a proper cold weather uniform during his convalescence, the men showed no sympathy. Oskar feared the "disgrace to the service" citation they issued would earn him an immediate recall to Russia once it reached his unit's headquarters.

---

[1] Raus and Newton, *Panzer Operations*, 249.
[2] Raus and Newton, *Panzer Operations*, 254.
[3] Raus and Newton, *Panzer Operations*, 255.
[4] Wikipedia contributors. "Piatykhatky, Kharkiv Oblast." *Wikipedia*, Wikipedia.org, 26 Jan. 2015, accessed 21 Apr. 2015.
[5] Jim Pool, "The Führer and Other Gifts," *Der Erste Zug: A Heer Living History Organization*, Dererstezug.com, accessed 20 Apr. 2015.

26 Shortages on the Home Front

THE FAMILIES OF FIGHTING MEN understood conditions were bad on the fronts, but few knew how gruesome the reality was because the Nazi propaganda machine in Berlin worked hard to keep it from them. Many families were distracted, or consumed, by their own problems. In Germany, day and night air raids on cities posed an ever-growing danger. For some, life was almost as grim as for the soldiers in the field. Rationing and shortages were a daily fact of life, particularly for people living in cities. Although rural communities also suffered wartime shortages of goods and fuel, fewer residents there went hungry because they could grow extra food in gardens or buy it from farmers.

Food wasn't a real concern for Maria and her neighbors in southern Moravia until after the war. In industrialized Germany rationing was strictly imposed and "Guns before Butter" was more than just a motto. Logically Herman Göring, the man the familiar expression is usually attributed to, should have been the originator because he played such a pivotal part in directing economic policy and forging a relationship between the Nazis and German capitalists before the war, yet another ranking Nazi, Rudolf Hess, actually coined it. Oddly enough, butter was one of the few foods available throughout the war while margarine, a butter substitute, became scarce.

Food in Germany was allotted to all civilians through buff-colored ration books containing stamps. Pregnant women received green ration books with extra stamps. The ration stamps inside the books were color coded to designate the type of food they could be used to purchase. Blue stamps were for meat, white for sugar, green for eggs, etc. They came in 10-, 25-, 50-, 100-, or 500-gram denominations, as appropriate for each category. Stamps were valid only within the district of issue, and soldiers home on furlough also needed stamps. Waiters removed the appropriate stamps from the ration books of customers who could afford to eat at a restaurant. The Allies tried to flood the market and disrupt the rationing system by dropping forged ration stamps from bombers, but the effort proved ineffective because the authorities imposed such a severe penalty for using forged stamps.

Coal, the main heating and cooking fuel, was also rationed. So was clothing, late in the war. Possessing a ration stamp for something and being able to buy were two different things. Users often spent hours in line waiting at several small specialized shops, since Germany had no supermarkets at that time. The availability of products varied regionally. Ration stamp food allotments decreased as the war went on and the daily calorie intake dropped. Potatoes remained Germany's main staple throughout the war, and that ration was normally adequate and dependable. Although the egg ration was small, eggs were also usually available, as was milk. But generous allotments of the latter went only to children. Fruit was often in short supply, and people craved jam. Plum jam inquiries became so common upon entering a grocery that they spawned a dark-humor catch phrase, "Der deutsche Gruß ist Pflaumenmus" (the German greeting is plum jam).[1] The fruit and vegetable shortage caused the government to distribute vitamins in pill form.

One product rationed almost immediately after the war began was coffee. When *Kaffeeersatz*, an imitation product made from roasted barley, chicory, and oats, failed to fill the desire for the real thing, coffee became a hot black market item. In 1941 it sold for about 40 reichsmark per kilo (2.2 pounds). By the final months of the war, its value was in the stratosphere. A kilo of coffee cost the equivalent of 20 liters (five gallons) of gasoline—itself an extremely hard-to-get black market item selling at 40 reichsmark per liter. As the war progressed, barter using various scarce black market products grew more common. Cigarettes, a currency throughout the war, assumed an even greater role after the war when the Americans arrived.[2]

Germany rationed bread too. The country needed to import a considerable amount of grain to feed its population adequately, but the war broke its supply chain. German seaports were blockaded and the war disrupted farming in the grain belt to the east. High quality grains became scarce, necessitating substitution with poorer grains. The inferior wartime bread was notorious for causing flatulence, and indoor air quality deteriorated. Selling bread after it was a day old also became a standard wartime practice because such bread was harder to chew and went further.[3]

Beer was also sometimes in short supply—less the result of a limited grain supply than a hops shortage. Much land formerly growing hops and barley was planted with wheat and rye to feed the country. Hence, as with bread, quality suffered. Breweries had little choice but to substitute lesser ingredients for the ones in short supply. Using weaker wort resulted in a beer with an alcohol content of less than two percent. It was known as *Dünnbier* or *Erntebier*, and Germans disdained the stuff. For Germans, degenerated beer was no small cross to bear. Production of quality beer in quantity didn't resume until three years after the war ended.[4]

The meat ration was small until 1944, when paradoxically near the war's end, it became readily available again. The explanation was simple. As German refugees fled the ever-nearing battle front to the east, they drove their cattle into Germany where the animals could be sold and slaughtered. For some reason sugar also reappeared during the final year of the war.[5]

◆

One shortage impossible to address through ration stamps was the availability of young men. Their absence had a profound effect in the Reich, particularly on women. The first to feel the shortage were the younger ones—women like Maria. They were of marriageable age but had no marriage prospects during the six years of war. Instead of starting families, these women were stuck doing men's work for years on end. Married women in their childbearing years were affected in the same way because they too were either unable to start a family or have more children.

Maria's employer, Alois Stöffel, received his induction notice in the latter part of 1940, about a year after the war began. During his three month-training period, he came home on leave twice. Maria's job situation improved temporarily when he took charge and performed the work he loved. Then, all too soon, he deployed to the Eastern Front and his father took over again. Aurelia was pregnant when Alois left, but the baby was not due for many months. The infant arrived stillborn, and the father never had the chance to come home and console his wife.

In September 1943 tragedy struck the family again. Word arrived that Alois lay hospitalized in Warsaw. He'd been wounded and serious complications had set in. Years later, Maria was no longer certain but thought his condition stemmed from a knee or leg wound suffered in Russia.

Maria assumed charge of the children and the farm as Aurelia and her father-in-law boarded a train to Poland to visit Alois in the hospital. While there, the thing they most dreaded occurred. On September 29, Alois died. His wife and father had to bury him in foreign soil instead of the ground he loved. At the time, Maria lamented that had there been any justice in the world his fate would have befallen Geidl, the first farmer she'd worked for, rather than this good man. However, Geidl was never called up because of his age. He remained in Wolframitz, free to make the lives of those around him miserable.

◆

Facts were another commodity in short supply throughout the Reich during this era, particularly in rural areas. What passed as news arrived via the government. Hitler was so impressed by the use of propaganda against Germany during the First World War that he made propaganda a top priority when he assumed power in 1933. The Foreign Radio Section (*Rundfunk Ausland*) became an important weapon in the Nazi proselytizing arsenal, as was apparent from the powerful 100-kilowatt transmitter complex built just outside of Berlin. Eventually the complex broadcasted in twelve languages. At its peak, 118 hours of programming in twelve languages spewed out over the shortwave frequencies each day. The United States, South America, South Africa, East Asia, South Asia, and eventually Central America were the prime targets.

The bulk of the broadcast material originated from a department having the candid but seemingly self-contradictory title of Ministry for Public Enlightenment and Propaganda. This ministry, headed by long-time Hitler loyalist Joseph Goebbels, operated divisions for the press, fine arts, theater, music, film, literature, and radio. Journalists and writers throughout the Reich were required to register with the appropriate department. Goebbels's propaganda efforts proved particularly effective in the German annexation of Austria and in precipitating the Munich Crisis. The later propaganda campaigns aimed at explaining away and minimizing the unending stream of military setbacks to a skeptical German public enjoyed less success.

Although the Nazis were not shy about transmitting broadcasts to foreign countries, like repressive regimes everywhere, they didn't care for the flip side of the coin—exposing their own population to outside broadcasts. Throughout the war, listening to foreign broadcasts was strictly forbidden. Violators even earned a name—*Feindhörer* (enemy-hearer). This criminal behavior was but one of many prohibitions under the broader category of *Volksschädlinge* (people pests). Violations included everything from property crimes such as looting during blackouts to "subverting the will of the German people." Offenders were subject to capital punishment. In one case late in the war, several Vienna postal employees were executed for stealing chocolate and soap from poorly wrapped packages intended for soldiers.

To further its own propaganda aims and at the same time thwart the Feindhörer, the government mass-produced a cheap radio known as the *Volksempfänger* (people's receiver). The original model cost the average worker about two weeks' wages. Later, a second model at half the price was introduced, and German black humor dubbed it the *Goebbels-Schnauze* (Goebbels's snout).[6] By design, neither picked up remote signals well; both were largely limited to tuning in the German government's approved stations. To further thwart listeners from receiving unauthorized English broadcasts, even with radios that worked the way they were supposed to, the Nazis jammed the BBC's European Service, the main foreign source of German news and information.

Hitler conferred with Goebbels almost daily to work out the best angle on the day's major developments. Goebbels then dispensed the sanctioned party line to his ministry underlings. All news stories submitted by journalists required official approval before being disseminated. Under this system, truth didn't have much of a chance.

The people's radio, Volksempfänger model VE301

In the Czech Protectorate the Germans confiscated short wave radios, but many Czechs had managed to secret theirs away. By 9 p.m., the news broadcast hour for the BBC and Radio Moscow, city bars, restaurants, and cafes would empty. The customers were at home with windows shut and shades drawn, tuning in their shortwave sets.[7]

Maria thought the Nazi propaganda effort was wasted because people quickly learned to read between the lines. Many just stopped wanting to know what was happening in the war once things began going badly. In her area few could follow the war on a day-to-day basis because they had no daily newspapers and not many people owned radios, even after the People's Receiver became available. The Stöffel household, being a little more prosperous than the average, bought one. Maria listened to news broadcasts occasionally, but not every day. During the growing season she didn't have time. Because the fields were near the Czech village of Bochtitz, getting there and back took considerable time, and after she returned, supper, chores, and cleaning up remained. The household didn't often gather around the radio for entertainment either as there wasn't much of interest to listen to.

Until the defeats in North Africa and the Battle of Stalingrad, when over a hundred and fifty thousand German families learned their soldier was either dead or wouldn't be returning home for a long time, the propaganda machine emphasized German military superiority. After the defeats the theme switched to patriotism. The propaganda also frequently mentioned the "Bolshevik horde" and Germany's role as the defender of Western European culture.

Like the Allies, Germany produced movie newsreels to preserve civilian morale and dispense propaganda. Maria couldn't recall any at the small movie theater she and her friends biked to occasionally on Sunday afternoons, but they surely must have played there. The Nazis were no slouches in funding quality propaganda. In the films, the producers made even the retreats and defeats look and sound like victory. Many examples survive today in various formats and can be viewed on the Internet.

◆

Maria noted that at the beginning of the war, more than a few men in Wolframitz expressed misgivings about Hitler's adventurism. They remembered the previous war all too well and knew how quickly things could go wrong. However, most residents were simple farmers who stoically accepted what they had little power to change. At first most families of soldiers were proud of what the German military accomplished. Later, when everyone realized the Nazis had overreached and momentum had reversed, many more began saying Hitler should never have invaded Russia. But of course they didn't say it openly.

Late in the war, all fit males from teenagers to men approaching their fifties were in uniform for the duration of the war. The standards for *fit*, loose to begin with, grew looser each year until they included nearly everyone able to walk. Maria explained that occasionally a soldier made it home on leave but wasn't there long. Over and over, after the men left they would write home for a time then never be heard from again. Every soldier's family dreaded the day a letter they'd sent would come back stamped with **VERMISST IM OSTEN** (missing in the East), **VERMISST AN DER RUSSICHEN KAMPFRONT** (missing on the Russian battle front), **GEFALLEN IM OSTEN** (fallen in the East), or **GEFALLEN FÜR FÜHRER UND VATERLAND** (died for the leader and the fatherland).

Maria's fiancé, like most local men inducted at the war's start, served in Battle Group North during the drive to take Leningrad. Some of the men died in the fighting; others froze to death or died of exposure beyond Estonia's Narva River during the bitterly cold winter of 1941–1942. They and most other soldiers on the Eastern Front experienced the same bitterly cold conditions General Raus described outside Moscow. Although a drive in Germany to collect warm clothing for soldiers was successful, the clothing didn't reach them because of the conditions and extended supply lines. Maria's young man was one of the men who didn't return. I don't know if she ever learned how he died. She never revealed his name; all she would say is that some things should stay private. This will just have to be one of them.

Information about the conditions the soldiers endured was hard to come by. During both world wars, all the major powers censored mail to prevent information such as the identity and location of a man's unit from falling into the hands of the enemy. Letters from soldiers were also censored to keep problems from recipients, even in America's military.[8] Governments didn't want the populace to know when their men were ill equipped, lacked supplies, or had suffered defeats. However, censorship wasn't foolproof.

Early in the war Maria and others in Wolframitz learned where their men were because one local soldier and his fiancé had devised a way to slip clues past the military censors. They'd plotted beforehand to write in tiny print beneath the stamp. After this soldier described how the men were starving and didn't have winter clothing and gear to deal with the intense cold, his fiancé knitted him gloves and other apparel. Then his letters stopped coming. She knew what it meant. Maria was well acquainted with the couple for they were both neighbors of her aunt in Klein Seelowitz. Few of the local men who'd gone to that inhospitable place beyond the Narva River returned. Aurelia Stöffel's brother, who married a good friend of Maria's and had four young children, was one of the men who died there. My father also experienced a winter in the Narva region, but his turn came later at the German exit instead of the entry. He too nearly ended up buried there, but many of his classmates and friends were not so lucky.

The war was going badly for Germany when Maria's brother, Eduard, finished his course of studies at Znaim and earned his teaching diploma. Eduard never had the opportunity to use that degree because in the spring of 1943 he too received his call to serve. Had Eduard been able to talk to, or receive an uncensored letter from his friends Oswald and Oskar, he'd have despaired, for they'd already experienced the utter hopelessness of Germany's situation. Oskar recalled the last letter he got from Eduard was in October 1942, shortly after his own induction.

Eduard's orders sent him to an armor training facility at St. Pölten, within the Vienna Wehrkreis. He reported to the 33rd Panzer Regiment of Panzer-Ersatz-Abteilung 33 where he completed both his basic and armor training. Maria recalled he returned home twice during this period by train on short leaves. Both times he walked from the station at Bochtitz to Wolframitz and stopped to visit. She then loaned him her bicycle so he could ride the rest of the way to Schömitz and more easily visit his friends and relatives.

Eduard Hajek during training at St. Pölten, Austria, prior to field deployment to 33rd Panzer Regiment on the Western Front

Eduard came home on leave one last time in the autumn after he completed his training. Maria couldn't recall the month, but never forgot what happened the day he returned her bicycle and said goodbye. The young soldier, clearly still just a boy, broke down and sobbed as he told her he didn't want to go to war for he knew he wouldn't return. It broke Maria's heart to see her brother, someone with such an abundance of promise, convinced his life was over before he ever tasted adulthood. His family members had done their best to talk him out of his fatalistic notion, yet he couldn't be dissuaded. Sadly, his pessimism was justified because he was fully aware how many local soldiers had already died or gone missing.

With the tight Nazi control, he had no alternative except to report to his unit. The papers of young males of military age were closely checked wherever they went by the shadowy Gestapo and military police. The Nazi enforcers were greatly feared because they were above the law and summarily shot or hanged deserters. These hard men excelled at their job. If fanaticism wasn't motivation enough, the threat of being sent to the front themselves provided incentive.

---

[1] Richard Grunberger, *The 12-Year Reich; a Social History of Nazi Germany, 1933-1945* (New York: Holt, Rinehart and Winston, 1971), 210.
[2] Grunberger, *The 12-Year Reich; a Social History of Nazi Germany, 1933-1945*, 205.
[3] Grunberger, *The 12-Year Reich; a Social History of Nazi Germany, 1933-1945*, 204.
[4] Lorenz Reiter, Personal communication.
[5] Grunberger, *The 12-Year Reich; a Social History of Nazi Germany, 1933-1945*, 205.
[6] Wikipedia contributors, "Volksempfänger," *Wikipedia*, Wikipedia.org, 4 Apr. 2015, accessed 21 Apr. 2015.
[7] Jan. Stránský, *East Wind over Prague*. (New York: Random House, 1951), 75.
[8] "Censorship—War Letters," *American Experience*, pbs.org, accessed 20 Apr. 2015.

27 Front Lines

WHEN EDUARD LEFT FOR THE ARMY IN 1943, the Reich's prospects had already turned from bad to worse, so Maria rarely listened to the radio anymore. By then the news broadcasts consisted of little more than *Rückmarsch*, the flip side of the *Vormarsch* (forward advance), that the propaganda ministry had constantly boasted of when the war began. The literal meaning of Rückmarsch is "rearward march," but to avoid the connotation of retreat the Nazi propagandists presented it in a way that conveyed the idea of strategic repositioning. They fooled few. People understood the word was a euphemism for *Rückzug* (retreat), a term conspicuously absent from the Nazi propaganda lexicon.

As he left to begin his service in 1943, Eduard, like every other Reich citizen, knew German forces had just suffered two major defeats. The first was the surrender of the 6th Army in February after Hitler decided to secure Stalingrad by ordering his mobile army to fight in a static urban setting. The other German defeat came when Hitler sent German troops to help their struggling ally, Italy, take control of the Suez Canal in North Africa. There, British and American forces defeated German and Italian troops in a series of engagements during the spring of 1943. Italy, Germany's main ally, imploded after these defeats and became a dangerous liability.

From that point on, Hitler's propaganda machine had a more difficult time duping the public. The populace became cynical. Rückmarsch entered the realm of German black humor with definitions such as "the process whereby a soldier returning from leave is met halfway by his division." The word distressed Maria for she saw Eduard and the other local soldiers being sacrificed for a lost cause as the overwhelming enemy numbers forced them ever rearward.

Had she and the public been aware of Hitler's mental deterioration, they'd have despaired even more. In his increasing derangement, he was fast losing trust in his military staff and taking over command. Early in the war his ambition and incompetence had led him to overcommit the military; now he was increasingly overriding the plans of his trained professionals. With all fronts collapsing, he needlessly doomed many thousands of men and destroyed whole armies by prohibiting strategic retreats until the force was largely annihilated. Everywhere, his vastly outnumbered and depleted forces lacked sufficient replacements, airpower, fuel, weapons, and ammunition to hold the enemy back. The best survival hope for frontline soldiers was a field leader with common sense, initiative, and a willingness to disobey orders.

America's assumption of a leading role in the war greatly complicated Hitler's problems. Germany could not match America's production of armaments and supplies. The United States provided enormous quantities of weaponry and materiel to Britain and the Soviet Union. After US fighter-plane and heavy-bomber production hit its stride, American and British planes dominated the skies over Germany and unleashed a massive bombing campaign directed at the fuel supply chain. When that was destroyed, the bombers concentrated on the Reich's already-strained industrial output and targeted both military and industrial sites. Once further raids did little more than reduce the debris to dust, the planners turned to bombing or firebombing civilian targets to demoralize the population. Berlin was bombed so intensely that German dark humor devised a new definition for a coward—a Berliner who volunteers for duty at the front.

In July 1943, with disaster looming on the Eastern Front, Hitler's forces also came under pressure from the south as America and Britain invaded Sicily. When the island was cleared of Italian and German troops, it became a springboard for invading the European mainland. After Allied bombers crippled Italy's industrial production, the civilian population decided it had had enough and turned on Mussolini and the German military machine. To avoid leaving the Reich's underbelly exposed, Hitler had no choice but to occupy the country and prop up the fascist government with German troops.

When the Allies opened a western front with their D-day invasion of France the following year, the Germans found themselves hard-pressed on three sides as well as from the air. This put a tremendous strain on their resources. The overwhelming Allied forces, with their seemingly limitless supplies of men, weapons, and fuel, pummeled the crippled German military and shrank the Reich's borders noticeably each week. Germany's already-crushing military casualties soared. Allied planes could strafe and carpet-bomb the Germans almost at will because of Germany's depleted air defenses. For German soldiers, the situation was a nightmare. With the Luftwaffe all but destroyed, planes were not available to protect resupply columns carrying essential replacement troops, munitions, and food. Vehicles often had to be abandoned for lack of fuel. Yet, a stubborn Hitler refused to heed his generals' advice to abandon indefensible territory and allow strategic pullbacks to better positions.

After Oskar's convalescent leave ended in January 1943, the last place he wanted to go was back to Russia. Throughout the journey to his new reserve unit at Rostock in northern Germany, he worried that the uniform citation he'd gotten in Vienna would land him right back there on the Eastern Front. On reporting, the first thing he asked the duty clerk about was the citation. He was tremendously relieved to hear: "Such messages go into the trash immediately."

For a few weeks, light duty at his new station allowed Oskar much time to rest and see movies. Then, new orders assigned him to an infantry company cobbled together from reserves. He and his new comrades found themselves on a train headed to the Western Front. At a stop in Belgium a fellow soldier in Oskar's car bought a huge box of cigarettes and distributed them among his fellow soldiers. However, the recipients soon learned the cigarettes contained something other than tobacco because it made them turn green. Rather than throw the whole lot away, the men decided to have some fun themselves. At a stop in France they tossed "cigarettes" out the windows and gleefully watched Frenchmen fall all over them.

The company's journey ended at the Bay of Douarnenez, near Brest, France, where Oskar and the others toiled quietly for weeks building coastal defenses they knew were pointless because the beach was too steep for the enemy to invade. The tranquility ended on June 6, 1944, when the news everyone had dreaded reached them. Early that morning, American and British soldiers landed on the beaches at Normandy, several hundred kilometers to the northeast. Oskar's company packed up immediately and headed to Normandy to reinforce the defenders. The trip took several days. Prowling American bombers and fighters filled the sky and made it too dangerous to move during daylight hours, so they had to travel at night and often on foot. By the time Oskar reached the fighting, the Allied bridgehead was well inland, despite the many Wehrmacht, Waffen SS, and Hitler Youth divisions trying to hold the enemy back. The company took up a position near the town of Lessay and dug in. Fighter-bombers roamed the sky from dawn to dusk and shot at anything that moved. Worse still was the shelling by heavy Allied naval guns that tore huge craters into the landscape around them every day.

For Oskar this new situation was deadlier than what he'd faced on the Eastern Front. Not only was the constant shelling, strafing, and bombing more intense and fearsome, the small fields, meadows, and hills hemmed in the infantry and made operation difficult and dangerous. Only occasionally did the terrain favor his company, like the time an

American unit rushed forward only to find itself surrounded on three sides by a swamp. Oskar didn't know where the higher-ups sent the gum-chewing soldiers they'd captured.

Most German losses came not from enemy bullets, but from air attacks and shelling by the American naval guns. The latter was feared the most, and Oskar vividly recalled one unforgettable shelling. He and a comical friend named Ottomar Groep were walking along on a road when the naval guns opened up. "Whole batteries fired at once," Oskar wrote. "I was lying in the rutted dirt road and wished I was small as a mouse." Tremendous explosions heaved the earth up all around him. It was the heaviest bombardment he ever experienced; he didn't dare so much as raise his head. After each detonation, he was certain the next would pulverize him. "In such a position only your guardian angel can help you, and you call out for him. But then quite suddenly it was over."

Oskar, covered with dirt but unhurt, shouted out for Ottomar, whom he thought had been killed. Ottomar, coated with dirt and grime from head to toe but still in one piece, appeared. The shock wave of an exploding shell had hurled him through the air and into the crater of another shell. If not for the crater, he said he'd surely have died. Oskar went on to say that in such a colossal shelling, a single guardian angel wasn't adequate and it took several to keep an infantryman alive. And his had come through again.

Not all German units stood their ground. The behavior of the 941st Infantry Regiment, which consisted mainly of older men with little education and a strong desire to get out of the war, galled Oskar and his companions. As other line units withdrew rearward in a coordinated pullback one night, the men of the 941st stayed in their holes to await the Americans. The following day, through binoculars, Oskar's company watched as the regiment raised a white flag. The action left a gap in the German lines and endangered everyone else.

As Oskar and Ottomar passed through Saint-Jores, a village already leveled by American shells and bombs, heavy artillery fire rained down and rearranged the rubble. The pair ducked inside a badly damaged church and took cover under the stairway to the pulpit as shells exploded everywhere around them. Before long, the remaining part of the roof collapsed. Oskar and his friend called upon every saint they could think of to save them this time. "Perhaps they heard us," he wrote, "because somehow we came out whole again." The town was deserted, most likely because the Americans had dropped leaflets warning the population to leave. Leaflets still lay strewn about everywhere. The only resident the two men encountered was a lone Frenchman hiding in a hole he didn't want to leave.

On July 20, 1944, a radio message informed field units of an assassination attempt on Hitler in his Prussian headquarters. Oskar and his friends wondered what repercussions this might have and whether it might end the war. But the assassins had merely wounded Hitler, and the fighting continued. The following day the Americans airdropped a huge number of leaflets on German positions. To counter Reich Marshal Herman Göring's assurance that merely a small clique had plotted to kill Hitler, the leaflets listed a long string of prior plots. Oskar picked up a leaflet to keep as a souvenir and stuck it inside his helmet, but it didn't survive long.

After the Hitler assassination attempt, the Americans pounded the German lines even harder than before. High-altitude heavy bombers carpet-bombed German positions throughout the day. Scout planes with smoke canisters marked the targets for the bombers. The mayhem and fear was overwhelming when trees shook violently and entire houses disappeared in clouds of debris in an instant. The only way Oskar could endure it was to press his hands over his ears. Despite the heavy smoke and dust, he could see the colored smoke marking new targets. Eventually, the American targeting moved further away, and he could breathe easier again.

The next day, the company dug in behind the cover of a hill. While Oskar was out of his foxhole picking up rations, artillery rounds exploded overhead in the trees. Rather than the typical high-explosive shells, these were white phosphorous shells that flung burning phosphorus everywhere. When a piece of shrapnel hit Oskar's right boot with numbing force, he thought for sure he'd lost his foot. But the pain was just from the impact. Back at his foxhole, he found his stationery and gear reduced to ash. The socks he'd washed earlier and hung in a nearby bush were still on fire. He cringed to imagine his fate had he not left the hole when he did. His guardian angel still seemed to be on the job.

At a new position behind an embankment the following evening, Oskar and Ottomar were startled by light machine-gun fire nearby. Shortly, the silhouettes of two *Amis* (Americans) appeared in the darkness. One threw a hand grenade. Oskar and his friend hit the ground and avoided injury. After the explosion, neither side cared to expose their position, so no shooting followed. Soon, the Yanks quietly withdrew. The next morning the Germans found a dead American officer nearby and surmised the two soldiers had been searching for him.

A couple days later, the company arrived at the town of Saint-Lô and was told to dig in. Near a house, Oskar and his friend discovered a pile of brush concealing an already existing foxhole that awaited new occupants. To save themselves some digging they dropped their gear into it and left to get some chow. On their return the gear was in a pile some distance from the hole. Two officers had evicted them and no amount of pleading could convince them to give it back. "So, what can an infantryman do?" Oskar wrote. "Nothing, except get out his shovel and dig himself a new hole. And if the ground is hard? Sweat, and then more sweat." Even though the eviction angered Oskar, it didn't keep him from asking himself, "Is my guardian angel looking out for me again?"

◆

July 25, 1944, proved a fateful day for Oskar. Early that morning, squadron after squadron of American bombers passed overhead and carpet-bombed the German lines. Oskar wrote that the havoc and pandemonium was indescribable as bombs rained down and exploded in rapid succession. German antiaircraft gunners fired back but only occasionally hit an enemy plane. The bombing persisted for hours because the Americans knew a large German force was concentrated in the area. Oskar, caught out of his foxhole when he saw the bombs closing in on his position, dashed for his hole and was just steps away when the earth boiled up violently around him.

The next thing Oskar knew, he was lying on the ground, helpless and unable to crawl toward his foxhole. He reached around to explore a warm sensation on his back, and when he looked at his arm, blood covered it. Each successive breath seemed to pump out more blood. The continuing fierce explosions around him made cries for help pointless until several minutes later when the bombing moved on. The responding medic cut open the back of Oskar's shirt and applied the dressing Oskar carried in his pack. When blood continued to gush out, he rolled Oskar onto his left side, hoping to lessen the flow. This only made it worse, so he bound Oskar's entire trunk with a large piece of cloth. Eventually the medic discovered much of the remaining flow came from two additional wounds, one on Oskar's arm and shoulder and the other on a buttock.

As Oskar lay there, he overheard the medic tell another man the bomb made a direct hit on the nearby brush pile and the two officers in the hole were no more. Oskar thanked his guardian angel again, even though his latest reprieve might be only temporary. Oskar asked whether or not Ottomar had also been protected by his guardian angel, but the medics didn't know. When the company commander appeared, the grim expression on his face told Oskar the captain thought he was looking at a dying man.

"Raise me up," Oskar said to one of the attendants when he felt blood pooling beneath him. In this position he saw a horse that had lost its front legs. Even in his own dire condition, Oskar's heart ached to see an animal suffer so. Mercifully, someone soon shot it. Eventually two soldiers brought a stretcher, eased Oskar onto it, and loaded him aboard a gig, a French two-wheeled cart pulled by a horse. After a painful ride to the dressing station located in a nearby house, soldiers placed Oskar on a table where a doctor administered a general anesthetic.

Oskar awoke with a tremendous thirst because of his blood loss. The medic told him patients with lung wounds weren't allowed liquids; they could only have their lips moistened. Oskar's thirst was so great that he begged another medic for a drink. This soldier brought him a cup of lemonade, which Oskar gulped down. The drink was satisfying, but only for a moment because it precipitated an alarming fever and great distress. Oskar asked for a doctor but got the division chaplain instead. Every soldier knew what this meant. After the priest muttered a few words that were supposed to be comforting, he promised to write Oskar's parents. Oskar couldn't understand how someone in his position could be so insensitive as to steal a wounded man's hope like that.

Which saints Oskar called upon next, he couldn't recall, but he refused to give up. Mercifully, he passed out when someone administered a sedative. He awoke some time later to the bedlam of American bombs striking the house. The soldier beside him, a man who'd taken a bullet in the stomach, was screaming in pain because a chunk of ceiling plaster had fallen on him. Oskar recalled little after that, other than slipping in and out of consciousness a number of times and receiving nothing further to drink.

Eventually medics loaded Oskar into an ambulance and drove him to a paratrooper unit's dressing station. From there, he moved on to a hospital in Rennes. Of this trip he remembered only that his pain during transport was excruciating. In Rennes he awoke in a large room where doctors and medics attended the wounded. They told him little, and he lost all sense of time. He had difficulty breathing and could barely move, so he tried not to think about how long his ordeal would persist. However, he never lost his will to live.

Through the open windows, Oskar could hear artillery shells landing ever nearer. When they fell close enough to rattle the windows, the staff placed patients on stretchers and began to remove them one by one until just Oskar and one other patient remained. The orderlies didn't return for a long time, causing Oskar to fear he'd been abandoned, shirtless and unable to move. Finally, a couple of soldiers came back for him and carried him down the stairs to an already crowded ambulance. Once the last patient was aboard, the vehicle headed for Le Mans. Oskar recalled but two things about this trip—the terrible road and a nun giving him candy to suck on in lieu of painkillers and sedatives, which couldn't be spared.

The jarring from potholes caused the wounded to cry out in pain repeatedly, despite the candy.

The stay in Le Mans was brief. The new patients were placed on beds in a facility already packed with the wounded. Oskar lay there shirtless and without any records or identification other than his dog tag. He'd even lost the German soldier's most vital document—the all-important Soldbuch. Not only was the Soldbuch his military ID and pay book, it contained a record of his military service and medical history. He felt his condition worsening because he'd had little actual medical care since the dressing station. The wound in his back was full of pus and blood, and his bandage hadn't been changed for three days. He wondered how much longer he could hold on. But soon he was in the back of still another ambulance and on the way to Paris, 250 kilometers away. As during the previous trip, sedatives and pain medication couldn't be spared, so the patients moaned or cried out with each bump. Oskar arrived in Paris at night and knows this only because one of the other men joked, "Paris by night, thousands of pretty legs!"

Oskar awoke in another large room crammed with casualties, both seriously and lightly injured. Here, in what he later learned was the Hotel de la Pitie, someone finally removed the shrapnel from his upper arm. However, smoking was allowed in the room and his lung wound flared up from the cigarette smoke. Eventually, a doctor moved him to a small room occupied by a single Waffen SS officer. There, Oskar recognized a pleasing, familiar dialect when the nurse who came to change the dressing on his buttock noticed the shrapnel wasn't deep and asked his permission to pull it from the wound with tweezers.

When he asked her where she came from, she replied, "Nikolsburg, Lower Danube." Nikolsburg was the district administrative seat for Schömitz.

After the nurse removed a 3-centimeter, triangular-shaped piece of metal from the wound, she cleaned it up and presented it to her patient as a keepsake. This left Oskar with just the largest piece of shrapnel, the chunk that had shattered two ribs and embedded itself in a lung near his spine. Although Oskar couldn't know it then, this souvenir whose outline resembled a shoe would remain with him forever and require him to carry an x-ray in order to pass through metal detectors and to regularly consult a pulmonary specialist. In 2010 he gleefully reported that after his most recent exam the doctor said, "I'd like to have those 86-year-old lungs when I'm your age. But without the shrapnel."

In the small hospital room during the course of a conversation, his officer roommate asked Oskar about his experiences in Russia. The man was astonished to hear Oskar had been at P'yatykhatky. "What! You were in the destroyed *Verwundetenzug* (wounded evacuee train)?" He couldn't believe any of the wounded had survived the Russian attack, much less gotten away under their own power. His own unit counterattacked and freed the second hospital train early the next morning. The odds that two strangers involved in one little skirmish on an enormous battle front with millions of soldiers should later meet and share the same hospital room on another huge front two thousand kilometers away were very small.

The SS officer told Oskar Russian soldiers captured the second train but left it intact. They attacked and destroyed the lead train because it was escaping. From the condition of the demolished train, he thought it a miracle that anyone on it survived. When Oskar asked whether the lone locomotive his group encountered during the night was on its way to meet the Waffen SS unit and retrieve the second train, his roommate confirmed it was. That engine evacuated the wounded the next day.

◆

Although the days were long and tedious for Oskar in the Paris military hospital, he slowly improved. Eventually the front neared again, necessitating another transfer. This time the evacuees were going all the way to Germany. On August 17 ambulances shuttled the patients to a train station and loaded them aboard a dedicated evacuation train. The relief among the wounded on the train turned to anxiety when evening arrived and the train still hadn't moved. Their fears became real when the patients heard shooting coming from the direction of the train depot. When the intensity of the firing increased and ricochets whistled through the air, the attendants turned off the subdued blackout lamps in the coaches. Oskar feared another P'yatykhatky. However, this train carried an armored car for protection and the soldiers manning its light flak gun began pounding the building the shots were coming from. Several resistance fighters hiding there had attacked the train to disable it.

Oskar was relieved to leave Paris behind the following day, but it was not the last place his heart palpitated on the journey. When the train stopped in a small town down the line, an air raid siren wailed as American fighter-bombers passed overhead. Several tracks away, the crew of an armored flak train made the mistake of firing at the bombers. Predictably, the planes turned around and attacked the flak train. Again, Oskar feared a P'yatykhatky assault—this time from the air. However, unlike in the Soviet Union, here the enemy usually respected red crosses. When the planes left, Oskar's train took on the flak train's freshly wounded.

The next problem lay just a few miles beyond the small town. American bombs had destroyed the track, so the train had to wait until a construction crew arrived and repaired it. Meanwhile, the doctors and medics had their hands full treating the wounded from the flak train.

The train was crammed with casualties, yet Oskar's compartment carried a woman passenger in civilian clothes. She'd boarded in Paris and unsuccessfully tried to coerce the doctors into providing her a compartment with no patients. Apparently she wanted to confer privately with several other civilians aboard the train. As Oskar gathered later from their hushed conversations, they were intelligence agents of some sort. They all disappeared as soon as the train touched German soil. And for good reason because even inside Germany the train was vulnerable to air attack. Prior to reaching the German border, the train experienced several more scares and air raid delays as it made its way through Reims, Namur, and Brussels. In Germany the wounded received a warm welcome, and Oskar collected his second Führerpaket. Oskar's journey lasted three days and ended at a hospital in Krefeld. Only there did he finally get to lie down in a bed again and receive treatment from doctors and nurses.

"You have a beard like a sailor," one of the nurses, a nun, told Oskar. The war had aged him, and he now looked more like a man of 30 than 20. Since the injury, an entire month had passed, but with the endless stream of new casualties, the attendants had been too busy to shave anyone. In Krefeld Oskar came to appreciate wearing clothes and having a toothbrush once more, but he most appreciated the stamina to get out of bed and stand up again.

All too soon the increasing air raid alarms sounding both night and day told Oskar the front was approaching once more and his days of safe haven here were numbered. When the ground fighting neared the hospital, fresh casualties arrived at the same time the staff was moving out the existing patients. With the Reich shrinking fast, the medical authorities had fewer and fewer places to send the wounded. On September 7 a hospital train delivered Oskar to Bad Harzburg in central Germany, a place not far from where his friend Oswald settled after the war. This hospital was formerly the Hotel Esplanade, and as at Krefeld, the staff took casualty care seriously. Oskar couldn't yet walk well enough to venture outdoors, but what he could do again was write home. His parents were overjoyed to get Oskar's letter because they'd heard nothing of him since the note from the division chaplain made them fear he was dying.

From his parents, Oskar learned that his brother Alfred, seriously wounded in Russia months earlier, was now recovering close to home in a Brünn military hospital. Siegfried, Oskar's younger brother, was now in uniform and had also been wounded at the front. And Oskar's father, who'd had surgery for stomach cancer the previous year, was not well. He'd improved initially, but the cancer had returned.

With the excellent care in Bad Harzburg, Oskar's recovery progressed. He celebrated his 20th birthday there. When he was fit enough to travel, he gladly transferred to a hospital in Brünn. On his November 7, 1944, arrival at Military Hospital IV, he received a special surprise. The nurse he handed his medical records to said, "Another Halusa just came out of surgery here." Oskar already knew his brother, Alfred, was in the same hospital, so he asked the soldier's forename. When she said "Siegfried," Oskar could hardly believe it.

"That's my brother!" he exclaimed excitedly. Oskar had been worried about Siegfried because he hadn't heard anything more of him since learning he'd been wounded at the front.

Oskar celebrating his 20th birthday in hospital at Bad Harzburg

The nurse informed Oskar his brother was still under anesthesia, but led him to the patient's room. The one eye visible under Siegfried's bandages popped open as his visitor approached the bed. Siegfried was still groggy, but like Oskar, was nonetheless overjoyed and amazed that they'd reunited under such circumstances. To have all three brothers recovering from wounds at the same hospital was unbelievable. Siegfried had taken shrapnel in his face, chest, eye, and hand. Surgeons had just removed a few metal fragments from his right eye with a magnet. Earlier, they'd extracted the shrapnel from his right arm and encased it in plaster.

Oskar's doctors needed an accurate diagnosis of his lung injury, so they sent him to Prague for a consultation with a specialist at a military hospital. Oskar had to wait there a full day to be seen because the specialist was busy performing cranial surgery. After studying the x-rays, the medical professor told Oskar surgery was risky because the metal chunk had embedded fragments of uniform in Oskar's chest cavity. Removal of the metal could result in sepsis (blood poisoning) if any fabric entered the lung during surgery. The doctor recommended watchful waiting, with surgery only if a compelling reason arose. He said the shrapnel would encapsulate over time and Oskar could live with it.

Oskar during 1944 Christmas leave following his convalescence

When Oskar neared the hospital in Brünn late that night, he could scarcely believe his eyes. Part of the building lay in ruins and was still burning after a bombing raid. There'd been casualties, so he had cause to wonder if his guardian angel had again protected him by the delay in Prague. After Oskar inquired about his brothers and learned they'd survived, a nurse instructed him to go home and return in a few days.

Eventually the doctors released both Oskar and Alfred to home care. In the following weeks the two brothers usually returned to Brünn together for follow-up treatment. At the end of December, Siegfried also came home to Schömitz for a few days, allowing the whole family to celebrate Christmas together. However, the joy was tempered by Oskar's father's stomach cancer. The holiday period was the last time Oskar saw his father.

◆

On January 2, 1945, Oskar bid his family goodbye yet again for he'd received orders to report back to the convalescent company of his military reserve unit in Rostock. Siegfried, still temporarily home from the hospital, took Oskar to the train station in Pohrlitz by horse and wagon. In Rostock Oskar's condition gained him a light duty assignment. But three weeks later he found himself at Stettin on the Oder River, in a new combat unit formed to fight the Red Army. The artillery rounds striking not far away told Oskar they were already uncomfortably close. Oddly enough, my father also was sent to that same general vicinity on the Oder about the same time.

Through a happy coincidence at the end of January, Oskar ran into a sergeant he knew. The guardian angel appeared to still be on the job because this friend soon helped him get reassigned to the Ambulantenzug (outpatient services platoon) of the III. Panzergrenadier Regiment "Feldherrnhalle" (3rd Motorized Infantry Regiment "Feldherrnhalle") in Parchim, many kilometers west of the Russian Front. The Feldherrnhalle regiment's name commemorated the site of Hitler's encounter with the Bavarian State Police the day after his attempted Beer Hall Putsch in Munich.

The outpatient unit primarily served the outpatient soldiers of the military hospital in Parchim, but provided other services as well. Oskar's new job was to distribute cold meals and rations in a barracks compound training very young recruits for the "final victory" that only the brainwashed could still believe in. To boost morale, patriotic slogans adorned the interior walls of these barracks and the recruits had to shout "Germany, awake!" after each marching-ditty stanza. For Oskar this duty was far better than the alternative of being bombed and shot at. Also, most field soldiers were living on short rations by this point of the war, but those on Oskar's base enjoyed plenty of food.

A letter from Oskar's mother arrived at the end of February, informing Oskar that his father had died on February 13. Although an official telegram didn't confirm the death until several weeks later, Oskar's company commander granted a 14-day special leave. Numerous delays during the journey consumed the first five days of the leave. Outside Magdeburg the train stopped to avoid an air raid in the city. For their safety, passengers had to disembark during the raid, which gave them a clear view of the explosions tearing up the city. Oskar shuddered to think what might have happened had the train been running a little faster. Countless bombs hit the rail station, so Oskar walked several kilometers to the other side of the damage so he could catch a train heading in his direction.

In Plauen his train was delayed when it ran over a packed refugee cart at a crossing. Only the cart's horses, which broke loose, survived. In limited visibility due to falling snow, the flagman at the crossing chose to open the barriers and allow one more cart to pass before the train arrived. The flagman misjudged the speed of the train and as a result, the unfortunate refugees suffered a disaster even worse than the one that cost them their home and property to the east.

On his walk home from the Pohrlitz train station, Oskar came across work parties digging antitank ditches along the road. Many of the workers were young girls. He couldn't resist inquiring who these trenches could possibly stop, for he knew the work was pointless and wouldn't present the Russians the least obstacle. This ominous reminder that the Red Army would soon reach his own homeland gave Oskar the chills. At the time, it didn't occur to him that Sudeten Germans had anything to fear from their own Czech countrymen.

In Schömitz, Oskar found his mother still locked in grief. Siegfried was back in his division's replacement unit, but Alfred's injuries had earned him a discharge. Anna, a hired girl from Ukraine, was also living in the house at the time, as well as a Serb POW. Schömitz was a depressed place. Of actual residents, only women, children, and old men were about. Many of the men in uniform were casualties by this late stage of the war, and very few of the rest were still in contact with their families. Several families had already lost two or three sons. Herr Mauer, the head teacher, had lost four. On top of this, the nearing front was driving ever more refugees before it.

The remainder of the 14-day leave passed quickly and Oskar's parting was especially hard on his mother, who worried about what would befall her separated family in the weeks to come. As Oskar said goodbye to his grandparents, who lived nearby, they made the sign of the cross on his forehead and said, "Go in God's name." Oskar believed they truly expected everyone in the family would reunite again after the war because they had beseeched the heavenly powers to deliver everyone home safely.

On leaving, Oskar took with him his Doxa *Firmungsuhr* (confirmation watch), a pocket watch on a gold chain. This proved fortuitous because otherwise he'd have lost it to thieving Czechs in the way Alfred lost his. Both boys had received one at their 1934 Whitsun confirmation in Vienna. Whitsun, or Pentecost, was a religious holiday important in the region since medieval times because it marked the beginning of a week in which serfs were free from service to their noble.

On the journey back to his duty station, the train passed through Brünn, Prague, and then Dresden. Oskar said his heart stopped when he saw the latter city. American and British bombers had firebombed Dresden on February 13, the same day his father died. The entire city center lay in charred ruins. No people were visible in the ruins and only chimneys and partial walls with empty gaping windows still stood. Everything else had burned and collapsed. For Oskar the sight brought to mind four eerie lines from Friedrich Schiller's "Song of the Bell":

> In the desolate window cells
> Horror broods;
> And from heaven the lofty clouds
> Peer within.[1]

Oskar had seen many battlefields and bombed German cities by this time, but nothing came close to matching the destruction in Dresden. This unfortified city teeming with refugees from the eastern territories had presented no military targets. The railroad tracks were quickly restored, but nothing else in the city was worth repairing. Officially, about 25,000 people died, but many Germans believe the number was much higher. No matter what the figure is, those who perished in the maelstrom suffered a horrible death. Not all of the victims died from fire; many were asphyxiated when the intense conflagration stripped the oxygen from the air. Workers incinerated all the bodies they could find, yet weeks later a terrible stench still hung over the city.

A number of American POWs were among those tasked with collecting and burning the bodies. One was Kurt Vonnegut Jr. who went on to achieve fame as a writer of dark humor. Vonnegut survived only because he and his fellow prisoners were housed underground in a former slaughterhouse. The Dresden experience scarred him for life. For years he struggled to incorporate his experience into a book and finally succeeded with his 1969 masterwork *Slaughterhouse-Five*.

The depressing scenes for Oskar didn't end with Dresden. The human tragedy was visible along the entire route. Refugees from the east were everywhere, and their misery was unimaginable. In one railway station he watched several Red Cross nurses try to coax a baby from a refugee woman's arms. "The child is dead," they kept telling the weeping mother, yet the woman wouldn't give up her frostbitten child. Similar heart-wrenching sights and dramas could be found in every city and town along the way. They were all packed with wretched people, mostly consisting of the elderly and women with children.

After three days of travel Oskar arrived back at Parchim and resumed feeding young soldiers. Where they came from and where they went, he didn't know. The fighting front neared again, and air raids occurred almost nightly. The Russians to the east were closest, but the Americans weren't much farther away to the west. It wasn't long before the regiment's administration dissolved, and when it went, the Ambulantenzug unit disintegrated. Oskar and his fellow workers hastily distributed the stock of underwear, uniforms, shoes, and food to area soldiers to keep the supplies from falling to the Russians. On May 1 when the radio announced Hitler was dead and military control had passed to Admiral Doenitz, the regional military command also fell apart. Soldiers reasoned they'd been forced to swear allegiance to Hitler, but they owed no allegiance to his successor. This effectively ended the fighting in Oskar's vicinity. For him, the war was finally over.

---

[1] Wikisource contributors, "The Lay of the Bell," *Wikisource*, En.wikisource.org, accessed 20 Apr. 2015.

28 The Curtain Closes

FOR MANY FAMILIES LATE IN THE WAR, the wait to learn the fate of their soldier became a purgatory. As the Allies annihilated ever more divisions, it was a rare Reich family that wasn't grieving for someone. Small communities such as Schömitz and Wolframitz, where everyone knew everyone else, never lacked soldiers to pray for at Sunday Mass. Reportedly there was only one tiny village in all of Germany that didn't lose a man in the war. Toward the end, few families still retained contact with men in the field. Even if the exhausted men did find time to write a letter, getting mail out was next to impossible in the chaos of constant pullbacks and the broken supply system. And mail from home seldom reached soldiers because of this same supply system breakdown, the frequent reshuffling of men between units, chaos in the rear area headquarters, and the destruction of the domestic transport system.

The families also had their own troubles, not the least of which was concern for their own fate. Maria knew no families who spoke English and listened to foreign broadcasts such as the British Broadcasting Corporation's World Service, so she and her neighbors were not aware that the Czech government-in-exile was saying and doing things with ominous implications for Sudeten Germans. The southern Moravian Germans had always gotten along with their Czech neighbors, so no one expected much trouble from that quarter. Everyone's focus was on the Red Army. With each dawn, families prayed the new day would be the last one of the war. Yet, the war dragged on for no good purpose. Although Hitler promised new secret wonder weapons that would stop the enemy and save the German cause, he had woefully few believers during the winter of 1944–1945.

Those waiting for a quick end to the war would have been aghast to learn that Hitler, probably due to the progression of Parkinson's disease, was so irrational and delusional in the final months that he ordered phantom divisions into battle and required both large and small forces to hold indefensible cities to the last man. His fearful generals could often only pretend to comply. Because Hitler was convinced both the German military and the German people had failed him, he had no qualms about bringing Germany down with him. In the last four months of the war, he and the fanatics around him sacrificed hundreds of thousands of fighting men and civilians to prolong their own survival.

Wolframitz's General Raus reported to Hitler less than two months before the latter's suicide. He'd met the führer three years earlier at Hitler's Eastern Front headquarters, Führerhauptquartier Werwolf, near Vinnytsia, Ukraine. This time he was appalled by Hitler's decrepit appearance: "I faced a physically broken-down, embittered, and suspicious man whom I scarcely recognized. The knowledge that Adolf Hitler—now only a human wreck—held the fate of the German people in his hands alone was a deep shock to me."[1,2]

Oddly enough, this meeting probably saved Raus's life for Hitler disliked the truthful assessment and had Raus sacked from his post as commander of the 3rd Panzer Army, which faced a Russian force outnumbering it by a ratio of perhaps twenty to one in Pomerania just 40 miles east of Berlin. In this post Raus would likely have been killed or taken prisoner by the Russians and never seen again.

Had the German residents of the eastern territories known earlier how dreadful the consequences were when Russian shock troops overran their homes, it is likely nearly all would have fled. Only after the war ended did fragments of the true picture emerge. Ethnic Germans were robbed, raped, and slaughtered with impunity, often in the cruelest ways imaginable. Whole cities were leveled by Soviet artillery. After towns and villages were ransacked they were frequently burned down. The columns of refugees clogging the roads to flee the violence were machine-gunned by soldiers, strafed by planes, or run over by tanks and trucks. The women, children, and old men clustering at Baltic Sea ports waiting for evacuation by ships of the German navy became Russian targets. Tens of thousands of those who made it onto ships died in the freezing water when their craft were deliberately targeted and sunk by Russian surface ships, fighter planes, and submarines.[3]

The German military fought hard with the meager supplies it had. The allied air attacks had left the Germans critically short of ammunition and fuel, and gasoline for civilian vehicles had dried up long before. The new German jet fighter-bombers were sometimes towed by horses on the runway to save fuel. Raus wrote, "Every [military] truck had to take a second empty in tow…passenger vehicles needed to be towed by trucks even during troop movements." Panzers sometimes had to be abandoned for lack of fuel.[4]

Coal-burning trains were used to bring in supplies, even dangerously close to the front. Heavy losses of rail tank cars often left the military unable to move the little fuel it had. When Raus learned of 70 tank cars stranded in Memel, a coastal city surrounded by the Red Army, he sought a way to get them out. One of his combat engineers calculated that if properly sealed the cars would float, so the general ordered them towed 110 miles across the Baltic Sea. The plan worked, but high seas caused several cars to break loose. Until recaptured, the cars raised alarms because their bobbing turret-like tops somewhat resembled Russian submarines.[5]

◆

All through April 1945 the residents of Wolframitz lived in fear of the war front rolling through their village. Whether or not they heard of people crucified to the sides of barns and families nailed to a kitchen table by their tongues and similar atrocities found by German soldiers after retaking villages from the Russians in Prussia,[6] I don't know. But such gruesomeness is not something I wanted to ask my mother about. However, Maria did tell me that at one point the uncertainty and danger caused her and three or four other young women to climb aboard a military truck taking a group of retreating German soldiers toward the west in mid-April. The soldiers, on their way through the village, frightened the women with the stories of what they'd seen or heard—the Red Army's brutal gang rape, torture, and murder of German women. They didn't need to emphasize that young women were especially at risk. While some people discounted the stories, the tales frightened Maria into getting onto the truck.

Germany was the destination. However, when the women realized the soldiers had little idea of how to get there and carried almost no food for the trip, they second-guessed their decision and decided they'd overreacted—that the danger from the Russians was exaggerated. Stories of the Red Horde's barbarism had circulated since the year before, but Germans had been manipulated by Hitler's propaganda machine for too long to fully trust anything. The uncertainty and risk of what lay ahead now led Maria and the others to believe they'd be better off confronting the danger inside their own homes, so not far out of town they stopped the truck, climbed off, and walked back to Wolframitz. Maria has no idea if the soldiers made it to their destination, yet in light of what subsequently happened to her she surely questioned many times her decision to remain behind.

The strict blackout implemented in the final weeks of the war ended all socializing after dark for Maria and her friends. In those days, she saw bomber formations of up to 100 planes pass overhead several times. Wolframitz presented no targets worth destroying, but her heart still raced on hearing the *whumph, whumph, whumph* of detonations in Mährisch Kromau, Nikolsburg, and Znaim. The violent flashes on the horizon during nighttime bombings were particularly frightening as she pictured the hell those explosions brought to the poor souls targeted. A Russian daylight bombing attack on Mährisch Kromau on the final day of the war struck her as particularly unconscionable. The attack killed many civilians, destroyed 116 houses, and damaged 360 more. The military necessity for such an attack had long since disappeared.

Nazi officials, politicians, and the well connected—the individuals who most deserved to be taken by the Russians—began fleeing to Germany and Austria as early as March. They loaded their most portable and valuable possessions on whatever transport they had and set off. Their conveyance was usually a farm wagon pulled by horses, for gasoline was almost impossible to get for civilian vehicles. The adage about rats fleeing a sinking ship was never more applicable. The suspected party member living in the house across the street from Maria was one of those who fled. One morning he was gone without a word to anyone. His neighbors speculated he and his Nazi son took flight together.

Maria confessed she and Aurelia Stöffel began to pack a wagon three or four times themselves. However, they always unloaded it again because unlike the wealthier people, they had no idea where safety lay. And without money or valuables to sell, they would have no resources to live on once they arrived. They could easily be more vulnerable as homeless refugees, especially if overtaken by the Red Army out in the countryside. When Anton Stöffel refused to leave with them in the wagon and strongly discouraged them from going themselves, flight became impossible anyway because the women couldn't handle the large unruly horses. Fear then took a back seat to denial as Maria convinced herself that in her home nothing terrible would happen. As a result, she, like many other Sudeten Germans with the same mentality, set themselves up to pay the bill for Hitler's arrogance and ambition.

Beginning in mid-April, Wolframitz and Schömitz residents heard Russian artillery fire every night coming from Pohrlitz, where the Red Army was encamped. Often, small arms fire sounded as well. What the Russians could possibly be shooting at baffled everyone, since all German resistance had ceased.

Everyone knew the Red Army wouldn't remain stationary forever, so they set about burning anything that might draw attention or invite reprisal. The people knew most Russian peasant soldiers couldn't read Russian, let alone German, so they didn't want to be shot for some ordinary document that happened to have a swastika rubber-stamped on it. An image of Hitler or a man in a German uniform might also draw attention, so Maria burned her Hitler-visit photo. People also frenziedly buried valuables in their gardens. Even furniture. They believed once everything blew over they'd simply go out and recover their property.

As Maria and the Stöffel family waited for something to happen, food stocks in the house dwindled. There'd always been enough to eat during the war because the family grew most of what it needed, and bought, borrowed, or bartered for what it didn't grow. But now the pantry held little since winter had barely ended and the growing season was just beginning. To stretch the pantry supplies, Maria and Aurelia resorted to butchering a litter of small pigs in the cellar at night, one by one. The Russians would surely eat them if they didn't. Some of the remaining pantry food they buried in the cellar in case their situation became really desperate later. The impending approach of the Russians made them worry that they might not even be able to tend crops that year.

In this fearful period, Wolframitz residents owning a wine cellar on the edge of town found a new use for it. The cellars, dug into a thick, hard sand layer, lined the cut banks on each side of the road. One right after another, they had entry doors over a small shaft leading into the interior. Anton Stöffel used to stroll to his cellar each evening to decant some wine from a barrel into a tall bottle jacketed in an insulating straw cover.

Maria and a good friend, Hermina, hid in the cellars a time or two when everyone feared the Red Army would shell the community at any moment. Many others did likewise. In anticipation of the hard times ahead, Maria and Mina also scraped out holes in the sand floor, filled them with emergency food and clothes, and then covered the holes with boards and spread sand over the top to conceal the caches. Aurelia, her two children, her mother, and Anton Stöffel slept there nearly every night before the close of the war.

Maria accompanied them there most evenings to help settle the children and then made her way back to the house after dark. Because of the blackout, the moonless or cloudy nights were so dark that she had to feel her way through an alley and enter the house by way of the back door. She returned so someone would be there in the morning to milk the cows and take care of the livestock. Someone had to do it, and neither Stöffel nor Aurelia stepped up. This went on for over two weeks.

Maria confessed that as perilous as her situation was, some people were far worse off. She particularly pitied the scraggy German soldiers hiding out around the wine cellars and elsewhere. Toward the end there were 50 or more of them. These gaunt, injured, starving men were stragglers who'd fallen behind in the retreat. They'd clawed and limped their way this far back from somewhere farther east, but were too exhausted to go on. The last of the passing military vehicles had left for Austria or Germany days before, so these men had nowhere to go. Other than the hapless defenders whose units had orders to stay behind at various positions and sacrifice themselves to give their comrades enough time to reach the American lines, they were the last soldiers left. She and everyone else knew their loved ones would likely never see the poor wretches again, not after the Russians got through with them. Maria felt bad that she had no food to spare for them.

---

[1] Raus and Tsouras, *Panzers on the Eastern Front General Erhard Raus and His Panzer Divisions in Russia, 1941-1945*, 27.

[2] Raus and Newton, *Panzer Operations*, 334.

[3] Wikipedia contributors. "MV Wilhelm Gustloff," *Wikipedia*, Wikipedia.org, 19 Apr. 2015, accessed 21 Apr. 2015.

[4] Raus and Newton, *Panzer Operations*, 304.

[5] Raus and Newton, *Panzer Operations*, 305.

[6] Marianne Schmeling, *Flee the Wolf: The Story of a Family's Miraculous Journey to Freedom* (Norfolk, Va.: Donning, 1978).

29 Another Peace Found Wanting

MAY 8, 1945, DAWNED as a splendid and unseasonably warm spring day in southern Moravia. Yet, the exceptional weather was not the reason the residents of Wolframitz would forever remember this Tuesday. It was unforgettable because of what happened shortly after word of Germany's unconditional surrender swept through the village.

The capitulation wasn't unexpected. The entire Reich knew Hitler had committed suicide a week earlier, just before Berlin was overrun by the Red Army. Although nearly all Reich Germans were relieved the war was over, its conclusion brought no joy. People had nothing to celebrate for many had lost everything, and everyone had lost something. Most breadwinners were wounded, dead, missing, or imprisoned somewhere. Without them, their families faced a grim future. In Germany most cities were heaps of rubble. When the wind blew, the air filled with grit, and when all was still, the air reeked of cadavers decaying under the debris. Little intact housing remained, utilities and sanitation systems were nonfunctional, and food was scarce. Everywhere, the homeless and displaced roamed in search of basic necessities. The knowledge that Germans could expect little sympathy or help from the rest of the world after what their madman had inflicted on Europe only added to the grimness.

Wolframitz hadn't been bombed and its pantries still held a little food, so living conditions there weren't ghastly as in much of Germany. However, the war's end brought dread because everyone knew the final accounting was imminent. The surrender meant the arrival of the Red Army in short order. The war might have officially ended, but Wolframitzers feared that the hostilities hadn't ceased.

When I was a child, my mother told me more than once the war ended in her town. It was true, though not quite in the sense I imagined. A Red Army battalion overran Wolframitz around 10 a.m. on the day the war in Europe ended. Wolframitzers shuttered their windows, locked their doors, and prayed while most of the Western world celebrated. Even so, none of them anticipated they'd just experienced the last moments of freedom they'd ever know in their village.

Locked inside her home, Maria didn't have long to wait before the mayhem began. Despite her fear and anxiety, curiosity drew her to the street-facing window. She heard the boisterous throng long before she saw it. Through the narrow slits of the shutter, she watched the barbarous, unruly mob of "liberating" soldiers swarm down the street—the same street their previous liberator had motored down five and a half years earlier. Had Wolframitzers been in a reflective mood, they might have noted how badly their liberations had always gone. This time there were no symbolic banners suspended on buildings in greeting or powerful leaders in grand touring cars. These liberators arrived on a crazy mix of transport. Some were in military vehicles, but most came on horses or horse-drawn wagons obviously stolen from farmers.

The wild horde was outfitted in motley uniform combinations. One author, recounting the arrival of the Russians in Prague wrote that the Red Army had no strict uniform regulations. The soldiers might be wearing khaki brown, blue, white, black, yellow, or red, and have pants of a different color. These combinations might mix summer and winter uniform. And the soldiers were crazy about flowers. They adorned their sidecar motorcycles with bushes and small trees, and every soldier wore a flower or branch in his cap, bootlaces, or buttonhole.[1]

Although everyone referred to the occupiers in Wolframitz as Russians, these men were Mongolians from the Asian part of the Soviet Empire. They weren't much larger than the younger local teens, yet their small stature belied their ferocity. These soldiers had no use for silly technicalities like a lack of resistance or the official end of the war. Although not a shot was fired against them, they didn't let that hinder the use of their guns.

Hundreds advanced wildly with their guns blazing as they looted, ransacked, and destroyed with gusto. Packs of men smashed down doors and swarmed into buildings. Inside, they acted like wild dogs in a butcher shop. What they couldn't wear or pocket, they threw on the farm wagons. Clocks, radios, jewelry, money, cameras, bicycles, furniture, food, tools, kitchen items—whatever struck their fancy, they carried off, even if its function wasn't known. Ticking things topped their list. Maria was glad she'd hidden her confirmation watch when she saw one soldier whose whole forearm was covered with wristwatches.

Maria's curiosity nearly got her killed. As she looked on, transfixed by the anarchy, a bullet shattered the window and splintered the door of the wooden wardrobe beside her. The near miss startled some sense into her. Aurelia and the children had hidden themselves long before the mob hit town; now Maria scrambled up into the attic and did the same.

In recalling the event decades later, Maria described the rest of the day as a blur of terror and worry. She awaited the splintering crash of the front door, but no violent intruders broke in that first day. The Stöffel house escaped the opening spasm of violence and looting because with several hundred houses to loot in the four villages, the plunderers didn't have time to hit them all before the stores of alcohol they encountered slowed them down. Intoxicated or not, the raiders knew the untouched houses weren't going anywhere.

I didn't press my mother about what happened when the Russians did come to her house. It was clear this topic was painful and she couldn't talk about it, either because she'd blocked out the memory or didn't want to revive it. She did say that between these thieves and the ones who followed, she lost nearly everything she owned, including her cherished confirmation watch.

At many houses the thieves took perverse pleasure in flinging everything they didn't want, or couldn't carry off, out the front door onto the road. Across the street at the residence abandoned by Maria's alleged Nazi neighbor, the soldiers smashed in the door, took what they wanted, and tossed the rest of the contents out. When Maria ventured out one morning before anyone was about, she stumbled across an 1897 Austrian cookbook bearing the title *Die Österreichische Küche*. The cover had been ripped off, and the book lay forlornly in the street amidst the broken furniture and other destroyed belongings. On impulse, she snatched it up and brought it home, despite whom it had once belonged to. The abused old book was a token of her culture and heritage. By the way my mother cherished that book until the end of her life, I'm sure the rescue also symbolized defiance.

The Soviet invasion showed Wolframitz residents how wrong they'd been to dismiss the stories of Red Army brutality. An even bigger mistake was to believe only the Russians posed a threat, for a second scourge followed on the heels of the Soviets. A ragtag mob of Czech men who called themselves communist partisans, or Revolutionary Guards (RG), arrived a few hours later. Sudeten Germans soon came to know them as Robber Guards. In some other areas of German-occupied territory such as the Balkans, the Eastern Front, and the Low Countries, partisans were resistance fighters who risked their lives when they actively opposed the German occupation and engaged in combat or sabotage. In the Sudetenland, the vast majority of Czechs who adopted the name did so only after any real danger had passed. They called themselves partisan to advance their looting and violence.

Maria and her fellow ethnic Germans knew that if those men had had previous thoughts of resisting the German occupation, they'd disguised it remarkably well by appearing friendly right until the end. Later, she and her fellow Sudeten Germans would learn that the Czech exile government, through foreign radio broadcasts, had begun exhorting Czechs to punish Germans long before the war ended. Beneš had been bent on revenge from the day the Munich Agreement was imposed on him. Getting rid of the Sudeten Germans entirely had been a top priority ever since.

◆

The internal Czech resistance movement throughout the war had done very little except pass information to Beneš in London and to the Czech communists in Moscow. Doing more risked Nazi reprisal and death. While he was in exile, to advance the goal of expelling his largest minority Beneš needed to stir up hatred of Germans inside the country, evoke sympathy from the outside world, and most importantly, sell the Allies on the idea that Czechs would no longer tolerate the Germans after the war. For the latter, he had to evoke some degree of Czech defiance and outrage.

The feeble Czech resistance within the Protectorate was unwilling to provoke the Nazis, so in 1941 the office of British Special Operations, in conjunction with Beneš, devised and implemented Operation Anthropoid. The Royal Air Force air dropped a Czech and a Slovak soldier into Czech territory to assassinate SS-Obergruppenführer and General of Police Reinhard Heydrich, the top ranking Nazi in the Protectorate of Bohemia and Moravia. His murder was certain to evoke severe reprisal by the Nazis, which would in turn stimulate outrage among the Czech citizenry. The two soldiers hid out for months before ambushing Heydrich in his car on the way to work. When the shooter's gun jammed, one of the pair lobbed a grenade, wounding Heydrich. The escape of the attackers triggered an enormous manhunt. The two men, along with several accomplices, died in a gun battle with German troops after one of their number betrayed his comrades when questioned by the Germans.[2]

Luck was with Beneš and the British. Although Heydrich's wounds were not life threatening, the blast introduced fragments of seat fabric into Heydrich's bloodstream and caused blood poisoning. He lingered for eight days before dying. The Nazis retaliated viciously as expected. They ordered the execution of all males over the age of 16 in a small village called Lidice when they learned the assassins received support there. The slaughter was carried out by the German Security Service. Village women and children were sent to concentration camps where most ultimately died. Altogether, 340 villagers lost their lives. The reprisal sent a strong message to other Czechs not to harbor agents of the resistance. The Nazis also arrested and killed at least two thousand political enemies and other members of the resistance at this time.

◆

Even had the southern Moravia Germans known of the hatred being stirred up by Beneš and his exile government, they'd probably still have discounted the idea of any danger from their neighbors because of crimes committed by Nazi leaders. After all, they'd had a cordial relationship with local Czechs for centuries. Even after the first wave of Czech looters arrived, neither Maria nor her neighbors were ready to believe the threat posed by them was as grave as that from the Russians. The first of the so-called partisans on the scene, young laborers from the nearby Czech villages, were only interested in looting.

The arrival of more hardened and violent plunderers in the form of gangs calling themselves partisans followed the Soviet soldiers and local Czech looters. These men didn't just pillage, they also assaulted and abused the defenseless residents. They moved from house to house and methodically cleaned out anything of value overlooked by the previous pillagers. The booty was thrown onto trucks and disappeared into the Protectorate. North of Prague the train line going into the city became known as the Alaska Express, which alluded to the Alaska Gold Rush and the gold diggers.[3]

Local looters comprehended how intent the Czech government was in punishing the Germans and soon found it easier to take the whole property rather than just belongings. This removed the need to haul booty away and at the same time provided a roof to sleep under and a leisurely existence. Of course, the best properties went first. Not all of the squatters stayed long term; some moved on or hopped to a better house when they found one. The new owners sometimes sent the former German owners packing, but most banished the resident family to one room and made their new slaves do their bidding as servants, cooks, and farm laborers. Oddly enough, most members of this new bourgeoisie claimed to be communists.

Wartime POW laborers, hired foreign farm workers, and the numerous Polish maids in their late teens and early twenties, also competed for loot. Because the maids had lived in their employers' houses and knew the hiding places intimately, they were in a prime position to fill their satchels. Many of them moved in with Russian soldiers who, like the Czech partisans, commandeered German houses.

The drinking may have spared some houses from looting the first day, but Wolframitz learned this reprieve came at a price. As the Russian soldiers began drinking, lust replaced looting. The initial wild shooting, theft, and destruction was bad enough, but the hunt for women was worse.

◆

Stalin requited Hitler's invasion and humiliation of the Soviet Union by declaring open season on Germans and their property in occupied territory and allowing his army to run rampant. The soldiers hadn't been paid in a long time because of the Soviet Union's insolvency, so the looting sanction also relieved pressure on Soviet paymasters and the national treasury. Communities like Wolframitz, occupied by battle-hardened frontline soldiers, paid the dearest price. Germans soon came up with a phrase to describe the plight they were in: "Deutsche sind Beute" (Germans are prey).

The occupation destroyed the sense of community that had existed in Wolframitz for most of a thousand years. The terror and lawlessness made Germans afraid to leave their houses. Families couldn't protect themselves, much less their relatives and neighbors. Each household was an island, helpless and isolated. Those Germans who hadn't acquired Czech masters couldn't lock their doors because all doors had been kicked in during the looting. Similar conditions prevailed throughout the Sudetenland.

The Wolframitz occupiers hit the wine cellars each evening, and the resulting drunkenness proved a nightly trial for Germans. Liquored-up soldiers stalked the streets in packs to find German females to rape. Some hunted on foot; others rode their stolen horses in the quest. The victims were usually gang-raped. Although pretty young women were the prime targets, all females from grandmothers to young girls were fair game. The assaults often happened in front of family members and small children. Everyone endured the violence and degradation. The villagers looked upon the Soviets as animals without a shred of decency.

It is true that some soldiers responded to Nazi atrocities committed in the invasion of the Soviet Union. However, it is also true that throughout the war the Red Army was encouraged to act violently by the likes of Moscow propagandist Ilya Ehrenburg, who prodigiously published articles not only in the leading Soviet newspapers *Pravda* and *Isvestia*, but also in the military newspaper *Red Star*. He repeatedly advocated treating all Germans as subhumans, as in this 1943 publication: "Germans are not human beings. From now on the word German means to us the most terrible oath...We shall not speak anymore...We shall kill. If you have not killed at least one German a day, you have wasted that day....If you kill one German, kill another—there is nothing more amusing for us than a heap of German corpses."[4]

Communities throughout the territories captured by the Russians experienced a rash of suicides, as documented in numerous books describing the atrocities in Central Europe at the end of the war. These reports come not only from Germans, but from other nationalities as well, including Allied POWs liberated in the Red Army's advance. POW reports such as the following were not uncommon. "In the district around our internment camp [Eastern Pomerania]…and hundreds of larger villages—Red soldiers during the first weeks of their occupation raped every woman and girl between the ages of 12 and 60. That sounds exaggerated but it is the simple truth."[5]

Some people were so affected by the violent crimes and horrible deaths that they saw suicide as the only way out. Sometimes, whole families perished when parents couldn't face the thought of their children being so horribly abused and injured. Others killed themselves because they'd lost everything meaningful in their lives.

In Wolframitz, the ill, those hurt through torture or assault, and females injured in sexual attacks had no medical care to fall back on because the sole physician, Dr. Johann Geidl, was confined to his house like everyone else. The old doctor, who walked slowly with the aid of a cane, was a well-respected man who for decades had tended both Germans and Czechs and treated them equally. He eventually committed suicide when he could no longer take the abuse of the partisans and was about to be thrown out of his home. Shortly after the occupation began, the partisans arrested many of the remaining local men and hauled them to camps in Mährisch Kromau or Znaim, where they were terribly mistreated. At least 11 local men and women died at the hands of the partisans in one way or another during this period. Oswald himself lost three cousins in this time.[6]

My mother talked about the events of May 8 and the dark days that followed only reluctantly and in the sparest detail. She confessed she feared reviving the memory of the brutality and terror because it would stalk her for days. She never revealed whether she'd been assaulted by the Russians. It is hard to imagine that many women, especially young and pretty ones, could have eluded the soldiers for months on end when even the dullest of the occupiers could learn in time where they lived. Yet, some women did evade them. Although I have to hope my mother was one, the question will forever remain unanswered. However, as will become evident, the Russian occupiers weren't the only rapists the women had to fear.

Maria maintained a constant vigilance. Hiding became second nature to her because when the Russians kicked at the front door, it was already too late to escape through the back. They'd long since learned to cover both entrances. Fortunately, they normally came only at night after drinking. If a woman made it out of her house, the darkness favored her. Farm fields provided hiding places, especially cornfields later in the growing season. The rapists usually didn't pursue their quarry beyond the village; they preferred to stick close to the source of the alcohol. Out in the countryside the women had an advantage over drunken Russians because they knew the fields and ditches.

In the struggle to avoid the soldiers, one factor in Maria's favor was the location of her residence. In one of my visits to Wolframitz, I explored the area behind the Stöffel Hof. Unlike many other houses in the village, it abutted farm fields to which Maria could flee.

At first the villagers thought the violence and brutality would eventually subside and the Russian officers would rein in their men. It didn't happen. Lawlessness prevailed and rape remained a danger throughout the months of Russian occupation. One frightening rumor Maria heard was that an enterprising group of soldiers kept a stable of women locked in a barn to spare themselves the effort of chasing victims down. But it wasn't just women who were at risk. Because the soldiers all carried guns, they also posed a danger to children and the few men still around. Anyone attempting to protect a family member faced being shot, and loaded weapons in the hands of drunks were prone to discharge accidentally.

Although partisans sometimes joined the Russian soldiers in their evening carousing, they largely partied on their own. Few Czechs openly carried guns because it made the Russians uneasy. However, guns were unnecessary to bully women, children and aged men. If a German should happen to raise a finger against a Czech, his or her life was in grave danger for the soldiers acted as the partisans' enforcers. Many of the partisans liked to exercise power themselves, even if their weapons were cruder. Fortunately, they didn't all dish out violence; some were content to enrich themselves with German property.

For the villagers, venturing out into the streets at night when the Russian soldiers and Czech partisans were most active remained dangerous throughout the occupation. The morning, when the occupiers were sleeping off their intoxication, was the time to do what needed doing. Germans stayed in their homes or in hiding places after dark unless an errand was truly unavoidable. The soldiers must have come to regret shooting out all the streetlights when they arrived, for lighting would have helped them navigate the streets better when drunk and made their hunt for women easier.

Germans who did leave their houses never dallied anywhere out of fear of Russians or Czechs, thus limiting contact with neighbors. As a result, news and information was hard to come by. However, this was only part of the reason people talked little to each other. When paths crossed, Wolframitzers feared they would arouse suspicion of plotting if they chatted. Any Polish girl or Czech who wished to settle an old score or cause mischief could report a German, should they want to humiliate or punish them. A German might also inform on others to curry favor with the occupiers.

The danger to Maria intensified the day a group of Russian soldiers took up residence next door. The occasion remained forever vivid in her mind. She told me of her terror when through a window she saw soldiers scurry to the back of her house. She expected the worst, but this day their objective lay elsewhere. They swarmed through her Hof, climbed up on a stall roof, and hopped over the wall to get to the back door of the adjoining house. The soldiers were unable to push open the well barricaded front door, so they smashed through the rear entrance. Although Maria was enormously relieved not to be the target, she feared for her neighbors and felt awful about being unable to help them.

She knew the family well but didn't learn what happened until 30 years later. When, in the presence of the whole family, one of the intruders pushed the wife to the floor to rape, the husband jumped on the attacker. The other soldiers pulled the husband off, put a gun to his head, and indicated they'd kill him if he moved another muscle. The man had not been away in the military because he was just above the cutoff age. After the woman was gang-raped, she, along with her husband and 12-year-old son were forced to watch the rape of her 17-year-old daughter, Henriet, known as Jetti. Afterward, the Russians decided the house was to their liking, so they booted the occupants out. Maria subsequently lost contact with the family. In the 1970s she learned the family fled to Klein Seelowitz and found refuge with relatives.

◆

Revenge wasn't the only purpose of the abuse advocated by self-appointed head of government-in-exile Edvard Beneš. To rid Czechoslovakia of Germans, it also served him to take German property and terrorize Germans so they would actually want to leave their homeland and have nothing to come back to. To encourage the Czech citizenry to participate in terror on a large scale, he guaranteed immunity from criminal liability. Beneš laid the foundation for this campaign early in his exile by vesting himself with the legislative authority to issue a set of punishing decrees applying to Sudeten Germans at war's end. Eventually 89 Beneš decrees, fleshed out with hundreds of pages of accompanying enforcement instructions, were codified into law. One of the decrees required all Sudeten Germans over the age of six to wear a white armband bearing a black letter N to identify the wearer as German. The N stood for *Němci*, the Czech word for "German." The armbands made wearers easily identifiable targets, as armbands had when the Nazis imposed a similar requirement on Jews years before.

After a Beneš speech in Brno (Ger. Brünn), on May 12, 1945, there could be no doubt of the president's aims. He paraphrased the words of German-hating Russian propagandist Ilya Ehrenburg: "In this war the German people ceased to be human! The German people ceased to be recognizable as humans! Now they look to us like a single large inhuman monster...we are resolved to definitively liquidate the German problem in our Republic."[7]

In Germany under Hitler, the degree of hatred necessary to carry out the violent persecution of Jews came only after it was cultivated and sanctioned. Beneš initiated a similar hate campaign against Germans during the war from London. The Communist Party of Czechoslovakia, which by war's end had largely destroyed all rival political parties, became a partner in the campaign. As soon as the German military was defanged at war's end, the communist cadre stepped up and demonstrated how to deal with Germans. Revenge became the vehicle driving mass participation, and free German property provided the fuel.

Condemnation of Beneš's final solution to the minority problem was so thoroughly suppressed that not until 1978 did disapprobation come from within. In an essay that he could only publish outside of the country, a Czech historian publicly criticized the Beneš decrees and the barbarity they'd produced. The author, Ján Mlynárik, denounced the buildup of hatred that led to mass liquidation and measures so ridiculously extreme that even the works of Mozart, Beethoven, Goethe, Schiller, Kant and Hegel were banned and the words for *German* and *Germany* could no longer be capitalized. Mlynárik charged that the cruel excesses had damaged the economy as well as moral values. His outspokenness earned him a jail sentence followed by exile.

The most controversial of the decrees, those stripping Sudeten Germans and Magyars of all human and property rights, are still on the books in both of Czechoslovakia's successor states, the Czech Republic and the Slovak Republic. In 1943 at the height of the war, Beneš traveled to Moscow to seek Stalin's support for his plan to eliminate unwanted minorities. He considered it advantageous to deal with Stalin because the Czech communists, the major political Czech power bloc, had fled to Moscow during the war. Beneš wanted to reduce dependence on the "unreliable" western democracies. Unfortunately, he trusted Stalin a bit too much. Hitler had deftly outmaneuvered Beneš five years earlier, and Stalin had no trouble doing the same.

Beneš won Stalin's approval, but at the cost of ceding great power to Moscow's Czech communist proxies. Before he left, he signed accords that bound future Czech economic, foreign, and military policy to the Kremlin. On Stalin's assurance of noninterference in the affairs of fellow Slavs, Beneš agreed to nationalize banks and industry, align his defense policy and military bases with Soviet needs, and standardize Czech military weapons and ammunition with those of the Soviet military. When Stalin later reneged on his noninterference pledge, the country found itself financially dependent upon the Soviet Union and no longer able to defend itself militarily. Stalin so easily made Czechoslovakia a Soviet satellite because the agreement Beneš signed removed the last two impediments to a takeover—capitalism and effective political opposition.

Stalin, who'd who callously killed millions in his own country, wasn't the least bothered by the idea of ethnic cleansing in Czechoslovakia and was only too happy to allow the Czechs to carry out their expulsion. He just didn't want to involve the Red Army in the process and risk alienating the western Allies before he could consolidate his power throughout Central and Eastern Europe.

Given a green light, Beneš set about creating the conditions necessary to make the Germans and Magyars want to leave. By the time the war neared its end, he had many of his decrees in place. The next step was to promote vengeance as every Czech patriot's duty. Although the Red Army never actively participated in the expulsion, it certainly helped the process along.

Beneš waited until the war was nearly over before he officially informed the British what he intended to do with his Germans and Hungarians. To sell his idea, he argued that the expulsion was necessary for humanitarian reasons—that the memory of Lidice and other injustices would cause riots and massacres if these people weren't stripped of all rights and expelled. Then, to the annoyance of the British government, which had supported him and other exiled Czechs throughout the war, Beneš moved his government-in-exile to Moscow. Only in April 1945, when the Slovak portion of the country was entirely in Russian hands, did Beneš venture to set foot in his country again. Compared to Hitler, who visited cities like Vienna, Prague, and Paris immediately after his troops arrived, Beneš was timid.

When Beneš assembled a provisional government in the Slovakian city of Košice, he promptly contradicted the reasons he'd given the British for removing his German minority and dropped all pretense of humanitarianism. Instead of acting to prevent massacres, he actively worked to incite them through hate speeches such as the one broadcast by radio in which he said, "Woe, woe, woe, thrice woe to the Germans, we will liquidate you!"[8] Yet, to the outside world the message would remain similar to that voiced in an August 1945 radio speech by Dr. Hubert Ripka—a Czech Foreign Affairs official—when he said, "We shall solve the [German] problem in a humane way as becomes a nation with an old humane tradition."[9]

To justify stripping the unwanted minorities of their property, Beneš labeled all Germans and Hungarians as politically unreliable. Similar proclamations, repeated endlessly by other members of the government, made all Germans and Magyars targets whether they'd supported the Nazis or not.

In Košice, Beneš also announced the formation of National Committees within every community. Under the umbrella of the National Front, these National Committees were tasked with providing local governance following the war. Since the communists were far better organized than any other political entity, they gained a disproportionate amount of control, which they subsequently used to win popular support.

Some communist committees, already organized, were tasked with coordinating resistance against the Nazis within Czechoslovakia. However, aside from some small actions in the mountainous area of north-central Slovakia and a weak and unsuccessful attempt to direct a mutiny by two Slovak Army divisions in 1944, the communists were unable to mount any coordinated resistance until the closing days of the war when the German military was near collapse. At that time they successfully engineered a general uprising in Prague. It was in the midst of this chaos that the brutal and indiscriminate revenge advocated by both Beneš and the communists began. The communists wanted a liberation conflict in Prague to forestall an American advance by General George Patton.[10] Beneš needed a bloody confrontation there to arouse nationalistic fervor and rally popular political support for his presidency.

This uprising needlessly cost many Czechs their lives, lives that would have been spared by waiting several days or honoring the withdrawal agreement that the fast disintegrating German military had already negotiated with Czech municipal leaders. Much of the vengeance wreaked on Germans was carried out against defenseless residents, wounded soldiers in hospitals, and disarmed soldiers who'd already surrendered their weapons.

President Beneš was no Mahatma Gandhi or Nelson Mandela. These leaders, after heading successful independence movements, used their authority to nonviolently amalgamate their minorities. During the course of the war, Beneš wrote: "In our country the end of this war will be written in blood. The Germans will be given back mercilessly and manifold everything they have committed in our lands since 1938. The whole nation will be caught up in this struggle; there will be no Czechoslovak who does not take just retribution."[11] His military commander-in-exile was even blunter, stating in a 1944 radio broadcast: "When our day comes, the whole nation will apply the old Hussite battle cry: 'Beat them, kill them, leave none alive.' "[12]

The Germans could only hope their neighbors would retain some moral conscience and resist taking part in the orgy of anti-German hysteria fostered by Beneš and his communist allies. A few Czechs took risks to help Germans, but sadly, the vast majority did not. Criminals, sadists, and sexual predators, along with ordinary citizens, took the inflammatory talk to heart and responded enthusiastically to deal with the fifth columnists and the minorities that their leaders-in-exile had branded as traitors. The promise of immunity for such acts of revenge excused the most horrendous of crimes—even those committed against children.

---

[1] Joseph Wechsberg, *Homecoming* (New York: A.A. Knopf, 1946), 19.
[2] Wikipedia contributors. "Operation Anthropoid," *Wikipedia*, Wikipedia.org, 15 Apr. 2015, accessed 21 Apr. 2015.
[3] Giles MacDonogh, *After the Reich: The Brutal History of the Allied Occupation* (Basic Books, 2009), 131.
[4] Alfred M De Zayas, *Nemesis at Potsdam: The Anglo-Americans and the Expulsion of the Germans: Background, Execution, Consequences* (London; Boston: Routledge & K. Paul, 1977), 65.
[5] De Zayas, *Nemesis at Potsdam*, 67.
[6] Oswald Lustig, "Personal Communication.," n.d.
[7] Johannes Rammund De Balliel-Lawrora, *The Myriad Chronicles* (Xlibris Corporation, 2010), 112.
[8] MacDonogh, *After the Reich*, 128.
[9] Great Britain, *British Documents on the Origins of the War, 1898-1914*, xxiv.
[10] Glaser, *Czecho-Slovakia*, 103.
[11] Balliel-Lawrora, *The Myriad Chronicles*, 112.
[12] Balliel-Lawrora, *The Myriad Chronicles*, 112.

30 Schömitz, Maria's Last Look

MY MOTHER TOLD ME the terrible things she saw happening in Wolframitz caused her to worry about the Luksch family and the Hajek children in Schömitz. Since Germans were no longer allowed to send mail and also couldn't pass messages through others because everyone was hiding indoors, the only way for her to learn how they'd fared was to go there herself. She thought it was the third Sunday after the war's end that she set out. Very early in the morning, while the occupiers were still sleeping off another night of raucous drinking and carousing, she retrieved her bicycle from its hiding place in the farmstead and brought it out through the Hof gate. After peering around carefully for Russians, Czechs, or Polish maids and satisfying herself that the way was clear, she set out as fast as she could pedal.

Maria recalled the ride vividly. She could still picture herself dressed lightly in her Sunday dirndl, for despite the ugly circumstances the warm and spring-like morning air promised a beautiful day. Although anxiety and tension stalked her the entire way, she encountered no one along the road. At the outskirts of Schömitz she slowed to check for danger ahead. The way looked clear, so she cautiously continued up the street. In passing through the village, she noted it didn't appear to have suffered the same degree of wanton destruction as Wolframitz, but the place no longer had a friendly feel. There was nothing carefree about it anymore. No doors or farmyard gates were casually ajar, and no farmers, housewives, or animals were outside.

When Maria knocked on the Luksch door, both she and her bicycle were whisked inside hurriedly. "Weren't you afraid to come?" Emma asked. Maria admitted she'd been scared, as any sane person would be, but said she'd made up her mind not to let the thugs dictate everything she could and couldn't do.

Then she and the family exchanged news of the events in their villages. Maria learned that the Red Army arrived in Schömitz at about the same time as in Wolframitz. On their heels, barely two hours later, came the thieving Czech partisans to compete in the ransacking and terrorizing of the village. In this process, they killed two men and injured several others. But because the Luksch family had wisely stayed inside their house, they didn't have the whole picture. I learned decades later from Oskar Halusa that Russians had also raped a 12- year-old girl and partisans had tortured a number of men. Oskar passed on an account of the latter event, written by Johann Caesar, the same man beaten black and blue in the Spielberg Castle by Czechs prior to the war. As bad as that earlier abuse had been, it paled in comparison to his postwar experience.

Not long after their arrival, the partisans stormed into the Gasthaus and announced they were looking for Johann Caesar, the innkeeper. As soon as Caesar replied, "That's me," they assaulted him. He had no idea what he'd done or what they wanted. After they stopped beating him, they dragged him off to house #10, the house that once belonged to the Jewish farmer, Dukes. Other armed partisans already held several German soldiers and a few other villagers there. Among the prisoners were Josef Bilek, who'd lost two sons in the war, and Josef Rodinger, the mayor. The Czech marauders had gone after Caesar because he was a hunter with a permit for a hunting rifle. They expected to find a rifle in his quarters, and when they didn't, tore the whole inn apart in a futile search. Eventually they found a French pistol Caesar's son brought back from France as a war souvenir while on leave recuperating from a wound. No one knew it was there because the son hadn't mentioned it.

Before long the partisans lugged a couch into the large room where the prisoners were held. Caesar recognized it for it belonged to the family of his in-laws up the street. The captives grew alarmed; they knew the couch hadn't been brought in for their comfort. And they soon found out they were correct. Each prisoner, in turn, was flung naked onto the couch to be beaten and tortured. Many Germans throughout the country reported that their Czech abusers took particular pleasure in stripping Germans naked before inflicting punishment. The purpose was not just to make blows more painful, but also to humiliate and dominate their victims. The couch placed the victims in a low, prostrate position so they could be struck harder from above. No prisoner left the sofa until he was bloody.

The beatings went on for days. Several of the prisoners became so despondent they sought to kill themselves to end the pain. Caesar, the oldest man there at 71, talked them out of it. Johann Rodinger, a soldier home on convalescent leave for a wound, was forced to help administer the beatings. Needless to say, the screams ensured that nearby neighbors suffered along with the victims because the agonized cries of pain penetrated the walls and closed windows.

Eventually the physical torture eased, only to be replaced by a new torment. At the beginning of June the captives were marched to Pohrlitz where thousands of German women, children, and the aged from the city of Brünn were being held. All Germans in Brünn had been driven from their homes two weeks earlier and brutally herded toward the Austrian border in what is known as the Brünn Death March. This appalling event resulted in the confinement of thousands of the expellees in Pohrlitz for weeks under the most abhorrent conditions. The sexual abuse, crowding, filth, and lack of adequate food and water resulted in a great loss of life. Although the deaths themselves did not much concern the Czech guards, these men realized the contagious diseases running rampant among the prisoners threatened their own safety. To get the dead buried quickly, they requested that partisans in surrounding villages send German prisoners to dig mass graves. The confined Schömitz men were part of the grave-digging detail.

Burying so many diseased, abused, and starved victims was dreadful and dangerous work. There seemed no escape for Caesar until one day his path crossed that of a fellow local innkeeper—a Czech whom Caesar knew well. This man quietly sent one of his workers to Schömitz to inform Caesar's family of their patriarch's whereabouts. When the messenger returned, Caesar learned his family had been deported to Austria along with many other Schömitzers. Without his family as hostages, the partisans had no leverage to keep him in Pohrlitz, so the old innkeeper decided to slip away at the first opportunity.

When Caesar saw his chance, he grabbed a vineyard hoe, slung it across his shoulder, and impersonated a farm laborer as he headed toward Nikolsburg and the Austrian border. To avoid undue attention, Caesar kept his eyes on the ground whenever he met anyone along the road, so he was horrified when someone in a horse carriage passing him shouted, "Hey, Mr. Caesar, where are you off to?"

Caesar looked up to see Tomas Sladek, a Czech from Schömitz, on his way to his daughter's wedding in Nikolsburg. To avoid giving anything away Caesar replied, "The Unterannowitz Vineyard."

The answer earned him a comfortable ride to the vineyard. Caesar knew the area because he'd bought wine for his inn there for years. On his arrival he asked a man he knew and trusted where he might cross the border discretely. In the early evening, near his destination, he ran into a Czech military patrol. When the soldiers questioned him, he told them he was working at the vineyard along the road, so they let him go. He pretended to work until they passed from sight. At dusk, with Austria just across the Thaya River, Caesar encountered another obstruction in his flight to freedom—the bridge he had to cross was heavily damaged. Yet, he was determined not to let that stop him. After waiting for the cover of darkness he approached the ruined structure. He had barely begun to scramble across when a Czech border police patrol intercepted him and demanded to know what he was doing.

Thinking quickly, he replied he was coming across to bring his daughter a vest, which he happened to have with him and could show them. As he hoped, they assumed he was sneaking into Czechoslovakia. They gave him a kick in the pants and told him to turn around and get the hell out of the Republic!

After outwitting them, Caesar thanked the heavens and clambered the rest of the way across. The Austrian police apprehended him on the far side. Fortunately, they were sympathetic and let him go. The refugee was now only 70 kilometers shy of his destination, but he faced another problem—money! The final leg of the journey to Vienna would force him to beg or steal if he hoped to eat. However, one of the policemen generously lent the exile 50 reichsmark.

◆

During Maria's Schömitz visit, the Luksch family either wasn't aware of the events in house #10, or chose not to tell Maria. She didn't learn of it until 2010 when I showed her a copy of Caesar's memoir shortly after I obtained it from Oskar in Vienna. With her progressing dementia, I was not certain she still recalled her old neighbor, Caesar. At the time of her Schömitz visit, the prisoners were still in the Dukes House, and she'd have passed right by it.

As elsewhere, the local contingent of partisans consisted largely of unskilled laborers who relished the opportunity to exhibit their newfound importance. In addition to looting and torturing helpless prisoners, they displayed their authority and frightened the Germans by informing them of their loss of civil liberties through the Beneš decrees. Maria learned from the Luksch family that the bike she'd kept hidden from the looters was no longer legal for her to have. The decrees prohibited Germans from possessing and using wheeled conveyances without the consent of Czech authorities. The punishment for this offense, like all offenses, could be severe.

When my mother described her visit, I didn't think to ask when she learned Germans were banned from sidewalks, pavement, park benches, trains, taverns, restaurants, and movie theaters. Or barred from shopping, except during certain restricted times.[1] Perhaps she never learned of the latter because it meant little to Germans in small villages after looters stole their household money and the government confiscated their bank accounts. Those who still had a little money risked a beating or worse if they ventured out. And since practically all shops in communities such as Wolframitz were German owned, they'd been ransacked and destroyed. In cities, where stores and markets were the main source of food, ration cards were eventually issued for Germans, but they were denied meat, cheese, eggs, milk, or fruit.[2]

Maria needed no reminder that lingering in Schömitz was risky. At the end of the hurried visit, she told the Luksch family she'd try to return soon to retrieve a few practical items as well as a few mementos of her grandmother. She knew most of Rosina's possessions had disappeared into the hands of Karolina's tenants over the years, and that plunderers had rifled through what remained. Emma promised to gather and stash away what she could find. Maria was reluctant to leave, but her new awareness of the illegal bicycle made a hurried return to Wolframitz pressing.

As she mounted her bike, she spotted a man gazing at her from near the school. It gave her a fright until she recognized him as her father. She hadn't seen him in some time and hurriedly rode to meet him. Maria couldn't recall what they talked about, but it could be little else but the dire situation and the family's safety. She'd have learned Maria's teen sisters had fled to Germany with the last retreating German soldiers, and that there was no word of Eduard and Erich. In the final months of the war when Hitler's arrogance, delusions, and incompetence had destroyed most of what remained of the Third Reich's military capability, he armed ever-older men and younger boys as well as men previously exempted as medically unfit. Such an untrained force stood no chance against artillery, tanks, and overwhelming numbers of seasoned Allied combat troops, but that appeared to be irrelevant to Hitler and those around him.

In early 1945 Maria's brother Erich and some 20 other area teens received an induction notice. The boys had no option but to comply since the Gestapo and military police enforcers were more than willing to shoot or hang shirkers right alongside military deserters. The portrait of Erich that I obtained from his siblings shows him in a uniform he likely received at a regional supply depot only days before he shipped out. The uniform is a 1936 field service tunic rarely issued anymore in 1945. His *Schirmmütze* (visor service cap) was likewise seldom seen so late in the war.[3] Manufacturing capacity and materials for military clothing were in such short supply, even though the production of civilian clothing had ceased throughout the Reich in 1943, that the Wehrmacht was reduced to issuing obsolete or recycled uniforms from warehoused stores along with recycled boots.[4]

Some of the boys in Erich's group were probably Hitler Youth. In the final months many such boys were grouped into fighting units and sent into battle with little or no training. Near the close of the war even boys as young as 10, and sometimes girls too, manned weapons in defensive lines. In what was possibly Hitler's last public appearance, 10 days before his death, he honored Hitler Youth boys for heroism in the defense of Berlin. Some of them were very young.

Erich Hajek shortly before his disappearance near the end of World War II

Erich was 18 when he was inducted. He hadn't been tapped earlier because he was too small to meet even the relaxed military requirements. Either he grew substantially or the requirements were sufficiently lowered at this time to snare him. According to his siblings, he was a boy full of life, one who lived for pranks and mischief. Whenever anything was afoot in the village, he was likely to be at the center of it.

The induction notice Erich received trapped him in a game beyond his control. His brother Eduard had not been heard from in months, and Erich had no desire to become the second casualty in his family. He was so much younger than Maria that she never got to know him as well as Eduard. Nevertheless, she anguished over him and thought it criminal that a few men in Berlin should have the power to keep on sacrificing boys for a lost cause.

Volkssturm inductees being shown how to use Panzerfaust antitank weapon near end of war

◆

On the ride back to Wolframitz, Maria worried about being seen on her bicycle, so she stuck to back lanes and ditches. The beautiful tree-lined roads she loved so much were now avenues of fear. She even avoided passing through Gubschitz, where in normal times she'd have stopped to visit with relatives and friends. Fortunately, luck was with her and she arrived back at her residence without incident. As oppressive as that house she called home had become, she was relieved to reach it.

Despite the ever present danger on the village streets, Maria soon resumed working in the fields. Someone had to do it if the household expected to eat, she explained, so she shouldered most of the responsibility. Everyone knew neither the Czech partisans nor the Soviets were going to feed Germans. To avoid trouble she left the house very early each morning. When Maria returned from the fields one day, she learned the household Polish maid who'd disappeared the day the Russians arrived had returned and shoved open the furniture-barricaded door of the house. Germans were forbidden to lock their doors, but even if they wanted to risk defying the ban, they couldn't because locks no longer worked. Nearly every door had been kicked in, so there was no stopping someone determined to enter.

Like many of the young women who came to work as maids during the war, their maid chose to move in with Russian soldiers rather than return to Poland. To Maria's relief, she hadn't moved in next door with the violent men who raped and tossed out their neighbors. Had she done so, Maria would have lived in constant fear that the girl would send the savage soldiers over.

This girl of little education and intelligence was canny enough to understand a return to Poland meant supporting herself through hard menial labor. Here, she could do well without working, for the consorts of soldiers and partisans lived off German booty, food, and alcohol. Nearly anything she wanted or needed was available for the taking. Aurelia, who was too frightened to ever leave the house, made no effort to prevent the theft of Maria's bicycle and entire wardrobe the day the girl shoved her way inside. Because the maid knew most of the hiding places in the farmstead, she cleaned out nearly everything Maria had stashed away. Losing the bicycle was the biggest blow because Maria had saved so long to buy it. The girl couldn't ride it herself; she took it for the Russians. Maria grew even more disgusted with cowardly Aurelia for offering no resistance to this simple girl who'd once been her servant.

A couple of weeks after her first visit, Maria again set out for Schömitz early on a Sunday morning. After the loss of the bicycle she had to go by foot. Again, she skirted around Gubschitz by way of little-used back roads and ditches. Although the trip took much longer this time, she again encountered no partisans or Russians.

At the Luksch house Maria bundled up the few remaining possessions Emma had gathered for her. Among the items were several sheets and embroidered pillowcases. One of the pillowcases from her grandmother was really old. Another had been her mother's. Not only were these items family keepsakes, they were also practical. Emma had also found several of the Maria's Handiweit school sewing projects.

As before, the exchange of news was hurried. Maria wanted to stay longer, but every extra minute made the return more perilous. As she skulked back through fields and roadside ditches, she was again both angered and pained that she couldn't use the roads her ancestors had built—roads she used to find so tranquil and lovely on sunny spring mornings. Although my mother didn't say so directly, I think she suspected she'd never be back and that she'd just seen her childhood village and home for the last time. By this point, many Sudeten Germans realized the longstanding cooperative relationship with the Czechs was damaged beyond repair.

Back in Wolframitz, Maria hid her small bundle of items under the hay in the rafters of the cow stall. Neither she nor any of the village residents could have imagined they would be reduced to concealing sheets and pillowcases in a barn. And there was little sign the situation was easing, as in some parts of the Czech areas where Soviet combat units were pulling out. Those pullbacks were a mixed blessing for on their way eastward these troops looted and raped much as they'd done earlier when moving in the other direction.

Like the partisans and other Czech squatters, the Red Army stayed on in Wolframitz. The nights remained long and terrifying because these men never ceased drinking and prowling the streets. Eventually, many Germans resumed attending church early on Sunday morning when they found they had a short grace period. Maria sometimes went, but didn't socialize or linger afterward as in the old days. The Czechs claimed Sunday as their special day, which made it dangerous for a German to remain outdoors. No doubt the newcomers felt the town belonged to them now, and they intended to stay. At first, when most of the new arrivals were from nearby Czech villages and were drawn by plunder, the celebrating hadn't been so frightening. But the later arrivals from the Czech core region had a harder edge. The Sunday partying began with drinking. After consuming wine from the German cellars, a nationalistic fervor seized the celebrants, and they promenaded up and down the street in wild celebration of their "victory" over the Germans. The revelry lasted well into the night.

The only defense Germans had was to hunker down out of sight inside their houses and barricade their doors with as much heavy furniture as possible. A face at a window risked attack from the revelers, so people peered through the slits of closed shutters instead. They didn't want to be taken by surprise. Germans didn't dare turn a light on after dark lest it draw the attention of the vicious mob. To some of these frightened people it surely seemed the Czechs were celebrating less a victory than the acquisition of status and property.

Maria, like all the other Sudeten Germans I interviewed or read of over the years, could never understand where this sudden surge of vindictiveness came from. Of all the countries of Europe caught up in the war, the Czech state was least affected and damaged. Its cities were scarcely touched by bombs, and its men hadn't died on battlefields. Of course, many Czechs harbored a deep hatred of the Nazis for the crimes they committed and others felt humiliated by their own failure to oppose the German takeover, but the Czech populace directed its vindictiveness against ordinary Germans as well as Nazis. The Sudeten Germans I have talked to said that in the reverse situation, after Hitler's takeover, they hadn't exacted revenge on their Czech neighbors for the previous two decades of oppression by Czech politicians and their enforcers.

In Wolframitz, where relatively few Germans had actively supported the Nazi Party, Maria hadn't experienced any animosity from local Czechs during the war. Nor had she ever heard of any sabotage, defiance, or resistance by Czechs. The Czechs she came into daily contact with throughout the war—people she worked with side by side in the fields—were content to have a job and be safely out of the war. The only case of resentment she came across involved a young man she worked with who had a gripe against their mutual employer, Anton Stöffel.

What was hardest for her to fathom was how certain Czechs could turn against the friends and neighbors they'd known and respected for years. Maria recalled a particularly pleasant young man, Karl, from a nearby village. He worked for a neighbor named Pfeffer, so she spoke with him often. Karl and Pfeffer got along very well, yet Karl stole Pfeffer's farm at the first opportunity. In Schömitz, Maria's father had been the best of friends with a Czech neighbor, yet this man and his son greedily claimed three or four German houses.

For years Maria's seamstress cousin, Marie Luksch, made clothes for a Czech family living in one of the Meierhof apartments. Sometimes she also baked cakes for their celebrations and special occasions. At war's end the family members, led by the wife, boldly barged into the Luksch house while everyone was present, rifled through the family's possessions, and stole whatever they wanted. "You'll just lose it anyway," the woman told the family. The house that should have been Maria's was similarly ransacked. Because Karolina had always forbidden Maria to remove anything from the house, the last of her grandmother's cherished mementos—the items she intended to reclaim one day when she had a place of her own—disappeared. Maria was especially upset over the loss of the childhood gifts she'd received from her Vienna relatives and a set of irreplaceable dishes passed down for generations.

---

[1] Norman M. Naimark, *Fires of Hatred: Ethnic Cleansing in Twentieth-Century Europe* (Cambridge, Mass.: Harvard University Press, 2001), 119.

[2] MacDonogh, *After the Reich*, 131.

[3] Michael Pruitt, Personal communication.

[4] Grunberger, *The 12-Year Reich; a Social History of Nazi Germany, 1933-1945*, 210.

31 Schömitz Occupied

THE FINAL DAYS OF THE WAR brought worry and indecision to Schömitz and Wolframitz. The Hajek family told me the German Army built a small base on the high ground late in the war between Schömitz and Lodenitz to provide warning of approaching American and British bombers. The soldiers manning the post billeted in various houses within their village. Two soldiers, a lieutenant and an enlisted man, boarded with the Hajeks for the final three months of the war. On the first of May, the day after Hitler killed himself in his bunker, most of the soldiers left so they would have time to reach the American lines for surrender. Like all German soldiers, the last thing they wanted was to become prisoners of the Russians. As they packed, they urged the girls of the village to leave with them on their trucks. The two soldiers living in the Hajek house tried to convince Johann and Karolina of the danger their three teenage girls faced when the Red Army arrived, but the parents kept Regina, Angela, and Hedi with them.

As the last two soldiers were about to drive away four days later, a neighbor who'd come to the house was shocked to find the girls still there. "Why haven't your daughters left yet? Do you want the Russians to rape them?" he reproached the parents. His own daughters had left with the first group.

The warning finally got through to Karolina, so the girls hurriedly packed and climbed aboard the truck. The soldiers knew they might not make it all the way to Germany before the war ended, so they intended to head south into Austria and then drive west through Austria to avoid being caught in Czech territory. The family was frightened enough now that even large uncertainties like when, where, and how the family members would find each other again after the war looked preferable to risking rape by the Soviet occupiers. Years after hearing this story, I was surprised to learn from Oskar Halusa that his mother fled with the Hajek girls on the same truck. With her husband dead, her daughter and war-injured son Alfred already in Vienna, and Oskar and Siegfried still in uniform somewhere, she no longer had a reason to stay.

The truck left the village on May 5. After several hundred kilometers, the group approached Bavaria where Germany juts into the northwest corner of Austria. After crossing the border, the soldiers intended to await the Americans at a military barracks in Passau, so the girls got off in the countryside outside the city. I was unable to learn if Frau Halusa got off at the same place but suspect she didn't because Hedi, the only surviving sister at the time of the interview, told me when the soldiers drove away the three teens stood at the side of the road, bewildered and unsure where they should go or what they should do.

Eventually they sought help at a village Burgermeister's house. The woman of the house feared her husband would be shot by the occupation forces if she harbored these undocumented refugees, so she directed them to a nearby farmhouse. The second family, apparently braver, boarded the girls for three weeks in exchange for farm labor. After a second stint of two or three weeks at a different farm, the girls trudged on, lugging their heavy suitcases until they became exhausted. Eventually they were steered to an American-run refugee camp where a kind woman from Brünn took them under her wing. She persuaded the American soldiers who ran the camp to give the girls light jobs, which provided them a little money for necessities.

After several days in the displaced persons (DP) camp, who should happen by but their Johann Onkel, the carpenter with whom the girls' brother Erich had apprenticed. Like nearly all German men his age, Johann had until recently worn a German uniform. He'd been one of the extraordinarily fortunate ones who not only managed to end up in the American sector of Germany, but also to chuck his uniform and avoid detention in a POW compound. He'd found a temporary place to bunk across the border in Austria.

As was the practice throughout Germany at this time, the DP camp posted an occupant roster near the gate. Nearly everyone in the country routinely scanned such lists to locate missing friends and relatives. When Johann came across the names of his nieces, he asked to speak to them. The girls were overjoyed when a messenger located them and asked if they'd like to see their uncle at the gate. Johann would have taken them with him right then, but the camp was under a typhus quarantine, and they couldn't leave until the next day when the quarantine ended.

Johann somehow got word to the families of Julius and Alois, his comfortably established older brothers in Vienna. One owned a jewelry store, and the other worked as the store's diamond cutter. The girls headed to Vienna as soon as their relatives made travel arrangements for them. Oskar's mother, who also ended up at the same refugee camp, joined her sister in Vienna.

After the girls escaped with the soldiers, Johann and Karolina had only their youngest child, Ernst, with them as they awaited the coming of the Russians, camped only six kilometers away in Pohrlitz for the previous month. Everyone in the village was aware of their presence because like Maria and the residents of Wolframitz, they heard the artillery firing almost nightly. They knew the Soviets could have walked over at any time. They'd have encountered only a few German soldiers, men who wished to do little more than throw down their weapons and survive the war. The Russians would also have found another defense unit even less determined to resist—the older men the Nazis had commandeered into an untrained force called the Volkssturm (People's Storm).

◆

By the summer of 1944, the Nazi leaders knew they faced defeat. The Russians were closing in on Germany from the east while the Americans and British were advancing through Italy from the south and France from the west. The attempt on the führer's life by military officers and government officials in July 1944 at Hitler's East Prussian Wolf's Lair field headquarters amplified their fear. Even as early as 1942, many army officers had believed Hitler was leading the country to disaster, but not enough of them were willing to step up and remove him. The failure of the Wolf's Lair assassination plot culminated in the execution of nearly 5,000 Germans by the Gestapo. The attempt failed because a Hitler aide inadvertently shoved the briefcase containing the bomb behind a heavy conference table leg with his foot. The table shielded Hitler from the worst of the blast.

This attempt, the most serious of more than 40 plots against Hitler, left the führer shaken. His health, both physical and mental, was already in rapid decline, but the bomb heightened his paranoia. Not only did he now lose all trust in his military staff, he also began to blame his long-suffering fighting men for letting him down and ruining his grand plans.

To slow the attackers closing in on Germany in 1944, Hitler ordered Martin Bormann to come up with six million new recruits. Even after tapping men who'd previously been classified unfit for military service or held critical jobs once considered protected, he met only a small part of the quota. In desperation, the Nazis dusted off a vague 20-year-old plan to raise a people's home guard called the Volksturm, and filled its ranks by conscripting those males between the age of 16 and 60 not already serving in some military capacity.

The shortage of time and resources assured that training was minimal or nonexistent. Fanaticism was to furnish what the new militia lacked in numbers and preparation. The bulk of the recruits came from the Hitler Youth. Because these boys had been indoctrinated since their early school years, many were idealistic enough to be fanatical. Tens of thousands of inexperienced boys were needlessly sacrificed when pitted against overwhelming numbers of battle-hardened, well-equipped Allied troops in the hopeless cause.

Near the end of the war, Reichsführer Heinrich Himmler collected many additional titles because of the ever-diminishing list of lieutenants Hitler still trusted. Intelligence, police, interior ministry, army armaments, V-rocket production, and concentration camp labor were just some of the departments Himmler took over. In October 1944, after assuming Volkssturm command, Himmler announced the plan to the German public in a radio broadcast. To evoke memories of the Landwehr and Landsturm reserve armies that liberated Germany from Napoleon in 1813, a background chorus in the studio sang the folksong "Volk ans Gewehr" ("People to Arms") as he spoke. His speech also alluded to resistance by a behind-the-lines Werewolf organization in parts of the Reich already occupied by the Allies.

Many Volkssturm units put 16- and 17-year-old Hitler Youth leaders in charge because the older men showed little enthusiasm for this new service. Sometimes teenage boys were in command of their fathers, uncles, or teachers. Real military uniforms and modern weapons were in short supply here and throughout the Reich, so in their stead Himmler issued black and red **DEUTSCHE WEHRMACHT** armbands and old weapons to the new conscripts. Schömitz didn't have a Hitler Youth chapter, so older men filled the Volkssturm ranks. Because of this new militia, Erich wasn't the last Hajek called up for military service. After Himmler's announcement, his father Johann and other older men in Schömitz were conscripted into the defense force. Johann was tapped to lead the village contingent because of his World War I military experience. The Volkssturm in Schömitz never had the slightest capacity or intent to offer resistance.

In addition to general defense, in the last month of the war Johann's men were ordered to help man an observation post at the army's small base on the high ground outside Schömitz. Their job was to look east toward Pohrlitz and report what the Red Army encamped there was up to. This was just more foolishness because the German Army was disintegrating and it made little difference what the Russians were doing. Whoever Johann reported to would be unable to do anything.

Fritz Haas, Karolina's brother and the owner of the house her family occupied, was in the Volkssturm too. Fritz was assigned to help man an antiaircraft flak gun in Lodenitz. His pronounced limp had exempted him from regular military service. With her distaste for the man evident, Maria said that she wasn't the only one who disliked Fritz's company. During the war years her sisters had to put up with him because he showed up at their house most days for lunch. One small compensation was that he sometimes brought melons grown at the Meierhof.

Days before the German surrender, Russian artillery destroyed both the Schömitz observation post and the Lodenitz flak battery. The barrage raised fear in the village, but no attack followed. The action was largely a token gesture because both the German military and the Volkssturm had already abandoned the sites. Without a doubt, before the Red Army arrived the Volkssturm men burned their armbands and "lost" whatever weapons they might have had.

◆

In the postwar occupation, tiny Schömitz was luckier than Wolframitz in one regard—its Red Army occupiers were not fierce combat soldiers. They specialized in communications. The Russian arrival was anticlimactic when compared to what went on in Wolframitz. Nevertheless, the residents feared the soldiers and were wary. Many women and the few girls who'd stayed behind hid during the first days. One farmer with a large cellar accommodated a group of them.

Like their comrades elsewhere, these occupiers too drank, stole, and destroyed, but the worst offenders in Schömitz were the Czechs who followed the Russians into town. Czech workers from the Meierhof had first crack at relieving the people of whatever money, jewelry, china, silver, bicycles, furniture, and food the soldiers hadn't taken. Not far behind the workers were looters from the nearby Czech villages. If Germans didn't voluntarily turn over their possessions, the freebooters took them forcibly. The arriving Czechs already knew looting was condoned.

Johann Caesar and the other men the partisans locked up and tortured weren't the only victims of violence. A group of partisans, or perhaps Russians, went after Paul Judex, one of the local large farm owners. After beating Judex severely, his captors forced him to run across a Meierhof field like a game animal while they shot at him. A bullet finally dropped him at the edge of a thicket. As he lay bleeding in the dirt, one of the men strode up and put a bullet through his head. Witnesses were uncertain if partisans or Russians were responsible because their uniforms looked alike from a distance. The incident severely frightened Johann and other men of the village for they knew the same could easily happen to them. Also killed was a woman, Agathe Titz. A Russian officer took away another woman, Zitta Predschly and her two children. None of them were ever heard from again.

Ernst Hajek, Eduard and Erich's younger brother, was a schoolboy at the time and remembered the soldiers well. He described them as surprisingly small men, not much taller than the rifles they carried. The villagers had little choice but to act friendly. For three weeks several of the soldiers showed up each morning at the Hajek house for a breakfast of oatmeal.

Ernst had lots of free time after the Russians arrived because school had been suspended. Instruction would have been impossible under such chaotic conditions even if Lehrer Mauer and his wife hadn't already fled to Vienna. For a boy, hanging around these foreign soldiers was exciting. Ernst soon learned they'd pay him with food to take home if he helped with small chores and assisted with their horses. Of course, the food had been stolen from other Germans, but it was food his family could use. Sometimes the soldiers also let him ride their stolen German horses. He particularly remembered accompanying the men to eat cherries from trees along the road to Lodenitz. No fruit was forbidden in such company.

◆

Several weeks into the occupation, Johann and many other village men were arrested because of their Volkssturm service and locked up in Znaim, the district administrative capital. This city where Gregor Mendel once taught had had a German majority until Beneš resettled Czechs there. The Nazis restored the balance by moving Czechs elsewhere, but after the war many Czechs returned and the city became an especially dangerous place for Germans. Many German civilians in the city were murdered. Others chose suicide rather than face the abuse their fellow residents endured.

The military barracks that once housed Johann's Austrian Army Regiment, as well as work camps where the Nazis had mistreated Jews, now became prisons for Germans. Some men from Wolframitz ended up here, where the sadistic Czech guards were fond of beating and torture. German men and women, packed into the camp buildings, endured harsh conditions and labored in work details. They lived on starvation rations and the guards abused them daily. As elsewhere, rape of German women was common and some females were even sold to Soviet soldiers by Czech guards for gasoline. Prisoners forced to spend the winter there suffered tremendously. Deaths were common.

Znaim also had a POW camp that held over 3,000 German soldiers. These men were mercilessly beaten and tortured. Many of the injured died or were executed. New prisoners were greeted with 120 to 180 whiplashes each. Thereafter, they were routinely beaten, maltreated, and sent out on labor details. SS, SA, and party members were beaten three times a day.[1]

After Johann's arrest, Karolina became too frightened to stay in her own house. Her dog barked almost constantly at night because of the many drunk Czechs and Russians prowling around. With Ernst in tow, she knocked on the Luksch door and begged the family to let her stay with them. She'd treated them and Maria shabbily for years, yet the family took her in. I would guess their kindness was more for the sake of the boy than the mother.

Johann was fortunate to be released from Znaim after only three weeks. Short as it was, the experience was more than enough for him. He'd learned what the capricious partisans were capable of and knew worse could easily follow. Two days after he came home the Hajeks, along with others from the village, fled across the Austrian border at night and walked to Vienna. There, Karolina's brother Julius took the family in. On arriving they were astonished and much relieved to learn that their three girls had recently arrived in Vienna from Bavaria and were with the family of Karolina's other brother, Alois. Alois had been in uniform and survived the war, but had yet to return home.

The Hajek family resided in Austria for nearly a year and spent their final months there near the town of Hollabrunn. By Allied agreement a large segment of Austria fell under Russian occupation, but most Germans there were not subjected to the same vicious treatment as were the Germans in the Sudetenland. The Hajek family saw this for themselves while staying in a house they and a few other Germans shared with several Russian women. The latter constantly stole from the Germans. Finally, an Austrian woman became angry enough to complain to a Russian officer. The officer stormed into the room the Russian women occupied and shouted something that caused them to practically fly out of the house. Unfortunately, none of the Germans understood Russian and didn't know what he'd threatened the thieving women with. In April 1946 the Hajek family packed up and moved to Germany.

◆

Oswald Lustig was one of the few men of his division who survived the fighting on the Eastern Front. At the end of the war, he trudged 350 kilometers with an open wound to get back to Germany. After he crossed the border, he became one of 45,000 men interned in a huge American POW camp on the German-Austrian border near Regensburg and Passau. A German-speaking American Jew forced him and the other prisoners to march four abreast as if on parade. With them were some young Italians who'd joined the SS. When one of these men stumbled out of the formation because he was weak and injured, an American hit him hard in the side. Oswald, also in poor condition, was struck as well, causing him to double over. Since he was now unable to walk, soldiers carried him into the camp enclosure. There, prisoners lived in depressions dug into the ground. He was dumped into one of these holes. He overheard someone say he was to be left there to die, but he defied the odds.

POW enclosure holding 116,000 men at Sinzig, Germany, on May 12, 1945. Oswald's camp was similar to this one.

The camp was nothing more than a wire-enclosed open field where prisoners slept on the ground, exposed to the elements. The hot summer weather made existence miserable. Groups of 12 men shared an inadequate portion of bread and water each day.

Under the harsh conditions, many prisoners became very sick and a substantial number died of typhus and other illnesses. About a dozen corpses were carried out each day. Oswald attributed his survival to resisting the overpowering urge to drink water from the contaminated mud puddles despite his extreme thirst. After two months, he heard that ethnic Germans were being released earlier than German nationals, so he told the authorities he was an Austrian from Linz. Oswald was given papers in four languages, English, French, Russian, and German, documenting his release.

He was finally released on August 8, three months after he'd been placed in the hole within the hellish open-air prison. His first and only thought was to check on his family in Gubschitz. He knew going back was dangerous because he'd been a German soldier and lacked any Czech identification. However, he thought he could pass as a Czech because he spoke Czech fluently. So he walked through Austria until he was south of his home. There, he sneaked across the border at a place where the guards made the rounds only every 15 minutes. He didn't use his release papers to avoid giving the guards an opportunity to arrest him.

A POW camp temporarily holding over 160,000 German POWs in 1945

Oswald found the situation in Gubschitz was not as terrible as he'd feared. The Russians had only abused one neighboring farmer. And no Czechs or Russians had yet ransacked his family's house, thanks to his father's good Czech friend, Franz Lang. Lang and the older Lustig had served together in the First World War on the Italian Front. Lustig had saved Lang's life and subsequently received a medal for bravery. Lang, who lived in Pohrlitz, never forgot his friend and visited the Lustig home each year.

Immediately after the German surrender, Lang had seen what other Czechs were doing to Germans and rushed to Gubschitz. To shield the family from looters, he moved in. But not long after Oswald returned, the partisans arrested Lang and took him away. Two days later they came back for Oswald's father and imprisoned him in Mährisch Kromau. From there they sent Herr Lustig on to Znaim and then to another camp. In that prison camp, which held boys as young as 14, the guards beat him and the other prisoners severely every day—often until the prisoners lost consciousness. The staff also tried prisoners and passed out sentences ranging from three to twelve years of hard labor. Oswald's father was sentenced to five years. The outcome of the process seemed to depend wholly on whether or not the partisan doling out the sentences liked the prisoner's looks. The trial and sentencing took less than five minutes.

Not long after the older Lustig's arrest, the partisans in Gubschitz returned in the middle of the night and gave Oswald, his sister, and their mother one hour to gather their documents and a few clothes. The trio was then taken to a rural Czech part of Moravia where they joined other Germans as slave laborers on Czech farms.

---

[1] Wilhelm Turnwald and Arbeitsgemeinschaft zur Wahrung Sudetendeutscher Interessen, *Dokumente zur Austreibung der Sudetendeutschen* (München: Selbstverlag der Arbeitsgemeinschaft zur Wahrung sudetendeutscher Interessen, 1951), report #369.

32 Oskar's Journey

AFTER THE AMBULANTENZUG UNIT dissolved on May 1, 1945, at Parchim in northern Germany, Oskar and several of his Ambulantenzug friends prepared themselves to head west toward the American lines, away from the advancing Russians. The men equipped themselves with backpacks crammed full of canned food but left all weapons behind. The roads were clogged with vehicles and equipment, so to make better time they headed across fields and that night slept in a barn near Neustadt. On May 3 the Americans arrived with huge bulldozers that shoved all vehicles and abandoned military hardware into the ditches so their own transport could pass. Because of all the armament and supplies the Americans brought, a rumor spread that they were going to fight the Russians. Of course, this turned out to be wishful thinking. At one point passing American soldiers gleefully held up hams and shouted, "Hitler is dead." For Oskar the dead meat taunt didn't sting; his war was over.

Oskar and his friends eventually joined a number of German soldiers already in the custody of the Americans. As the guards escorted Oskar's group westward, their lines fell in with endless other columns of German soldiers. After a night spent sleeping on the ground in the forest near a campfire, Oskar saw a black American soldier first steal a bracelet from the arm of a woman passing on the road and then frisk passing German soldiers for valuables. To save his confirmation watch, Oskar feigned answering nature's call in the woods. There, he tied the pocket watch to a string, fastened the other end to a trouser button, and lowered the watch down into a pant leg. The soldier, who by then had collected numerous wristwatches on both arms, didn't find the watch when he searched Oskar.

From the start, Oskar and the others had intended to slip away at some point, disguise themselves as civilians, and make their way home. Toward this end, they'd brought military road maps in addition to food. However, as the number of POWs around them grew, they abandoned this plan. Too many other German soldiers had already tried it and the Americans were dealing harshly with them. After two days of walking, the captive group, which now numbered 15,000, reached a delousing station at Lauenburg. Here, men missing limbs or in obvious need of medical attention were separated and taken to a hospital. The rest scraped shallow sleeping pits and settled in. Although rain fell during the night and turned the campsite into muck, the prisoners had to remain there and endure the miserable conditions for several days. Oskar was better off than many for he still had canned meat in his backpack.

On May 12 trucks arrived and transported the prisoners across the Elbe River to a complex near Munster in the Lüneburg Heath, where they were turned over to the British Army. The facility had been a large German military training area, so the early arrivals found bunks in the stables and barracks. However, when the prisoner population swelled to 60,000 to become one of the largest POW camps in Germany, the buildings could no longer accommodate everyone. As a relief measure, the British appropriated large tents from a nearby tent factory. Oskar was lucky enough to be assigned to the work party retrieving them and used the opportunity to grab a smaller tent designed for 10 men.

He spent the rest of his confinement in this tent, along with seven others. Initially the daily food ration consisted of a few biscuits and a small can of meat—a very meager diet. Soldiers are inventive in such situations. To make the rations more palatable the group used a few primitive tools to fashion some basic cooking equipment. Their handiwork was subsequently admired by the British guards.

Because the POWs had nothing to fill their time, they organized evening entertainment, religious services, and courses in English. In Russia Oskar had enjoyed carving various motifs on hazel branches with a pocketknife, so he did something similar here to kill time. He carved assorted designs on stout sticks he collected, inscribed the place and date, mounted T-handles, and produced several handsome souvenir walking staffs. One made it home with him despite all the difficulties he faced after his release.

After Oskar found several aluminum panels from one of the old barracks buildings, he fashioned small storage cases out of them. With a pair of plaster scissors, a pocketknife, a hammer, and a nail file, he fabricated a basic box. On the lid he engraved a mountain pasture scene, using a nail. As a finishing touch, he cut three Edelweiss-flower-shaped pieces out of the aluminum material, engraved them, and fastened the flowers to the lid with rivets of the same material. Then he made smaller cases for his shaving kit and a few other items that would stow neatly in the box. He acquired enough skill in making edelweiss flowers that his friends asked him to make some flowers for them too. By the time he was released, he'd finished three boxes and took them all with him when he left. One he presented to his sister Lotte. Another went to a cousin, and the third he kept for himself as a souvenir of his captivity.

Oskar was able to haul his handiwork with him because while procuring the tent he also scrounged several pieces of tent fabric. Like every German soldier, he carried a needle and thread, which he used to make a bag to stow his items. He also fashioned a pair of shorts from another piece. He was never bored in his confinement and didn't come down with the emotional distress soldiers called cabin fever. For many men, living without work and purpose brought on this psychological condition. One of the men in the tent ignored Oskar's advice to stay busy and spent most of his time staring at the ceiling, and as a result, went a little crazy.

After the tent factory excursion, Oskar left the camp only once during his stay. The occasion was another work detail to unload cans of gasoline from a railroad car. So many prisoners volunteered for these work parties to stem their boredom that another chance never arose. During Oskar's trip outside the camp, local farmers brought the prisoners a warm meal—a welcome respite from the tiresome and meager camp rations, which typically consisted of small portions of Kommissbrot (dark German bread baked from rye and wheat as army rations), potatoes, and corned beef. This menu was occasionally supplemented with a little butter, cheese, or other ingredients.

◆

About two months after the establishment of the camp, the administrators began a conditional release program to ease the German labor shortage and spare Britain the expense of having to feed and care for so many prisoners. On July 13, after filling out a form and undergoing a medical examination, Oskar and his comrades walked out of the camp, discharge papers in hand. A British military truck transported them to an area west of Hanover near the Dutch border to help harvest grain. The party consisted mainly of Austrians, men who couldn't return to their homeland because it was occupied by the Soviets. Oskar was assigned to work for a small farmer who treated him admirably.

The adequate food helped him regain some of the weight he'd lost in the first month. Particularly wonderful was eating honey on his bread for breakfast again. Relations with the locals were strained at first because the Austrian dialect is so different from the Low German spoken in that area, but once everyone adjusted, the Austrians became popular in the village. Not only did Oskar help with the grain harvest, he also learned how to harvest peat, a job possible only during the summer. Peat was cut into cubes with a spade and then stacked and dried for use as stove fuel or livestock bedding. The peat came from a beautiful heather tract. It seemed to offer a surface solid enough to drive over while in bloom, but, as Oskar discovered when he almost lost a horse and wagon in it one day, the solidity was deceptive.

Oskar had long worried about his family, and when he read newspaper accounts of the Sudetenland expulsion, his concern grew. The lack of letters made him wonder if his family members were even still alive. At first the outside world knew nothing of what was happening in the Sudetenland. Later, word leaked out that Czechs had seized all German property and required Germans to wear identifying armbands. Such monstrous behavior was almost beyond Oskar's comprehension. When he'd been home in March, a month before the Russians arrived, he'd seen no sign of Czech hostility.

Oskar knew that German newspapers and radio broadcasts couldn't criticize what was happening in the east because of the terrible things Germany had done under Hitler. Also, Germany had lost the war it started, and only the victors' views and moral judgments were allowed to be presented. The hatred displayed by Czechs and the other East Europeans was not open to condemnation. Yet, word of the terrible misdeeds occurring in the east gradually spread. Former soldiers like Oskar could only imagine their own fate had the Czechs, Poles, or Russians taken them. Only later did Oskar learn the extent of the unbelievable cruelties inflicted on Germans in the Sudetenland by Czech partisans and mobs.

The autumn weather was mild and the work tolerable, but the Austrians longed for their families and ached to go home. Oskar's situation was different from that of his comrades since he no longer had a home to return to. However, he did have many relatives in Vienna and Upper Austria who were Austrian nationals, so when most of the harvest work was complete in October, he said goodbye to his employer and left with the other Austrians. For their journey, the farmers loaded them up with food.

The first part of the trip was particularly difficult since few war-damaged rail lines heading south had yet been repaired. A few short passenger rail segments were operational, but the service was irregular and limited. Consequently, the trains were extremely crowded. Often, no space was available, so the group waited for trucks or trains heading in their direction and sneaked aboard. Usually this meant hiding in loads of dirty coal or coke. These rides were usually short because the American military police frequently checked transport vehicles and ejected stowaways. Then, after a night on the floor of a train station waiting room, the men would await another opportunity and do it all over again. On the train station walls they always scanned the many signs and messages posted by the legions of displaced refugees searching for their relatives or friends.

Eventually the group arrived in Passau, with Austria just across the border. There, on a railroad station wall, Oskar spotted the name of a Lodenitz farmer he knew. In the hope of learning something of his own family, he hurriedly took a train to this farmer's town, where the Lodenitz family told him his mother was in the Somme Barracks in Passau, the very city he'd just come from. These expellees also described the horrors of the expulsion and warned him not to return home for the Czechs would lock him up.

Oskar rushed back to Passau, but like the Hajek girls' Uncle Johann, discovered the Somme Barracks camp was under quarantine. Back at the train station Oskar now found a note left by his brother Siegfried, announcing he'd gone to stay with his uncle in Steyr (Upper Austria). It turned out that Siegfried had also had come here after his release from captivity and had tried unsuccessfully to collect their mother from the Passau camp.

When Oskar set out to join his brother in Austria, the border guards wouldn't let him pass. His discharge papers, which listed his home as the "Lower Danube Region," authorized entry only into the Russian Occupation Zone of Austria, not the American Zone. To remedy this he went to an American military administrative center to change his home address on the discharge certificate to Wels, Austria, the nearest rail station stop to his uncle's farm. The process took several days, but the papers cleared his entry into Upper Austria and earned him a free one-way rail ticket. Nine days after arrival in Passau, he finally stepped off the train in Wels. When he sought directions, an old man recognized his uncle's name and directed him to the farm. Those last few kilometers were again on foot, but Oskar didn't mind.

Although the front door of the house was ajar when he arrived, he knocked anyway. From within, a girl's voice called, "Come in." Inside, Oskar found Siegfried, his uncle and family, a cousin and her mother, and several other expellees from the homeland. The emotional welcome Oskar received was overwhelming and never forgotten.

33 Life Under the Knife

MEANWHILE BACK IN WOLFRAMITZ, the Germans continued to live in fear and terror. At the house next to Maria's, the daytime was usually quiet while the Russian soldiers slept off their hangovers and attended to their military duties, but nighttime was a different story. Every evening, as the drinking and rowdiness resumed, Maria's anxiety and fear spiked. Because of the dangerous soldiers next door, she and Aurelia stayed vigilant and out of sight. The Stöffel boy was too young to understand what was happening, and the girl was just a toddler, but both children picked up the women's fear and became subdued, as did all the village children. Because parents constantly feared for their children, they never let them out of their sight.

Maria never learned if the soldiers next door were always the same ones or whether different individuals came and went. Even more so than in the Nazi days, curiosity was dangerous. However, others told her at least some of the local cadre rotated to Vienna regularly. Fortunately for Maria, most of the Russians chose houses in Klein Seelowitz, the most prosperous of the clustered villages. Maria never saw any Russian civilians; all the occupiers were Mongolians in uniform.

Since the front door could no longer be locked, the two women kept a wooden wardrobe against the front door. That barrier wouldn't stop men determined to get in, so Maria slept fully clothed every night in case she had to run and hide. Maria's good friend Mina, who'd helped her bury supplies in the wine cellar in the war's closing days, also knew all about sleeping in her clothes. She spent weeks camped out in a cornfield when a partisan with a gun moved into her house. After taking a house, many partisans forced any attractive females living there to become their bed partners. Exceptionally attractive Mina was a magnet for such men.

Many women submitted because they were threatened with harm or were too frightened to say no. Often women had no choice because other family members were held hostage. Mina courageously spurned the partisan and refused to have anything to do with him. She was fortunate he didn't use his gun on her, but shortly after she rejected him a Russian soldier stalked her. She speculated the Czech had set him on her for revenge. As a result, Mina was in constant peril.

In Mina's home the soldier and his friends put a pistol to her father's chest and threatened to kill him if he didn't tell them where his daughter was. He insisted he didn't know. To protect Mina, he was prepared to sacrifice his own life. In the end they didn't kill him, probably at the behest of the resident partisan. Without his farmer slave, the Czech had no one to work the farm. After the incident with the soldiers, the father sometimes hid too. Although he was beyond the point where he feared for his own life, out of concern for his daughter he couldn't ignore the consequences of defiance.

Other men too tried to protect their women. Maria had heard somewhere that several men were so desperate to protect their wives and daughters from being gang-raped that they hid them in a cellar and bricked up the entrance.

◆

Most southern Moravian households had little food left following the war. Stocks were seasonally low after the winter, gardens were not yet producing, and pantries had been raided by the occupiers. Flour and other necessities were no longer attainable, either from shops or from neighbors. The people thrown out of their homes by the Russians and partisans were even worse off for they'd lost all reserves and now needed to rely on relatives and friends.

The looters stole not just valuables and food, but also ordinary household items like cooking pots and utensils—items important for survival. Germans had a hard time protecting anything when the thieves had the entire day to devote to theft. Many villagers had to leave their homes during daylight hours to work the fields or tend outlying gardens so they, or their new masters, could eat. Prior to the fall 1945 harvest, the partisans were not yet numerous enough to claim every farm, so some German farmers had still planted fields for themselves that year and harvested those crops despite the danger and difficulty.

Maria was one of the people who labored dutifully in the fields. She confessed that at first, like many others, she was in denial as to how serious Czechs were about taking everything, so she worked hard to make sure she and the children would have enough food to make it through the next winter. With nearly all men gone now, farming was more grueling than ever. As before, neighbors pitched in to aid each other when they could. Maria often assisted Mina in the fields, and Mina returned the favor. The two friends also helped each other milk the cows until the cows were taken away. The work in the fields was exhausting, but out there Maria and Mina felt more secure than in their homes.

Only after the harvest, when the crops were in the Hof storage bins, did the farmers who still had their land learn they'd been tricked into believing at least some of the crop would actually be theirs. At this time droves of new Czechs descended to snatch up the unclaimed land along with the harvest. That year's crop was the last the Moravian Sudeten German farmers ever planted in the belief it was their own. After 800 years of uninterrupted farming, the cycle ended. Because many of the new owners couldn't discern a plow from a hay rake and didn't intend to work the land themselves, German slave labor planted and harvested one more crop in 1946.

Through the early months of the occupation, farmers had held out hope of keeping their land because the livestock not stolen or devoured in the initial violence remained untouched. But after the 1945 harvest was complete, reality set in. At the Stöffel house, the partisans had helped themselves to the geese early on but left the two milk cows, so the children had milk. And the horses, probably because they were too large for the small Mongolians to handle, remained as well. Without the horses, harvesting wouldn't have been possible.

However, after the harvest the remaining livestock was collected and taken away. In the eastern part of the country the Czechs supplied the Russians with Germans to act as herdsmen to drive the assembled animals to the Soviet Union on foot. The herdsmen who survived often didn't return for months. Around Wolframitz, livestock met a different fate. Klein Seelowitz had a large flour mill, which the Russians decided to put to better use. With German labor, they converted the mill into a slaughterhouse and proceeded to butcher the large farm animals rounded up after the harvest. Many girls and women toiled in the slaughterhouse every day. Cutting up and packing all the meat was backbreaking, dirty work. The Russians shipped the meat to Vienna, and then presumably much of it journeyed on to the Soviet Union.

This enterprise may have been one reason most of the Russians and their sycophants chose to live in Klein Seelowitz. They, their Polish girlfriends, and the partisans ate well there. The slaughter meant the end of milk for German children. The eradication of livestock was so thorough that even Lucy, the Stöffel family's 20-year-old, much-loved, gentle pet of an old horse was seized one day and taken to the slaughterhouse. She'd been used only for light work or riding in her later years. Maria, the children, and Aurelia all cried.

◆

At the beginning of the occupation, Maria thought Aurelia would pitch in and share the work and risk. The mutual hardship and her reduced circumstances had put the two of them on a more equal footing. But Aurelia again shirked her responsibilities and refused to go outdoors, much less work in the fields. Her cowardice meant all outside chores and errands fell to Maria. At first Maria complied for the sake of the children. Later, she had no choice because after the harvest Aurelia became intimate with a Czech partisan fully 10 years younger than her. Aurelia regained some of her former status by willingly becoming this man's mistress when he moved in. Maria thought it detestable for a widowed mother of two small children to sully herself in that way.

The new domestic arrangement meant additional household duties for Maria, both in the morning and after she finished her exhausting farm labor each day. Aurelia's new status allowed her to forgo much of the modest amount of work she had actually been doing since the occupation began. For Maria it was like a return to the old days when she wasn't free to get on with her other duties, or on Sundays enjoy her day off, because Aurelia hadn't yet bathed the children or cooked breakfast. Maria did the extra work because she'd become attached to the children, especially the little boy. He wasn't hers, yet for all practical purposes, she'd raised him.

The work and injustice wasn't all that wore Maria down. The daily effort of finding enough to eat was also a trial. At times the resident partisan brought food for more than just himself, and Aurelia then cooked it for him to stay in his favor. However, this didn't happen often.

Maria was in a bizarre position because only she was able to talk to the man. Aurelia didn't understand a word of Czech, and the partisan didn't speak German. Their relationship worked solely because Aurelia was weak and pliable. Maria disliked eating at the same table with this pair every day, yet had no choice. At least the man treated the children decently. And his presence had one benefit—it bestowed a certain degree of protection from intruders, both Russian and Czech.

One day the partisan showed up with a pair of workhorses that could only have come from some other German farm. This was bad news for Maria. Not only did she now have to tend the animals daily, she also had to resume working with Anton Stöffel in the fields. The Czech was another of the "communists" with capitalist dreams of living large off the farm he intended to operate through the sweat of others.

◆

Some Czech partisans were crueler masters than others. Just up the street, the man who took over the house of Franz and Theresia Eisenstein, Oswald Lustig's grandparents, proved a demon. In his new position of authority, the former farm laborer made life for the previous owners a hell. He used the old couple as his slaves and allotted them a cramped storage room to live in. Outside of their duties, they weren't allowed in the main part of the house. If Theresia needed a bit of flour, sugar, or lard from her own cupboard, she had to ask permission. Whenever the Czech felt the urge, he beat Franz, a man in his seventies.

In February 1946 Franz and Theresia, like Maria, learned at an outdoor assembly that they were soon to be expelled. Because they didn't know where they'd end up or what would happen to them, they desperately longed to see the family one last time. Somehow they learned where Oswald, his sister, and their mother worked as field slaves and got a message to them requesting them to come to Wolframitz. It wasn't practical for all three to go, but the Czech farmer for whom Oswald worked was a reasonable man and loaned Oswald his bicycle for the journey to Wolframitz. The trip was risky for Oswald, but he removed his identifying armband and set out.

At his grandparents' house, his home for years while a schoolboy, Oswald knocked and asked to enter. The new owner refused to allow him in. Instead, he fetched the old couple, shoved them outside, and slammed the door. As the three talked, Oswald's grandfather slipped his Sunday shoes from beneath his jacket and asked Oswald to take them out of the country when he was expelled. Franz knew the Czech wouldn't allow him to keep the shoes if he learned of them. They were just shoes, but apparently they represented the only meaningful possession the old man had left.

At this point the Czech flung open the door and ripped the shoes from the old man's hands. He'd had his ear to the door the whole time. After flinging the shoes down in front of Theresia, who'd begun to cry, he cursed in German and shouted, "Didn't you know everything belongs to me now?" He ended his tirade by striking the old man.

Before Oswald could react, a second Czech approached. Now both men berated Oswald for daring to come to Wolframitz. Their threats tipped Oswald off that they intended to steal the bicycle and send him to the prison camp in Mährisch Kromau. Oswald's Czech fluency saved him. The men backed off because he convinced them that they themselves would go to jail if they stole a Czech's bicycle. As he rode away, the pair shouted curses at both him and the farmer who'd loaned him the bike.[1]

◆

Oswald had been lucky to make it all the way back to Moravia from Germany without Czech identification papers after his release from the American POW camp in August 1945. If caught, he'd have joined the unfortunate German military captives unable to reach the American lines at war's end. As harsh as his American internment had been, under the Czechs and Soviet his experience would have been much worse. Maria learned of the gruesome torture of two such soldiers from friends living near the police station. Her friends heard the pitiable cries of these men when Czechs ripped their teeth out with pliers.

After the war's end, Maria saw many emaciated and ragged German soldiers destined for a POW camp in Mährisch Kromau as they were herded through Wolframitz. Toward the end of 1945, she would have occasion to see for herself what the partisans, police, and Czech soldiers did to the men at this camp. Many prisoners could be seen on the streets of the town daily as guards delivered them to their labor details. Their haggard, beaten faces betrayed their lost hope. She found it hard to contain the pity she felt for these humiliated men, but neither she nor any other German could help them. These prisoners were not meant to survive their ordeal. Those who didn't die through torture and beatings were starved and worked to death. Maria's loathing of the "brave partisans" who hadn't lifted a finger in resistance during the entire six years of German control, but now mistreated helpless soldiers, stayed with her for the rest of her life.

At first the German population expected the anarchy to subside and the beatings, rapes, and thieving to taper off. But the optimism dissipated as the lawlessness and violence continued. From Maria's perspective, the Russian soldiers doled out most of the terror and viciousness in the beginning, but the partisans asserted themselves and eventually surpassed the Russians in cruelty. For Maria, one particular event early in the occupation cemented this perception.

After the opening spasm of violence, if any Wolframitz Germans still wondered what more the occupiers could do to them, they didn't have to wait long to find out. On May 12 a town crier strode through the streets shouting out a message as he beat the small drum suspended from his neck. Because neither the new Gemeindediener nor his message was German, most Germans had to ask others what he was saying. The message raised enormous anxiety and fear. All Germans were ordered to assemble in the Marktplatz. The captive audience of women, children, and old men with the N-emblazoned white armbands gathered at the appointed time. Throughout living memory, the small Marktplatz in Wolframitz had been the site of markets, festivals, holidays, and weddings—a place of commerce, celebration, and laughter. The Czech partisans clearly intended to turn it into something else, and the crowd of several hundred dreaded what this might be as they were herded into a large semicircle facing the wall of a building called the Doktorhaus.

The strutting unskilled laborers who called themselves partisans were eager to demonstrate that they, not the armed Soviet soldiers looking on, were in charge. They began by haranguing the captive audience with communist and antifascist slogans in Czech. Few in the frightened crowd understood what they were shouting. Under different circumstances, the performance might have been comical. But not today. The assembled crowd feared what was to come. When the preliminaries ended and audience anxiety ran high, the partisans ordered all eyes to the front. Those of young children too. The crowd then quickly figured out someone was about to be severely punished.

The assembled Germans knew that the people truly deserving punishment had long since fled to Germany or Austria, so they had reason to fear. No one yet knew how the partisans made decisions or who amongst them was in charge. They did recognize that under mob rule, revenge and retribution replaced law, trials, evidence, and defense arguments. Anyone dragged to the center of the semicircle was certain to be in deep trouble. Their suspicions were confirmed when they learned they were about to witness an execution. They felt it was bad enough that adults were forced to watch such a brutal spectacle, but to inflict such a thing on innocent children was unconscionable.

Maria expected to recognize whoever the partisans chose for punishment but was shocked to find it was her close neighbor, Gustav Smrczek, who was led out from the entrance of the city hall and placed against the wall. Gustav, a city official in his fifties, lived one house away from Maria. She learned later that his Polish maid, a girl who'd found herself a Soviet boyfriend right after the Red Army's arrival, was responsible. When the partisans had driven a loudspeaker-equipped vehicle through the village and announced all firearms were to be turned in, she saw a chance to impress her new boyfriend by denouncing her employer. Smrczek had an antique, silver-plated, nonfunctioning pistol—a gift from one of his sons—in his house. Maria knew all three of his sons, particularly the two closest to her own age, Rheinhold and Schintzy. Schintzy and the youngest boy, Alfred, had died in the war. Gustav either forgot about the pistol or, in keeping it as a cherished reminder of his son, assumed the Czech fanatics would realize it wasn't a real weapon.

As the Czechs escorted Gustav to his execution, his wife Julia ran out from among the spectators, held her husband, and shouted to the executioners, "If you are going to shoot him, I want to die with him." Maria knew Julia was already despondent over the loss of her sons, and if she lost her husband too, she'd have little left to live for. The partisans obliged Julia and lined her up in front of the wall next to Gustav.

Several Czechs fired at the couple with their machine pistols. Maria said they targeted Gustav first, and Julia had a screaming spasm before her turn came. Oswald Lustig heard the victims were shot at the same time and fell together. Julia died before she hit the ground, but because Gustav still moved, a Czech partisan walked up, put his gun to Gustav's head, and pulled the trigger. Gustav's head bounced once before it came to rest.

Seeing their neighbors die so gruesomely with a shower of tissue and blood made the onlookers cry and shriek. The sickening spectacle distressed my mother enough that she still found it difficult to talk about half a century later. She'd worked hard to erase it from consciousness and didn't want to give it new life.

When the crowd was sent home, several old German men were ordered to stuff the bodies into burlap sacks and cart them off. Maria never learned where the remains ended up because curiosity was dangerous. A safe guess would be an unmarked grave in a field outside of town.

The partisans had turned into the very monsters they pretended to have resisted and defeated. They proclaimed themselves communists, but became the new Nazis in all but name. All they lacked was a fancy Nazi uniform, but not for want of trying. Many resorted to wearing parts of old German uniforms, most commonly those of Germany's Afrika Korps from early in the war. The villagers could have been forgiven for thinking these men would have felt right at home in black Gestapo uniforms, even though there was a difference in how the two groups operated. The Gestapo preferred working in the shadows whereas the partisans relished the limelight and public blood sport.

◆

Fortunately, not everyone arrested by the partisans and the Czech police could be shot in the head without repercussions. Beneš knew the deaths of too many Germans would in time evoke censure in the western press, so he dealt with them in other ways. Locking them up was one way. Most Germans arrested in Wolframitz and Schömitz were initially taken to Mährisch Kromau. In addition to a POW lockup, that town also had a prison camp for women and another for men not in uniform. Maria discovered that Geidl, the first farmer she worked for, was sent there. She never learned if he'd been charged with anything; as far as she knew he hadn't been a Nazi.

As in camps throughout Czechoslovakia, in Mährisch Kromau men were beaten, abused, and forced to work hard on starvation rations. In many camps a popular pastime for the guards was to force two facing rows of men to strike each other until bloody. Several Wolframitz men were known to have perished in Mährisch Kromau camps from abuse and torture. At least one was shot, but I am uncertain whether or not he was one of 11 area German men that Oswald reported were executed in the Schlosspark (castle park) on June 2, 1945 after being forced to dig their own graves.[2] Had I been aware of this incident the day I enjoyed a bit of sunshine in this park in 2010, I'm sure it would have caused some reflection.

German soldiers who survived their initial encounter with the partisans and Red Army in the vicinity of Wolframitz were taken to the POW camp in Mährisch Kromau. The best these men could hope for was a quick death. Most endured prolonged torture, beatings, abusive labor details, and starvation before they died or were sent elsewhere.

Prisons run by criminals and sadists existed throughout the country. Many survivor accounts detail the unimaginable brutality inflicted on POWs. They were shot, beaten, and tortured everywhere. In Prague, where 50,000 wounded German soldiers were hospitalized, partisans and civilian mobs invaded hospital trains and wards, robbed the patients, and ripped off bandages to inflict more pain when they delivered blows to open wounds and amputated stumps. Mobs threw many patients out of upper floor windows. In the streets crowds attacked unarmed prisoners with hammers, pipes, clubs, and whatever was at hand. Many soldiers in Prague were roasted alive over bonfires as they hung suspended upside down from lamp posts. Such human torches greeted President Beneš in his triumphant return to Prague.

This is not to say civilians, even children, were treated kindlier. In many camps and prisons, Czechs could walk in off the street and deliver a slow and painful death to a German of their choice. In Prague's Pankrác prison, where the Nazis had committed their own share of crimes, visiting Russians received a special treat—they got to watch a German being flogged to death.[3] In the years following the war, thousands of reports detailing the inhuman cruelties inflicted on Germans during this period were filed by survivors and still exist in German archives. A small portion of these reports were published in the 1950s.[4,5]

◆

Late in her life, Maria revealed she'd learned about the Mährisch Kromau POW camp some months into the occupation when she was herself arrested and taken to the women's prison camp by horse cart. Maria was never informed of the charges against her, but she was certain she was sent there for the same reason most of her fellow inmates were. In her case someone with a score to settle had lied to the partisans and told them she was a Nazi sympathizer.

She knew but one individual who held a grudge against her. During the war, Anton Stöffel had somehow wronged a young Czech Maria knew slightly. This man subsequently initiated legal proceedings against Stöffel. Maria couldn't remember what the case had been about and probably hadn't even fully understood it at the time. She'd been dragged into the Vienna court proceedings because Stöffel's two Czech ex-wives refused to get involved, and Maria was the only Czech-speaking person in the extended household. At the time, it gave her a chance to see her Vienna relatives. Stöffel assumed she'd testify favorably for him, so when he lost the case, he angrily blamed Maria for failing to provide him the proper testimony. She'd done nothing more than answer truthfully, but in Stöffel's mind she'd sided with the Czech.

During the occupation, Stöffel was arrested when the same Czech again filed a complaint. Maria was convinced that, being the vindictive person he was, Stöffel sniffed an opportunity to win his dismissal and get some revenge in the bargain. She had no proof, but in her mind the suspicious circumstance of his release at the time of her own arrest was too much of a coincidence.

On arrival in Mährisch Kromau, Maria found most of the town lay in ruins for on the final night of the war it had been bombed by Soviet planes.[6] The cart dropped Maria off at a former military camp where about a hundred other women from all over the district were imprisoned. In many camps, guards routinely and repeatedly raped women prisoners or sold access to them. Maria didn't say how much of this activity she found in her camp. The living quarters were filthy old barracks, overrun with fleas. The fleas, meager rations, and crude conditions made life there grim, but much worse than the living conditions was the proximity to a large, old leather factory converted into a torture center for German POWs. Every day she saw these poor soldiers with their hollow cheeks, sunken eyes, and vacant expressions, standing inside the fence. They were skin and bone. Yet, it was what took place out of sight inside the building that made her camp most unbearable. She couldn't block out the agonized screams of the men being beaten and tortured night and day.

Maria bonded with another prisoner during her confinement, a Czech woman about her own age with two children at home. Like most other inmates there, she had been anonymously accused of aiding the Nazis. Maria believed her new friend when she denied any collaboration. The two of them were together for several weeks before the woman was released.

Each morning, the guards assigned the inmates to a labor detail and delivered them to the work site. Escape was impossible. Prisoners had nowhere to hide and no one to turn to for help, since all Germans in the country were captives in one way or another. Maria was lucky in her assignments. Much of the time she drew household duty rather than street repair or ditch digging. She said her Czech fluency was probably the reason. The job required interaction with Czechs. Through most of her imprisonment she worked for a white-collar communist family that enjoyed privileges denied ordinary Czechs. Not only did these people have access to better food and household goods, they also enjoyed a nice, new bourgeoisie house liberated from a German family. The maid service was one way the privileged of the new classless society could enjoy a bit more comfort than ordinary workers.

The family treated Maria decently enough and gave her some food, although not as much as she'd have liked. In the course of her assignment, the couple's married daughter, husband, and grandchild decided they too wanted to enjoy the same lifestyle, so they moved in. Like the older couple, they brought with them many nice possessions they'd recently acquired. The daughter had no homemaking skills and was lazy, like Aurelia. This woman didn't know how to cook and "couldn't even darn socks," so Maria had to tend to her needs as well.

Just as mysteriously as Maria had been arrested, she was released two or three months later. However, she wasn't allowed to go anywhere but back to Wolframitz and the unpleasant domestic situation there. She was happy to see the children again, but residing in the same house as Aurelia and her boyfriend was every bit as grating as before, and the frightening Russians still lived next door. She was also distressed to once again live near Anton Stöffel, the man she was convinced had concocted the lies that sent her to the prison camp.

Recalling the camp ordeal was understandably stressful for my mother so I didn't press her for more details. However, not long after our chat I discovered why she hadn't disclosed her imprisonment sooner. She knew doing so could lay bare the secret she'd so carefully guarded throughout her adult life because of the unbearable shame she believed it carried.

---

[1] Oswald Lustig, Personal Communication.
[2] Oswald Lustig, Personal Communication.
[3] MacDonogh, *After the Reich*, 137.
[4] Arbeitsgemeinschaft zur Wahrung Sudetendeutscher Interessen and Wilhelm Turnwald, *Documents on the Expulsion of the Sudeten Germans* (Munich: University Press, 1953).
[5] Theodor Schieder, Germany (West), and Flüchtlinge und Kriegsgeschädigte Bundesministerium für Vertriebene, *Documents on the Expulsion of the Germans from Eastern-Central-Europe, Vol. IV* (Bonn: Federal Ministry for Expellees, Refugees and War Victims, 1958).
[6] Wikipedia contributors. "Moravský Krumlov," *Wikipedia*, Wikipedia.org, 26 Feb. 2015, accessed 21 Apr. 2015.

34 The Secret

MARIA'S FAILURE TO REVEAL the hellish arrest and prison camp experience earlier both astonished and puzzled me. At first I believed she'd kept it to herself because it was another of those painful experiences she didn't wish to revive for fear it would leave her with distressing intrusive thoughts and keep her up at night. But then some new information dovetailed with other parts of her story and made me realize she'd had a completely different and more compelling reason for holding it back.

Maria's memory was already spotty when I learned of her experience, and she could no longer recall just when the imprisonment occurred or when she was expelled from Czechoslovakia. But from records and sources collected during a trip to Germany, combined with what I already knew, I figured out the approximate date of her expulsion. The key was the date of her release from the Mährisch Kromau prison camp, which I found in a yellowed and flimsy Czech document Maria had among her possessions. Examination and translation of this paper also provided further insight into other traumatic events she had kept to herself over the years—events that comprised the secret she thought she'd successfully hidden since 1946.

Unbeknownst to Maria, I'd already learned a portion of this secret years before. Once I recognized how her imprisonment and her secret were connected, I could comprehend why she'd kept the incarceration in Mährisch Kromau to herself. I would like to think I'm not betraying a trust in writing about this since, like most other women of her generation in the same situation, she only buried this part of her past because it provoked deep shame. I am talking about rape. A number of German victims of Russian rapists during and after the war wrote about their experiences anonymously, but it wasn't until 2010 that a German woman broke the taboo and publicly identified herself as a victim. In a news interview she spoke openly about the assaults and how they damaged her life. Psychologists call the experience of women such as her and Maria a "double trauma" because aside from the act of violence itself, they have to keep it hidden.[1] Lamentably, Maria passed on without accepting the notion that most people who heard her story would not attach shame to her.

I learned a little about what had happened to Maria 40 years after the fact in Germany because my father thought someone besides himself should know before he died. He was convinced Maria would never reveal it herself. The occasion was a family visit to Bavaria and the village my parents lived in after the war. While there, my father discreetly took my sister, my wife, and me to a tightly packed parish cemetery in the nearby town of Teisendorf. Next to a masonry wall near the back of the cemetery, in a section reserved for infants, my father pointed to a small, plain stone marking the grave of Renate Hajek. She was born in 1946 and died later the same year.

"She's your sister," Fidel told us. We were stunned. None of us wrote down the details from the tombstone or even took a photo. It was one of those solemn, inviolable occasions when doing something like that seemed crass. When I revisited the cemetery years later, the remains and the stone had been removed as is customary in many space-constrained cemeteries in Europe. But through parish and government records, I learned Renate lived a mere six months and 23 days.

My sister and I were even more shocked when our father told us Renate was the result of a rape by Czechs in Czechoslovakia at the end of the war. Of course, I regret not having asked more questions then, but my father was clearly uncomfortable talking about it, and the subject appeared too sensitive and taboo to delve into any deeper at the time. Having just the sketch, as opposed to the detailed painting, seemed adequate at the time. My sister and I walked away knowing we too now had a secret to keep—one demanding a pretense of ignorance in conversations with our mother. I assumed that someday, under the right circumstances, I'd bring up the subject with her or she'd raise it herself.

Neither happened in the next two decades even though I presented Maria repeated opportunities to talk about the ordeal. Eventually I concluded she wasn't going to disclose anything about it voluntarily. By then, I could no longer bear to confess how long I'd already known, and I didn't want her angry with my father for divulging her secret. Then several years after my father died, Maria surprised me one day by saying she'd held something back. It was written down and tucked it away to be found after she died, she said. This made me even more reluctant to disclose that I already knew what it was.

Later, with Maria's memory in evident decline, I knew I had to finally broach the delicate subject. When I explained how I'd learned of Renate, her reaction was more subdued than I expected. While the rape obviously still persisted as a source of humiliation and sadness, the dementia had blunted her emotions as well as her memory.

♦

Because of the distress of the original trauma, the passage of over 60 years, and her advancing dementia, I knew my mother's story would have gaps. When she began to tell me what happened, I realized that, as with the death of her fiancé, her innermost feelings were too private to bare.

Not long after Maria told me her story, her health problems necessitated a move to an assisted living facility and then later a nursing home. With no hope she'd ever return to her house, I helped pare down her possessions and ready her house for sale. Because twice in her life she'd lost nearly everything she owned and held dear, she'd found it difficult to throw things away, particularly in her later years. So, sorting through her belongings to find the written revelation she said she'd left was no small task. Stashed throughout the house were old letters, notes, greeting cards, recipes, and not surprisingly, bedding. I carefully sifted through everything but failed to find the note she had claimed to have left. By then she no longer had any recollection of leaving a note. Over the next year I gently brought up the subject of Renate, the camp, and assault a couple more times in the hope she'd remember other details, but those memories were now irretrievably lost.

For Maria, the occupation was a time when fear and terror never took a holiday. Each day was just another block of time to survive, so she probably didn't firmly anchor her experiences to calendar dates. With the onset of dementia, Maria lost even more of her ability to associate dates with events. However, by combining the new information I'd gathered from records in Germany with what she'd already told me, I could put together the following picture.

Maria said the ordeal began when several partisans rounded up a group of young women. Working backwards from the date of Renate's birth told me this had occurred only days after the war ended and the Czech partisans arrived in Wolframitz. Although the women might have been collared during the early home invasions and looting, it appears more likely to me that they were corralled a few days later when the wave of frenzied looting was over, things had settled down a little, and everyone was assembled in the Marktplatz for the executions. Whenever it was, Maria and the others were surely terrified as they were marched out of the village because their group consisted only of young women. After a couple hours of walking, the captives arrived at a site beyond Lodenitz near two neighboring Czech villages. Because the captors knew where they were going and obviously had a purpose, I am guessing the men came from these communities. If so, Maria may have recognized some of them because she'd come here for dances and other social events many times in the past years and the locals belonged to the same Lodenitz parish as Maria had when younger.

On arrival the women were immediately put to work cleaning abandoned munitions left behind by the German military. It was grimy, hard work but the women must have been greatly relieved to find they'd been brought there merely to toil at a labor site. At the end of the day, the partisans took the prisoners to a house in one of the villages and told them they needed living quarters because the work would continue for some time. Inside the house, the prisoners were confined to one large room—a room Maria described as having "not one stick of furniture." Their guards brought them a little food but didn't allow them a table to eat at. These men were intent on making Germans suffer.

The women were given no bedding, so they slept on the cold, bare floor in their dirty clothes. In the morning after a night of broken sleep on the painfully hard surface, the partisans led their captives back to the work site. This exhausting, uncomfortable routine continued for several days, but if the work and harsh conditions had been the worst they encountered, the experience would have remained just another hardship and not a nightmare. Over the weekend the women's initial fears came to fruition. During the night, a group of Czech men swarmed into the room and gang-raped the captives.

Locked inside that room, the women couldn't even wash after the attackers left. Maria didn't talk about how they coped, but the rest of the night was surely long and unimaginably frightening as she and the others huddled together on the cold floor. In the morning the traumatized prisoners were herded back to the work site as if nothing unusual had happened. Although Maria didn't elaborate on her feelings at the time, I can guess she and the others must have feared the attack would be repeated and that the rapists might even kill them. By this time they surely knew President Beneš had guaranteed Czechs they wouldn't be prosecuted for any act of punishment committed against Germans. When rape, torture, and murder were no longer crimes, Germans became disposable.

"When I think about it, it's so, so sad." Maria sighed after losing the struggle to find words adequate to describe how terrifying and humiliating the experience had been and how violated she'd felt. Talking about it was painful for her, and she feared that she'd again be haunted by distressful thoughts at night. Although this discomfited me for reviving her distress, I sensed my mother did gain a little relief in finally unburdening herself of the secret. Still, I wasn't sure she had unburdened herself completely. For many years after I first learned about the occupation and the extent of the lawlessness, I wondered if Maria had been raped. Then, after I learned about her rape and the child that came of it, I wondered if my mother had been through the horror more than once. If so, she never let on, and I never asked. All she ever said was that the Russian soldiers and partisans remained a danger to females in Wolframitz throughout the occupation. Surely, it was difficult for young women to avoid these predators for months on end, but I like to think Maria's early trauma not only had her sleeping in fields many nights, but also left her hyper-vigilant and ready to flee at any time.

I can only imagine how difficult a time my mother had when she realized she was carrying a fetus fathered by an anonymous, violent thug. Coming to terms with such a burden would have been dreadful enough in a civil time, but during her pregnancy Maria did not have rape counseling, medical care, an adequate diet, or the constant support of friends. Her daily companions were a woman she despised and a Czech gold digger. During the last two or three months of the pregnancy her company was fellow prisoners. Throughout her pregnancy, she had to work hard. First, it was manual farm labor and then domestic service as an inmate in a filthy prison camp. Luckily, no medical complications developed, and she had a healthy baby. Maria's friends in Bavaria, people who knew her infant too, assured me Maria loved Renate dearly in spite of the ugly circumstances surrounding the conception.

After I'd located the date of Renate's birth and determined that the rape occurred shortly after the war ended, I realized the reasons for Maria's visit to Schömitz were probably more complicated than she'd let on. She'd surely gone there out of concern for the Hajek children and the Luksch family as she told me, but I think she herself needed comforting because of the trauma she'd just experienced. The Luksch family members were the people who had loved and supported her most.

◆

The documents my mother had in her possession, records obtained more recently in Germany, and interviews with people acquainted with Maria and Renate after their 1946 arrival in Bavaria helped me establish the following timeline of events. Renate was born in Mährisch Kromau early in 1946 toward the end of my mother's confinement in the prison camp. The date and place of birth, as determined from entries recorded after Maria's arrival in Germany, gave new significance to a Czech record that Maria had kept through the years. It was a form typed on a partial sheet of flimsy newsprint and came with several handwritten notations and signatures in ink. The poor quality paper had yellowed and become fragile, but remained legible. A translation of the document showed it to be Maria's release permit from the Mährisch Kromau (Cz. Moravský Krumlov) camp, dated shortly after Renate was born. Renate's birth in the camp explained why Maria had refrained from telling me about her confinement for so many years. She wanted to avoid having to answer further questions about it for fear she might reveal some part of her secret. The record and what it revealed also help explain why Maria so despised Anton Stöffel, for what kind of a man would falsely and maliciously send a heavily pregnant rape victim to such a place?

The release form directed Maria to return to her former residence in Olbramovice, the Czech name for Wolframitz. It ordered her to report to the Czech police station upon arrival. The release was stamped, dated, and signed by the camp commander, and subsequently by an officer in Olbramovice. The translation reads:

> Headquarters of detainee camp
> Moravský Krumlov.
>
> *Hajkova Marie*, born…*1919* is released from the detainee camp in Mor. Krumlov with the order to remain within a reachable distance of her existing residence in *Olbramovice 65*, county Mor. Krumlov.
>
> In addition she must comply with the relevant rules and restrictions that are decreed for Germans.
>
> Mor. Krumlov, 7 February 1946.
> Commander of the detainee camp,
> Ranking Officer Burián
> *Burián* [signature]
>
> *And she also cancels her food rations, which she received in here.*
>
> [reverse side]
>
> I confirm that Marie Hajkova reported herself on 11 February 1946 at local headquarters after she was released from the detainee camp.
>
> Olbramovice, 11 February 1946.
> Commander of the headquarters
> procurator, Constable Schwarz
> *Strážm Schwarz* [signature]

When Maria finished telling me about the rape she said, "That's why I hate the Czechs." She'd said before that she hated them, but I'd always assumed the reaction stemmed from her collective experience after the war. After this I had no doubt about the source of her most toxic memories. Of course, she never hated all Czechs and said as much at other times. She knew they hadn't all approved of the malicious treatment.

---

[1] Susanne Beyer, "Harrowing Memoir: German Woman Writes Ground-Breaking Account of WW2 Rape," *Spiegel Online*, Spiegel.de/international, 26 Feb. 2010.

35 The Czech Final Solution

THE BULK OF CZECHOSLOVAKIA'S massive ethnic cleansing occurred in two waves. The initial phase, known as the Wild Expulsion, began in May 1945, months before the Allies were ready to even discuss relocation, and it continued until August. Beneš and his communist National Committees, the self-appointed government, acted quickly to kill and eject the unwanted Germans and Hungarians at war's end because the postwar chaos and the strong anti-German sentiment prevailing in the West provided cover for their actions.

Strident populist speeches and outrageous propaganda, the same tools employed by Hitler and Stalin, worked their evil once again. Beneš and his cronies inflamed the public and exhorted it to drive out or kill the Sudeten Germans as revenge for their so-called collaboration with Hitler in taking over Czechoslovakia. Many Czechs and Slovaks responded enthusiastically. They armed themselves with clubs, whips, chains, and other weapons, and used them prodigiously. Sadistic and greedy mobs of civilians and partisans, assisted by the police and the reconstituted Czech military, invaded homes and businesses throughout the country to steal, terrorize, and throw out the unwanted minorities.

The victims of the Wild Expulsion typically had only minutes to bundle up a little food and clothing. Armed thugs and criminals, most of whom had only just added their names to the communist roll, called themselves resistance fighters and engaged in brutal orgies of retaliation. They herded defenseless women, children, and the aged out of the country like cattle. Young and old alike were whipped, beaten, robbed, and raped along the way. In many locales throughout Czechoslovakia, Germans were tortured and killed in the most appalling and sadistic ways imaginable, both by locals and outside gangs of communist toughs. The killers commonly disposed of the bodies in mass graves or dumped them into rivers.

Countless Germans were injured in assaults and beatings and no small number died of their injuries later in Germany. The injured overwhelmed German hospitals already full of civilian casualties of the Allied bombing campaign and wounded soldiers. Very few expellees escaped with anything of value to sustain them later because their belongings had been rifled through repeatedly. Although these actions received little mention in the western press, by late summer Beneš had to temporarily suspend the exodus because the maltreatment was so extreme and widespread that the country risked condemnation from the West.

The Allied Potsdam conference in July and August 1945 formally addressed the banishment of Germans and other minorities from Central and Eastern Europe when the leaders of the Big Three powers—Harry Truman, Joseph Stalin, and Clement Attlee—conferred. Truman, Roosevelt's vice president, had assumed the office of president when Roosevelt died of a cerebral hemorrhage in April 1945. Atlee succeeded Churchill after the Labour Party won the majority of seats in Parliament in July 1945. The three leaders signed off on a joint agreement that stipulated, "Any transfers that take place should be effected in an orderly and humane manner." Beneš likely wouldn't have received approval for the German expulsion had the Lidice massacre by the Nazis not occurred and aroused strong sympathy for Czechs in the west. After the war when the planners of the Reinhard Heydrich assassination that provoked the Lidice massacre came under criticism by Czechs because it should have been obvious such a murder would cost a great number of Czech lives, Beneš allegedly covered up his involvement.[1]

The second round of expulsions began in mid-January 1946. By then most of the remaining Germans had suffered so grievously that they wanted out as quickly as possible. Yet, a few were still in denial and thought the expulsion wouldn't actually apply to them. Maria's fraternal aunt in Klein Seelowitz thought being married to a Czech exempted her, despite her daughter having been a youth leader in the girls' Nazi youth organization, Bund Deutscher Mädel. Maria was fond of her aunt's husband, a friendly tailor who spoke fluent German.

The aunt never refused her daughter anything. But during the occupation, when Maria tried to borrow a shoe brush from the woman because the ones in her house were all stolen, she learned her aunt's generosity extended only to her daughter. She wouldn't loan Maria even such a trifling item. When expulsion became a certainty for everyone else, the woman had the temerity to beg other Germans for the valued items they'd buried to keep them from the looters. She argued that they'd lose their belongings anyway when they left. The items she collected, she reburied in her own yard in the belief she'd be able to hang on to them because of her Czech husband and name. In the end, she too was expelled and lost everything.

Although the Czech partners of expelled Germans often stayed behind, some were so disgusted by what was happening that they preferred to get out as well. Maria's uncle wanted no part of this new Czechoslovakia, but another family Maria knew did split up. Alois

Stöffel's brother had to leave, but his Czech wife chose to remain with their two children and the farm. After Moscow's proxy communists seized power in 1948 and confiscated private land, people like this woman probably questioned their decision.

◆

In February 1946 the partisans again ordered all Germans in Wolframitz to the Marktplatz, just as before when they'd been assembled to witness the executions. This time no killing spectacle awaited them. Rather, they were told that all Germans would be expelled in stages. Those selected to leave on the first train then heard their names read.

The initial stage of this second expulsion wave got rid of the aged, infirm, and women with small children—the people of least use to the Czechs. Three additional transports followed over the coming months. Because the expellees left at different times and ended up in scattered locations, this process separated families, neighbors, and friends. Trains dumped the hapless refugees into a broken Germany to join millions of other displaced persons (DPs) jostling for food and shelter. Although this dumping served Beneš by emptying Czechoslovakia of his unwanted minorities, it also advanced Stalin's aims. Not only did the ethnic cleansing empty the border areas of people, providing Stalin space to build military bases and fortify borders for permanent control of Czechoslovakia, it also created enough chaos and impoverishment in Germany to make it easy for the Red Army to step in and take over the entire country should the western Allies pull out as Stalin expected..

The Germans scheduled for removal in the later transports continued to toil as slave laborers for their Czech masters. The established Czech farmers, as well as the new ones, now had difficulty finding Czechs willing to perform the grueling labor because the former workers were now flush with their own property and goods. When the final bit of value was extracted from these Germans, mostly women and older men, they too were expelled. Their departure near the end of 1946 marked the end of the thousand-year German farming culture in Wolframitz, Schömitz, and hundreds of other locales throughout the Sudetenland.

Expellees could officially take out 40 kilograms of possessions, excluding valuables such as jewelry, watches, and bank savings books, but the Red Army, partisans, East European laborers, and ordinary Czechs had already relieved most Germans of their valuables and greatly pared down the rest of their possessions and property. People who'd spent their entire lives toiling to build up a little security for their old age and a legacy for their children exited with only a few clothes, bedding, and some mementos. Many people couldn't scrape together enough to fill the 40 kg allotment. The people who'd been booted from their homes by Russians, Czechs, or Slovaks departed with nothing.

In practice, expellees were limited by what they could carry. Old people and children couldn't tote much. Exhaustion, malnutrition, and injuries restricted others. The expelled were technically allowed to take out a small reichsmark allowance, but the few who had any money left after buying food or paying bribes needed considerable luck getting it past the sticky-fingered guards during multiple searches in the exit ordeal. Not uncommonly, guards removed family photographs from bags and threw them away. What all expellees brought out in quantity were scars, both physical and emotional.

◆

After the looting, Maria didn't have much left to bring out beyond the baby given her by the partisans. Carrying a month-old infant made the journey much more demanding in the primitive, unsanitary conditions and the cold of winter. However, she'd bonded strongly with the baby and carried on under the difficult circumstances. Knowing her love of children, I doubt she could have been more strongly attached to tiny Renate had the infant been fathered by a man she loved.

When the February departure time came around, Maria and the others whose names were called at the assembly in Wolframitz were shuttled to a camp in the village of Misslitz to await a train. Mothering a newborn in a filthy, crowded camp was a wretched experience. Maria recalled spending about a week there under conditions reminiscent of the prison camp she'd left not long before. However, in this camp she was not under arrest and knew the stay was temporary.

The train that arrived consisted of cattle cars. Thirty to 40 people and their belongings were jammed into each car. Although the travel distance wasn't great, confinement in a crowded, drafty cattle car without access to running water or a toilet made the two-day journey seem infinite. Maria lacked adequate supplies to care for a baby needing diaper changes. Between the infrequent stops, a hole in the floor or a bucket served as a communal toilet for men and women alike. These were the "humane conditions" Beneš had agreed to provide in order to win official Allied approval for the expulsion.

Between Maria's preoccupation with her baby during the expulsion and the burden of dementia late in life when I interviewed her, Maria couldn't tell me anything more about the trip other than the train stopped in Prague. Fortunately for her, the weather was relatively mild at the time, and the destination was southern, rather than northern, Germany. Many expellees succumbed to exposure or their injuries on other expulsion trains. A great many needed hospitalization or died after reaching Germany. Various accounts describe the arrival of children with frostbite or old people and women in labor frozen to the floor of freight cars by their leaking body fluids.[2]

Between January and November 1946, over a thousand trains like Maria's, carrying an average of 1200 people each, discarded their cargo of newly minted DPs from Czechoslovakia at the German border. By December most of the 3.2 million Sudeten Germans alive at the end of the war had been removed. Only about 250,000 remained behind. Most of them were held back for their skills. Yet, these "valued" workers didn't receive any special treatment. They too suffered abuse, lost their homes and possessions, and worked without pay wherever they were sent.

For Maria, leaving the land of her ancestors should have been difficult. Under different circumstances it would have been, but the relief she felt at escaping the monsters who'd turned her homeland into a vicious hell was too great. Despite the uncertainties, she believed the worst of what lay ahead would still be better than what she'd just left. The slave labor and terror-filled nights of sleeping in her clothes beside a window were over. Even though she expected her next residence to be another crowded camp, she would no longer feel a constant gnawing fear in the pit of her stomach.

The governance of Germany was in a state of transition when Maria arrived. At the Yalta and Potsdam conferences in February and July 1945, the Allied leaders agreed to divide Germany into four occupation zones. German dark humor described the division: Britain got the ruins, France got the wine, Russia got the agriculture, and the United States got the scenery. The location of the four-power jointly occupied administrative capital, Berlin—110 miles inside the Soviet zone—quickly became a major headache for the western powers. The United States, Britain, and France operated their zones cooperatively and in a manner that would punish the Germans but allow an occupied and defanged Germany to recover eventually. Stalin, on the other hand, chose to impoverish his zone and make it wholly dependent on the Soviet Union. Toward this end, the Soviets dismantled and hauled away anything and everything of value in the name of reparation. When the three western Allies requested talks in 1946 and 1947 to reunite Germany, the Soviets refused to participate, and Cold War hostility took root.

Fortunately, Maria's train took her to Bavaria in the American zone. Although life there was no picnic, the expellees discharged in the Soviet East German zone had it much rougher. DPs in the "workers' paradise" faced many years of hardship unless they had the foresight and energy to leave while it was still possible.

Gerd Hanak, who has worked to preserve southern Moravian memories and history, was a boy of 10 living in a village not far from Wolframitz at the time of the expulsion. The Hanak family was expelled three or four months after Maria. Gerd's young age gave him a different perspective on the trip. Except for the terminus beyond the border, his route was likely almost identical to Maria's. The following is a translation of his account of his family's Sudetenland exit:

> It must have been June 20, 1946, when we were loaded onto cattle cars at the train station in Misslitz. Each car held 30 people and their luggage. Our baggage was piled high on the left side of the car so there would be room for the people. The expellees in our car consisted mainly of my family and relatives, along with a few others from the village. Because the weather was good the loading door was kept open, with just a bar across the opening for safety. The trip was a history lesson, for while we children crouched by the door my Uncle Edmund talked about what was moving past our door outside.
>
> When the train crossed the famous Kanitz Bridge, Edmund explained it was built by Alexandre Gustave Eiffel, the railroad bridge builder best known for designing the Eiffel Tower, built it. On our arrival in Brünn, he pointed out the Spielberg Castle, where everyone had heard the Czechs carried out gruesome tortures. Then in Prague, while crossing the Moldau River I distinctly remember my uncle telling the children to look carefully at Hradschin (Cz. Hradčany) Castle because "who knows if and when we will ever get to see it again." One man wouldn't for certain. Sadly, during the trip my godfather, Johann Bauer, died. I next saw it again 46 years later.
>
> The train stopped at times to give the "passengers" access to latrines. No one wanted to escape, but to prevent it an honor guard of heavily armed sentries always watched. These men are probably still proud of their heroic deeds!
>
> Eventually the train crossed the border at Furth im Walde, and at last our group was in Germany. In Nuremberg it began to rain, but from the train the attention was on the city for it was all in ruins. On the train platform I found a 10,000 pengö banknote, which I

kept for years as a secret treasure even though the Hungarian currency was so inflated the note was worthless. Only a month later the pengö was replaced by the forint at a rate of 400 quintillion pengö to one forint. The pengö still holds the world record for hyperinflation.

Sometime after the train resumed its journey and passed through Würzburg, I had a terrible scare. Outside, a military convoy passed and I noticed the vehicles were emblazoned with a large star. For a moment I thought we'd been delivered to the Russian Zone instead of the American Zone because I didn't realize that, like the Red Army, the American Army also marked its vehicles with a star. However, theirs was white, not red.[3]

Unlike Gerd, Maria never again set foot in Czechoslovakia or in the Czech Republic successor state that formed after the Slovaks broke with the Czechs a second time in 1992. But she didn't ever want to return. Her homeland was no longer the same place, and she wanted nothing to do with those who had defiled everything she'd held dear. When I brought Schömitz and Wolframitz back to her in the form of photos, she was interested in seeing the place again, but clearly no longer regarded these villages as home. Maria's sisters, as well as both Oswald and Oskar, did return for visits after the collapse of the Soviet Union in 1989. The decay and blight in their once carefully tended, vibrant communities shocked them. They described the villages as bleak and joyless places devoid of activity. Some of the villages they passed through were barely a step removed from ghost towns. When they described the deteriorated state of houses once occupied by relatives, neighbors, and friends and the empty gaps where houses had once stood, I had to wonder if even a man as duplicitous and unfeeling as Beneš would have carried out his expulsion had he known the great harm it would cause his country.

---

[1] Dědinová, *Edvard Beneš the Liquidator*, 241.
[2] Douglas, *Orderly and Humane*, 194.
[3] "Ankunft und Empfang," *Europas-mitte*, Europas-mitte.de, accessed 20 Apr. 2015.

36 Germany with Tears

HEIMATVERTRIEBENE AND VERTRIEBENE are the terms Germans applied to ethnic-German displaced persons expelled from their homelands to the east. As the reception system became organized, all these people were destined for camps, at least in the short term. I asked Maria too late in her life to describe her entry into Germany. She no longer recalled where she crossed the border or how much time she spent in reception and transition camps. In her fog of dementia, about the only thing she recalled was encountering her first Americans. She was surprised to find so few. However, by this time the US Army had already occupied Bavaria for nearly a year and most of its soldiers had pulled back into bases and turned the social service duties over to international agencies and the Germans themselves.

Maria and her fellow Sudetenland expellees were denied refugee status. Allied Armed Forces commander General Eisenhower and his deputy, General Lucius Clay, believed in collective guilt and wanted to punish all Germans for the war and the Holocaust. Since Germany had started the war, they thought all Germans deserved to suffer. Consequently the Allies and the Office of Military Government, United States (OMGUS) defined refugees as non-Germans displaced by the war. The differentiation assured foreign aid assisted only Allied POWs, foreign DPs, and concentration camp survivors. The Heimatvertriebenen, along with native Germans, were denied international aid.

The Allied resettlement and relief effort for officially recognized refugees was turned over to the United Nations Relief and Rehabilitation Administration (UNRRA), an internationally staffed agency. When UNRAA was organized in 1943, planners had no inkling that after the war some ten million ethnic Germans would be coming to Germany, where eight million outsiders already were. The latter were supposed to be leaving, but they too needed food, housing, and care until they could be resettled or repatriated. Consequently, the scale of the problem overwhelmed the ill prepared agency. The effect of the United States foreign aid restrictions meant only non-Germans received adequate food.

The chaotic situation the occupying military had created by its bombing campaign and now had to contend with in German cities is almost unimaginable today. In describing the situation months after the war had ended, one historian quoted a noted German bishop: "Thousands of bodies are hanging in the trees in the woods around Berlin and nobody bothers to cut them down. Thousands of corpses are carried into the sea by the Oder and Elbe Rivers—one doesn't notice it any longer. Thousands and thousands are starving in the highways...Children roam the highways alone, their parents shot, dead, lost."[1]

Thousands of camps arose throughout Germany to deal with the transient, roiling mass of humanity. The authorities set up some of the camps; others formed spontaneously. Not uncommonly, former military bases, industrial buildings, and warehouses became make-do camps. Hidden munitions factories became refugee camps, and even open ground was settled by the enterprising to cooperatively grow food.

A November 12, 1946, story in the New York Times described the drastic situation posed by the influx of ethnic German expellees: "Bavaria bears the brunt of this human dumping operation as far as deportations from Czechoslovakia are concerned, since two-thirds of the migration to the American zone remains here.... The Germans are the end product of one of the few clauses of the Potsdam Agreement that have been carried out. If Bavarian figures hold good throughout the country, immigration amounts to more than a fifth of the native population, or the equivalent of about thirty million added to the population of the United States in less than a year."

The correspondent went on to say: "If Allied statesmen had imagined how heavily this wandering mass of helpless people would beat upon themselves they couldn't have assumed so casually the moral and historic responsibility for the most unhuman decision [ethnic cleansing] ever made by governments dedicated to the defense of human rights."

American policy mandated Jews get exceptional treatment, so Jewish refugees and repatriated Jews were given top priority. The army expected 100,000 of them to arrive by the end of winter 1945.[2] UNRAA prioritization gave non-German refugees the next highest status. Native Germans occupied the lowest spot and ethnic German DPs were barely above them. Since no German republic existed anymore, both of the latter two groups were left to the care of the individual German states, all of whom were impoverished. The state of Bavaria responded by creating an expellee authority and somehow constructed 1,153 camps. When the trains from Czechoslovakia began arriving at the end of January 1946, up to 10,000 new arrivals each day needed food and shelter. The influx created a nightmarish problem in a region already subsisting on starvation rations.

The Allied authorities grew terrified once they comprehended the enormity of the situation. In Bavaria the US Third Army's chief of staff was quoted as saying: "I can't see with a couple more million coming in, how there is going to be room. Even stacking them on top of one another, the facilities are going to be really busting."[3]

Rural areas were left to absorb the newcomers; the destroyed cities simply couldn't handle them. The statistics for Berlin illustrate why. An OMGUS Berlin Sector report stated that of the 1.5 million dwelling units in the city in 1939, only 20 percent remained undamaged by mid-1944, and the bombing continued for nearly another year. The takeover of many of the relatively intact buildings for troop housing and offices by occupying forces didn't help matters. Building new dwellings to relieve the strain looked impossible for many years because of all the debris. One report estimated that "ten trains of fifty cars each could leave the city daily, fully loaded with rubble—and Berlin's debris would still not be cleared for sixteen years." The report went on to state that even building at the rate of the big 1927 to 1937 construction boom, just getting back to the prewar supply of units would take 20 years.[4]

Of the 16 million homes that existed in Germany before the war, four million were destroyed by Allied bombs. Another four million were damaged. Half of all schools were damaged or destroyed, as was 40 percent of Germany's infrastructure and factory capacity. The answer the occupiers came up with was *Trümmerfrauen* (rubble women). Had Maria been sent to a city, she'd probably have been one too for the Allied powers removed restrictive measures protecting women in the labor force and ordered urban women between 15 and 50 years of age to participate in the postwar cleanup. The job fell to women because at the time Germany had seven million more women than men.

Private enterprises were usually granted the contracts to remove bombed buildings. Along with the contracts came a permit to employ women to do the work. The ragged Trümmerfrauen worked in all weather on these often dangerous structures. With their simple demolition tools, mainly picks and hand winches, they reduced the remnants to single bricks that could be reused. A line of women passed the bricks to the street to be cleaned and stacked. They also salvaged other useable material like beams, sinks, fixtures, and pipes. The unusable debris was moved with wheelbarrows and wagons and then taken away by truck.[5] Some of the rubble was used to make new bricks or to fill bomb craters in the streets, but most was dumped at sites that became huge mounds the Germans called Trümmerberge (rubble mountains). Most major German cities have at least one such hill. Berlin has several. The majority of these landmarks became recreation areas or parks.[6]

The food shortage meant working Germans previously living on 3,000 calories per day had to make do with a fraction of that. Urban Germans existing on these starvation rations became malnourished and vulnerable to disease. Children and adults picking through garbage cans were an everyday sight throughout the country. The truly desperate chewed on leather and licked the paste off wallpaper to find nourishment. The specter of a food crisis and mass starvation was frightening to the Allied command because a large number of deaths would bring about severe criticism. This fear prompted the alteration of the official policy disallowing the feeding of Germans and expellees from Allied food stocks.

At the end of the war when OMGUS wanted to punish Germans, its occupation forces had been ordered to throw out uneaten and surplus food rather than share it with starving Germans. The order even prohibited military spouses from feeding their German maids. Although this rule was widely ignored, the wives still weren't allowed to give the maids food for their families. American mess halls couldn't simply throw out waste. The dumped food had to be made inedible in some way to keep Germans from scrounging it from garbage containers and dumps.

The American leadership was so determined to punish Germans that when the American Mennonites, Quakers, and the Red Cross collected food to help Germans get through the upcoming winter of 1945, the authorities returned the donations and told the agencies to use them elsewhere. The US State Department also prohibited foreign governments and agencies from sending food and even stopped the Catholic Church from shipping food for German infants. Swiss food trains were turned back at the border. Food aid that did somehow make it through was confiscated and withheld in some areas. The military authorities went so far as to curtail fertilizer production and to keep German fishing boats in port to prevent them from fishing.[7,8]

By October 1945 the American military government finally recognized Germans would be lucky to average 1,250 calories per day with the food supplies on hand. Since approximately 2,000 calories per day were necessary to stay alive during the winter in unheated dwellings, the OMGUS prepared for food riots, and General Eisenhower even discussed shooting Germans if necessary to preserve order.

The divergence in living standards between the occupiers and the occupied was so enormous that after a Jewish publisher from Britain toured the British Zone late in 1945, he published a small volume consisting largely of photographs that illustrated the human side of the tragedy in a way that words couldn't. He wrote: "The plain fact is that there are two worlds in Germany today, the world of the conquered and the world of the conquerors. They meet at the peripheries, but their hearts beat in an inhuman isolation."[9]

Back in the United States, opposition to the draconian food policy mounted, and a few politicians began to speak out when news stories and photos depicted the extent of the suffering. However, by then it was too late to build up supplies in time for winter. In early autumn General Clay finally acknowledged the seriousness of the situation and admitted many Germans had already died of exposure, starvation, and disease when he said, "The death rate in many places has increased several fold, and infant mortality is approaching 65 percent in many places. By the spring of 1946, German observers expect that epidemics and malnutrition will claim 2.5 to 3 million victims between the Oder and Elbe."[10]

The domestic criticism in America forced the OMGUS to alter its food policy. The generals, fearing a starvation disaster would invite a comparison to Nazi crimes of starving undesirable populations, in November hastily announced a ration increase to 1,500 calories. They knew the small improvement wouldn't make a real difference, but the earlier strict ban on aid had left reserve stocks too low to do more. The ration for Germans worked out to three medium potatoes, five and a half slices of bread, three tablespoons of cereal, and one teaspoon of sugar and fat daily. About 80 percent of the calories came from the starchy bread and potatoes. By comparison, American soldiers in Germany received 4,000 calories, Americans back home 3,200, and the people of Britain 2,900. While the Germans were consuming their 1,500 calories, the foreign DPs in the American sector of Germany got 2,600. Ironically, imprisoned Nazis were allotted 2,200 calories because of international conventions on the treatment of prisoners! Ultimately, to assist the neediest Germans, the military set up a number of field kitchens. However, those receiving the meals were charged ration coupons. In the crisis the US State Department began to allow private relief agencies to send limited supplies to Germany.[11]

As bad as the situation was for German civilians, it was worse for most German POWs. At war's end, General Eisenhower classified the bulk of German prisoners as Disarmed Enemy Forces to sidestep the Geneva Convention terms for the treatment of prisoners. During the war, when Germany still had some leverage because it held US POWs, the US military fed German POWs adequately. After the Germans lost their leverage, calling German military prisoners something other than POWs allowed the US command to drastically cut their rations. In their weakened condition under close confinement, many thousands of these men died, particularly in the French and American zones. My father avoided incarceration in such a camp, but most German soldiers did not. The generals kept the International Red Cross out of the Allied POW camps and didn't permit them to supplement the food of the prisoners. In the fall of 1945, after numerous appeals, the Red Cross finally obtained limited access to British and French camps and were allowed to provide some aid. However, the American military didn't ease its policy until February 1946. Many times during that winter, the Red Cross reported prisoners being held in appalling conditions.

The sudden return of 250,000 German POWs from North America during the winter of 1945 further strained the food shortage. These men were to be turned over to the French, but the POWs the French held already were so malnourished that they were expected to die over the winter. The situation compelled General Eisenhower to free his captives so the existing food stocks could keep the French prisoners alive.

A critical coal shortage compounded the misery in Germany during the winter of 1945 because coal was the main fuel used to heat homes. Although coal production increased somewhat before winter's onset, the transport system was still too broken to deliver the coal in the quantities needed. The military government seized the entire available coal supply, but by December the American Zone had barely enough stockpiled to keep trains and vital public utilities operating. Unless people were able to scavenge a bit of wood to burn, they did without heat and cooked food. A lot of furniture went up the chimney that winter. Not uncommonly, children were required to bring a piece of wood to school each day to help heat their classroom.

Starving Germans and the military government alike breathed a sigh of relief when spring arrived. They'd averted disaster only because the winter was one of the mildest on record. Had it been cold, the outcome would probably have been a catastrophe still noted today. As serious as the food shortage was that winter, it was worse the next because a summer drought resulted in a very poor harvest. The winter of 1946–1947 struck with a fury and lasted through March. The *Hungerwinter*, one of the names by which it came to be known, was one of the coldest in living memory and is still noted by those who experienced it. The average German calorie intake ranged from 1,000 to 1,500 calories per day that winter and the still persistent coal shortage aggravated the population's misery. Tens of thousands of Germans perished as a result of the conditions.

[1] Ralph Franklin Keeling, *Gruesome Harvest: The Allies' Postwar War against the German People* (Marietta, Ga, The Truth At Last, 2001), 62.
[2] Earl Frederick Ziemke and Center of Military History, *The U.S. Army in the Occupation of Germany, 1944-1946*, Army Historical Series (Washington, D.C: Center of Military History, United States Army : For sale by the Supt. of Docs., U.S. G.P.O, 1975), 416.
[3] Ziemke and Center of Military History, *The U.S. Army in the Occupation of Germany, 1944-1946*, 409.
[4] Office of Military Government US Sector Berlin, *A Four Year Report: July 1, 1945–September 1, 1949*, archive.org, 51.
[5] Wikipedia contributors, "Trümmerfrau," *Wikipedia*, Wikipedia.org, 14 Feb. 2015, accessed 21 Apr. 2015.
[6] Wikipedia contributors, "Schuttberg," *Wikipedia*, Wikipedia.org, 17 Jan. 2015, accessed 21 Apr. 2015.
[7] James Bacque, *Crimes and Mercies: The Fate of German Civilians under Allied Occupation 1944-1950* (London: Warner, 1998), 91.
[8] Wikipedia contributors, "Food in occupied Germany," *Wikipedia*, Wikipedia.org, 19 Apr. 2015, accessed 21 Apr. 2015.
[9] Victor Gollancz, *In Darkest Germany* (Hinsdale, Ill.: H. Regnery Co., 1947), 98.
[10] "Food in occupied Germany."
[11] "Food in occupied Germany."

37 Identity Entanglement

ALTHOUGH THE EVIDENCE SUGGESTS my mother arrived in Germany early in March 1946, I was unable to find any records bearing the precise date. Neither could I learn where she crossed the border. But wherever it was, she'd have encountered the same harsh conditions plaguing much of Germany that winter. Coping with a food shortage, a lack of fuel for heat, and crowded transit camps while trying to care for a tiny baby must have been daunting for her.

The screening and classification process at reception facilities typically confined displaced persons to temporary quarters for 10 days or more. There, aid workers ascertained people's medical condition, job skills, ability to work, and political history. Following this assessment, administrative authorities dispersed the expellees to various rural areas where the housing was still intact. After that, the DPs became the burden of their new community and drew rations from the community's stocks.

For the newly arrived, the issuance of identity papers was crucial to resettlement. Without papers life was difficult, if not impossible. Food, shelter, and work all depended upon proper identification. Like many of the Heimatvertriebenen, Maria arrived with few papers, and her child came with none at all because the Czechoslovak government didn't bother issuing birth certificates for German babies after the war. Maria had only her own birth certificate, a school report card, a valueless bank deposit book, the Czech prison camp release notice, and the Ahnenpass the Nazis had required to prove racial purity. The latter was minus its cover because Maria didn't want to risk trouble exiting Czechoslovakia with a document bearing a prominent swastika on the front.

The county office in the Bavarian town of Teisendorf provided me a copy of a form with the heading: "*Flüchtlingsschein* (refugee registration) issued by the office of Der Flüchtlingkommissar des Landkreises Laufen." The translation reads: "Maria Hajek, farm worker from Wolframitz, Czechoslovakia, arrived on transport number 2 on March 28, 1946, with the following family members: Renate Hajek, daughter, born 1946 in Mährisch Kromau. They were settled in the municipality of Holzhausen near Teisendorf. The named have been deloused and medically examined. Their ration books were issued by the municipality on April 8, 1946. They are to lodge according to established guidelines. The accommodated have been given directives to follow."

Beyond the dates and vital statistics, this document is telling for two actions all expellees were subject to upon arrival in Germany—delousing and medical examination. The lessons of General Typhus and the devastation of Napoleon's armies were never forgotten in Western Europe. Lice are a danger to civilians as well as soldiers. They can be deadlier than bullets and bombs when feces of lice harboring the microscopic typhus parasite enter a bite or cut. The typhus agent is pandemic to Central and Eastern Europe, so when the Czechs, Poles, and others confined expellees in unsanitary conditions, lice flourished and hitched a ride to Germany. America had devised a method of control during the war when it discovered DDT effectively killed lice. They used the chemical extensively in Germany, but DDT didn't kill louse eggs, so follow-up treatments were necessary to wipe out any newly hatched insects. Occupants of the trains got a dusting at the border and then twice more during the resettlement process.

A medical examination was necessary to isolate not only potentially contagious diseases, but also to assess physical condition for the assignment of housing and work. The physical assessment was especially necessary for work assignments because of the makeup of the group. The following news clip from the April 27, 1946, issue of an OMGUS news publication called *News of Germany* describes the situation for just one small district in Bavaria: "About 30,000 Germans, most of them from Czechoslovakia, have been accepted in the district of the Land Labor Office for Upper Bavaria from November 1945 until the end of March 1946. In March alone, more than 16,000 persons were accepted, three-fourths of them being women and children. Of the 16,000, only 438 were men aged from 26 to 35 years of age."

◆

In October 1945 intelligence sources informed General Eisenhower's aide, General Clay, that he should expect a total of ten million, not nine million, ethnic Germans expelled from the east. And 65 to 70 percent of them had already been deported. Germany was receiving 500 to 600 thousand per month; more than 40 percent were children. Most of the expellees were in poor condition. The majority of arriving adults were unable to work because they were old or ill, had physical disabilities, needed to care for their dependents, or suffered from malnutrition. These were daunting numbers.[1]

The same situation existed in the British Zone. There, the effort to cope with the expulsions from the east was called Operation Swallow. Whether this name was intentionally literal or not, *swallow* describes what Germany needed to do with these people. One official put it bluntly when he said, "The population transferred was largely human wreckage."[2]

Everyone involved knew these expellees presented a huge burden to whoever had to accept them. Beneš and the Czechoslovaks particularly infuriated the authorities because they deliberately held back miners as well as specialized and skilled working-age men. The refugee population consisted primarily of abused, infirm, and dependent transferees. Angry American officials demanded that Czechoslovakia return one working-age man with each family, but the Czech government ignored the call.

The Polish government acted similarly. For political reasons, Germany's neighbors to the east wanted to rid themselves of their Germans as quickly as possible. They'd worked out quota agreements, but after falling into the Soviet orbit they cheated by over allotting whenever they could get away with it. In one instance, Poland dumped 80,000 people at the border from unauthorized trains and left the DPs to find their own way across.[3]

A sizeable proportion of the expellee population required immediate hospitalization or institutionalization. However, hospitals and asylums near the border were so jammed that the authorities often had to send the people needing prompt care farther into the interior of Germany. The already acute British Sector housing shortage worsened when many Polish Jews, including those just freed from concentration camps, fled Poland because they were being mistreated and killed by their fellow Poles. The housing shortfall was further aggravated when many displaced Poles in Germany refused to go home.[4]

The economic impacts of the expellee crisis were multiple. Because the western Allies had to care for and feed so many DPs, money and resources were drained from the recovery process. The overwhelming need to transport refugees all over the country on the crippled rail system left much of the rolling stock and track unavailable for the huge infrastructure-rebuilding effort required for Germany to house, feed, and heat the homes of everyone now living there.

◆

The earliest of Maria's German records were stamped **LAUFEN**. Besides being the name of a *Landkreis* (US county equivalent), Laufen was also the name of the town serving as its administrative seat. These official stamps suggest Maria was processed, given her medical exam, and deloused for the final time in Laufen. The heart of the town lies within a very sharp bend in the Salzach River. Directly across this stream sits the Austrian town of Oberndorf, once a part of Laufen. In a church there the Christmas carol "Silent Night" was first sung in 1818. In the just-concluded war, a 15th century Laufen castle and an adjunct facility at nearby Tittmoning served as a POW camp for Allied officers early in the war. Captured American officers, including Jews and blacks, lived reasonably well there on the Red Cross packages that supplemented their German rations. Later, the installation became Ilag VII, a camp for many of the 2,000 American civilians trapped in Europe by the war. The camp also housed the British men removed from Britain's Channel Islands, Jersey and Guernsey, after the islands were seized by Germany during the war,

Many of the top Nazi leaders were familiar with Laufen because of a small Luftwaffe airfield there. Hitler and others often landed here when they traveled to their chalets at Berchtesgaden. From the tiny Ainring rail station, they boarded a train to Berchtesgaden, 18 kilometers away. In the war's final months, the airfield became the home base for Jagdverband 44, a squadron of Messerschmitt Me262A-1a jet fighters. The Messerschmitt, the world's first jet combat aircraft, enjoyed a five-to-one kill ratio against Allied planes. However, partly due to Hitler's meddling in the jet's design capabilities, the production of these planes was too low and came along too late in the war to affect the outcome.

German Messerschmitt Me262A-1a jet fighter

Laufen might also have had another camp or two that Maria could have transited. A brief citation in a 1947 English newsletter for American and British Zone aid workers in Germany noted: "Two UNRRA barracks burned at Laufen, Bavaria, with a loss of RM [reichsmark] 550,000." And a reference from an oral history project called *A Survivor Remembers*, by

Berek Latarus, noted that a Jewish work camp survivor recalled "walking through this little town, Laufen, in May 1945 when some farmers came running out on the highway shouting, 'The war is over!' There was an army camp not far from there, and it became a DP camp."

Maria received two important identification documents in Laufen. A small booklet with **FLÜCHTLINGS-AUSWEIS** (refugee identity) printed in large letters across the front was dated May 8. The document bore an identity number and fingerprint, Maria's vital statistics, and four rubber stamps, one of which was autographed by the local official representing the Bavarian commissioner for expellees.

The most interesting part of the document was a line I'd ignored until late in the writing of this book. I'd previously dismissed this heavily inked out line, sandwiched between my mother's information and two subsequent rows she'd later filled with the pertinent information about my younger sister and me. I'd always assumed she'd blacked out something entered in error. Only during the search for documentation of her expulsion journey did I guess what the cross-out must conceal. Enlargement and software enhancement exposed the text just enough to make out Renate's name and birth date, which my mother had hidden to obviate later questions and to preserve her secret. Perhaps it was also a gesture, though surely a futile one, to avoid a painful reminder of the rape and her dead baby.

◆

All four major Allied Powers instituted denazification programs, and agreed to try the top Nazis at Nurnberg. But they had differing ideas about how to deal with the lower level party members and officials. Russia took care of its Nazis in the same brutal way it dealt with other enemies of the state. The western Allies, in an effort to identify and label their offenders, applied what might be termed totalitarian democracy. Their path required revised identity cards. In Bavaria under American rule, the resulting frenzy of documentation began in April 1946 and applied to all refugees age 14 and above. The replacement ID was more concise, durable, and difficult to forge. Maria received her new *Deutsche Kennkarte* (German identity card) in September 1946. The document title, as well as the heading for each line within the ID, appeared in four languages—German, English, French, and Russian.

The form was printed on textured gray cardstock folded in half to make a four-page, passport-sized document. Page three bore two fingerprints as well as an affixed photo rubberstamped at two corners to prevent photo substitution. The top line of page four read: "Von der zuständigen Behörde einzutragen" (Issued by the competent authority).

Beneath was the notation: "Official decision pursuant to Law for liberation from Nazism and Militarism of 5 March 1946" in each of the four languages of the occupiers.

At least until the cold war began and the new Communist enemy replaced the old Nazi enemy, the left-side margin of the back page carried the most important piece of information—the bearer's denazification status. Each ID had a hole punched through one or more of the boxes that corresponded to the determination. The Americans, the prime movers behind implementing the rigorous classification procedure, prodded the British and French occupation authorities to adopt the same scheme. The two allies complied but administered their denazification a little less enthusiastically than the United States.

A form popularly called the *Fragebogen* (questionnaire) was the instrument used to gather the necessary personal information about an individual's Nazi activity during the Third Reich era. In the British and French zones, the Fragebogen was only required of certain individuals, but initially in the American zone it had to be completed by all adult Germans and ethnic German DPs. Later, the rules were relaxed. Lying could result in criminal penalties. The risk of being caught was considerable because, quite surprisingly, the Nazis had failed to destroy the Party registry before the end of the war. Persons with an active Nazi background could expect a hearing in a denazification court.

While the British purged German libraries and the Russians brutalized their captive population and printed a closely spaced 526-page book listing banned literature, the American denazification took the form of a bureaucratic inquisition. The lengthy 131-question Fragebogen came to be feared as well as ridiculed by Germans. The reasons are not hard to understand considering some of the questions. For example, question 18 on the first page read, "List any titles of nobility ever held by you, or your wife, or the grandparents of either of you." Another question asked for a list of every published work, speech, and lecture delivered since 1923, along with the date, subject, and audience. A thorough answer required a recall spanning 23 years. The form also asked for a list of all trips outside Germany and the names of persons visited there. Naturally, German dark humor couldn't help but pose additional questions such as: "Did you play with toy soldiers as a child? If so, what regiment?"

This denazification process, which was controversial even among the Allies, left former Nazi Party members struggling to rid themselves of their damaging past. An answer for many was what became known as the *Persilschein* (Persil ticket). The term had come to mean a "clean bill of health" because Persil was a common laundry detergent in Germany. It took on a new meaning when the Allies began to issue a document called

Certificate of Good Standing to suspected offenders who obtained written statements from their victims attesting to the applicant's good reputation or conduct. A person with such a certificate was now scrubbed clean and could rejoin society, obtain housing, resume a previous occupation, or participate in business. Of course, the Persilschein opened the denazification process to abuse.

As might be imagined, the Fragebogen process created a logistical nightmare—one costly to administer. In the American Zone where about ten million forms needed to be processed, the task overwhelmed the administrative centers. To cope, the authorities kept altering the program. In the third and final phase, implementation was turned over to the Germans. From the rubber stamp and signature dated July 1947 on Maria's ID card, I know it wasn't punched with a classification until many months after issuance, confirming how badly the process was bogged down.

To ease the strain, Germans born between January 1919 and March 1928 received a youth amnesty in late 1946, with high-level offenders excepted. People born after March 1928 were already exempt from completing the questionnaire. These changes removed two million names from the Nazi rolls. The administrators reasoned that most party members in this age group automatically joined the party because they'd been indoctrinated from a young age through Hitler Youth. A subsequent Christmas amnesty for little Nazis (small-fry, low-income offenders) removed another 800,000.

When the Germans took over the program, a new questionnaire came into use. The two-page *Meldebogen* (declaration form) consisted primarily of a list of Nazi organizations to which the respondent admitted or denied membership in.

The Law for Liberation from National Socialism and Militarism of March 5, 1946 directive that turned denazification over to the Germans placed all Germans into one of five classes. These were:

> I. *Hauptschuldige*: major offenders
> II. *Belastete (Aktivisten, Militaristen, Nutznießer)*: offenders (activists, militarists, profiteers)
> III. *Minderbelastete (Bewährungsgruppe)*: lesser offenders (probationers)
> IV. *Mitläufer*: followers
> V. *Entlastete*: active resisters and persons exonerated

On the back of the gray Kennkarte ID the hole punched in the boxes numbered 1, 2, 3, and 5 denoted the holder's classification. Numbers 1 through 3 branded the bearer as some type of Nazi. Box 4 was never punched as everyone in class IV automatically had hole 5 punched. Thus, this box lumped together everyone not sanctioned—Nazi resisters, the exonerated, minor party followers, and those given amnesty. Boxes 6 to 15 indicated various sanctions and conditions. For example, number 12 prohibited employment as a teacher, preacher, editor, writer, or radio commentator.

Maria's ID had box 5 punched. She'd never been politically active or a party member, and was young enough at the time of the Nazi takeover to be amnestied. Under the strictest interpretation, this should have relegated her, along with the majority of Reich Germans, to class IV status—not politically active, but not an active resister.

As might be expected, not everyone who had actively resisted the Nazis was happy with the idea of sharing the box 5 designation. In a legal case that attracted much attention, two newspaper editors who qualified as class V resisters refused to have hole 5 punched on their IDs because they objected to being lumped in with the Class IV followers. As a result, the rules were changed. Class V persons were allowed to get a new ID if they objected to having hole 5 punched. However, since most Germans were very poor then and new IDs cost one deutsche mark, they could instead cover the hole and have their ID stamped **POLITISCH ÜBERPRÜFT** (politically verified).

The screening forms and subsequent investigations resulted in three and a half million indictments and nearly a million legal proceedings in West Germany. Unfortunately, I was unaware of this extensive denazification process when my parents were still alive, or I'd have asked them about their own experiences with the process. My father, who adapted more readily to America, had long since tossed out all of his old German documents.

In their zone, the Soviets had no use for the West's denazification program. They relied on the same tried-and-true methods they'd always used to get rid of their enemies, undesirables, and political rivals. Their Nazis, suspected Nazis, and all other real, imagined, or potential enemies were dealt with much more cheaply and efficiently. They simply had the Soviet NKVD lock prisoners in concentration camps. Quite conveniently, an abundant supply of such camps was ready and waiting. It was only necessary to replace the signs over the gates. Approximately 43,000 people perished in these camps.

---

[1] MacDonogh, *After the Reich*, 184.
[2] Douglas, *Orderly and Humane*, 200.
[3] Douglas, *Orderly and Humane*, 102.
[4] Douglas, *Orderly and Humane*, 198.

38 Wimmern, a New Beginning

MARIA AND HER BABY arrived in her assigned Bavarian village along with four other *Flüchtling* (refugee) women. In 2010 a lifelong Wimmern resident known as *die Bachter Nanni* by her neighbors (for reasons explained shortly) described their coming. Nanni, a young teen at the time, still vividly remembered this day because the newcomers were more than an idle curiosity. They came from a different culture, spoke an unfamiliar dialect, and posed a threat to the static little village. The threat was change! I don't know if these women were the first expellees assigned to the village, but they were certainly not the last. Not only would the new arrivals substantially boost the local population, they would also sit at the family table and voice their views—no small thing in an insulated, conservative community. But it wasn't just the villagers who had concerns. The newcomers were just as reluctant to move into the house of strangers as the strangers were to accept them.

Nanni remembered that these women, dropped off on the main road passing through the village, had begun their journey at a camp in Landkreis Znaim. Besides Maria and Renate, the group consisted of two unrelated young women and their mothers. Maria and one of the young women, Nessi, quickly became good friends. The following year I too developed a connection to Nessi because she was a midwife and assisted Maria at my birth.

Shortly before Maria's arrival in Germany, the Allied Control Council (joint military administrative council drawn from all four occupying powers) issued Act Number 18, or the *Wohnungsgesetz* (housing law), to cope with the severe housing shortage. The Act mandated that local governments set up housing departments to help homeless Germans find accommodations. It compelled local authorities to confiscate living space in existing dwellings and to come down especially hard on Nazi and war criminal landlords.

This housing law required every dwelling in the village to board expellees. The new arrivals were pre-assigned to their residence so they merely needed to locate the house and settle in. I never thought to ask my mother about her fears and expectations, but with so many unknowns ahead, and bad rooming experiences in the past, her anxiety undoubtedly ran high.

The new situation was trying in other ways too. Not only was Maria penniless, she didn't have the run of the house as she did in Wolframitz. Her home for the foreseeable future was a small bedroom. As difficult as her adjustment was, arriving as a pauper and living in a shared bedroom was even harder for the two older women who came with Maria. The memory of their own homes and gardens was still fresh and they knew they could no longer hope to rebuild their lives the way younger refugees could.

Nanni recalled their sad plight with a story. Not long after arriving, Nessi's mother came to Nanni's house and asked for a pan of milk. On the way back to her room the new situation and the humiliation of having to beg overwhelmed the poor woman. She broke down in the middle of the road and wailed, "I want to go home!" The devastated, homesick woman couldn't quite grasp that home no longer existed. The other older woman in the group, who came from the Banat region of Yugoslavia, insisted the landlord paint her room blue, a color she favored in the house she'd lost. Of the newcomers, Maria remained in the village longest. The other four women eventually moved on to situations in other Bavarian communities.

Most of the natives were friendly and accepting of Maria and the others. But not all. Several resented the refugees and treated them accordingly. In their minds the expellees weren't real Germans because they spoke another dialect and had different customs. However, after these residents came to know the newcomers better, they realized they'd overreacted and changed their attitude.

Initial resentment of refugees was common throughout Germany and also extended to bombed-out, native-German city dwellers resettled in smaller communities. Sometimes the issue was religion when Protestants came to Catholic communities and vice versa. Although most expellees had enjoyed a standard of living and education similar to that of native Germans, some local Germans believed the expellees to be backward or dirty because of their condition upon arrival.

One factor offsetting the resentment of having to house strangers was compensation. House owners collected rent, and precious few couldn't use a little extra money. Relief agencies assisted the displaced persons unable to work. Those physically capable of work paid their keep out of wages from an outside job or by working for the owner.

◆

The quaint farming village of Wimmern, only 10 or 11 houses and some 75 residents, was but a fraction of the size of even tiny Schömitz, but its grand setting compensated for its size. Wimmern boasted a 1200-year-old onion-dome church and lovely traditional Bavarian farmhouses, but its prime feature was the view. *Picturesque* understates the spectacular setting. From the village's perch at the crest of a hill, every house enjoyed a breathtaking panorama of the Bavarian Alps across the valley to the south as well as the highest part of the Austrian Alps. A mere 20 kilometers to the east lay the Austrian border and the historic city of Salzburg.

The village was a cluster of farm houses and barns, too small to support any real stores. A room within the house next door to Maria served as the village tavern, and a few basic groceries were available at another house. The real shopping was done in the market town of Teisendorf, three kilometers away.

Maria's quarters offered a partial view of the Alps from two small, east-facing windows. Although the room was upstairs, the stairway led down to a hallway and the front door so she didn't need to pass through the owner's living area on entry or exit.

If Maria needed any reminder of who'd set in motion the events resulting in her presence in Germany, she had merely to gaze down the valley toward the southeast from her windows. There, on a clear day she could see Obersalzberg, the valley where Hitler, Göring, Goebbels, Bormann, Speer, and other important Nazis had built grand homes.

◆

Hitler discovered the Obersalzberg mountain retreat area of the Bavarian Alps above the town of Berchtesgaden in 1923. A few years later, he finished writing *Mein Kampf* there following his prison release. Because the book popularized his ideology and turned him into a wealthy man after he acquired part ownership of Standarte GmbH & Herold Press, the publisher, Hitler was able to afford a retreat home in Obersalzberg. As his power and influence grew, he directed Nazi Party Secretary Martin Bormann to secure ever more land. Many owners were reluctant to part with their property and needed a little persuasion. The owner of a hotel near Hitler's house held out until a detention of several weeks at Dachau caused him to change his mind. Before the Nazi accumulation was finished, the party had earned the enmity of many local residents.

In the construction of the complex that grew around Hitler's house, workers demolished over fifty buildings, including houses, hotels, and a sanatorium for handicapped children. In the thirties, Hitler enormously expanded his modest house and turned the surroundings into his private park. The finished structure, Schloss Berghof, comprised 60 rooms filled with expensive furniture, rugs, and art. The enormous cost befitted the führer's ego.

The complex eventually swelled to 80 buildings and included SS barracks, administrative offices, a hotel for important visitors, and a large greenhouse to satisfy Hitler's vegetarian diet all year round. The huge facility required many workers, so their housing added to the size of the place. The development's capstone was the Kehlsteinhaus, also known as Hitler's Eagle's Nest. This chalet, built 3,000 feet above the main compound atop an adjoining mountaintop, commanded a stupendous view. Martin Bormann, whose control over access to Hitler lent him enormous power, commissioned it for Hitler's 50th birthday at enormous expense. The project cost the lives of 12 of the 3,000 construction workers who labored at the project around the clock for 13 months.

The access road with its five tunnels was an engineering marvel and cost some 200 million in 2009 inflation-adjusted dollars. The road ended on a small plateau 400 feet below the chalet. From there a tunnel led to an elegant elevator finished in polished brass and the final leg of the ascent. Today tourists can either hike a trail or take a bus from a parking lot where the SS Barracks once stood to the chalet 2600 feet above. At the Kehlsteinhaus sightseers can get a meal and a beer while taking in the panoramic view. While I recommend the hike, the ride too offers breathtaking views from the dedicated buses with special engines and brakes. The irony is that the expense and effort of the construction was largely a waste. Hitler felt claustrophobic in the tunnel and feared the heights at the top, so he seldom used the place. When he did, he stayed only a few minutes.

Toward the end of the war Allied intelligence feared Hitler might retreat to an Alpine redoubt in the mountains, so the military bombed the Obersalzberg complex. The mountaintop Kehlsteinhaus survived the war intact because, unlike the lower compound and Hitler's mansion, it was too small and elusive a target to hit with bombs. Upon arriving at the main compound, American and French troops found Hitler's mansion hit by two bombs and largely destroyed. Although already ransacked by locals, the soldiers scoured the place for souvenirs then blew up the remains. To prevent the site from becoming a Hitler memorial, the military declared it off limits to Germans. In 1952, OMGUS returned Obersalzberg to German control but made removal of the remaining Nazi ruins a condition of the transfer. At this time the last of the wreckage—the SS barracks and the houses belonging to Göring and Bormann—disappeared. However, an American military presence remained because commanders had noted the same stunning setting that attracted Hitler and used the locale as a recreation area for its occupation troops.

Today an organization called the Institute of Contemporary History operates a museum on the site of the lower complex. Dokumentation Obersalzberg's entry brochure describes the museum as "a permanent exhibition detailing the history of Obersalzberg and the Nazi dictatorship." The extensive exhibit particularly recounts the grim story of the Nazi era and the local takeover. One of the few surviving structural units of Hitler's compound is a bunker complex accessed from the lower level of the exhibit. The tunnels are of incredible scale and are a must-see.

◆

On my first Obersalzberg visit in the 1970s a local resident told me the Soviets rolled up the heavy communication cable connecting the complex to Berlin and hauled it back to Russia. He was probably right, considering the major portion of the cable's route ran through the Russian zone where the Soviet occupiers took everything potentially useful and shipped it east. They dismantled thousands of factories and stole whole companies. It was not unheard of that the company workers were also sent east or that owners were charged shipping costs. At the Leipzig Zoo, first the feed for the animals was taken and then later the animals themselves.[1]

The Brandenburg Opel truck plant was an example of the process. Workers disassembled the entire factory for transport to the Soviet Union. However, the dismantling of this factory, like many other industrial sites, was so sloppy that no one at the other end had any idea how to fit the parts fit back together again. The material then rusted or rotted away.[2] Although haphazardly dismantled factories might have been too complex to put back into service, telephone cable was not. A safe assumption is these lines soon carried Stalin's military messages instead of Hitler's.

The failure of the Russians to reassemble some factories like the Opel plant doesn't mean they didn't ever produce German-engineered products like Opels. When the Soviets also demanded the Rüsselsheim Opel truck factory in the US Zone, they were turned down. But the Americans did foolishly turn over the tools, dies, jigs, and drawings for Opel's Kadett car when the Russians pleaded they needed to provide local employment by producing the car at an Opel subsidiary plant in Leipzig within the Russian Zone. Leipzig production never happened, but the next year the Moskvitch 400 came out of a Moscow auto plant. The car looked suspiciously like the Kadett in every detail. Three years later when the Soviets wished to export their car to Belgium, one of their selling points was the ready availability of replacement parts from Opel in Germany.[3]

◆

In early 1946 German consumers had little money and stores had little to sell, but everyone required at least some shop items. Maria and the other

Wimmern residents, when they had any money, bought them in Teisendorf, 45 minutes away by foot. For centuries the town was under the dominion of nearby Salzburg, Austria, the birthplace of Wolfgang Amadeus Mozart. Until late in the 18th century, Salzburg and the surrounding area was an independent state reigned by a prince-archbishop. Salt mining made the city prosperous enough to allow its archbishop to rule like a monarch over towns in his domain. Because Teisendorf sat astride a major salt transport road where it intersected another road, the settlement prospered as a market city. When the Austrian-German border inconveniently separated the two communities after the Napoleonic period, Teisendorf was cleaved from Salzburg.

Left: Teisendorf memorial to fallen soldiers of both world wars. Right: One of four interior plaques engraved with a long list of the local war dead.

Being practical men, in 1800 the town burghers had the sense to appear in the city's marketplace and surrender Teisendorf to Napoleon's advancing forces before fighting could cause destruction. On May 3, 1945, the mayor and city council again showed the same foresight and raised the white flag of surrender when a unit of General George Patton's Third Army approached. The residents were sick of the war and knew what could happen to their town if they didn't act. They merely had to look to nearby Salzburg. Between 1944 and the end of the war, American and British planes bombed the city 16 times. Much of the historic center lay in ruins and 531 people lost their lives. Even closer to Teisendorf and just days before Teisendorf's May 3 surrender, bombs also flattened most of Freilassing.

Aside from the fine scenery, Maria was fortunate to be assigned to Wimmern because it was a farming village where rations weren't as meager as in German urban areas. However, she quickly came to hate both the job and living in her employer's house. For the third time since leaving Schömitz, she was stuck with a demanding and unreasonable boss. Like Aurelia, her new farmer was comfortable with the notion of work only when it was done by others. The farmer, known by his house name of Schmidt, accomplished little through his own efforts. With an infant to look after, Maria couldn't work full time. When she did work, she had to find others to take care of Renate. Sometimes she enlisted Nanni and her older teenage sister, but more often the babysitter was Schmidt's mother in the room adjoining Maria's.

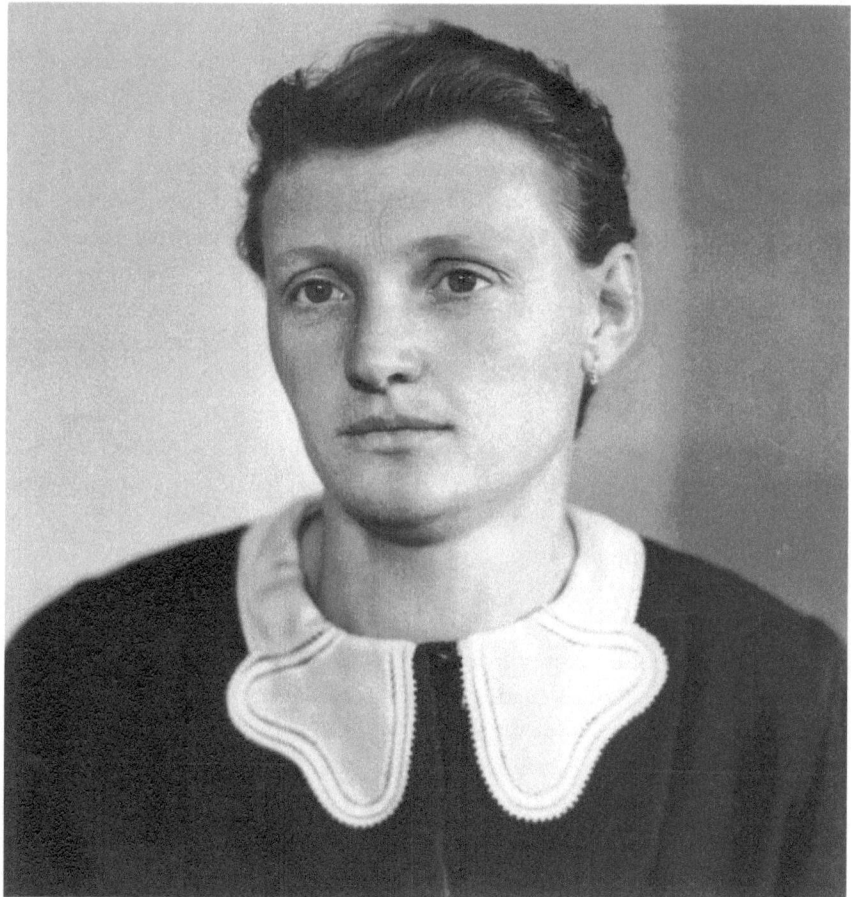

Maria in Wimmern

Although the extreme housing shortage prevented Maria from moving elsewhere in the earliest years after arrival, she was never obligated to work for Schmidt. But because every village swarmed with DPs, no other suitable jobs were available locally. Working in Teisendorf would have been out of the question because just the walk back and forth took over an hour, so she stayed in her job.

Maria experienced two life-changing events during her first year in Wimmern. One was Renate's death. The other was meeting a young man. Like Maria, he was an ethnic German from a rural German village to the east who'd found a home in Wimmern after the war. This man would become her husband and my father. I never learned the precise circumstances of their meeting, but in such a tiny village it was impossible for two people to remain unknown to each other for long. Maria, as a young and lonely single woman thrust into a new country where the dialect was so different from her Austrian-flavored German that it sounded like a foreign language, would have quickly encountered this fellow DP because he spoke a *Schwäbish* dialect she easily understood. It also didn't hurt that he was a charming and handsome young man with dark hair and hazel eyes.

Maria's early impression of Fidel Eipert wasn't entirely favorable. Because their paths sometimes crossed while working in the fields, she knew he was a hard worker. But more than once she'd seen him wander tipsily to his house after a bout of card playing. And she thought he was a flirt because she'd also seen him in his lederhosen and white knee socks, strolling back from Teisendorf with his arms wrapped around various girls.

However, in his defense I must say that after the war such behavior wasn't unusual in men who'd returned. Because many young women hadn't enjoyed the companionship of men for years and so many men had died or had yet to return home, the men who came back readily found female companionship.

The vestibule of the village onion-dome church attests to Wimmern's great loss of men. Out of less than a hundred residents, 10 names are inscribed on a stone plaque. Four of the dead on that list have the same surname. A twin plaque carries the names of the village World War I dead, and its list is nearly as long.

Interestingly, the names on the plaques do not correspond to the Wimmern names most commonly heard there. In the area's small rural communities, residents know each other by their house names rather than by their real surnames. When taken together with the German fondness for shortening or changing first names to nicknames, it should not be surprising to learn that Maria's next door neighbor, Anna Mösenlechner, became *die Bachter Nanni* after she and her husband took over the family dairy farm. Even though Anna's family had lived there for many years,

Left: Village of Wimmern's 600-year-old St. Laurentius Catholic Church. Right: Foyer of church bearing plaques listing toll of war dead from each world war.

they and the house kept the name passed down with the house, Bachter. For the same reason, Fidel knew the farmer he worked for as Brunner, even though this wasn't the man's real name. Longstanding tradition or not, the post office in Teisendorf doesn't play along and insists mail show the recipient's actual surname and house number.

Lenz and wife, Anni, in 2010

Maria's neighbors on the side opposite the Bachter house became close lifelong friends of my mother and father. Their son, Lenz, and his wife remain family friends today. In the late 1940s, Lenz and I were among the few young children in the village. On my last visit, Lenz took great pleasure in explaining the oddities the use of house names introduced. Although his family had been known by their house name of Meisner, their real name is Reiter. Not too distant from their residence lives a family named Schmidt but known by their house name of Reiter. Meanwhile the family next door to Lenz, the place Maria lived, is called Schmidt, even though that is not the family's real surname. It can be very confusing.

Although Fidel worked for Brunner, he frequently also helped other farmers and took on nonfarm side jobs as well. He arrived in Wimmern a day or two after Germany's May 8, 1945, surrender and immediately found work by knocking on doors. He'd chosen this small out-of-the-way place because he expected few American MPs to be prowling about looking for German ex-soldiers here. He'd likely have chosen a different village had he known the very type of POW camp he was trying to stay out of would spring up within sight of his house. But by arriving when he did, he not only beat the rush for housing during the expellee resettlement process, he also found his farming experience in demand during the labor-intensive growing season.

Although Fidel didn't have years of exposure to the traumatizing brutal ferocity of the fighting fronts, he was nevertheless an Eastern Front combat veteran who needed to readjust to peacetime life. What Maria failed to understand was that the girls and the beer drinking was a necessary part of Fidel's transition passage back to normal life. Soldiers who'd seen action needed to decompress, drive out the demons, and make up for lost time. His whole generation had missed out on the carefree days of young adulthood and independence because of the Nazi regimentation and the war.

Fidel's partying and carousing wasn't solely driven by his readjustment. He was also needed to block out what he'd lost. His tally was substantial. Many of his classmates and friends from Romania were now rotting under Soviet earth. Fidel's only brother lay in some unmarked mass grave after catching a Russian bullet in central Berlin at the very end of the war. And his sister, a young mother, toiled away in some unknown part of the Soviet Union after she'd been hauled off in a freight car as a slave laborer during the winter. Fidel had no illusions about her chances of survival for he'd experienced a winter in the region himself. Her punishment came only months after a Russian officer in a Romanian farm field callously executed her unarmed husband. Fidel himself was barred from returning to his homeland, seeing his family, or reclaiming his farm. The new Moscow-controlled puppet government of Romania considered the men the former government had sent to the German military as enemies of the state and subject to death. Fidel didn't know if he'd ever see his mother, relatives, and acquaintances again.

Fidel also kept a secret, as I mentioned at the beginning of this narrative. I suspect it may have caused some survivor guilt feelings after he learned just how few of his old friends and military comrades had survived the war. The story behind his secret, Fidel's childhood and war experiences, his life in Wimmern with my mother, and the family's transplantation to America will follow in another volume.

◆

I've never seen a photo of my sister Renate, and as far as I know, none exists. My mother couldn't afford a portrait after she arrived in Germany, and any friends or neighbors in Wimmern who owned a camera would have found film, like most other consumer goods, hard to come by in the first year or two after the war. All I have to picture my sister is a verbal description provided by Bachter Nanni, 64 years after Renate's death.

Nanni fondly recalled the child and described her as a *fichts Kind* (a happy, likeable child) with round eyes, blond hair, and a beaming broad face that smiled a lot. She was a pleasant baby to mind. Nanni said she and her teen sister fought over which of them got to babysit Renate when Maria asked. Lenz remembered his grandmother telling him even Schmidt, although not actually fond of the child, did tolerate her until he and his wife adopted a small girl themselves. Then he resented having Renate around because she took attention away from his own daughter. His feelings were obvious to everyone in the village, and they considered his attitude shameful. Sadly, the adoption inadvertently played a role in Renate's demise.

According to Maria, Schmidt and his new wife had lived upstairs in the house until shortly before her arrival. Then Schmidt's mother gave the house and farm to her son and took the upstairs room next to Maria's. In rural Bavaria, like in Maria's homeland, sons commonly delayed marriage until they inherited their family's land. However, Schmidt's widowed mother was a generous soul and gave her son his inheritance while he was still a young man. Maria saw it as a big mistake because Schmidt, although adopted as a young child himself, showed no gratitude to his mother and treated her shabbily.

Times were hard for all Germans in the postwar period. They learned to get by on very little and as a result came to appreciate small things formerly taken for granted. One was sweet treats, a rarity for children shortly after the war. In recalling those days, Nanni related the following story. She'd been selected to carry the candle in the traditional procession for the baptism of her uncle's new baby and eagerly looked forward to the ceremony. Young people sought this honor because afterwards ceremony participants got to indulge in confections. However, Nanni's sister coveted those treats so much that she offered to trade her precious rabbit with 10 babies for the pleasure of carrying the candle and earning the treats. Nanni thought hard about the offer before accepting.

Although all families were economizing, Schmidt took it to an extreme and didn't allow his own mother, who'd given him the farm, even an apple from one of his trees. Only after all the fruit was picked could she have an apple if it lay on the ground. Everything she needed, she had to ask for. Schmidt demanded much of his mother, but denied the poor woman any say in household or farm matters. Although Maria found Schmidt's wife annoying at times too, she was basically a good person and Maria felt sorry for her in having to put up with such a beastly man. The woman worked outside the home as a maid in another household, so Maria sometimes helped her out by babysitting her child.

Schmidt's kindly mother frequently helped Maria. Unfortunately, her son's stinginess prevented her from giving Maria any housekeeping items. Later, after Maria married Fidel, and my sister and I came along, this kindly woman allowed Maria to store some of our family's food in her room because Maria's was so cramped. After I grew old enough to provide amusement to a somewhat older child like Lenz, he frequently came up to our room to play. In his later years Lenz could still picture that room—the small table against the wall to the right of the doorway, the tiny open space beyond, and the bunk bed to the left of the door. I was too young to recall anything but my mother's stove, a simple electric hotplate parked on the table.

Schmidt was so extraordinarily stingy that Maria couldn't help but shake her head and chuckle over some of his antics when she described them to me, although the experiences had been anything but amusing at the time. Maria recalled he grew angry when she visited with her friends the Reiters because he believed she was cheating him whenever she wasn't working. His gross eating habits were another of Maria's recollections and one of the hardest things for her to bear at the time. Until she married she had no means of cooking for herself, so she ate at the Schmidt table.

"They were both slobs. When the Schmidts butchered one of their hogs, they would eat and eat that meat, even after it started to stink. But they never seemed to get sick from it," she exclaimed.

Schmidt was so tight that even sick hens that died were butchered and cooked. He also insisted the vinegar from the cucumber salad be saved and reused day after day. Maria laughed when she told me how this led to a revolt when two ex-soldiers, a Prussian and a Moravian, also roomed in the house. One day while everyone was together eating, the Prussian reached his limit. Rudolf got up from the table, took the container with the used vinegar, and poured it down the drain. But of all Schmidt's eating practices, his habit of eating soup from the serving pot most turned Maria's stomach. On one occasion she got so sick from something served at his table that the doctor pumped her stomach.

Lenz confessed he never had much love for Schmidt and his capers either. He particularly recalled one occasion during his boyhood when Schmidt started his noisy tractor almost directly below Lenz's bedroom at five in the morning and for some reason had to leave it running while he went in for breakfast. The noise kept Lenz from getting back to sleep, and the tractor exhaust drifting in through the window made him nauseous.

Nanni in 2010

Schmidt's doings were always good for a laugh around the village. Another story I heard came from Nanni and related to Schmidt's bulk in later years. He was very fat, in contrast to his thin brother. One day the pair of them set off together for another village in a small car. Because the roads in this part of Bavaria are narrow and curvy, when the brothers rounded a tight curve too fast the off-balance car rolled and landed on its side in a wheat field. Neither brother was seriously injured, but heavy Schmidt had landed atop his brother. Because the fat man couldn't get out of the tiny car, his poor brother had to endure the crushing weight until help arrived.

Despite the poverty and her repellent employer, Maria was much better off than she'd been in Wolframitz. She no longer had to sleep in her clothes, hide her possessions, or fear denunciation and arrest. Life gradually grew normal again and gave her hope the future would be even better for her and Renate. But in mid-August, barely five months after arriving in Germany, the unthinkable happened and she lived every parent's worst nightmare.

Renate caught a skin rash from the Schmidt child. No one remembered the exact details, but the little girls were together from time to time when Maria, Schmidt's mother, or others cared for them. One afternoon Renate's cheeks and neck swelled. Maria, and the neighbors she consulted, thought the child had caught the mumps until early evening when Renate began to show signs of distress. The symptoms ran their course in a shockingly short time. Before Maria could bundle the baby up and rush her to a doctor, Renate's condition worsened precipitously and she died.

In 2010, in Germany, I learned more about Renate's death. Nanni said the baby's passing had touched her deeply at the time. She explained that in those days families didn't send the deceased to a funeral home; the body was prepared for burial at home and removed quickly. The law required burial the following day because the health authorities feared infectious disease outbreaks due to substandard living conditions and malnutrition. This requirement was hard on families. From what Nanni told me, I'm sure everything happened so fast that the baby was gone and in the ground before Maria could fully absorb what happened.

After friends washed, dressed, and wrapped Renate's tiny body, Nanni's sister carried her to Teisendorf. I am guessing she asked to do it as act of love. The walk was three kilometers by the shortest route and largely downhill, with a steep ravine to cross not far outside of town. Today a bridge and a paved road span the ravine, but in those days crossing the ravine meant dropping down one side, hopping a creek, and climbing back up the other side. Nanni didn't say, but I am sure others also accompanied the body. Maria almost certainly wouldn't have been among them. Her neighbors and friends would have been tending the stricken mother in her room. I can only imagine how distressed my mother felt after all she'd endured in Czechoslovakia while carrying that baby inside her. To survive it all and then lose the child to a silent and invisible killer through the course of an afternoon in the relative safety of Germany must have seemed grossly unjust.

Bachter Nanni's sister, Marie, as a teen with the author and his baby sister, circa 1950

According to the St. Andreas Parish register in Teisendorf, the funeral mass took place three days after Renate's death. The cause of death in the register was meningitis. However, the record dated August 19 in the Holzhausen district recorder's office attributed the death more specifically to Pÿodermie, which indicates the body was examined by a doctor or medical examiner before burial. Pÿodermie is a rapidly evolving ulcer of the skin. After helping me collect these records, Lenz took me to his doctor so I might get a better understanding of the term. The doctor explained the symptoms described by Nanni, taken together with the Pÿodermie diagnosis, told him it was a staphylococcus infection that led to sepsis. Sepsis results when an infection penetrates the skin via a cut or sore and leads to a rapidly spreading infection within internal tissues or the bloodstream.

I don't know how my mother worked through this personal tragedy or how long the process took. Perhaps her keeping Renate a secret for the remainder of her life says something about how deeply this momentous change in her life affected her. But life did go on for her, as it had for her own mother after losing Maria's sister to a contagious disease. My father stepped into Maria's life about this time. Although she'd been acquainted with him for months already, I don't know exactly when the romantic spark struck. Their courtship is another thing about which I regret never having asked my father when he was alive or questioned my mother when she still had her memory.

Although my mother's story is not yet complete, at this point it merges with my father's and becomes the story of two lives intertwined, for she soon married and became a mother again. The telling will recommence in the volume to follow at the point where my father's story and hers converge.

---

[1] Anne Applebaum, *Iron Curtain: The Crushing of Eastern Europe, 1944-1956* (New York: Doubleday, 2012), 33.

[2] Wikipedia contributors, "Opel," *Wikipedia*, Wikipedia.org, 19 Apr. 2015, accessed 21 Apr. 2015.

[3] "Opel."

39 Aftermath—An Accounting

Maria's Cookbook and the Written Record

The trashed Austrian cookbook my mother salvaged after the Russian and Czech looters ransacked Wolframitz is one of the few mementos she brought out of the Sudetenland. The book accompanied her to Germany, went with her to America, and remained in her kitchen until she entered an assisted-living facility near the end of her life. In the book she'd jotted in German: "A souvenir from my home; Schömitz in Sudmähren; beautiful and unique District of Nickolsburg." The cookbook, a few photographs, several embroidered pillowcases, a couple of sheets, and a sampling of the school sewing projects her cousin Emma retrieved from Maria's grandmother's house in Schömitz were all she had left of her possessions; everything else was stolen.

Although this cookbook earned a reprieve, most other German books did not because the destruction of the printed word is intrinsic to ethnic cleansing. I saw an example for myself in Bosnia and Herzegovina in 2003 when I passed through a still uneasy Sarajevo several years after the Bosnian War ended. The Serb nationalists had targeted and destroyed the Bosnian National Library, which had housed the vast majority of Bosnia's historical archives. I encountered another instance of record destruction while researching Johann Hajek's World War I military service records. The Czechoslovak government apparently destroyed the military and pension records of Sudeten Germans who'd served Austria in the war—records that by treaty were turned over to Czechoslovakia for safekeeping after Versailles. In Czechoslovakia and other Central and East European countries, destruction of the written record even extended to cemeteries, where German gravestones were sometimes removed and used as building material or crushed for road gravel.

In Schömitz the Czech partisans tried to destroy all German books and documents to clear the village records of a German history. They largely succeeded. However, one thoughtful and brave soul rescued 120 school record books and smuggled them out of Czechoslovakia. They contained the family records of every child attending the German school since 1853. These records ended up in the hands of Oskar Halusa, who laboriously compiled a catalog of all the German children and their families.

Eduard Hajek

Eduard, true to his premonition that he wouldn't return once he reported to his combat unit, died some months after he arrived on the Western Front. Neither Maria nor anyone else in his family got a letter from this likeable, intelligent young man following his last training leave. Through inquiries to the Red Cross, his siblings learned in 1964 that Eduard died in France in 1944. However, from my own inquiry to the Red Cross in 2002, I discovered that he actually died of wounds in Bardenberg, Germany on March 2, 1945, the day after his 21st birthday. Bardenberg is near Aachen, the first city in Germany captured by the Allies (October 1944).

Grave of Eduard Hajek lying among 32,000 others inside Holland on the German border at Deutscher Soldatenfriedhof Ysselsteyn

To me, the lack of letters from Eduard to his family in the months before his death suggests he was seriously wounded either before or during the Battle for Aachen, and spent the months between the capture of Aachen and his death as an injured POW. Eduard lies buried in the Deutscher Soldatenfriedhof Ysselsteyn (German Soldier Cemetery Ysselsteyn) on Holland's side of its border with Germany. The German War Graves Commission administers this cemetery of 32,000 graves, which consolidated the remains of all German soldiers who died in Holland or nearby on the German side of the border. Around 6,000 graves hold unidentified soldiers. Nearly 3,000 German military war dead were reburied here after the Battle of the Bulge in the Ardennes and Hürtgenwald. The cemetery is also the resting place of 85 German soldiers from World War I. The commission still adds new graves as World War II remains are unearthed in construction sites.

Quite appropriately, the cemetery's infrastructure includes meeting facilities for German and Dutch youth groups. Eduard, who never had a chance to apply his education as a teacher, would have approved having his grave here among many others so that the vast sea of crosses could convey to future generations the true cost of war.

The Hajek Family

Maria's brother Erich, who was last seen leaving the Schömitz area on the back of a military truck along with about 20 other teens in the desperate Nazi manpower call-up of early 1945, was never heard from again. Nor were any of the other boys. Erich's Uncle Julius in Vienna made many inquiries but learned nothing. The boy's siblings suspect the truck didn't even reach its initial destination. Erich and the others were probably captured and executed by the Russians and now lie in a long-forgotten mass grave somewhere.

About a year after Johann, Karolina, and their youngest child, Ernst, escaped Czechoslovakia on foot and reunited with their three daughters in Austria, the family resettled in Germany. The survivors and descendants reside there today. I met my grandfather Johann only once. Or rather he met me, for I was a toddler and too young to remember him when my mother took me by train to visit the family. As an adult on trips to Germany in the 1970s, I twice had an opportunity to meet him but chose not to. My mother urged me to see him, but at the time I resented him for the benign neglect he'd shown her. I now regret the decision for I realize surely his war experiences had turned him into the man he was. I'd judged him too harshly.

My mother always got on well with Tanti Pauli, her stepmother's sister. My wife and I once visited this woman in her modest apartment in a small, old stone castle in Germany. Unfortunately, I was ignorant of most of the family history back then and consequently didn't ask questions. However, I have visited Maria's half siblings several times since then and collected what information and photos I could. Maria's sister Regina and her husband, Anton, visited my parents at the family farm in Iowa once and enjoyed themselves tremendously. Anton spent much of the war as a POW in Indiana after the North Africa campaign and relished revisiting America as a free man.

The Lustig Family

Oswald Lustig, along with his mother and sister, were expelled from Czechoslovakia in 1946. From his new home in Germany, Oswald returned to southern Moravia several times when it again became possible after the fall of the Iron Curtain in 1989, and extensively documented the villages, culture, and people he'd known in his childhood to preserve their memory. When I visited him, he told me that Eduard had a girlfriend named Mitzi, who never forgot Eddo, but tragically, also died young. Mitzi's sister, Franziska, whom Oswald was fond of, died a gruesome death at the hands of Czech partisans.

Oswald's father served one year of the harsh labor sentence the Czechs imposed on him before he too was expelled from the country. He joined his family in Germany, but in that year of imprisonment his captors had ruined his health through starvation and repeated beatings. He was unable to work again and didn't live much longer.

The crude Czech farm laborer who took Oswald's grandparents' house and abused the old couple died at the not-so-old age of 58. Oswald noted the man had an ironically appropriate inscription on his gravestone, **VŠE CO MILOVALI POTREBENO ZDE JEST** (Everything that one loves, one must leave here). In the end none of what he stole remained with him for long.

The Halusa Family
The Austrian government granted Oskar Halusa and his brother Siegfried a resident permit because their prior agricultural training and experience were of value to Austria's rebuilding effort. Oskar married, had children, and worked as a civil servant in Vienna, his new home.

After the closure of the Somme Barracks camp in Passau, Oskar's mother joined a sister in Vienna but couldn't find work there. To remain in Austria among her relatives, she took a job as a housekeeper in Steyr, Upper Austria. Oskar's siblings Alfred and Lotte, who fled Schömitz shortly before the Red Army arrived, also settled in Vienna.

The Luksch Family
All four Luksch family members were expelled to Germany where they lived out their lives. Marie and Emma never married and have no descendants. My mother reconnected with the family in Germany following the expulsion and remained in touch as long as they lived.

Henriet
Maria's 17-year-old next-door neighbor Henriet, who was raped by Red Army soldiers in Wolframitz, and her family found shelter with relatives after the soldiers threw them out of their house. Maria never saw her or her family again in Moravia, but Henriet visited Maria in her home in Bavaria several years after the expulsion. Somehow she located my mother through the incredible word-of-mouth network that developed in Germany during the time of broken infrastructure and displaced people.

Only then did Maria get the full story of what happened the night the Russian soldiers invaded Henriet's house and raped her and her mother.

Johann Caesar
Shortly after the old innkeeper escaped the gruesome burial detail in Czechoslovakia and joined his family in Austria, Caesar tracked down the border policeman who lent him the money to finish his odyssey and happily repaid him. Caesar began a new life and lived another nine years. But his gravestone in Vienna is surrounded by the headstones of strangers, not those of ancestors in his homeland as he'd expected throughout most of his life.

Mina
Mina, the friend who hid with Maria in the wine cellar and later camped out in a cornfield to escape the Russian rapist, resettled in Bavaria. I met Mina in 1974 when I accompanied my mother to Mina's home, but because I knew nothing of her history then, missed an opportunity to collect a most interesting story.

The Stöffel Family
Aurelia Stöffel, Maria's employer, housemate, and nemesis, resettled in Bavaria and eventually remarried. Maria visited Aurelia once years later but only because she'd been attached to the children and wanted to find out how they were doing. Maria confided that even then she felt like strangling the woman.

Surprisingly, Maria once encountered Anton Stöffel near Wimmern as she walked along a road. Stöffel tried to start up a conversation but Maria ignored him and continued on. After all the pain and aggravation he'd caused her, she had nothing to say to him. He'd lost everything he'd ever worked for and was separated from his grandchildren, but Maria couldn't work up any sympathy for the man she believed responsible for the false accusation that resulted in her camp confinement. The once-arrogant landowner was reduced to doing menial farm labor for someone else so he could eat.

The Geidl Family
During the Russian occupation Emilie Geidl told Maria that Czechs had taken her husband away, but she didn't know his whereabouts. Later in Germany, Maria spotted Emilie from a train window once but was unable to get off to learn how the children had fared. Coming across people from her small village in this new setting felt strange. When she told me about seeing Emilie, she also recalled once encountering several children from Wolframitz on a train. Although Maria never heard what became of Geidl himself, she had a good idea

of what happened to his dangerous kicking horses. A safe guess was they ended up on some Russian tables via the Red Army's slaughterhouse. More recently, after it was too late to tell Maria, I learned from another source that Geidl had survived his detention and was expelled to Germany.

Lehrer Mauer
Through the years Maria occasionally reminisced about her old school teacher, Rudolph Mauer. He and his wife lost four of their five sons in the war. And then their young daughter Erica, the girl Maria sometimes entertained after school, succumbed to tuberculosis near the end of the war. Only Rudi, Maria's classmate and the physically smallest of the five boys, survived. Maria and Rudi reconnected decades later but only via letters. He told her it was a shame she'd ended up in America, so far from their homeland. Maria last saw him shortly before the war ended when he somehow reached home. He fled to Vienna with his parents just before the Red Army occupied Schömitz. If they hadn't left, the partisans would surely have tortured, or killed, both Rudi and his father.

Several years before Maria died, her sisters told her they had run across a student report card from one of Rudolph Mauer's classes in an exhibit called *Heimstreffen* (Home Reunion) in an Austrian *Heimatmuseum* (homeland museum) and were surprised to find it was Maria's. Maria was pleased that at least a few people had been able to bring out mementos of the old existence for without such artifacts Sudeten Germans would have only their memories.

The Neuspiel Family
Maria believed for decades that the Nazis had snatched up this Jewish family in Schömitz. She was happy to learn from one of her sisters late in life that the Neuspiels had fled during the night and were not taken by the Gestapo. They escaped to the Czech protectorate with many of their most prized possessions. I didn't learn where the parents or Ilse, the daughter, ended up, but Oskar Halusa told me one of the sons, Erwin, wrote to an old acquaintance in Germany from Israel and passed along "Greetings to all Schömitzers." Willibald, the other son, went to America.

The Village of Wolframitz
The majority of Wolframitz's former residents who could be located after the war, some 400, settled in Germany. Another 26 called Austria home. When Czechs finished appropriating the German houses, the cluster of four adjoining villages lost their centuries-old names, traditions, and identity and became a municipality called Olbramovice. Many houses

were demolished after suffering neglect, decay, and abandonment. Today this village has gradually become tidy once again, but is a sleepy shadow of its vibrant former self.

The Village of Schömitz

Out of a population of 500, Schömitz lost 24 men on the battlefield during the Second World War. Czech partisans or Russian soldiers killed five residents in the war's aftermath. Like residents of neighboring Wolframitz, most Schömitzers began their lives anew in Germany after the expulsion. The village, which now appears on maps as Šumice, withered and lost much of its population and vitality. In Oskar Halusa's *Heimatbuch* (homeland remembrance) booklet, he wrote that on his first return visit in 1990 he and his family were shocked at the decrepit state of Schömitz. Buildings were vacant, yards lay in ruins, farm buildings were rotting, and Hof walls were collapsing. Neglect was everywhere. Between my own two visits in 2003 and 2010, the condition of the village noticeably improved. Property prices were low enough to induce people willing to commute to their jobs in Brno (Ger. Brünn) to buy and renovate houses there.

Miskogel, the park like wooded recreational hill in the distance, no longer exists. The Czechs expanded a stone quarry, and the hill all but disappeared.

The Volkschule building still stands but now serves other purposes. The school would probably have died of natural causes in the age of consolidation anyway, but it was alive and well until the end of the war. Oskar's Heimatbuch, *Schömitz*, noted that the final entry in the school's logbook, dated March 1945, showed head teacher Mauer still on the job. His upper-level class learned of the Turk army at the gates of Vienna in 1683 at the very time the Red Army was poised to reach those gates in 1945. The Turks abandoned the 1683 siege, and the Viennese subsequently melted down 180 captured Turkish cannons to cast the second largest swinging bell in Europe, but history didn't repeat itself with the Russians. Incidentally, that bell is one of 23 bells hanging in St. Stephen's Cathedral, the place where Ludwig van Beethoven realized the extent of his deafness when he noticed birds hurriedly exiting a bell tower but couldn't hear the bells.

Stripped of their self-sufficiency and economic viability under Beneš and his communist successors, the villages declined and lost their charm. Schömitz, Wolframitz, and the surrounding villages stood in stark contrast to the prosperous communities across the border in Austria, where the residents retained continuity with the past and had no communist central planners to contend with. In the joyless Czech villages, I saw few people on the streets and sidewalks because many of the young people had left for jobs elsewhere. On my 2003 visit to Schömitz, a Czech resident of Maria's generation led me to the house of Maria's grandmother. He'd attended the German school for a time and been a classmate of one of Maria's brothers. The man told me his two children worked in Germany and returned only for occasional visits.

I wondered whether the irony of the situation was as obvious to him as to me. The same Czech government that still denied it had done anything wrong by killing and expelling the Germans now relied on the descendants of these people for jobs. Of course, succeeding Czech generations had nothing to do with the expulsion and barely knew anything about it. Their school history texts told them the Allied Powers made the decision to expel and ordered Prague to carry it out. Beneš, and the communist leaders who followed him, lived by the principle that political expediency is more important than the historical truth.

The Village of Gubshitz
When return visits became possible in 1990, Oswald Lustig experienced resentment and harassment whenever he appeared in his former village of Gubschitz. On one of his later visits, he and his wife were taking street measurements in order to draw an accurate map of the village for one of his remembrance books when the mayor threatened to jail them if they didn't leave. They left, but a car followed them. That night, Oswald received a suspicious phone call at 11 p.m. in his Brno hotel room, warning him of danger to his car parked outside. When he peeked through the window, he saw the two men who'd followed him hiding in the shadows, holding clubs. These thugs intended to assault this man nearing 80 years of age when he came out to check on his car.

Austria
The Allies bombed Vienna 52 times during the war, leaving 3,000 bomb craters in the landscape and a fifth of the city's housing destroyed. One source even claimed only 41 civilian vehicles survived the air raids.[1]

As in Germany, the Allies divided Austria's territory into four occupation zones and jointly administered the city of Vienna at World War II's end. A Stalin-picked communist puppet government waited in the wings when the Russian troops crossed the border into Austrian territory in the spring of 1945. However, an Austrian politician, Karl Renner, formed a provisional coalition government and induced a Russian general to persuade Stalin to recognize his coalition. Stalin believed he could control Renner and subvert his government since the most important of Renner's cabinet posts were in the hands of communists. Yet Renner, the 18th child of a poor Sudetenland family, defied the odds and kept Austria from falling into the Soviet orbit even though the three western Allies didn't trust or recognize his government for months after it assumed power.

However, Renner couldn't take all the credit for keeping Austria independent—he got considerable help from the Russians. In the first weeks of the occupation, nearly the entire population turned against the Red Army because its soldiers engaged in so much drunkenness, sexual violence, and crime. In November 1945 the Soviets were shocked to find they polled only five percent of the vote in a national election. Under the parliamentary system the communists in the cabinet lost their positions. Stalin expressed his anger by dismantling a vast amount of Austria's manufacturing capacity and hauling it to the Soviet Union. The following year he appropriated many businesses in the Russian Zone and incorporated them into a single enterprise operated for profit. The endeavor was temporarily competitive, but only because it refused to pay Austrian taxes. The gains, of course, went to Moscow.

Most of Austria's agriculture and oil fell in the Russian Zone, so like Germany, Austria went hungry and cold the first two or three years after the war. However, Austrians didn't suffer to the same extent as Germans. The country gradually eased out the Russians and saw the last occupation troops leave in 1955.

Adolf Hitler

The führer committed suicide on April 30, 1945. He'd married his long-time companion, Eva Braun, just 40 hours earlier. Braun chose to die with him rather than flee, as Hitler urged. The vaunted Thousand Year Reich endured a mere 12 years and four months, but in that time Hitler's vision and reckless ambition caused untold harm and suffering throughout Europe. Near the end of his life, Hitler was no longer the cunning, calculating politician he'd been earlier in his career. If not insane then, the Parkinson's disease, and possibly other conditions, almost certainly impaired him mentally.[2] The Parkinson's diagnosis alone would explain his later physical deterioration and personality characteristics such as "mental rigidity, extreme inflexibility, and insupportable pedantry." He was also described as having an "antisocial personality disorder with lack of ethical and social values, a deeply rooted tendency to betray others and to deceive himself."[3]

The argument about whether he was deranged throughout his career or simply evil persists to this day and will never be resolved. His megalomania, inability to form close attachments, sexual insufficiency, and bizarre attachment to his mother are often used to argue the former. Rumor holds that he carried his mother's photo wherever he went and it was in his hand when he bit down on the cyanide capsule and put a bullet through his temple.

Joseph Stalin
After World War II the western Allies allowed Stalin, the man who helped trigger World War II by forming a pact with Hitler and dividing up Poland, to not only keep the part of Poland he seized, but to also help himself to most of the rest of Eastern and Central Europe. Stalin remained in power until his death in March 1953. Some historians think he was poisoned, but most attribute his death to a major stroke. He spent his last days in agony. His doctors were unavailable to treat him because he'd arrested them in his latest paranoiac purge.

Although Stalin is still a cult figure and hero to many Russians today despite his culpability in the death of millions of Soviet citizens, some of his insider contemporaries held him in contempt. Nikita Khrushchev, Stalin's successor, insisted the man whose name meant "man of steel" was a coward. Khrushchev charged that to avoid direct blame, Stalin never put his signature on any document. In his memoirs, Khrushchev wrote, "Stalin...was paralyzed by his fear of Hitler, like a rabbit in front of a boa constrictor."[4] He also asserted Stalin suffered a nervous breakdown when the German military neared Moscow in 1941. Although his empire held together several times longer than Hitler's, in 1989 it too crumbled.

General Erhard Raus
After Hitler dismissed Raus from his command on March 10, 1945, the general was given a reserve status. In May he surrendered to the American Army and was an Allied POW until 1948. During that time he, along with other generals, produced several historical manuscripts for the American military. Because a record of armor tactics used against the Red Army became more valuable during the Cold War, he continued to write for the Americans after his release, with his greatest output from 1950 to 1952. Raus was a humble man, so unfortunately never published a book of his personal memoirs like a number of other German generals. Raus died in Vienna in 1956.

Edvard Beneš and Czechoslovakia
After gaining their independence, Czechs idolized their country's two founders, Masaryk and Beneš. Neither man had acted nobly in his wartime lobbying or at Versailles, but both wished to preserve their prominent and favorable positions in Czech history. Beneš's chicanery in manufacturing false documents was particularly egregious, so he established wide scale censorship, confiscation of newspapers, and the Protection of the Republic

Act of 1923. Among the Act's 306 punishable offences were several aimed at ensuring that "the history" would always be presented "correctly." The Act criminalized unfavorable coverage of the country's founders and threatened violators with charges such as incitement of racial hatred and military treason. The subjugation of criticism did not seem to strike him as odd behavior in an open democracy.

In part, after World War II this earlier repression of truth allowed Beneš to blame the birds he'd locked in the cage for the mess on the birdcage floor when he condemned all Sudeten Germans as traitors, issued the punishing Beneš Decrees, and obtained Allied approval to ethnically cleanse Czechoslovakia "in an orderly and humane manner." Neither the western press nor the Allied leaders found it hypocritical that the regional instability he and Masaryk had created drove the Sudeten Germans into Hitler's hands and helped ignite the Second World War. Neither did the victors see any hypocrisy when Beneš, at the very time he was directing a massive terror and ethnic-cleansing drive at home, sent an ambassador to help found the United Nations in order to ensure a just life for all.

Beneš's eventual undoing was the 1943 Czechoslovak-Soviet Treaty of Alliance agreement he'd reached with Stalin. While trying to regain control over Czechoslovakia's government after World War II, Beneš discovered that in signing this pact behind the backs of the western Allies, he'd given his "friend" Stalin overall control of the government by allowing Stalin to stack the most powerful positions in the new government with Kremlin proxies.

Beneš's coalition government of Democrats and communists ended abruptly in February 1948. The communist party had lost much of its popular support by then and was in danger of being marginalized, so its Moscow-controlled leaders staged a coup. Unfortunately, Beneš had little time to experience life after the "final victory of socialism" that he helped bring about, since he died only three months after losing power.

The Beneš Decrees

The shameful decrees, which became law when the Czechoslovak government began vigorously pursuing and punishing Nazi criminals, are still on the books as of this writing. They serve to keep Sudeten Germans from filing claims to try to get back their property in Czechoslovakia's two successor states. The decrees also still protect the few remaining Czech and Slovak citizens who tortured, murdered, and raped Germans.

In 2009 the Czech Republic endorsed the International Criminal Court (ICC), formed to prosecute war crimes committed in countries deliberately shielding war criminals. Had such a court existed after World War II,

President Beneš should have easily qualified as a defendant if Bosnian Serb leader Radovan Karadzic is any example. Karadzic ordered the ethnic cleansing of Bosnian Muslims from Bosnia at the time of Yugoslavia's breakup. Despite Czech approval of the ICC, no one in the Czech government was willing to admit to the criminality of their own country's more massive and brutal ethnic cleansing.

Central and Eastern Europe

Czechoslovakia was not the only nation in Central and Eastern Europe to lose its independence. All Soviet-liberated territory, with the exception of Austria, became firmly shackled to Moscow behind Stalin's Iron Curtain. Historian Norman Davies described just how tight the Soviet hold was:

> Layer after layer after layer of interlocking political control mechanisms enabled Moscow to hold its dependents in check at every turn. And if one check snapped there were plenty of others in reserve. Moscow's allies were not merely held by a collar around the neck; they were held by a leash on the collar, a chain on the leash, a handler on the chain, a collar and lead on the handler, a handler's handler, and, for safety's sake, a muzzle on the mouth, blinkers on the eyes, and a set of trip-wires fastened to the paws and tail. In the parlance of Soviet dog-handling they called it fraternal assistance.[5]

The Eastern Bloc finally began to disintegrate in 1989 after deep Soviet economic troubles forced a liberalization of policies and weakened the authoritarian glue that held the empire together. The Soviet Union itself collapsed in 1991 and its former republics gained, or regained, independence.

Sarajevo

If Johann Hajek were still alive, he probably wouldn't be surprised to learn that Sarajevo, where he first went to war in 1914, is currently the capital of a tiny artificially constructed country known as Bosnia and Herzegovina and remains troubled 100 years later. Although the Bosnians, Croats, and Serbs are still divided, the unrest today probably stems more from government stagnation, corruption, and high unemployment.

In January 2014, the German publication Der Spiegel reexamined this messy spot on the map and the source of its current problems. Despite the mixed metaphors, the following excerpt sums up its recent history: "When former Communist leader Marshal Josip Tito, the man Stalin called a 'megalomaniacal dwarf', ruled Yugoslavia from 1945 to 1980, he managed to contain the ethnic centrifugal forces. But the dams definitely burst after 1991. In Belgrade the Serbs—with the support of their traditional protectors, the Russians—pursued their goal of establishing a Greater Serbia. Meanwhile, Karadžić executed his policy of "ethnic cleansing' on Bosnian soil."[6]

The Spiegel story points out the ultimate source of the problems today: "The two parts of Bosnia and Herzegovina and a multinational district has been divided into 10 cantons run by a total of 180 ministers. Administrative costs consume up to two-thirds of the national budget. Consensus among the different parts of the country and ethnic groups cannot be achieved on even the most fundamental issues, such as the rights of minorities."

And in a final irony, as I write this, an Austrian is once again in charge, just as when World War I began. He is the country's highest ranking civilian authority as the European Union's Special Representative for Bosnia and Herzegovina.

The Red Army

Soviet soldiers were trained for mass commitment, and the number of lives expended was of little concern to the Kremlin. Embedded commissars and NKVD barrier troops placed behind their lines guaranteed they wouldn't fall back because the danger of death from the rear was no less than from the enemy to the front. For the most part Soviet soldiers fought bravely under difficult circumstances and sometimes poor leadership. Over eight and a half million Soviet soldiers died and 18 million suffered wounds in World War II.

However, these liberators quickly wore out their welcome in the Czech lands and the other occupied territories after the war. This was in no small part due to the high crime rate they brought with them and their lack of courtesy in not leaving after the liberating was finished. Moscow, like Prague, held a hard line on prosecuting German military war criminals and punished many German soldiers, but seldom penalized the criminals in the Red Army.

In Czechoslovakia, Beneš's treaties with Stalin allowed the Russians to stay for the next 45 years. In early 1990, shortly after the fall of the Berlin Wall and the collapse of the Iron Curtain, I saw Soviet officers still commuting to work on the Prague subway. However, out on the street and outside military bases, the Soviet Army (as the Red Army was called after 1946) was clearly packing up. Ordinary soldiers sold Soviet uniforms, gear, and Russian rubles on sidewalks as tourist souvenirs to supplement their miserable pay.

The Rape Epidemic

Rape occurs in all wars. Interestingly, in World War II the German command enforced discipline and German soldiers committed relatively few rapes. The opposite was true in the Red Army. Russian propagandists openly encouraged it. Although the Kremlin leaders avoided an official sanction of rape, it was tolerated at all levels and soldiers were promised the conquered women to make them fight harder. It was said that the first troops in got the watches, the second group got the females, and the rest had to settle for the leftovers. While the Soviet soldiers raped wherever they were and even Russian women fell victim, German women suffered most. In Russian-occupied German territory rape was part of everyday life. In some areas the savagery wasn't seriously curtailed until four years after the war ended. Although no one knows how many German women were raped, a figure of two million is often used.

On taking Berlin the Russian commander told his troops the city's women were theirs. At this time up to 80 percent of the city's population was female. British officers reaching the city were stunned to find lakes full of women who'd committed suicide after sexual assault. Young girls, old women, nurses, and even nuns were fair game. Many were gang-raped and raped on multiple occasions. Some victims were so badly injured that they didn't survive the attack. Many others picked up venereal diseases, which ran rampant among the attackers. For the women, there were no antibiotics. The majority of resulting pregnancies were terminated in painful abortions under the most unsanitary conditions. Nevertheless, up to 200,000 "Russian" babies were born to German women.[7]

After a European inspection tour, US Senator James Eastland said in a December 1945 speech: "The virtue of womanhood and the value of human life...are the very cheapest thing in Russian-occupied Germany today." To illustrate his point, he read from a priest's letter that had been smuggled out of Breslau, Germany: "In unending succession were girls, women and nuns violated...not merely in secret, in hidden corners, but in the sight of everybody, even in churches, in the streets and in public places were nuns, women and even eight-year-old girls attacked again and again. Mothers were violated before the eyes of their children; girls in the presence of their brothers; nuns, in the sight of pupils, were outraged again and again to their very death and even as corpses."[8]

The horror Berlin suffered had already been visited upon countless cities and towns such as Königsberg and Danzig to the east. Survivors who fled East and West Prussia reported women assaulted after such cruelties were even nailed to doors or wagon carts. A priest from Danzig wrote they "violated eight-year-old girls and shot boys who tried to shield their mothers."[9]

The Red Army wasn't alone in this crime. Poles, Czechs, partisans of all stripes, and gangs of freed Russian POWs raped throughout Central and Eastern Europe. Allied soldiers did so as well, particularly near the end of the war in French and German territory, but never to the extent of the Red Army. The US Army enforced the policy against it when possible. At least 50 soldiers were hanged for the crime.[10] After fighting in Europe ended, the incidence of rape by Allied soldiers fell precipitously, but not because of a sudden outbreak of virtue. The decline in chaos lessened opportunity, and sex could be purchased from starving German women for shoes, medicine, soap, or morsels of food. Even children turned to prostitution to survive.[11]

Germany

During the Cold War the western Allies combined the American, British, and French Zones and formed the nation of West Germany. The Russian Zone became East Germany. Throughout the Cold War, America and its allies confronted the Soviet Union's ambition to control all of Germany and Western Europe. The struggle led to the formation of two military alliances: the North Atlantic Treaty Organization (NATO) in the West and the Warsaw Pact Alliance in the East.

To prevent Germans from leaving, the Soviets ordered their East German satellite state to build a fortified fence and minefield along the entire border. However, isolating the administrative island of West Berlin within East Germany wasn't possible without also cutting off much of East Germany's rail service. Thus, a migration loophole open for East Germans remained open until 1961 when a rail bypass around West Berlin was completed. At that time the Communists separated East and West Berlin by building what they called the Anti-Fascist Protection Rampart. The rest of the world knew the barrier as the Berlin Wall. A few gates in the Wall finally opened on November 9, 1989, at a time when the communist governments of the Central and Eastern European countries were rapidly losing control. Sledgehammer-armed citizens, popularly dubbed *Mauerspechte* (wall woodpeckers), hastened the liberation process by creating a number of unauthorized border crossings. Less than a year later the two countries officially reunited. Germany went on to become the economic powerhouse of Europe.

The Sudetenland

Clearly, the music died in the Sudeten German borderlands in 1945. Gone are the innovative and industrious farmers, the vineyards, the gardens, and the fruit-tree-lined roads. Gone are the Volkschulen, the gymnastics organizations with their sports areas, the community choruses, and the cultural organizations. And gone are the cooperatives, the village craftsmen, the shops, the festivals, the dances, the hunts, the inns, and the holiday traditions. What remains are houses and largely vacant streets. Much change would have occurred anyway in the course of modernization, but if Beneš hadn't sold Czechoslovakia's soul to Stalin to win approval for his eviction of all Germans, a postwar fate more like Austria's is imaginable.

Of the Czechs who scooped up the German farms, few had a love for the land or knowledge of it, so little attachment formed. Fittingly, the new owners too lost their farms when the communist government created its vast collective farm system. The Czechs who snapped up free houses in rural communities likewise did not appreciate the dwellings as did those who'd inherited a family legacy or worked and saved to buy the home. Predictably, many buildings fell into disrepair. Some were never occupied, and others rotted away after neglect or abandonment. A sense of community does not form instantly when almost everyone is a stranger and knows their neighbors are thieves.

Entire industries, and many local economies, collapsed after Beneš's shortsighted political motives eliminated the industrious German farmers, businessmen, and skilled workers. Parts of the country turned into economic wastelands, and many old villages disappeared from the records. By 1965 over 500 Sudeten villages had vanished. Some dried up because the communist government couldn't get Czech workers to remain in them despite cash subsidies. Others were in the way of collectivization. Bulldozers and matches eradicated them, and little or no physical sign of their existence remains.

Brüx (now called Most), a city of 30,000 residents before the war, provides an example of what happened. When its many Germans were driven out, the city remained half empty and stood neglected for years. By the 1960s the city became less valuable than the coalfield it sat astride, so the communist regime allowed it to be destroyed in the filming of a war movie, *The Bridge at Remagen*. A replacement Most now sits at another site.

The vast majority of displaced Sudeten Germans became West Germans. A smaller number settled in Austria and other countries. Despite the bitterness many of these people felt towards Czechs for what occurred, many still contributed money to help restore the churches and monuments in their old homeland. Oswald Lustig and Oskar Halusa, like many others, did so not because they thought they'd ever get back any stolen property, but to preserve what was dear to them and their ancestors. In 2003 I saw a prime example of this in the village of Lodenitz where my mother attended Sunday morning Mass throughout her childhood. The parish priest there told me contributions from former German residents paid for much of the refurbishment going on at the time.

The Sudetenland Farms

Through her middle years, Maria held out hope of compensation for her plot of Schömitz land. She knew the money wouldn't amount to much. Rather, she would have valued the symbolic recognition of a wrong and an acknowledgement of the great suffering borne by Sudeten Germans. Neither she nor any of her fellow expellees ever realized this hope.

Following the loss of the German farmers, agricultural production fell precipitously. Much land went to ruin or was left untended. After the 1948 coup, when the communists dropped the last pretense of democracy and seized power, the new government bundled nearly all farmland into collective farms, or *kolkhozy*, as the Czechs' Soviet masters called them. The German land was collectivized first. Even the Meierhof enterprise lost its identity.

When the individual parcels were merged to create giant fields, most farm lanes, landmarks, and other traces of character were obliterated. The once carefully tended vineyards, fruit and nut trees, berry bushes, and vegetable patches were wastefully cleared and burned. Thereafter, the land that had nurtured numerous largely self-sufficient villages for centuries was tended by uncaring laborers with no personal stake in the production process. This system of agriculture failed miserably.

The collectivization continued through the sixties and eventually encompassed 95 percent of all agricultural land in Czechoslovakia. The high cost of subsidizing workers to keep them on the farms was but one problem. The soil itself was often degraded through poor management, bad practices, and toxic contamination because the system fostered corruption. Farm managers could too easily be induced to look the other way as contaminated or diluted fertilizer and chemicals were applied.

The agricultural landscape was so altered that in the nineties, when the new political reality reopened the border and enabled expelled Germans to visit their former *Heimat* (homeland), the original farmers could no longer find their fields for lack of landmarks.

Sudeten German History and Geography

Today the Sudetenland exists only on historical maps and as a fading memory in the heads of its former residents. After the Sudetenland's moment of fame at the onset of World War II passed, its relevance diminished and the territory became little more than a historical footnote. The press largely ignored the extreme savagery unleashed on Germans there after the war and neither the scale nor barbarity of the ethnic cleansing received much mention in the history books. Germans have long since acknowledged the great sins committed during the Nazi era, but in Czechoslovakia's successor states, as in Russia, there persists a strong resistance to acknowledging the wrongs of the past. The regional history taught in Czech schools since the war contains a large gap. The topic remains a victor's history, which is defined as the misrepresentation that occurs when nationalistic interests override the truth. The surviving Sudeten Germans and their descendants might rightfully point out this policy is at odds with the Czech Republic's lofty motto, "Pravda vítězí" (The truth shall prevail).

Notably, a few Czechs braved criticism and spoke out over the years. Ján Mlynárik, a Slovak historian exiled from Czechoslovakia in the early 1980s, was an early critic of the Czech Communist government. He contended the extreme theft of German property taught the nation to steal and undermined its morality. František Hanzlik, a Czech military historian asserted the vicious first expulsion wave, the Wild Expulsion, was a government-sponsored program that officials subsequently covered up. Czech journalist and writer Sidonia Dedina aimed much of her criticism at the architect of the ethnic cleansing, Edvard Beneš. In the forward of a book which is part historical novel and part investigative journalism, she calls Beneš "a disaster of a man" who "today...would have to stand trial before an international tribunal for war crimes, or crimes against humanity."[12]

More recently, various Czech politicians have in one way or another tepidly expressed regret for various aspects of the expulsion but not officially apologized. When in 2013 Czech President Miloš Zeman said Sudeten Germans should be grateful they were merely expelled from their homeland, Czech prime minister Petr Nečas tried to smooth things over by acknowledging before the Bavarian Parliament that the forcible expulsion of millions of ethnic Germans from his country was wrong. However, his words again fell short of the apology the Sudeten German survivors and descendants demand. The reluctance to take this final step is perhaps politically understandable, considering a 2011 survey of Czechs showed 42 percent still believed the expulsion of Sudeten Germans just. The good news is that this is down from 52 percent in 1995.[13]

The Numbers

Nearly two million Reich soldiers became prisoners in Czechoslovakia at the time of Germany's surrender. The majority ended up in Russian captivity, where many perished under ghastly conditions. Of the survivors, many were too physically damaged to ever work again. The Czechs also imprisoned many POWs, but precise numbers are hard to come by because of the initial secrecy and lack of record keeping. Refugee affidavits report that once disarmed, those captives not machine gunned in groups, executed individually, or killed by mobs endured extreme and prolonged pain at the hands of the Czech military and paramilitaries.

About 180,000 Sudeten Germans in uniform died in battle or in captivity. Approximately 10,000 Sudeten German civilians perished in the wartime hostilities. Some were caught in the fighting, but the majority died in Allied bombing raids on Sudeten cities. Another thousand or more died resisting the Nazis.

The number of deaths resulting from the occupation and expulsion are controversial even today. The figures draw both defenders and critics. Heimatortskartei (HOK) für Sudetendeutsche, a German charitable organization whose stated mission was family reunification, undertook an extensive accounting of Sudetenland ethnic Germans over several decades after the war and assembled a refugee database to account for all Sudeten Germans. Of the 3,295,000 within Czechoslovakia before the expulsion, the HOK claimed it had determined the fate of all but 225,000. Many of the latter group may have survived but could not be located. By HOK numbers some 165,000 Sudeten Germans were killed directly in the expulsion period between May 1945 and October 1946. It says another 105,000 died from the consequences of the expulsion, for an overall total of 270,000 dead, not including the 180,000 military deaths mentioned above. Many of these expulsion deaths were said to have occurred in Germany from the effects of starvation and abuse in Czechoslovakia. The German government's Federal Statistical Office developed similar numbers during this period.

Various historians, commissions, and Czech interest groups who insist that only witnessed deaths can be included state that these estimates are highly biased and include people who died of natural causes or were bilingual Czechs who spoke German. At the time of this writing the Czech government, like its predecessor communist government, maintains that only about 19,000 Germans died in the expulsion and only another 6,000 died of violence. A joint German and Czech commission in 1995 estimated the number of civilian deaths in Czechoslovakia as between 15,000 and 30,000 persons.[14]

The critics of such commissions and government groups contend that the resultant numbers are highly political and discount the vast database and the statistical methods employed in the German studies. Given the chaos, the nationwide scale of the violence, and the secrecy employed by many of the killers, the standard of using only witnessed deaths vastly understates the total. One academic criticism of such reports states the low-end numbers come from using incredibly exact standards and only include death certificates issued by Czech administrators in concentration camps and elsewhere. Obviously, the authorities had no desire to leave in the public record the number of deaths they were responsible for by issuing such certificates.

Furthermore, critics of the low figures charge that not all existing Czech records were accessed.[15]

For Central and Eastern Europe as a whole, out of some ten million expelled ethnic Germans, and up to another five million who fled prior to the expulsions, between one-half and two and a half million perished. Again, there can be no agreement on a number when political interests are at stake. Many historians claim the higher figures cannot be supported. Other stakeholders who claim to be in a position to have the best numbers—the German government at various times, the German Red Cross, and several nongovernment organizations—believe the actual number falls between two and two and a half million civilians.

Whatever the figure, few in the West knew or cared at the time. An exception was British philosopher and Nobel Peace Prize winner, Bertrand Russell. During the war crime trials in Nuremberg, he pointed out the hypocrisy in trying Nazi defendants for "deportation and other inhumane acts against civilians" while the Allies simultaneously engaged in that very practice on a much larger scale. In October 1945 he wrote: "In eastern Europe now mass deportations are being carried out by our allies on an unprecedented scale, and an apparently deliberate attempt is being made to exterminate many millions of Germans, not by gas, but by depriving them of their homes and of food, leaving them to die by slow and agonizing starvation. This is not done as an act of war, but as a part of a deliberate policy of 'peace.' "[16,17]

Maria

In the wake of World War I, Maria's childhood was not an easy or a placid one. Her mother died when she was less than two years, so she could never remember mother's love. In short order she also lost her father through the lingering effects of his war trauma and his domineering new wife's refusal to accept a stepchild. Maria was then raised by an impoverished grandmother and had to help care for six younger stepsiblings at the bidding of her stepmother in order to be allowed to maintain some relationship with her father. Thus the child's early life was less than carefree. When Maria's grandmother died, her stepmother claimed the house Maria expected to inherit and a few months later sent the 15-year-old to live in another village among strangers and work as a farm laborer. Despite these tribulations, Maria retained many fond childhood memories because she grew up among supportive relatives and friends.

At the close of Maria's teen years, Hitler's war of expansion deprived her of the carefree days young adults should know before the responsibility and worries of adulthood. The war robbed Maria of her fiancé and removed an entire generation of young men from her community. The reign of violent assault, terror, and theft that followed in the postwar Soviet occupation left Maria with toxic memories and burdened her with a rape baby. As with most of her fellow Sudeten Germans, the severe anguish and emotional toll of the mistreatment imparted an ire that would never quite dissipate. Only after the Czechoslovak government's ethnic cleansing campaign expelled Maria to a ruined Germany full of resettlement camps, poverty, and cramped living conditions could she again begin to feel safe.

Maria in her 80s posing in an old hat

Despite the poverty and adversity in Maria's early life in the Sudetenland, she considered herself rich in terms of friends, culture, and heritage. Although she mourned the loss of her homeland the rest of her life, the intangible wealth and grounding it imbued allowed her to regain her balance. My mother was not without happiness and fulfillment after her expulsion and the death of Renate, but many conversations with her about her early years convinced me a part of her remained behind in the Sudetenland.

The remainder of my mother's story, the part that occurs after she married my father and their stories merged, follows in the companion volume relaying my father's parallel chronicle. In short, after marrying, she bore my sister and me and then courageously transplanted her family to North America after six years in Bavaria. In the United States, she had two more children and found a new life in rural Iowa after a short sojourn in Tulelake, California, a place that must have brought back disquieting memories because it was the site of a large World War II Japanese-American internment camp. Her adjustment to farm life proved difficult because unlike in most of rural Europe, farm wives in North America lived semi-isolated lives out on the land. She sorely missed village life and having her friends and relatives around her. Nevertheless, she regained her equilibrium, made many new friends, devoted great energy to the raising of her children, and survived a bout of breast cancer in midlife. By the time I was grown and had left home, she'd come to embrace the country life enough to want to remain on the family farm into her 80s. She died at the venerable age of 91.

---

[1] Wikipedia contributors, "Bombing of Vienna in World War II," *Wikipedia*, Wikipedia.org, 9 Feb. 2015, accessed 21 Apr. 2015.

[2] Fischer, *Hitler and America*, 241.

[3] F Gerstenbrand and E Karamat, "Adolf Hitler's Parkinson's Disease and an Attempt to Analyse His Personality Structure," *European Journal of Neurology: The Official Journal of the European Federation of Neurological Societies* 6, no. 2 (March 1999): 121–127.

[4] Nikita Sergeevich Khrushchev, *Khrushchev Remembers*, 1st ed. (Boston: Little, Brown, 1970), 180.

[5] Norman Davies, *Heart of Europe: A Short History of Poland*, corr. ed., Oxford Paperbacks (Oxford [Oxfordshire] ; New York: Oxford University Press, 1986), 84.

[6] Walter Mayr, "The Bosnian Knot: Conflicts Unchanged in Birthplace of WWI," *Spiegel Online*, Spiegel.de/international, 16 Jan. 2014.

[7] MacDonogh, *After the Reich*, 114.

[8] Ralph Franklin Keeling, *Gruesome Harvest*, 54.

[9] Ralph Franklin Keeling, *Gruesome Harvest*, 54.

[10] Wikipedia contributors, "Capital punishment by the United States military," *Wikipedia*, Wikipedia.org, 16 Apr. 2015, accessed 20 Apr. 2015.

[11] Ralph Franklin Keeling, *Gruesome Harvest*, 64.

[12] Dědinová, *Edvard Beneš the Liquidator*.

[13] "The Expulsion of Sudeten Germans Is Still Raw," *The Economist*, Economist.com, 7 May 2013, accessed 20 Apr. 2015.

[14] Wikipedia contributors, "Expulsion of Germans from Czechoslovakia," *Wikipedia*, Wikipedia.org, 13 June 2015, accessed 10 July 2015.

[15] Karl Cordell and Stefan Wolff, *Germany, Poland and the Czech Republic Since Reunification: Ostpolitik Revisited* (Routledge, 2004), 112.

[16] De Zayas, *Nemesis at Potsdam*, 108.

[17] Bertrand Russell, *Yours Faithfully, Bertrand Russell: A Life Long Fight for Peace, Justice, and Truth in Letters to the Editor* (Open Court Publishing, 2002), 162.

Addenda

More About World War I: Ignition

In the early 1900s, Serbia, along with Bulgaria, Greece, and Montenegro, attained independence from the Ottoman Empire. Serbian nationalists wanted to also unite Serbia with other south Slavic populations still outside their borders. One such region was Austrian-held Bosnia with its substantial population of ethnic Serbs. A Serbian terrorist organization calling itself the Black Hand hoped to accomplish this by provoking an Austrian reprisal serious enough to rile Bosnian Serbs into revolting and joining its independent neighbor Serbia. Serbian nationalists were only too willing to task members of the Black Hand with killing Archduke Franz Ferdinand of Austria.

The Black Hand had evolved from a Serbian nationalist organization that hoped to instigate a war of liberation using anti-Austrian propaganda and sabotage. The group needed the backing of Russia, since Serbia couldn't hope to win such a war on its own. When Russia declared itself unwilling to go to war over this issue, Austria gained enough leverage to compel the Serbian government to break up the organization. The disbanded group's leaders promptly formed the more secretive Black Hand. In the new organization, district committees took their orders from an executive committee led by a Serbian military commander with the code name Apis. The name came from an ancient Egyptian bull deity who served as an intermediary between humans and an all-powerful god.

Apis feared that as soon as Archduke Franz Ferdinand acceded to the throne he intended to grant the Empire's ethnic Serbians enough autonomy to make pan-Serbian unity very difficult for his nationalist organization. When Apis learned Ferdinand would visit Bosnia, he bypassed the executive committee and launched a plan to kill Ferdinand. The means to carry out the mission fell into Apis's lap when a scrawny high school student with ties to a group that called itself Young Bosnia approached one of his agents. The student, Gavrilo Princip, and several other young men he had already recruited to help with the task were then armed and trained in Serbia. On the day of Ferdinand's visit, Princip dispersed himself and six other assassins along the publicly announced motorcade route.

An emissary of the Serbian prime minister as well as Austria's own spies warned Ferdinand he was in danger, but the archduke refused to cancel his appearance. Despite the threat, the security arrangements for Ferdinand's visit made by the Austrian military governor of Bosnia were surprisingly lax. Relatively few policemen guarded the route on that June 28 Sunday morning when the six-car motorcade wound its way through the city. The open-top royal car belonged to a member of the archduke's retinue, Count Franz von Harrach. Harrach rode in front with the chauffeur while the governor, Ferdinand, and Ferdinand's wife, Sophie, occupied the back seat. As the archduke proceeded along a major thoroughfare, Appel Quay, to the city hall where he was to deliver a speech, the Black Hand assassins, armed with Browning pistols and small grenade-sized bombs from the Serbian State Arsenal, positioned themselves along the route.

The first two students failed to shoot or lob a bomb, but the third student along the route asked a policeman which car was Ferdinand's before he flung his bomb. After the device exploded near the trailing car and injured many, including the man carrying the archduke's speech, the attacker swallowed a cyanide capsule and ran into the adjoining river. However, he vomited up the bitter poison, and failed to escape the angry pursuers in the inches-deep stream.

The upset archduke continued to the city hall. There, after he wiped off the blood-spattered pages of his speech that had been retrieved from the bombed car, he delivered his address and then insisted on visiting his injured aides in the hospital.[1] The governor directed the motorcade to return along Appel Quay because it was straight and allowed a higher speed. As the vehicles set out, Count von Harrach positioned himself protectively on the left running board of the car next to the archduke. When the police in the lead car mistakenly turned onto a side street, the archduke's driver followed. As soon as the governor recognized the error, he ordered the driver to stop and turn around.

Princip, finding himself only feet from the car with no one between him and the occupants when the car stopped, stepped forward and fired two shots with his pistol. The first bullet hit Sophie in the abdomen, and the second passed through Ferdinand's uniform collar and severed a jugular vein. When Sophie slumped over, the archduke had just enough time to plead with his beloved wife not to die before he himself passed out. The driver frantically extricated the car and sped to the governor's residence, but both Ferdinand and Sophie were dead by the time they were carried inside.[2,3]

From a detached viewpoint the archduke, as an excellent marksman, would surely have been astounded that two such wild shots could each prove fatal so quickly. Had he been armed and aware of what was happening, Princip might have been the one to take a bullet, for the previous year as a guest of British King George V at Windsor, Ferdinand's shooting skill allowed him to bring down a disproportionate share of the estimated 4,500 pheasants and 1,000 ducks the party of five bagged in three days of shooting.[4]

More About World War I: Factors Leading to Conflict
The pre-war German government, under the near-absolute rule of Kaiser Wilhelm II, was wary of a rising leftist influence and realized the heightened nationalism that comes with war could help stem this drift. Germany, with the largest and best army in Europe, was also engaged in a naval arms race with Britain to counter the latter's decisive sea dominance. Navies were the key to acquiring colonies and expanding foreign industrial markets, and Germany's leadership was not averse to using its expanding fleet to help the economy.

Russia, after a poor military showing against Japan in the 1905 Russo-Japanese War to dominate Manchuria and Korea, needed to boost its international standing and influence. The empire had recently reformed and rapidly expanded its military, so the tsar was confident he would profit from a conflict.

In Austria-Hungary, the Habsburgs believed their forces could easily overwhelm Serbia's much smaller army and punish the country for Franz Ferdinand's assassination.. The resulting victory would then help unify their empire.

In France, the leftist government faced strong right-wing opposition and still stewed over the loss of territory upon the unification of Germany in 1871. President Poincaré believed that French forces were in a strong position militarily and might never again find conditions so favorable. The French left expected to regain both votes and lost territory through a clash with its neighbor, Germany. Although France was prepared to fight Germany, it couldn't afford to initiate a war without losing vital British support through a defensive pact made with Britain, but Poincaré was not averse to having the war start elsewhere.[5]

Imperialism also played an important role in the onset of war. The European powers each realized that the least costly way to acquire the natural resources they required to keep their industries competitive was to hold on to, and if possible increase, their colonial possessions. All the powers were certain a war would benefit their colonial interest, and, as a result, remained suspicious of each other's foreign intentions.

Germany, with only a few minor colonies, was especially mistrusted. Britain, which controlled one-fourth of the world at the time, was particularly worried about the proximity of one of Germany's colonies, Southwest Africa (now Namibia), to Britain's vast gold and diamond resources in South Africa. London was also concerned about Germany's plan to build a Berlin-to-Iraq railroad, which would open a major trade route to the Persian Gulf and threaten Britain's trade monopoly there. Although France, Britain, and Russia also had differences among themselves with respect to colonial interests, fear of Germany's intentions unsettled them the most.[6,7]

On July 23, 1914, a month after the assassination of Archduke Ferdinand, Austria presented Serbia with an ultimatum. To the consternation of the Serbs, who insisted that their own ongoing investigation of the assassination was adequate, the Austrians demanded acceptance of an Austro-Hungarian inquiry. Austria also demanded that Serbia curb all anti-Austrian propaganda and root out terrorist organizations such as the Black Hand. The nature of the demands, and the stipulation that the answer must come within 48 hours, made refusal to comply almost a foregone conclusion.

More About World War I: Two Lesser Known Fronts of the Great War
Militarily, the Triple Alliance of Germany, Austro-Hungary, Italy, and several smaller allies got off to a shaky start in the war because of an earlier major misunderstanding. Although Germany had long before agreed to stand by Austria in a justified Austrian attack on Serbia, it expected Austria to hold off on this offensive and turn the bulk of its military against the large Russian army in Poland to the north. This would free Germany to finish off France before engaging the Russians. However, Austrian planners counted on Germany to shoulder most of the fight against Russia. At the last minute the Austrians realized they had little choice other than to hurriedly mobilize against the freshly deployed Russian army. Yet, they refused to delay the attack on Serbia.

The German war plan called for a quick victory against France, and then a rapid transport of most of the fighting force to its East Prussian province to engage the Russians. To overwhelm France, Germany intended to seize Belgium as a staging ground for an invasion of France. Unfortunately for the Germans, this action had the unintended consequence of drawing the British into the fight before Germany could take France. The English feared the proximity of the Germans across the English Channel and opted to honor a treaty to defend Belgium. When the allied French and British forces stopped the Germans not far short of Paris at the Battle of the Marne, the Germans had but one army free to defend their territory in East Prussia. However, the German commanders facing the Russians found that despite the overwhelming size of the opposition army, the Russians failed to use their advantage and attacked only with scattered units. This handed the Germans a stunning victory when the vastly outnumbered German Eighth Army destroyed the Russian Second Army at Tannenberg. German mobility then made it possible for that same army to engage and defeat the Russian First Army. The Russians never recovered on this part of the eastern front.

Just as in the war of 1905, the Russian field forces underperformed on the battlefield despite a large numerical superiority. The reforms instituted before the war began failed in large part because bureaucratic squabbles between various governmental ministries and the military left the army without a unified supreme command. The resulting internal civil war raging within the Russian military leadership effectively split the troops into two forces that refused to coordinate operations. One fought the Germans and the other, the Austro-Hungarians.

The Russian army also suffered from a deficient general command staff, a shortage of competent senior field officers, and an undertrained infantry. Military leaders throughout Europe at that time believed it took 10 years of service to make a good soldier. The two- or three-year term the conscripts served was too short to train them in anything but simple maneuvers. Since 1912 the Russian military academy had taught officers only two movements, advance and pullback, so the only tactic field commanders had was to send large masses of men against the enemy line. The new weapons—machine guns, accurate artillery, and infantry rifles that fired many times per minute—effectively cut the Russians down. The Russian Army was also hindered by a lack of modern communication equipment, poor artillery support, and an outmoded dependence on highly vulnerable cavalry units.

◆

With Germany unable to confront Russia on the scale it planned at the outset of the war, Austro-Hungary had to scramble to change its war plan. The reassignment and transport of much of Austria's military manpower to the Russian Front left far fewer soldiers to overwhelm Serbia. Still, on paper the Austrian force of 270,000 was much stronger than the standing Serb force, which numbered 180,000. So the Austrian chief of staff, Count Franz Xaver Joseph Conrad von Hötzendorf, confidently pressed the attack in the belief that he could take Serbia within a month or two.

Marshal Radomir Putnik, a man in poor health, commanded the Serb military forces. Ironically, at the start of hostilities Putnik was under treatment in a hospital within the Austrian Empire. The

Austrians arrested Putnik at the war's start but released him a short time later. They did this ostensibly as a gesture of courtliness, but it is likely the Austrians let him go in the belief that such a sick man couldn't possibly be a competent commander. The release proved to be a huge mistake. Putnik effectively led the outgunned Serb army from a hospital room while Conrad, whose task was admittedly more difficult because he was dealing with larger forces as well as directing two fronts simultaneously, bungled both the Austrian mobilization and the conduct of the war that followed.

The Serbian campaign was a disaster for Austria. At the end of 1914, after months of fighting, the army found itself back where it began because Putnik drew in the invaders to stretch their supply lines before he counterattacked. Although by the time the fighting ended, Serb casualties amounted to 170,000 dead, wounded, missing, or captured, Austro-Hungary paid even more dearly. It lost nearly 230,000 men in this corner of the war.

Unlike their German allies, the Austrians also fared poorly against the tsar's forces. The Austrian military inflicted enormous losses on the Russians, but at such a huge cost to themselves that they could never replace all their own losses. Particularly hard hit was the field officer corps. In 1916 alone, the incompetence of the Austrian high command resulted in a million casualties on the Russian front. The dire situation didn't improve until the Germans stepped in and assumed the lead under a merged command. The German staff had little sympathy for Austria and blamed it for not investing enough in war preparation. General Erich Ludendorff, the top German war strategist and the most powerful man in Germany in 1917 and 1918, later wrote that having Austria for an ally was like being "shackled to a corpse."

In coordination with the German and Bulgarian armies, Austro-Hungary finally took Serbia late in 1915. But several months earlier, Italy had changed sides and attacked the Austrians in the Alps. Although the Austrians had troubles enough, their soldiers fought more effectively here than did the Italians who outnumbered them. The difficult mountainous terrain left the Italian Army only one major attack point—the widest stretch of the Isonzo River Valley. In this valley, one battle sometimes blended into another, leaving historians to wrestle with the problem of 12 Battles of the Isonzo. As elsewhere, losses were high on both sides. The nature of the terrain and the static position of the armies meant trench warfare took root much like on the Western Front, but the geology made for one important difference. Exploding shells proved far more deadly here because the rocky soil sent so much extra shrapnel flying.

More About World War I: Versailles—A Flawed Process

French Prime Minister Georges Clemenceau, by then an old man, was elected president of the Versailles Peace Conference in 1919 because France was the host country and Clemenceau, who spoke English, could communicate directly with his American and British counterparts. Clemenceau had based his whole political career largely on one issue that can be summed up in the words of a contemporary journalist observer: "He hated Germany and he hated Germans; to him they were incarnate bad, all of a piece, the eternal enemy. To him there was only one future, that of a France secure forever against a repetition of the assault."[8]

Clemenceau delegated the Austrian territory settlement duties to his deputy, André Tardieu, a man who would later serve as France's Prime Minister himself. Tardieu hated Germans nearly as much as Clemenceau did. Unfortunately for the Habsburgs, Tardieu was also interested in gutting their empire. Because this meshed with the interests of Edvard Beneš, an ultranationalist Czech delegate, the two men worked hand in glove.

The conference was rife with misleading documents and maps designed to buttress arguments, and no one used them better than Beneš. With one document, *Memoire III*, he "underestimated the number of Germans in Bohemia by one million" and employed a forged map to prove the German areas were not contiguous.[9]

The earlier bowing and scraping accorded Wilson by the other Allied leaders, and the lip service paid to his "right to self-determination" talk, largely ceased after the need for American money and troops disappeared. In the end the French leaders got their revenge against the Germans and Austrians, and in the bargain planted a deeply indebted ally, Czechoslovakia, between the two defeated foes.

Not only the Czechs got their way. The Kingdom of Hungary's neighbors, who demanded most of Hungary's territory and people, also received what they asked for. The American delegation sided with Hungary in its request for plebiscites to decide the fate of the affected areas. However, everyone knew the residents of these regions would overwhelmingly vote to remain part of Hungary. The British and French delegations wanted a weak Hungary so they refused to permit any balloting. Allowing a vote would also have set a dangerous precedent—one tacitly acknowledged by Tardieu when he defended his stand by stating he had a choice of organizing plebiscites or creating Czechoslovakia. From the first, he stated that they would show no pity to Hungary, and he stuck to his word. He saw to it that the thousand-year-old kingdom lost 71.4 percent of its territory to hostile neighbors Czechoslovakia, Romania, and Serbia.

The economic consequences were devastating. Hungary lost the majority of its paved roads, railroads, industry, financial firms, and natural resources. The kingdom also lost half of its 10 largest cities and nearly two-thirds of its population—a prescription for economic ruin if there ever was one. In the Austro-Hungarian Empire, Hungary as the breadbasket and Austria as the industrial center had complemented each other and allowed the whole region to prosper. Removing the bulk of the Empire's natural resources and key pieces of its road and rail network sabotaged the economy of the entire region. With Hungary's huge grain mills stranded and Austria stripped of its industry, banks, and skilled work force, Central Europe was knocked into a severe depression.

Hungary's representatives were not even invited to Paris until the dismemberment was all but formalized. Even the least deserving ally, Romania, who'd performed miserably in the fighting and supported the Allies only halfheartedly, was awarded a huge chunk of the very valuable Banat that it lobbied for. This award changed the nationality of the other Johann, my paternal grandfather. Soon after his homecoming from the Great War, he found himself a Romanian instead of a Hungarian.

Beneš, when asked how many Hungarians would fall under Czech rule if his demands were met, answered 350,000. The real census figure was more than double that. He also misrepresented the geography to extend the Czech border and leave Hungary militarily indefensible. However, his most flagrant fraudulent assertion was to claim a stretch of the Danube as the border with Hungary when he knew that land was 95 percent ethnic Hungarian. This placed another 415,000 Magyars inside Czechoslovakia.

Romania's chief delegate was no less dishonest in the quest for Transylvania. He drastically understated the region's Hungarian population and claimed it contained only one million Hungarians when the true number was nearly double that. When challenged by the American Secretary of State, Tardieu cut the Secretary off and declared that the concession had been studied with care and would stand.

◆

Slovakia proved yet another story of deceit. To gain the popular support of Slovaks before the peace conference, the Czech nationalists repeatedly pledged their new joint republic would be a real federation and not just a smaller Czech-led Austrian Empire. Still, the Czechs didn't rely entirely on quiet acquiescence. At the very time that Beneš was assuring the Allies that his new country would model itself on Switzerland and its ethnic Cantons in democratic structure and tolerance, behind the scenes he ruthlessly suppressed the minority voice in his "republic" to prevent contradictory testimony from getting in his way. In ordering the Czech military to occupy Slovakia, his heavy-handedness caused most Slovaks to quickly turn against the union.

The Slovaks were a devoutly Catholic people with a history of choosing priests as leaders. Their most influential leader at the time was Monsignor Andre Hlinka. Hlinka had been a supporter of the Czech-Slovak state until his Czech "partners" invaded and militarily occupied Slovakia. When he realized how this Slovak "autonomy" was going to work, he attempted to go to Paris and inform the delegates that Slovaks now wanted out of the union. The Czech police refused to issue Hlinka an exit visa, but he managed to sneak across the border into Poland to seek a visa there. However, due to the strong influence of the French Embassy in Warsaw, Poland too denied him. With help from a future pope, Pius the Eleventh, Hlinka and his party surreptitiously slipped through Croatia, Italy, and Switzerland, often going without shelter, food, or sleep. When Hlinka finally arrived in Paris three months later and took refuge in a monastery, he immediately asked to meet with the only delegates he trusted—the Americans. Unfortunately, by then the critical decisions had already been made.

Stephen Bonsal, a journalist who later won a Pulitzer Prize for a book about the proceedings in Versailles, was President Wilson's personal Versailles translator at the time and was assigned to be Hlinka's contact. Bonsal met secretly with Hlinka in his small monastery cell in September 1919 after Hlinka's friends showed Bonsal a letter from General Štefánik, a man Bonsal knew and admired. Štefánik was a highly decorated Slovak patriot and military pilot who'd died tragically several months earlier. During the war this scientist and Renaissance man rose to the rank of General of the French army and became the Czechoslovak provisional government's Minister of War. He'd been a guiding member of the Czechoslovak resistance government against the Austrians and a strong backer of Czechoslovakian statehood until the Czechs occupied their so-called Slovakian partner's territory. Štefánik had then confronted Beneš and after a fierce argument severed all ties with the man.

No one knows if Hlinka was correct when he asserted that Beneš's agents killed Štefánik as he returned to Slovakia, but Štefánik's death was very convenient and occurred under suspicious circumstances six months after the war's end. The official explanation was that his plane was mistaken for a hostile Hungarian plane and shot down by Czech troops. Hlinka charged that Štefánik was executed after he landed. Before his death, Štefánik had entrusted Hlinka with the letter that led to the meeting with Bonsal. It said, "Do what you can for my friends...secure for them an interview with the president or Colonel House [Edward

House, President Wilson's chief negotiator and aide at Versailles]. I can guarantee the absolute veracity of what they will have to say."[10]

Among other things, Hlinka told Bonsal that the Slovak people's fear of Lenin's Communists allowed the Czechs to convince them that only a merger of Czech and Slovak lands could fend off the threat. They were promised the union was only temporary and if things didn't work out, the Slovaks could go their own way. But the Slovaks quickly learned otherwise. Hlinka said, "In this short time [three months] we suffered more from the high-handed Czechs than we did from the Magyars in a thousand years."[11] The Pittsburgh Agreement that supposedly guaranteed both Slovak representation and autonomy got the Slovaks nothing.

Not long after this meeting, the French quietly expelled Hlinka and sent him back to Slovakia. There, Hlinka decided the only way he could maintain a voice was to run for a seat in the new parliament. However, before the election a midnight raid by Czech police ended that idea. The beatings and mistreatment Hlinka received in prison permanently damaged his health. Because Bonsal admired Beneš, his interpretation of events didn't completely agree with Hlinka's, but nevertheless he came away with a high enough opinion of the man to write "I think of him as the most sympathetic of the many agents of the scattered and disinherited ethnic fragments with whom I was brought in touch."[12]

At Versailles, President Wilson reacted strongly when he learned that Masaryk had misled him about the fraternity between the Czechs and Slovaks. Shortly thereafter, Wilson tersely interrupted a Beneš speech to declare that he'd never dismissed the idea of a Slovak referendum as needless. Beneš brushed aside the American protestations with an arrogant argument about the lunacy of creating chaotic little nations in that corner of Europe.

More About How the Minorities Fared in the New Czechoslovakian State: Reality Czech

Czechoslovakia's founders made many lofty promises about strong constitutional rights for minority citizens when they sought support for their proposed new country at Versailles. However, the government ignored these promises from the moment the borders became official. Although Sudeten Germans were most affected, the autonomy pledged to the Slovaks—a Slovak administration, parliament, and courts—never materialized either. The people who Masaryk had called Czechs in different clothes were never granted autonomy because Masaryk and Beneš knew that if allowed any leeway, the Slovaks would do the very thing the Czech nationalists had done: agitate for their own state.

In government, Czech domination was assured from the outset because Czechs were overrepresented. The Germans, despite being the country's largest minority group, received little meaningful voice. Czechs filled nearly every administrative post with any authority, to the exclusion of Slovaks, Germans, and Hungarians. Only some of the lowest level administrators at the local level were chosen from minority ranks.

When Prague showed no signs of implementing the Swiss-like tolerance Beneš promised, on March 4, 1919, German demonstrators throughout the Sudetenland gathered to show their support for self-determination. Czech soldiers crushed the gatherings by firing on the crowds. Many people were wounded and 54 died. This suppression of such a basic democratic freedom proved to most Germans that the government did not intend to sustain a balance of rights between Czechs and Germans.

An assembly under the control of Masaryk and Beneš drafted the 1920 constitution without a popular referendum. It received no Sudeten German input despite the fact that Germans had contributed two-thirds of the country's economy and a quarter of the population. Administrative policies undermined the constitution's promises that educational and cultural institutions would be maintained in proportion to population and that minorities had the right to keep their traditional language in everyday life, schools, and dealings with the government. Germans were squeezed in a vice as Prague continued to apply the minority protections in reverse by bringing ever more "minority" Czechs into the German areas to smother the German language and culture. Bohemian Germans were particularly outraged when the most sacred of Sudeten German national territory, their ancient forestland in Western Bohemia along the German border, was nationalized for "security reasons." The story was much the same in the Hungarian areas.

The Land Control Act, the legislation codifying the confiscation of estates larger than 150 hectares of tillable land or 250 hectares of total land from "foreigners" and the Roman Catholic Church, was another provocation. The seized land was to be parceled out to the landless, but it went almost exclusively to landless Czechs, not landless Germans, Hungarians, or Slovaks. The measure did little more than bring Czechs into minority areas. This so-called agrarian reform settled 170,000 Czechs in Slovak areas between 1921 and 1925.[13]

Nearly a decade into Czech statehood, Beneš boasted to a Swiss journalist how he'd gone about changing the ethnic makeup of communities. "The dominant power always has the power to change the ethnic character of towns by stationing troops, civil servants, industry, banks in them…we have done this," he said.[14] He stated this method had worked in Brno (Ger. Brünn), a city once almost entirely German but now rapidly becoming Czech. The Germans became a voting minority there in 1919 when Prague incorporated 23 largely Czech municipalities into Greater Brno. Košice (Hung. Kassa), once a Hungarian city, was likewise altered to become a Slovak city.

Another redistribution scheme imposed a capital levy to appropriate up to 30 percent of a household's property value and savings.[15] The burden of this tax fell disproportionately on the German population since it contained many of the middle class professionals, skilled workers, managers, intellectuals, and businessmen. Another law made Czech the only official language to be used in all communications with the authorities. This reneged on the pledge that allowed Germans to keep using their traditional language for such dealings and violated the main provisions of the Treaty on the Protection of Minorities, which Czechoslovakia had been required to write into its constitution at Versailles.[16]

Other incendiary actions placed German companies in Czech hands, nationalized businesses, and reduced the powers of local government in the minority areas. These actions, along with the enactment of policies affecting student funding, tariffs, investment, transport, currency exchange, and trade essentially bankrupted the once prosperous German population. By the mid-1930s, German unemployment reached 30 percent—five times the Czech rate. Social welfare benefits, which were controlled by unsympathetic Czech civil servants, largely eluded the German unemployed. Pensions and support for widows, orphans, and disabled veterans within the minority population were likewise reduced or cut. Germans protested with numerous pleas and petitions, to no avail.

Many victims of this harassment and deprivation became desperate for relief from this system that treated them as undesirable aliens in their own homeland. They understood that the pledge Masaryk and Beneš had made to emulate the Swiss model of government had been nothing more than a confidence trick to lock up the most valuable prizes of the Austrian Empire. Politically, the result was predictable. Sudeten Germans gravitated to Sudeten German nationalistic parties. Like the chicanery at Versailles, this important chapter was expunged from Czech history and has only begun to appear recently.

More About Putzi: Hitler's "Friend"
Hanfstaengl's father was a highly connected, wealthy German publisher who'd entertained well-known personages like Mark Twain and Richard Strauss at his Munich mansion. Putzi's mother was the daughter of William Heine, a German emigrant who served as a Union Army officer

in the US Civil War, and was related to a general who took part in Lincoln's funeral.[17]

Putzi grew up in Germany and then graduated from Harvard in 1909, where he achieved some fame as a pianist. At Harvard he became best known as a cheerleader who led rousing fight songs at football pep rallies. This left him uniquely suited to later convert the Harvard cheers into Nazi rally cries for Hitler. After graduation, Putzi managed an art gallery in New York, a branch of the family business. Putzi's talents lay as much in meeting important people as in music or business. He once even played the piano in the White House for Teddy Roosevelt. Among his other acquaintances were Walter Lippman, John Reed, Franklin Roosevelt, William Randolph Hearst, Winston Churchill, and Charlie Chaplin. Putzi returned to Bavaria during the early twenties where he heard Hitler at beer halls and rallies. He quickly wormed his way into Hitler's inner circle and became a close and important Hitler friend who advanced the führer's sophistication and introduced him to influential people.

Putzi soon came to know most of the important Nazis, but he had met Heinrich Himmler, the powerful leader of Hitler's SS and Gestapo, long before he'd ever heard of Hitler. He liked to joke that on the occasion Himmler "had a pacifier in his mouth." Himmler's father had been Putzi's schoolteacher, and Himmler was just a toddler when Putzi met him.[18]

When Hitler became so important that Putzi was no longer of use, Hitler cast him aside. Even though now scorned by Hitler, when Hanfstaengl returned to New York for a visit in 1934 he believed he was scoring propaganda points for the Third Reich and ingratiating himself with Hitler by allowing himself to be photographed shaking hands with a Jewish judge. But Hitler became furious.

Nevertheless, Putzi was determined to worm his way back into the führer's good graces. In 1937 he thought he'd won such an opportunity when asked by Hitler to undertake a special flight mission to Spain, where the Nazis were supporting fellow fascists in a civil war against a communist opposition. After a few minutes in the air, the pilot summoned his passenger to the cockpit and explained to Hanfstaengl that his mission was to parachute behind enemy lines in order to work as an agent for Spain's fascist dictator, Francisco Franco. Hanfstaengl, realizing such an assignment was a suicide mission, grew terrified and talked the pilot into feigning engine trouble while still over German territory. According to Hitler's trusted confidant, Albert Speer,[19] and Hanfstaengl's own memoir,[20] the "mission" was an elaborate practical joke dreamed up by Hitler's lieutenant, Herman Göring, and approved by

Hitler. Portions of the prank were even filmed for Hitler's amusement.

Back on the ground, the would-be agent sneaked away in a taxi and made his escape to Switzerland by train. At his Swiss hotel, Hanfstaengl received a letter from Göring explaining that the whole thing had been a joke and his desertion would be forgiven if he came back. However, Hanfstaengl no longer trusted the pair and eventually ended up in North America, helping the Americans. Before leaving Europe he managed to get his son out of Germany. This son served in the US Army during the war.

More About Hitler: The Führer's Love Life
When Hitler reached his mid-thirties, success and power made him attractive to a variety of women, yet he pursued only relationships with teenage girls. Perhaps this should not be surprising for he'd been insecure since puberty. The extent is described by August Kubizek, the only friend Hitler had during his teen years. Between the age of 16 and 20, Hitler professed an extraordinary love for a girl named Stefanie Isak and sometimes stalked her. Not once in these four years could he work up the nerve to utter a single word to her. The highlight of the relationship occurred when Hitler caught a rose the girl tossed from her carriage during a flower festival. Kubizek said the idealized love would have shattered had the two ever spoken. Hitler entertained elaborate fantasies of Stefanie. For a time, his fantasies involved kidnapping and elopement. When he realized he'd have no means to support his Stefanie, the illusion turned to suicide, with Stefanie dying with him.[21]

Hitler's sex life is likely to remain a fertile field for discussion because facts are in such short supply. Even after his stature as a powerful leader and celebrity gave him access to countless women, his disturbed makeup prevented him from ever becoming much of a ladies' man. He had numerous superficial dalliances, but just three women—Eva Braun, Mimi Reiter, and Geli Raubal—were known to have been deeply involved with him. Perhaps because they were impressionable teens when he first drew them in, all three subsequently became troubled and attempted suicide. Eva Braun's two attempts have already been described. Geli did succeed in killing herself, if the rumors of murder are discounted.

Mimi, perhaps Hitler's only true love, tried to hang herself but lived because a relative intervened. After a short failed marriage—one from which Hitler helped extract her by dispatching his personal lawyer to handle the divorce—a message from "Wolf" in 1931 was enough to draw her back to his apartment. Following a night together, Hitler told Mimi he still loved her and wanted her as his lover, but his mission to save Germany still kept him from marrying her. She replied she'd accept nothing less than marriage and walked out. Hitler reportedly said in response, "All women ever think of is having babies."

Mimi later remarried. This time she chose a military officer. When her husband died during the war, Hitler sent her 100 roses. Mimi saw Hitler one last time in 1938. By this time he'd found Eva Braun. When Mimi asked her Wolf if he was happy, he replied that if the question referred to Eva, the answer was no.

In Obersalzberg, where Hitler built his large house and SS-secured compound, the relationship with his niece, Angela (Geli) Raubal, developed. Geli, with her Viennese allure, perhaps reminded Hitler of his unattainable teenage love in Linz. Geli was a flirt and despite her uncle's possessiveness and strict control, managed to carry on a brief romance under Hitler's nose with his long-time chauffeur. And probably others too. Yet somehow, despite Geli's resentment, she could still feel jealousy when she learned Hitler had been taking 17-year-old Eva Braun for rides in his car. Eva worked in the shop of his official photographer and friend, Heinrich Hoffman.

When Geli shot herself, not everyone believed the official "self-inflicted" ruling because Hitler had enough influence with the police by then to make any inconvenient evidence disappear. Just before Hitler had departed for Hamburg the day of the shooting, a tremendous argument occurred after he ordered Geli to cancel a planned trip to Vienna with her friends.

Vicious rumors sprang up: the suicide came after Hitler had beaten Geli, Geli was pregnant by Hitler and unable to bear the shame, and Geli felt trapped in the relationship and despaired because she was unable to escape. Another rumor had Hitler killing her via a Nazi lackey because she'd become an embarrassing liability and had even threatened to blackmail Hitler. These suspicions cropped up because the suicide weapon was Hitler's personal revolver, a weapon he rarely failed to carry with him. Misgivings also arose because at the time of the argument, quite conveniently, only one servant was present and he was deaf.

Despite Hitler's deep depression, or perhaps because of it, the relationship with Eva Braun developed. The girl had just graduated from a convent school when she met Hitler. She continued to see him despite the disapproval of her Catholic family, who disliked both Hitler's politics and the great age difference. Braun didn't know at the time that she would be doomed to spend most of the next 14 years "waiting for Hitler." The nature of their sexual relationship, or whether they even had one, is not clear.

The facts surrounding Hitler's relationship with Renate Müller, one of the top German film actresses of the period, are also murky. Hitler may have first met her at a Danish film location, or she might simply have been "invited" to the führer's quarters. Joseph Goebbels, Hitler's propaganda minister, relentlessly prodded her to star in his propaganda films. He even tried to match her up with Hitler to form the perfect Aryan couple.

Müller found herself constantly shadowed by Gestapo agents. Her story ended tragically after she tried to shake herself free of the Nazis. Dark rumors emerged in 1937: she had a Jewish lover, she was disgusted with Hitler, and she possessed a damaging knowledge of Hitler's sadomasochistic sex life. Following her death that same year, the Nazis laid the blame on epilepsy and a morphine addiction. Later it emerged that she jumped or was pushed from the window of her residence building shortly after the arrival of several SS operatives.

---

[1] Morton, *Thunder at Twilight*, 246.
[2] Joachim Remak, *The Origins of World War I, 1871-1914*, Berkshire Studies in History (New York: Holt, Rinehart and Winston, 1967).
[3] "The Balkan Causes of World War One," *First World War.com: a multimedia history of world war one*, Firstworldwar.com, accessed 20 Apr. 2015.
[4] Morton, *Thunder at Twilight*, 128.
[5] Wikipedia contributors, "Causes of World War I," *Wikipedia*, Wikipedia.com, 1 Apr. 2015, accessed 20 Apr. 2015.
[6] Bernadotte Everly Schmitt, *The Coming of the War, 1914* (New York, London: C. Scribner's sons, 1930).
[7] Sidney Bradshaw Fay, *The Origins of the World War*, 2d ed. (New York: Macmillan, 1935).
[8] Burlingame, *Victory without Peace*, 188.
[9] Glaser, *Czecho-Slovakia*, 24.
[10] Stephen Bonsal, *Suitors and Suppliants; the Little Nations at Versailles* (New York: Prentice-Hall, 1946), 157.
[11] Bonsal, *Suitors and Suppliants; the Little Nations at Versailles*, 160.
[12] Bonsal, *Suitors and Suppliants; the Little Nations at Versailles*, 165.
[13] Glaser, *Czecho-Slovakia*, 29.
[14] Henry Bogdan, *From Warsaw to Sofia: A History of Eastern Europe* (Santa Fe, N.M., USA: Pro Libertate Pub, 1989), 223.
[15] "Migration Citizenship Education—Polish and German Expulsion," *Migration Citizenship Education*, Migrationeducation.org, accessed 20 Apr. 2015.
[16] Bogdan, *From Warsaw to Sofia*, 220.
[17] "From the S&S archives: He Played Piano for Hitler—and FDR," *Stars and Stripes*, Stripes.com, 23 Feb. 1971, accessed 20 Apr. 2015.
[18] "*From the S&S Archives: He Played Piano for Hitler—and FDR.*"
[19] Albert Speer, *Inside the Third Reich: Memoirs* (New York: Macmillan, 1970), 126.
[20] Hanfstaengl, *Unheard Witness*, 287.
[21] Kubizek, *Young Hitler, the Story of Our Friendship*; Translated from the German by E.V. Anderson [pseud.] With an Introd. by H.R. Trevor-Roper, 34.

Author's Note

Reviews and comments are much appreciated. If you enjoyed *The Secret She Buried: A Perilous Odyssey Through the Time of Hitler* (also available as an e-book), please consider posting an online review. Watch ericheipert.com for the upcoming companion volume recounting the parallel story of my father through World War II. And check out my novels.

About the Author

Erich, after spending his first five years in Germany, became an Iowa farm boy who eventually left tractors behind to earn a PhD in immunology. Not long after moving to the Pacific Northwest, he hung up his white lab coat to pursue other interests. Today time not spent with his family is divvied among coaching vision-impaired athletes in the sport of goalball, hiking the American West, traveling, playing bocce, and writing.

Works of fiction by the author

Books for young or not-so-young adults who relish adventure, youthful heroes, wry humor, a real plot, and a pinch of romance.

Guy Going Under

Guy just wanted to win a girl a little beyond his reach. He didn't plan to get himself, and a too-smart girl he couldn't stand, trapped in a cave with a gruesome historical secret.

Learn more about **Guy Going Under** and how to buy an e-book or paperback at ericheipert.com.

Butterfly Powder and the Mountains of Iowa

In 1960s rural Iowa, meet underachiever and improbable hero Gilbert Perles, the train he comes to call his own, an alluring girl named Alice, and the rival he would later re-encounter in a new and unexpected setting—war-torn Vietnam.

Learn more about **Butterfly Powder** and how to buy an e-book or paperback at ericheipert.com at ericheipert.com.

Image Attributions

Note: Unattributed images belong to Erich Eipert or members of his family and may not be reused without permission.

Chapter 2
Location of Lee County; modified from "Map of Iowa highlighting Lee County" by David Benbennick; 2006, public domain; commons.wikimedia.org

Chapter 3
1930 distribution of the 83 million Germans; derived from: Lange-Diercke – Sächsischer Schulatlas, circa 1930; by anonymous; public domain; commons.wikimedia.org

Linguistic map of German areas of settlement in Central Europe; The development of the German linguistic area; by Rex Germanus; Creative Commons Attribution-Share Alike 3.0; commons.wikimedia.org

Sudeten German areas of Bohemia and Moravia; modified from image by Georg Nickol, NICKOLdesign; used by permission of Georg Nickol; schloss-hartheim.at/projekt-sudetenland-protektorat/en/history.htm

Wolframitz marketplace tower; used by permission of Oswald Lustig

Chapter 5
Diagrammatic illustration of European alliances; modified from WWIchartX; Creative Commons Attribution-Share Alike 4.0; commons.wikimedia.org

The 2nd battalion of Austria's 99th Infantry Regiment; used by permission of Oskar Halusa

Austrian troops positioned in a shallow trench; Great War Primary Document Archive: Photos of the Great War; by unknown; used by permission; gwpda.org/photos

Austrian mountain troops scaling a rock face; Austro-Hungarian mountain corps during World War I, 1915, by unknown Austro-Hungarian officer; public domain; commons.wikimedia.org

Chapter 7
The regions of Europe; Grossgliederung_Europas; by Ständiger Ausschuss für geographische Namen; Creative Commons Attribution-Share Alike 3.0; commons.wikimedia.org

Chapter 8
Edvard Beneš; by unknown; United States Library of Congress; public domain; commons.wikimedia.org

Tomáš Masaryk; Podobiznu presidentovu dle fotografie z roku 1918; public domain; commons.wikimedia.org

Chapter 9
Chaotic state of rail yard in Trento, Italy; copy from war museum Kötschach-Mauthen (Austria); by unknown; public domain; commons.wikimedia.org

Image Attributions 355

Chapter 10
German territorial losses from two world wars (1919-1945); Germanborders; by Adam Carr, Renata3; public domain; commons.wikimedia.org
New national boundaries after the dissolution of Austria-Hungary; The partition of Austria-Hungary showing the boundaries as defined in the treaties; by unknown; Wikimedia Commons; public domain; commons.wikimedia.org

Chapter 12
Narrow strip fields; used by permission of Oswald Lustig
Undated postcard of Schömitz street scene; used by permission of Oskar Halusa

Chapter 13
Reproduction of 1676 Semnytz (Schömitz) village seal/drawing of the Schömitz village crest; used by permission of Oskar Halusa

Chapter 14
1927 Dedication of new water works; used by permission of Oskar Halusa

Chapter 15
Route of Graf Zeppelin 1929 global circumnavigation; Weltrundfahrt Map 1929; by Rlandmann; Creative Commons Attribution-Share Alike 3.0; commons.wikimedia.org

Chapter 16
The crowded Bürgerbräukeller beer hall; Bundesarchiv Bild 146-1978-004-12A; by Heinrich Hoffmann; German Federal Archives; Creative Commons Attribution-Share Alike 3.0; commons.wikimedia.org
Putzi Hanfstaengl, Hitler, and Herman Göring; Bundesarchiv Bild 102-14080; by unknown; German Federal Archive; Creative Commons Attribution-Share Alike 3.0; commons.wikimedia.org

Chapter 20
Map of Czech bunker line near Wolframitz; used by permission of Oskar Halusa

Chapter 21
Hitler's arrival in Wolframitz; used by permission of Oswald Lustig
Hitler curtly acknowledges crowd in front of Wolframitz Rathaus; used by permission of Oswald Lustig
Interior courtyard of Schloss Kromau; by Heinrich Hoffman; public domain

Chapter 22
At the teacher training school in Znaim; used by permission of Hajek family

Chapter 25
Area of Europe still under German control; Nazi Occupied Europe September 1943 Map; by Female bodybuilder enthusiast; Creative Commons Attribution-Share Alike 3.0; commons.wikimedia.org

Chapter 26
The people's radio; Volksempfänger VE301W; by Baujahr, 1933; Creative Commons Attribution-Share Alike 3.0; commons.wikimedia.org
Eduard Hajek during training at St. Pölten/[Eduard] prior to field deployment; used by permission of Hajek family

Chapter 27
Oskar celebrating his 20th birthday in hospital; used by permission of Oskar Halusa
Oskar during 1944 Christmas leave; used by permission of Oskar Halusa

Chapter 30
Erich Hajek shortly before his disappearance; used by permission of Hajek family
Volkssturm inductees being shown how to use Panzerfaust; German Federal Archives; by unknown; Creative Commons Attribution-Share Alike 3.0; commons.wikimedia.org

Chapter 31
POW enclosure holding 116,000 men at Sinzig; Prisoner of war transient enclosure at Sinzig; Department of Defense; public domain
A POW camp temporarily holding over 160,000 German POWs; Camp for German prisoners of war. Unidentified location in Germany; Department of Defense; public domain; commons.wikimedia.org

Chapter 37
German Messerschmitt Me262A-1a jet fighter; modified from Flugzeug Me 262A auf Flugplatz; German Federal Archive; Creative Commons Attribution-Share Alike 3.0; commons.wikimedia.org

www.ingramcontent.com/pod-product-compliance
Lightning Source LLC
Chambersburg PA
CBHW020638300426
44112CB00007B/160